ELECTRONIC MONUMENTS

Electronic Mediations

Katherine Hayles, Mark Poster, and Samuel Weber, series editors

Electronic Mediations, Volume 15

ELECTRONIC MONUMENTS

Gregory L. Ulmer

University of Minnesota Press
Minneapolis • London

MINNESOTA

An earlier version of chapter 1 appeared as "Metaphoric Rocks: A Psycho-geography of Tourism and Monumentality," *Postmodern Culture* 4, no. 3 (1994); copyright The Johns Hopkins University Press; reprinted with permission of The Johns Hopkins University Press. Chapter 2 was first published as "Traffic of the Spheres" in *Car Crash Culture,* edited by Mikita Brottman (New York: Palgrave Macmillan, 2002), 327–43; reprinted with permission of Palgrave Macmillan. Chapter 6 was first published as "The Upsilon Project: A Post-Tragic Testimonial," in *Psychoanalysis and Performance,* edited by Adrian Kear and Patrick Campbell (New York: Routledge, 2001), 203–17. Chapter 7 was first published as "The Miranda Warnings," in *Hyper/Text/Theory,* edited by George P. Landow (Baltimore: The Johns Hopkins University Press, 1994), 345–77; reprinted with permission of The Johns Hopkins University Press.

Published by the University of Minnesota Press
111 Third Avenue South, Suite 290
Minneapolis, MN 55401-2520
http://www.upress.umn.edu

Library of Congress Cataloging-in-Publication Data

Ulmer, Gregory L., 1944–
    Electronic monuments / Gregory L. Ulmer.
      p.   cm. — (Electronic mediations ; v. 15)
    Includes bibliographical references and index.
    ISBN 0-8166-4582-5 (hc : alk. paper) — ISBN 0-8166-4583-3 (pb : alk. paper)
    1. Internet in education—United States.   2. Instructional systems—Design—United States.   3. Human-computer interaction—United States.
    I. Title. II. Series.
    LB1044.87.U44 2006

                        2005013462

Printed in the United States of America on acid-free paper

The University of Minnesota is an equal-opportunity educator and employer.

12 11 10 09 08 07 06 05   10 9 8 7 6 5 4 3 2 1

This little essay is a great declaration of war; and regarding the sounding out of Idols, this time they are not just Idols of the age, but eternal Idols, which are here touched with a hammer as with a tuning fork: there are altogether no older, no more convinced, no more puffed-up Idols—and none more hollow. That does not prevent them from being those in which people have the most faith.

—*Friedrich Nietzsche,* Twilight of the Idols

Contents

PREFACE

NEWSWEEK MAGAZINE published a commemorative issue in fall 2001, titled "Spirit of America," devoted to the event and aftermath of September 11, 2001 (9/11). Richard M. Smith, chairman and editor-in-chief of the magazine, wrote the preface for the issue.

On September 11, an act of hate changed all our lives, but amid the horror of those moments, and in the days and weeks since, there have been thousands—millions—of individual acts of bravery and generosity, acts that testified to our profound sense of community. Ordinary people made extraordinary contributions. America's elected officials rose to the challenge. Spiritual leaders brought comfort and wisdom. A renewed sense of patriotism united the country, reaffirming our shared values of kindness, tolerance, diversity and liberty. This special issue of *Newsweek* commemorates the spirit of America. In words and pictures, we tell the stories that have touched all of us: of the workers, the leaders, the heroes, the citizens around the country and the world who gave of themselves. Together, they brought hope and healing. We also offer remembrances of some of the missing and dead. They number in the thousands, but each life—and each loss—was unique.

Figure 1. Will Pappenheimer, "Twin Towers Tuning Fork."

The special issue calls attention to the power of catastrophes to motivate collective as well as individual reflection on the meaning and purpose of life. The links between catastrophe and memory are biological, of course, but also cultural. The legendary beginning of ancient mnemotechniques is associated with the ability of Simonides to identify the bodies of a large group of party guests crushed beyond recognition in a collapsed building by recalling the order in which they were seated around the dinner table. Memory and identity have evolved with the changes in the language apparatus of civilization. The disaster of 9/11 occurred at a time of apparatus shift—the emergence of a global electrate world out of a modern literate society. The notions of spirit and the imagined community of America were already undergoing mutation at the time of the terrorist attacks, themselves motivated apparently as protests by representatives of a religious (oral) world displaced over the past millennium by scientific civilization. One of the fundamental features of Islamic culture is aniconism (the rejection of images). The attack on the twin towers—understood internationally as symbols of American power—was an act of iconoclasm.

One of the defining issues of twenty-first-century America concerns the future of Ground Zero. "The site of the World Trade Center is now a vast empty hole in the ground, some six to seven stories deep and some 16 acres in area," states the booklet distributed to participants attending the "Listening to the City" meeting convened in New York, July 20, 2002, by the Regional Plan Association on behalf of the Lower Manhattan Development Corporation (LMDC). Under the slogan "remember and rebuild," organizers promised that the planning and decision-making process would be "open and inclusive." The statement of principles distributed at the meeting declared the mission of the LMDC to be the renewal of Lower Manhattan as a symbol of our nation's resilience. "The entire nation has embraced New York, and we have responded by vowing to rebuild our city—not as it was, but better than it was before." "Our most important priority," it continues, is "to create a permanent memorial on the World Trade Center site that appropriately honors those who were lost, while reaffirming the democratic ideals that came under attack on September 11. Millions of people will journey to Lower Manhattan each year to visit what will be a world-class memorial in an area steeped in historical significance and filled with cultural treasures—including the Statue of Liberty and Ellis Island. Just steps from the World Trade Center site is St. Paul's Chapel, where George Washington prayed for the wisdom to lead a fragile nation."

We are now in a time of aftermath. It may be that our moment will find its closest analogies with such situations as Germany in the Napoleonic period. The modern university was founded in Germany by intellectuals and others who were shocked by the defeats suffered at the hands of the revolutionary French armies. The Germans wanted to understand collectively what happened and to overcome the deficiencies of their circumstances. The history of the German nation that follows that moment perhaps makes this example a cautionary tale. Another such moment was provoked by the event of Sputnik, when the Soviets beat the United States into outer space. This event shocked the American nation and motivated a massive recommitment to education, including the creation of the National Defense Education Act that paid my way to graduate school in the field of comparative literature. The story of the American space program is still unfolding, marked recently by the destruction of the shuttle *Columbia* and President Bush's interest in manned trips to Mars. Does 9/11 constitute a similar trauma for the nation? Will it provoke a turn to the institution of education as part of its collective response to understanding the 9/11 disaster?

The proposals and project presented in *Electronic Monuments* (EM) constitute one possible response that education might make, taking up the democratic spirit of the LMDC mission statement by calling attention to an experiment in progress at the University of Florida. The experiment involves testing a new practice of education for a civilization of the Internet in the form of an online consultancy called the EmerAgency. Initiated in the courses and research of a creative arts group, the Florida Research Ensemble (FRE), the EmerAgency is a conceptual umbrella organization created to coordinate and to lend coherence to experiments in adapting arts and letters education to the Internet and to the digital or computing revolution in general. The first element in the project is a challenge to the dominant characterization in our disciplines of the new media world as a "society of the spectacle" that necessarily destroys the civic sphere of modern democratic republics (as argued in theoretical texts), or as a "matrix" in which monsters farm humans for their corporeal energy while enslaving their minds through virtual reality cyberspace (as in science fiction films). Grammatology (the history and theory of writing) reads these negative critiques as confirmation of the interdependence of technology, social institutions, and individual identity formation (the social machine of language). The current modes of collective and individual identity—the nation-state and individual selfhood—are as much a part of an apparatus of literacy as are printed books, library archives, and all the related practices of schooling, which is to say that they are not stable or permanent modes of identity.

The lesson of history is that there will be change in the fundamental realities of our lives associated with the transformation of the language apparatus, but this change is not determined in advance, and the specifics of equipment, institutionalization, and behaviors remain to be invented. The spirit of America was in question with or without 9/11, since that to which the phrase refers was undergoing mostly invisible, slow-motion "catastrophe" in its adaptation to emergent "electracy" (electracy is to the digital image apparatus what literacy is to alphabetic print). The destruction of the World Trade Center in New York City has brought the question of the spirit of America to the fore. The meaning and coherence of this spirit is assumed to be given and consistent by the journalists and planners. It is the question of the "imagined community" (as Benedict Anderson called it): America as idea is open to further invention. Is it true, as the editor of *Newsweek* claimed, that the shared values of America today are kindness, tolerance, diversity, and liberty? Are these values the ones most relevant to the experience of being American?

September 11 has most of the earmarks of what the urbanist Paul Virilio called the "general accident"—an accident that happens everywhere in the world simultaneously, related to the existence of the Internet. The global effects of the terrorist attack on the world economy bear out the ecological nature of contemporary existence. Virilio blames the digital apparatus in general, and the Internet in particular, for creating the conditions that both make a general accident possible and prohibit or destroy the civic or public sphere needed for maintaining a free democratic society capable of responding to such a disaster. The EmerAgency experiment addresses this challenge by developing an institutional practice precisely for an Internet civic sphere. Specifically, the practice is a means through which the full intelligence of education as an institution might become part of a writable collective memory by transforming commemoration into a mode of active collective reasoning. For the EmerAgency, the Internet is an inhabitable monument.

The New Consultancy

I first tested the EmerAgency in a seminar taught in a networked classroom, motivated by the grammatological analogy that showed that electracy is an apparatus, meaning that learning how to use images in education was a matter not only of form and technology but also of institutional invention. As the history of the vanguard arts and entertainments shows, a new form requires a new institutional setting if it is to become practical. I introduced a conceptual institution as a practice for the Internet. Its practical purpose in the course was to get the students to think outside the confines of academic discourse, to address the potential that the Internet provides of delivering disciplinary knowledge to points of need in the community outside the university. To call it "conceptual" (alluding to conceptual art) suggests that the EmerAgency may achieve part of its function simply by circulating as an idea, without being actualized in literal terms. For the seminar it was a thought experiment, a fictional frame for the online projects.

The EmerAgency is a distributed, virtual, online consulting agency, meaning that emeragents (or simply "egents," to signal that we are concerned with the changes affecting human agency in electracy) are self-declared consultants without portfolio. At this stage it serves as an umbrella term for collaboration among colleagues, students, and public schools. The EmerAgency in principle coordinates the collaboration among teachers, volunteers, and partner organizations, across the levels of schooling, to add an Internet dimension to a curriculum that would give public schools a new voice as a "fifth estate" in our society. At present, public policy formation is worked out in politics among the three branches of government and journalism, as influenced behind the scenes by competing corporate and private interests. These interests hire consultants, almost exclusively experts based in the empirical disciplines of instrumental reason (as one would expect in the literate apparatus committed to enlightenment science). The EmerAgency is a deconstruction of conventional consulting, meaning that it appropriates this existing and familiar practice for delivering expert knowledge to sites of need, and transforms it with a different usage. The intent is to include citizens (netizens) as witnesses called to testify in hearings leading to problem discovery and policy solutions.

The chief alteration in deconstructive consulting (deconsulting for short) is to add to instrumental knowledge the knowledge and methods of the liberal and fine arts disciplines. A further alteration is including amateurs and ordinary citizens among the experts, especially students. A consultation involves coordinating school curriculum with public policy formation via the Internet. A correspondence is arranged aligning subject matter in the curriculum (history, geography, ecology, political science, literature, chemistry, physics, and the like), problems both recognized and unrecognized (officially) in the community (drugs, unemployment, crime, pollution, terrorism, child abuse, alcoholism, and the like), and public policy. What the EmerAgency adds to the existing arrangement is this dimension of the fifth estate whose purpose is to witness, monitor, the process relating knowledge, problems, and politics. The plan is to test the principle that observation alters what is observed (and the observer as well). Students perform "testimony" relating their own situations and learning to the public issues by means not of expertise but art and aesthetic devices. This witnessing influences the process through the awareness on the part of the four estates that their behavior and decisions are being monitored (countersurveillance).

The approach of the EmerAgency to these circumstances is pedagogical—not simply to declare immediately a commemorative plan, since a 9/11 memorial is a means to address the greater ends of inventing electracy. The larger questions about electracy as an apparatus—a social machine—are evoked through the details of a practical experiment. The experiment is partly conceptual (provisional, hypothetical, a thought experiment). At the same time, the project models a use of the Internet that has been performed as a curriculum for media studies and as various kinds of art projects (installation, CD-ROM, video, performance). It is an invitation for invention and a call to action of a kind that draws on all the resources of disciplinary knowledge in a time of emergency.

The Vernacular Memorial

The writing practice described in this book—the MEmorial—is intended to be to the networked classroom what the argumentative issue paper is to the literate classroom. The MEmorial is a hybrid: as a composite of text and image, it combines features of the topical essay and the vernacular shrines that in recent years have become a common folk response to the disasters that befall a community. The street shrines to 9/11 scattered throughout the New York City area represent this trend.

> Under a bridge in Brooklyn, a small table is covered in bricks, candles, a cross
> and a flag in memory of Department of Transportation workers who died
> in the attack on the World Trade Center. Across town, a statue of the Virgin
> Mary stands before sympathy notes and photos of two firefighters also killed
> on Sept. 11. It's been almost a year since terrorists flew two jetliners into the
> twin towers, yet the makeshift shrines set out to honor the more than 2,800

victims still dot the city's streets. "This was such a huge tragedy that everyone felt they could mourn in their own neighborhood. The wide dispersion of the shrines is unique," said Steve Zeitlin, Director of City Lore, a non-profit group dedicated to recording urban folklore. Their survival depends on public participation and cooperation. Each tends to have a shrine keeper, who covers paper objects with plastic and replaces burned-out candles and wilted flower bouquets. Each exists with the consent of landlords or city officials. (*Gainesville Sun,* August 31, 2002)

The objects left at the Vietnam Wall, or the crosses and bouquets displayed after each of the school shootings, are among the better documented instances of this commemorative vernacular. A function of the EmerAgency is to put this spontaneous mourning behavior into relationship with school research, and through the new transinstitutional reach of the Internet contribute to a new dimension of the civic sphere.

That the time is right for the democratization of monumentality represented by the MEmorial is suggested by the fact that a figure such as the radio polemicist Rush Limbaugh alluded (ironically) to the possibility: "One or two Americans a day are dying in Iraq. Why are we getting a daily Iraq death update when we don't get daily drowning death updates or fire death updates or pedestrian updates, accidents, this kind, when the numbers are clearly far greater than what is happening in Iraq?" (http://www.salon.com/opinion/conason/2003/07/22/uday/index.html). Curtis White, in an excerpt published in *Harper's* from *The Middle Mind: Why Americans Don't Think for Themselves* (San Francisco: Harper, 2003), is even more explicit: "This faith [in the raw ideology of technical progress] must be maintained in the face of the fact that 42,000 citizens of the United States die annually in traffic accidents, never mind the hundreds of thousands who are injured. . . . Every ten years we wipe out the population of four cities the size of the one in which I live, Bloomington-Normal, Illinois. Dead. And we leave a population the equivalent of a major metropolitan area (close to three million) as walking wounded, carting around the pain of pins in their ankles, knees like pudding, and ruptured vertebrae. Where is the memorial to those deaths and wounds? How many millions of human beings lost on the roadside over the last century? These numbers dwarf the losses in wars like Vietnam and Korea, and yet they are the result of a 'rationalizing' of our communities and our lives" (*Harper's Magazine,* August 2003, 20).

The appropriate site for mourning these "unremarkable" disasters is the Internet as living monument. Mourning is a behavior of both individual and collective identity formation, psychologically and socially. Tourism plays an important role at both levels and contributes to the invention and maintenance of American national identity. The EmerAgency syncretizes this aspect of tourism as the invention of symbolic capital with certain features of post-structural theory to produce a hybrid practice for the Internet that democratizes both institutions (entertainment and discipline). The mood of the book is that of a conceptual or hypothetical proposal for a virtual consultancy. The design of a MEmorial is just one method of this consultancy, but the one to which this entire book is devoted. The immediately practical application of the project has been tested in my undergraduate and graduate seminars taught in a networked classroom, in which the entire course is constructed around the design and testing of electronic monumentality. EM recounts the genesis of the EmerAgency leading to the performance of a cybermemorial (or rather, a MEmorial) for 9/11. The discussion includes some features of a guide or manual so that others may test this practice for themselves.

This book reflects my teaching and research over the past several decades. The MEmorial project has been tested by my graduate and undergraduate students in a series of classes taught in the Networked Writing Environment at the University of Florida as a way to organize courses on new media culture using the Web as the medium of instruction. Although EM makes no attempt to simulate Web design, a collection of representative MEmorials by students is accessible at http://www.nwe.ufl.edu/~gulmer ("Mystory Myseum"). This book continues my research program, especially the work on the mystory in *Teletheory: Grammatology in the Age of Video* (1989), and on chorography in *Heuretics: The Logic of Invention* (1994). Working with the Florida Research Ensemble (Barbara Jo Revelle, John Craig Freeman, William Tilson, and Will Pappenheimer), I tested chorography and the EmerAgency in a consultation on the Miami River, Miami, Florida, in "Miami Virtue: Psychogeography of the Virtual City" (book in progress). An experimental textbook formulated the consultancy in pedagogical terms in *Internet Invention: From Literacy to Electracy* (2003). EM takes up the new consultancy where *Internet Invention* leaves off. The project was explored as well with students of the European Graduate School, Saas-fee, Switzerland (thanks to Wolfgang Schirmacher). EM is meant to stand on its own and to be used in a variety of ways, from its most modest claims as a way to teach courses dealing with the Internet to its most ambitious claim as a practice for a virtual civic sphere, sustaining an electrate imagined community for a global "America."

INTRODUCTION
THE EMERAGENCY

The Internet Accident

This book proposes an institutional practice—the MEmorial—that allows students and citizens to use the Internet as a civic sphere. The MEmorial and its institutionalization in the EmerAgency as a new kind of consultancy are a response to concerns formulated most forcefully by Paul Virilio, who describes the Internet as the potential source of a general accident:

> Today, the new technologies convey a certain type of accident, one that is no longer local and precisely situated, like the sinking of the Titanic or the derailment of a train, but general, an accident that immediately affects the entire world. This is quite obvious when we are told that the Internet has a worldwide vocation. Yet the accident of the Internet, or that of other technologies of the same nature, also represents the emergence of a total—not to say integral—accident. And that situation has no reference. We don't know yet, perhaps with the exception of the stock market crash, what an integral accident could be, an accident that would involve everyone at the same time. (1999, 12)

Virilio's argument is that teletechnologies, through their instantaneous interactivity, have produced a single time—real time—whose milieu is speed. This unprecedented immediacy and ubiquity make democracy impossible, he argues. Public space in real time becomes an image in some medium—photography, cinema, television. These images replace the trajectories of the city, the face-to-face interaction of the public sphere, and the encounter of subject with object in the agora, the forum. The question he raises is whether a virtual city is possible—whether it is possible to urbanize real time. "If the answer is no, then a general accident is inevitable, the accident of history, the accident of accidents that Epicurus spoke of regarding history. If we are not capable of urbanizing the real time of exchange, in other words the live city-world, the city-world in real time, through the globalization of telecommunications, then both history and politics will be called into question. This is an extraordinary drama" (40).

Virilio does not claim that the general accident is inevitable. Rather, he poses this possibility as a general emergency. The danger that he sketches begins with the formation of the mental map that each person develops. The threat to freedom, he says, begins with the reduction and impoverishment of this mental picture. As an urbanist he locates the source of the crisis as the displacement of the real city by the telecity, the loss of a lived public space in favor of a virtual gathering on the Internet (45). The weakening of the borders of identity associated with this reduced mental map is the subject formation that Scott Bukatman called "terminal identity":

> Body and image become one: a dissolution of real and representation, certainly, but also of the boundaries between internal and external, as the interiorized hallucination becomes the public spectacle of the Videodrome program. Here *Videodrome* echoes *The Simulacra,* in which a character's psychosis results in a physical transformation. . . . In the postspectacle society delineated by Baudrillard, all such boundaries will dissolve, will become irrelevant through the imperatives of the model of communication (simultaneous transmission and reception): "In any case, we will have to suffer this new state of things, this forced extroversion of all interiority, this forced injection of all exteriority that the categorical imperative of communication literally signifies" (Baudrillard, *The Ecstasy of Communication*). . . . The subject has "no halo of private protection, not even his own body, to protect him anymore." (1993, 92)

What looks like a generalized schizophrenia from the point of view of literacy, however, is understood in electrate terms as symptoms of a change in subjectivation intrinsic to the new apparatus. In electracy, for better or worse, the borders of identity—of the group subject (between individual and collective)—become writable.

Virilio's conviction is that we must not be seduced by the tele- or cinecity, but must recover the living city, the polis. "If there is a solution possible today, it lies in reorganizing the place of communal life" (1999, 52). The first step he claims is to counter the image by re-creating speech, recovering language, and writing (87). Meanwhile, that which makes this condition intelligible is the accident, which is an inverted miracle in that it has the effect of revelation ("when you invent the ship you invent the shipwreck" [89]). The most important aspect of Virilio's argument from the point of view of electracy is his claim that the new technologies of the spectacle (that is, the technologies associated with the apparatus of electracy) produced the conditions of a "knowledge accident" in which each invention includes its own catastrophe. The accident of accidents at the level of knowledge involves the very category formation of literacy itself invented by the classical Greeks.

The EmerAgency experiment responds to Virilio's warning not by retreating to the literate industrial city, but by designing a practice to address the loss of borders experienced in the virtual city. As a consultancy its point of intervention is precisely at the level of the circulation of values. The claim is that the new category system (the new metaphysics) emerging within electracy is capable of making an object of study of the metaphysics of literacy, and hence of "getting up to speed" with the accident of time. The unconscious or machinic dimension of the literate knowledge accident becomes accessible to reason again within the holistic category of the electrate chora.

Information Infrastructure

The EmerAgency is an online consultancy whose purpose is to develop an Internet practice that responds to the challenge posed by Virilio. The basic premise of the EmerAgency is that problems, no less than the policies devised to address them, are social constructions. Problem and policy formation, that is, are special cases of Western metaphysics in general, meaning literacy and the ontology of categories, concepts, and topics.

> Problems come into discourse and therefore into existence as reinforcement of ideologies, not simply because they are there or because they are important for well-being. They signify who are virtuous and useful and who are dangerous or inadequate, which actions will be rewarded and which penalized. They constitute people as subjects with particular kinds of aspirations, self-concepts and fears and they create beliefs about the relative importance of events and objects. They are critical in determining who exercises authority and who accepts it. They construct areas of immunity from concern because those areas are not seen as problems. Like leaders and enemies, they define

the contours of the social world, not in the same way for everyone, but in the light of the diverse situations from which people respond to the political spectacle. (Edelman 1988, 12–13)

In other words, within literacy problems are treated as topics. Ian Hacking noted, for example, that "women refugees" is posited as a category or idea, with certain consequences. "Ideas do not exist in a vacuum. They inhabit a social setting. Let us call that the matrix within which an idea, a concept or kind, is formed. 'Matrix' is no more perfect for my purpose than the word 'idea.' It derives from the word for 'womb,' but it has acquired a lot of other senses—in advanced algebra for example. The matrix in which the idea of the woman refugee is formed is a complex of institutions, advocates, newspaper articles, lawyers, court decisions, immigration proceedings. Not to mention the material infrastructure, barriers, passports, uniforms, counters at airports, detention centers, courthouses, holiday camps for refugee children" (1999, 10). "Matrix" is interesting in our context since it resonates with one of Plato's metaphors for chora. The implication is that one needs to grasp not one problem, but the matrix as a whole within which such an idea makes sense. Chora is a holistic ordering of topics into an electrate image system of categories.

Problem entities become images, Joseph Gusfield argued in a discussion of the idea of drunk drivers created as public facts:

> They constitute a public reality in two senses. First, these are facts which are shared by many people in the society who have no, or very little, personal knowledge of individual cases making up the aggregated facts. As public facts, they are not peculiar to any particular class, cultural group, or educational status. Second, they compose a public reality in being an aggregated fact rather than the events involving particular people. They are not about anyone but about a society—the United States. Because such facts are not records of individual events but are rather aggregations of data, amassed and presented, the "discovery" of public facts is a process of social organizations. Someone must engage in monitoring, recording, aggregating, analyzing, and transmitting the separate and individual events into the public reality of "auto accidents and deaths." At every stage in this process human choices of selection and interpretation operate. (1981, 37)

Through the EmerAgency, egents may help "compose" public facts.

It is a matter of the relations among ideology and values, politics and morality. "Multiple voices and silences are represented in any scheme that attempts to sort out the world. No one classification organizes reality for everyone" (Bowker and Star 2000, 41). Bowker and Star warn that this inevitable interdependence of policy and metaphysics becomes dangerous in a condition of "convergence"—when the system disappears as such. "This blindness occurs by changing the world such that the system's description of reality becomes true. . . . It will be impossible to think or act otherwise" (49). A community will not notice when it has reached convergence until there is a breakdown in the system (34), when its solutions fail to pass a reality check. The events of 9/11 may be considered one such reality check. The single greatest determinant of policy formation is the dominant value paradigm. "For any problem at the regime or macro-level of discussion and analysis there are remarkably few alternatives actually under debate. In the United States a powerful and enduring political culture (as distinct from an arguably much more variegated popular culture) helps to whittle down the range of 'legitimate' alternatives to a pitiful few long before any quasi-pluralist 'conflict' over problem definition ever ensues" (Bosso 1994, 184).

The challenge for the EmerAgency is to develop an approach to policy formation that opens a new perspective on literate society by means of a category formation native to the image apparatus of electracy. Given the interdependence of category and policy noted above, the task of this study is to take up the question of the public sphere by proposing a new civic practice, specific to image technologies organized into the apparatus of electracy, and operating logically with a speed that matches the accelerated conditions of a wired planet.

Electronic Monumentality

The project introduced in this book is a pilot, concerned first of all with establishing the EmerAgency (an Internet consultancy) as a practice for education in the society of the spectacle. The hypothesis of electronic monumentality is that commemoration is a fundamental experience joining individual and collective identity, which must be adapted in any case to the emerging apparatus of electracy. All the concerns about the decline of the public sphere or the destruction of civic life caused by the society of the spectacle (which is how electracy is conceived from the point of view of literacy), are focused by the question of commemoration: how a collectivity remembers who or what it is. The proposal of this book is that the Internet makes it possible for monumentality to become a primary site of self-knowledge both individual and collective, and hence a site supporting a new politics and ethics, as well as a new dimension of education. Electronic monumentality provides the basis for a virtual public sphere capable of producing public policy decisions that take into account the dromosphere. The MEmorial makes it possible for monumentality to go "live."

The conventional assignment in a college composition course assumes a twenty-five-hundred-year history of the literate apparatus. We take for granted that, as most college handbooks say, arguments focus on issues about which there is some debate. "A position paper assignment will typically ask you, first, to choose an issue in which you are interested; second, to argue a position on one side or another of the issue; and third, to support your claims with evidence, which you locate through research" (Fulwiler and Hayakawa 1994, 127). This description can trace its pedigree back to Aristotle. The purpose of the paper is to persuade other people to agree with a particular point of view (128). The certainty of how to produce this persuasive effect is based on a method invented in Plato's academy and developed as the institutional practice for transforming information stored in libraries into knowledge in the experience of individual writers. A. P. Martinich summarizes some of the most widely used tactics of analytical (conceptual) writing:

> Dilemmas are useful for setting out problems. A dilemma makes obvious some contradictory aspects of widely held beliefs. Since dilemmas need to be solved by some means, some methods of problem solving need to be discussed.
>
> *Reductio ad absurdum* is one of these methods. It is a way of proving one's own thesis indirectly by showing that the denial of that thesis is absurd and hence false. Since the direct opposite of your thesis is absurd and false, your own thesis must be true.
>
> A counterexample is a way of showing that some proposed solution or thesis is not a correct one; it shows that something is incorrect without showing directly what particular solution or thesis is correct. The method of counter-examples is a method of criticism, not theory construction.
>
> Dialectical reasoning is a way of thinking that can be adapted to a way of structuring an essay. It begins with a simple and unqualified thesis, subjects it to criticism, revises and reformulates it several times until a complex, sophisticated and adequate thesis is arrived at. Dialectical writing, which is an orderly record of dialectical reasoning, is a kind of intellectual travelogue, in which all the important side-trips are recorded as adventures necessary for reaching the traveler's ultimate destination.
>
> Dialectical reasoning can also be used as a rhetorical tactic in doing something called "analyzing a concept." Conceptual analysis is the task of breaking down a complex concept into simpler components, just as chemical analysis is breaking down a complex chemical into simpler ones.
>
> All of the [tactics] concern ways of clarifying and making essays more precise. A basic way of getting clear about things is to divide them into dif-ferent categories, that is, to distinguish them. Making a distinction often requires defining one's terms because the terms often depend upon having a precise meaning. Perhaps the most basic way of being clear and precise is to define a word or phrase. (1996, 96–97)

It is easy to imagine a host of issues related to the multitude of public problems itemized and tracked in the mass media. A point of continuity between literate and electrate education is this interest in public issues as a basis for student projects. These conventions of educational practice provide a context for the EmerAgency and the MEmorial, offered here as prototypes for a learning practice that is to electracy what the argumentative essay is to literacy. The relationship of the MEmorial to the essay is not one of opposition but supplement. The MEmorial takes up where the conventional paper leaves off.

Apparatus Analogy

The context for this proposal is the need for a compositional practice capable of supporting learning with digital media, to do for the Internet and hypermedia what the essay did for the library and argumentative writing. The invention of this new practice involves grammatology. Grammatology as a method works by analogy, using comparisons with the transition from orality to literacy to organize inquiry into the transition from literacy to electracy under way in our own time. The following list reviews the features of each apparatus:

- The matrix of orality includes the technology of natural language (lest it be forgotten that the symbol system of spoken language was itself an invention); the institution of religion with its mnemonic practice of ritual; the tribe as collective identity; and the individual experience of identity as spirit (thought experienced as the voice of a god or spirit outside of oneself).
- Literacy includes the technology of alphabetic writing, culminating in print; the institution of school (origins in Plato's academy, Aristotle's lyceum, and the library at Alexandria, founded by Aristotle's student Alexander the Great) with its practice of method (dialectic: analysis and synthesis); the nation-state as the ultimate order of collective print identity; and the individual experience of identity as selfhood.
- Electracy is most obviously emerging as a technology, with the continuing evolution of digital media and the merger of the various business organizations overseeing their delivery to society (telephone, television, and related information utilities). If one recalls that the technological shift from literacy to electracy began in the nineteenth century with the invention of photography, followed by other new means of recording and transmission—phonograph, telegraph—it is easier to appreciate that the institution most responsible for producing the rhetorical practices for digital memory is entertainment.

Our analogy suggests that a form and practice (institution) of writing will emerge within electracy that are native to the new apparatus. The Internet consultancy is not a rival to journalism or to science and engineering, but an experimental search for this new way of relating thinking and language.

A question sustained from one apparatus to the next is: why do things go wrong? why do we make mistakes despite our best efforts to assure desired and intended outcomes of our actions? The ultimate collective response to this question in orality is religion, and in literacy is science. Religious rituals addressed problems by appeasing the gods. Oral peoples consulted diviners to help resolve personal problems. In literacy, scientific consulting addresses problems directly by discovering their material causes and providing material remedies. Electracy has not been around long enough to have produced its ultimate response, but it is working on one, primarily in the institution of entertainment.

The Mise-en-Scène of Disaster

Tragedy as a form is an oral-literate hybrid—performed as part of a religious ritual festival (such rituals being the central institutionalized mnemonic practice of orality), while employing the new technology of writing (the plays are scripted) and introducing innovations, such as the individual actors apart from the chorus, made possible by the new order of memory. Commentators have shown that literacy in general and tragedy in particular were important factors in the transformation of Greek collective identity from a group of allied tribes to a city-state (Hermassi 1977). Individuals were beginning to experience themselves as autonomous beings with a clearly defined inner experience apart from the external and outwardly directed relations with the tribe and the gods in nature. Within this process the tragedies addressed the problematic of error in a preconceptual way, since categorization by concept was still to be invented, or had yet to be codified by Plato and made accessible or learnable by means of the practice of method introduced in Plato's academy and refined in Aristotle's lyceum.

The aspect of tragedy of most interest in our context is (in Greek) *ATH* (*até* in lowercase), which means "blindness" or "foolishness" in an individual, and "calamity" or "disaster" in a collectivity (Doyle 1984). The effect of literacy just beginning to be felt and explored as Greece assimilated alphabetic writing was a new power of abstraction that made it possible to analyze and compare actions and statements, making visible certain patterns that were unintelligible and unnoticed using oral means. Tragedy in its preconceptual style dramatized foolish mistakes, actions without knowledge or understanding (blindness) and their consequences for the community (the prototype being *Oedipus Rex* by Sophocles). The specific feature of tragedy known as *até* has to do with the hero losing control, being overwhelmed temporarily by a passion, taken or possessed from without, and producing an action that might be trivial in itself but had catastrophic consequences not only for the hero but also for the community as a whole. If the story of Oedipus slaying his father at a crossroads was remade in a contemporary version, it could be dramatized as an incident of road rage. A trivial example in our own time is Mike Tyson biting the ear of Evander Holyfield (he "ate" his ear)—foolishness without catastrophe. More serious is the Bill Clinton–Monica Lewinsky affair, whose consequences are still playing out. The basic insight of *ATH*—that a seemingly inconsequential detail of behavior may have unforeseen and immense consequences for the community—is echoed in chaos theory (the butterfly effect).

A premise of the EmerAgency is that *até* continues to be a factor in our own time, even if theater and the genre of tragedy are no longer adequate expressions of it. Indeed, the history of literacy is in part a record of the gradual shifting of our struggle with *até* from tragedy to consulting, from being a matter of destiny or chance to a matter of knowledge and control. The tendency of science has been to eliminate to the greatest degree possible the role of chance or fortune in our experience, with the turning point that tipped the balance in favor of control being Machiavelli's *The Prince*. In our post-Enlightenment moment, this movement seems to have overreached itself, gone too far, and is in need of a different state of mind. It is important at a fundamental level of survival to formulate a new way to notice and attend to *ATH* in electracy, distinct from but without replacing tragedy and consulting (problem solving).

Electracy

Grammatology shows by analogy the nature of the challenge facing educators dealing with the emergence of a new apparatus (electracy) that will be as different from literacy ultimately as literacy is different from orality—different not only technologically but also institutionally and behaviorally. However inevitable, changes do not happen instantly, and their nature is not determined in advance (no technological determinism). The history of writing has put a name and date on nearly every modification that brought us from the Eleusinian mysteries to rocket science. The record shows that societal adaptations other than those followed in the West are possible. Since we have some choice in the matter and some responsibility for the outcome, what direction should we take? What policies should we adopt to guide our collective self-overcoming?

From theater through philosophy to modern science, literacy has addressed the problem of individual ignorance but has not done as well in ameliorating societal ignorance. The challenge of education within literacy has been to figure out how to translate individual learning into social formations. Socrates (to continue the oversimplifications of this rapid sketch) discovered contradiction by applying literate reasoning to the oral lifeworld. In *Euthyphro*, for example, Socrates demonstrated that his interlocutor's reasoning about piety and impiety (motivating Euthyphro's decision to prosecute his father for murder) is filled with contradictions. Socrates employs a new practice, a device of literacy—the definition—which Aristotle eventually perfected in his dialectical topics. Socrates asked Euthyphro to define his terms, and the result revealed different meanings in different contexts. Euthyphro was not happy about the proof that he did not seem to know what he was doing or why, no more than did most other Athenians, who voted one fine day to martyr this first literate subject.

Plato did not start a religion to commemorate Socrates (which would have been an oral response to the great man's career). Rather, he invented the institutional means for reproducing dialectical reasoning in a method that could be taught and learned by ordinary people so that they would not keep making the same mistakes. Socrates never wrote, Havelock noted, but his reasoning was literate. An ordinary person could duplicate Socrates' feat only with the help of a prosthesis, such as the cheat sheet that Phaedrus had up his sleeve when he arrived for his lesson with Socrates, an event recorded in the first discourse on method in the Western tradition.

After twenty-five hundred years of schooling, we have made some progress as individuals in our powers of analysis. Science as an institution found a way to do for literate knowledge what the church did for oral spirituality—focus and augment individual work through collaborative group organization. Translating these collective adaptations into the political realm has proved difficult in both cases. An individual's power of abstraction, for example, helps her understand the direct connection between cleanliness and health. At the collective level, however, we fail to grasp the contradiction in the fact that the factories producing our soaps are polluting our habitat. Even if we notice the relationship between the production of goods and the increase in pollution, collectively we are nearly helpless to do anything about it. We are a collective Euthyphro.

A goal of electracy is easy to state in this grammatological context: to do for the community as a whole what literacy did for the individuals within the community. Could a community go to school collectively? Should we imagine the United States of America (in the persona of Uncle Sam) positioned in a corner of an electrate history class wearing a dunce cap? The Internet is the place of this scene of instruction, and the EmerAgency provides the pedagogy for group subjects. If the literate apparatus produced subjectivation in the mode of individual selves organized collectively in democratic nation-states, electracy seems to allow the possibility of a group subjectivation with a self-conscious interface between individual and collective. The sacred sociology of Georges Bataille and his colleagues briefly united in the Collège de Sociologie explored this peculiar condition. More recently Félix Guattari focused his research on the group subject:

> At least three types of problems prompt us to enlarge the definition of subjectivity beyond the classical opposition between individual subject and society, and in so doing, revise the models of the unconscious currently in circulation: The irruption of subjective factors at the forefront of current events, the massive development of machinic productions of subjectivity and, finally, the recent prominence of ethological and ecological perspectives on human subjectivity. Subjective factors have always held an important place in the course of history. But it seems that with the global diffusion of the mass media they are beginning to play a dominant role. The immense movement unleashed by the Chinese students at Tiananmen Square obviously had as the goal the slogans of political democratization. But it is equally certain that the contagious affective charges it bore far surpassed simple ideological demands. A whole lifestyle, collective ethic and conception of social relations (derived largely from Western images) were set into motion. (1995, 1–2)

The challenge of the EmerAgency is to design a practice capable of educating this group subject. The difficulty of this challenge should not be underestimated, since this subject thinks in the dimension of the unconscious.

Testimony

A MEmorial witnesses (monitors) a disaster in progress. The principles guiding the composition of a scene of witness have been transformed in our discipline through the historical precedent of the Holocaust. The MEmorial tests a modality (testimony) that has been heavily theorized in cultural studies. Shoshana Felman reminded us that "testimony is the literary—or discursive—mode par excellence of our times, and that our era can precisely be defined as the age of testimony. 'If the Greeks invented tragedy, the Romans the epistle, and the Renaissance the sonnet,' writes Elie Wiesel, 'our generation invented a new literature, that of testimony'" (1995, 17). Ours may be the age of testimony, but this is not to say that anyone knows how to witness. The prototype of the witness for Felman (and many others) is the victim of the Holocaust. Such persons, to the extent that they suffer the effects of post-traumatic stress disorder (PTSD), are literally not able to testify, thus pointing to a "crisis of truth" that may be generalized as a description of our present condition. "For the attempt to understand trauma brings one repeatedly to this peculiar paradox: that in trauma the greatest confrontation with reality may also occur as an absolute numbing to it, that immediacy, paradoxically enough, may take the form of belatedness. Economic and psychological explanations never quite seem to match the full implications of this strange fact. . . . The impact of an event in which 'no trace of a registration of any kind is left in the psyche, instead, a void, a hole is found'" (Caruth 1995, 6). This ultimate collective shipwreck manifests a collapse of witnessing and as such poses a fundamental challenge to the very nature of commemoration (an institutionalized procedure for remote experience): "History was taking place with no witness: it was also the very circumstance of being inside the event that made unthinkable the very notion that a witness could exist" (7).

A practice of collective pedagogy must deal with the extreme condition of postmodern memory—PTSD: a separation of memory from consciousness, a storing and placing of memory "outside" inside. Lyotard explained the great impact of trivial details on persons living this condition in terms of the temporality of shock: The first blow is received, deposited, but is not set to work (it exceeds and overwhelms the shock-defense of the individual and so is not processed in ordinary memory). At a later time, the second blow is triggered by an encounter with some detail, some marginal fragment associated with the original trauma, that triggers the affect (Lyotard 1990, 15–16). The repetition compulsion in which shock victims obsessively relive an expelled memory is a grotesque cousin of epiphany.

The important point is that within the condition of shock there can be no recognition of the sort associated with epiphany or tragedy (anagnorisis) as conventionally understood. Indeed, the very reductionism associated with utilitarian consulting is itself a defense formation. "It will be a question of making understood that the unveiled is never the truth (since the unveiled is always the veiled, as the named is always the betrayal of the unnamable)" (Lyotard 1990, 60). Testimony in Lyotard then relies on a certain kind of feeling that has been theorized in terms of the unconscious. This feeling bears witness to shock-work:

> What is a feeling that is not felt by anyone? What is this "anyone"? How can I [Freud] asks, even be led on the path of this insane hypothesis if there exists no witness? Is not the affected the only witness to the affect? . . . It is not that the speaker cannot make himself understood; he himself does not hear anything. We are confronted with a silence that does not make itself heard as silence. Something, however, will make itself understood, "later." That which will not have been introduced will have been "acted," acted out, "enacted," played out, in the end—and thus represented. But without the subject recognizing it. It will be represented as something that has never been presented. . . . This will be understood as feeling, fear, anxiety, feeling of a threatening excess whose motive is obviously not in the present context. And how can this site be localized without passing through a "memory," without alleging the existence of a reserve where this site has been retained, in non-localized and nonlocalizable fashion, and without consciousness having been

informed about it? This sudden feeling is as good as a testimony, through its unsettling strangeness, which "from the exterior" lies in reserve in the interior, hidden away and from where it can on occasion depart to return from the outside to assail the mind as if it were issued not from it but from the incidental situation. (12–13)

A premise of the EmerAgency is that the exceptional state, the extremity of PTSD, in fact characterizes the general condition of experience in the society of the spectacle. Lyotard's analysis, after all, is not that different from the account of shock produced by the modern city registered by Baudelaire in *Paris Spleen*. Concerns about "compassion fatigue"—the failure of citizens to be affected by or at least moved to action in response to the daily rehearsal of worldwide misery—is only the latest annotation of the alienation that informs the human condition of modernity. This "feeling not felt by anyone" is the dimension of experience that the Internet as a prosthesis of memory may address (this feeling becomes accessible to experience in testimony). The foreclosure of emotion in shock falls within the set of recognition, including the recognition of interpellation that goes without saying. The fundamental difference between ancient and modern epiphany is that in the latter the experience of insight is understood as a misrecognition, which is to say that the unconscious is involved. Our approach to electracy, in any case, assumes that the Internet is a prosthesis of the body-mind, adding to cognitive science the dimension of the unconscious (interpolating between consciousness and the neural brain the dimension of drive and desire). We may not be able to think the unconscious directly (intuitively), but we may write it.

The Mediated Witness

The EmerAgency goal is a practice for consultants with only mediated access to the data of problems. A preliminary question concerns how to adapt the lived, direct experience (as victim, eyewitness, or bystander) of disaster to a practice treating mediated experience. It is the difference between testimony and testimonial. "Testimonial" in epistemological terms refers to a second-hand mode of access to knowledge or information about the world (our information comes to us used) rather than through one's own senses or intuitions. The compassion fatigue affecting media consumers of reported disasters is a manifestation of the limits of conventional commemoration. The relevance of the Holocaust lesson for the EmerAgency is that the practices of commercial media perform this very collapse of witnessing. Kevin Robins (in *Into the Image*) argued that the formal design of popular culture communication functions for the society as a whole the way psychological defenses function for an individual. The immense amount of knowledge about disaster is supplied to us by our media in a way that is unreceivable at the level of belief (hence the reliance on fetish-logic: I know, but still . . .). Such is the scission of our time—the disjunct between knowledge and experience, between collective history and individual existence.

If modernity established that there was no position of safety from which to observe the "shipwreck of life," postmodernity put in question the status of the subject itself, whether victim or spectator, individual or collective. Alexander Düttmann, for example, proposed that AIDS could serve as an update of the Holocaust prototype, a "paradigm of the contemporary social-economic-political-technical state of the western world, which necessarily includes its relationship to other worlds" (1996, 5). Analyzing the position of various AIDS activists, Düttmann takes a radical stance regarding the proper function of testimony as a refusal of the comforts and safety of identity. Against all proposals for making sense of this condition, including the identity politics of the homosexual community ("I am out; therefore I am"), or even if it is only to take AIDS as the sign of the meaning that is missing from the world, Düttmann (in a study that originated in Derrida's seminar) insists on a position of Being-not-one-with-AIDS, which may be reduced to Being-not-one as such: the collapse of the subject and with it the possibility of selfhood, of the subject coinciding with itself.

> Giving testimony comes about because there can no more be a communication of what is testified to than there can be any simultaneity with Being-not-one. Giving testimony does not communicate anything; it has no communicable content. It does not testify to anything definite that could be handed down in the form of a content; it does not tell a story or history; no historiography can rely on it. Perhaps in the time of AIDS a way of giving testimony, a marking of Being-not-one, comes about that communicates nothing and erases itself because such a paradoxical making must always also be understood as the attempt to exhibit Being-not-one as such. Only when this exhibition is thought can one perhaps speak of a duty and a responsibility to give testimony. (Düttmann 1996, 76)

The rationale for this more radical stance of refusal to speak from any position of identity, to testify rather to the collapse of such positions, is an acknowledgment of trauma as the defining condition of our culture. In this view testimonial would not be a *conscientization* but a defense (a response of the unconscious, a repression). The position would not be that of one-who-knows but of one-who-is-in-shock.

Jacques Derrida pointed out that testimony (like interpellation) functions in the modality of faith rather than of truth. As such it shares none of the assumptions of scientific proof. "An invincible desire for justice is linked to this expectation. By definition, the latter is not and ought not to be certain of anything, either through knowledge, consciousness, conscience, foreseeability or any kind of program as such. This abstract messianicity belongs from the very beginning to the experience of faith, of believing, or a credit that is irreducible to knowledge and of a trust that 'founds' all relation to the other in testimony" (Derrida 1996, 18). Writing in the context of Blanchot's last book, *L'instant de ma mort,* in which Blanchot recounted an experience of facing a firing squad during the German occupation of France, Derrida insists on the paradoxical or aporetic status of this instance or example. Blanchot as witness promised to tell the truth, yet the promise necessarily is haunted by the possibility of the lie, such that testimony and fiction share a border. Did the incident really happen, or is Blanchot belatedly making a political credential for himself? "If this possibility were effectively excluded, if the testimony became proof, information, certitude or archive, it would lose its function as testimony. To remain testimony, it must therefore let itself be haunted. It must allow itself to be parasited by that which it excludes from its interior core, the possibility, at least, of literature" (Derrida 1998, 31).

The EmerAgency is a deconstructed consultancy, meaning that it is simultaneously an immanent critique of conventional consulting and an experiment in an alternative mode that adapts arts and letters knowledge to a practice supportive of a virtual civic sphere. The hypothesis is that the non-empirical, noninstrumentalist disciplines do not replace scientific knowledge or literacy in general, but supplement it in a practical way. A basic strategy of deconstruction is to address the binary opposition structuring the concept, ordering the object of study (consulting, in this case). Students encounter the opposition in the distinction between pure and applied research. As one guide to research in the humanities puts it, "You risk a mistake if you make a problem in the world the problem you try to solve in your research. No research paper can solve the problem of [9/11], but good research might give us knowledge that could help us solve it. Research problems involve only what we don't know or fully understand. So write your paper not to solve the problem of [9/11], but to solve the problem that there is something about [9/11] that we don't know or understand, something that we need to know before we can deal with it" (Booth, Colomb, and Williams 1995 , 55). Encultured into a society that prizes instrumental reason, beginning researchers "try to cobble the solution of a research problem onto the solution of a practical problem"; they try to make pure research seem like applied research (57). The dilemma of testimony adds the further complication that there is something about 9/11 that we cannot know as such. The MEmorial brings the unconscious into consulting.

Heuretics

Part of becoming an egent and making a MEmorial is learning how this project was generated (an example that is generalizable, transportable to other conditions calling for invention). The EmerAgency is a heuretic invention. In *Heuretics* (1994a) I generated a hypermedia rhetoric (choragraphy) using the heuristic discovered through an analysis of the tradition of discourses on method, from Plato's *Phaedrus* to Breton's Surrealist manifesto. The logic of "invention" (heuretics) includes both the rhetorical sense of *inventio* (collecting the commonplaces of what to say and how to say it) and the creative sense of innovation. A comparative study of a sample of discourses on method revealed a poetics: however different each method was, they all manifested a set of operations summarized in the acronym CATTt (Contrast-Analogy-Theory-Target-tale). We do not yet know how to commemorate 9/11, or any disaster, as a practice of electrate learning. We may generate a method for this practice by choosing materials for each category of the CATTt.

We are using the literate method to bootstrap an electrate practice. The outcome depends on what is used to fill the slots of the CATTt. I will give an overview of my choices, with the understanding that different choices are possible, and the design I propose is relative to these choices. The dilemma for the EmerAgency is that it is a post-Enlightenment consultancy: it hopes to improve the world, but fears that it will only make things worse. To summarize briefly for now, the CATTt generating the MEmorial includes the following relays:

Contrast: The most important approaches to changing society, posed as a continuum between the poles formed by conventional or empirical consulting on one end of the spectrum, and revolutionary politics on the other, whether reactionary or progressive (right wing or left wing). At one extreme is instrumental reason that tinkers only with the utilitarian aspects of the lifeworld, meaning that it confines itself largely to treating symptoms or effects rather than causes of public problems. At the other extreme is revolutionary politics, with its assumption that there may be no solution to any one problem without solving all problems at once (starting over with a clean slate).

Analogy: Tourism as an institution, including both the behavior of families vacationing at tourist destinations and the work of booster organizations inventing these destinations by designing and building attractions. The analogy provides not a template or model but a relay orienting us in the direction of the practice we are inventing.

Theory: Poststructural philosophy, criticism, and art, especially French theory, particularly the work of Georges Bataille, but also Jacques Derrida,

Gilles Deleuze, Félix Guattari, Jean-François Lyotard, and Maurice Blanchot, among others. The comprehensive term for the peculiar mode of poststructural theory I am using is "choragraphy."

Target: The Internet in particular, and the apparatus of digital new media in general. The target supplies the terms of the problem that is the reason justifying the creation of a new method or poetics: it identifies the requirements calling for invention in the first place. Our target is the Internet as a potential civic sphere and the need for a practice of writing native to this institutional arrangement.

Tale: The EmerAgency. In the tradition of the discourse on method that began with Plato's *Phaedrus* and extends into contemporary philosophy, the syncretizing of the four content generators (CATT) took place in the proposal for some concrete, material practice whose performance would produce the kind of work called for by the conditions addressed in the CATT. The CATT inventories have no form of their own, and must be couched in some specific form to integrate them into coherence. The tale in part dramatizes what it explains. The EmerAgency institution and the MEmorial practice enact this synthesis in *Electronic Monuments* as a discourse on method. It is intended to be taken both literally and figuratively.

ASSIGNMENT

This book is devoted to one assignment: design an electrate commemoration—a MEmorial—for a disaster; it does not have to be for 9/11, the event that stands in for any event of loss whose mourning helps define a community. The immediate goal of this assignment is to develop a familiarity with the Web site and the Internet as media of an emergent language apparatus. The long-range goal is to "improve the world"; or, if not to improve the world, then to understand in what way the human world is irreparable.

Foreshadowing

The first part of the book introduces the project of electronic monumentality within the larger context of learning how to write in a society of the spectacle, in which the image and word have become inseparable. The method proposes a hybrid of tourism and expert consulting as an interface metaphor accessing the logic of a civic sphere within an image civilization. The first chapter begins the hybrid invention by extrapolating from Mount Rushmore to Florida Rushmore, an electronic monument to be constructed at the State Geological Park near Gainesville, Florida. The related online tourist museum celebrates the contributions that tourist inventions have made to the formation of American national identity. MEmorials commemorate as sacrifices the losses that occur in the society that may be ascribed to the persistence of certain value-behaviors such as the use of automobiles, cigarettes, handguns, and the like. The second chapter introduces the prototype of a MEmorial. It commemorates the sacrifice represented by traffic fatalities. The proposal form presenting the MEmorial evokes a tradition that includes everything from the satire of Jonathan Swift's "A Modest Proposal" to the pragmatics of the NAMES project AIDS Quilt. A MEmorial, in other words, is critical, relying on a performative method to overcome "compassion fatigue."

The second part of the book is a workshop placing the MEmorial in the context of journalism, critical theory, and fine arts precedents, models, and relays. The MEmorial inquiry begins (in chapter 3) with the monitoring of journalism in search of a story that stings or disturbs the designer. This procedure is contextualized in an archive of examples showing some of the possibilities to be found among artists and writers who used news events as points of departure for specific works. The fourth chapter focuses on one news event as a case study, featuring an archive of documents that demonstrate a path of displacement away from a lived event through the spectacle (image culture) into a theory of how to map this passage between the personal private and collective public registers.

The third part extends, tests, and demonstrates the principles proposed in the first two parts. The MEmorial is a practice developed for a new institutionalization of civic life online (beginning with the Internet as a virtual public sphere). The biggest change in the imagined community predicted by the theory is the transvaluation of guiding values from ideal principles (abstractions) embodied in narratives to abject behaviors *(abjections)* emblematized in images. In electracy we have to be concerned not only with the spirit but with the body of "America." Chapters 5 and 6 take up an extensive development of a particular MEmorial consulting on policies related to child abuse. The chapters simulate the work of conductive inference—related to Deleuze's *concetto,* showing how images gather information into unstable categories. A MEmorial is proposed—Upsilon Alarm—to be linked to Space Mirror, the Astronaut Memorial at Cape Canaveral.

The fourth part generalizes from the documents of Upsilon Alarm to an electrate category of "justice." Chapter 7 experiments with the theoretical capacities of the impersonation alluded to in that emblematic parable, the Turing test. Chapter 8 documents my collaboration with the artist Will Pappenheimer and the Florida Research Ensemble on a MEmorial for 9/11. The emphasis throughout is on demonstrating the process of invention, so that the theoretical rationale and practical rhetorical operations are grounded always in a specific application, generalizable to other issues and projects. The conclusion introduces a plan for the appropriation of divination forms as an interface by means of which citizens could consult the collective wisdom of Internet databases. This updated hybrid of Western and non-Western epistemologies facilitates the self-consciousness of a (potentially) global group subject.

Part I

Theory Tours

With the revolution in the electromagnetic transmission of images, of sound and information, you could say that the traffic accident finally has a future since, above and beyond the classic accidents of rail, air, sea, or road, we will soon see the emergence of the accident to end all accidents, in other words, the traffic of the generalized accident which will then largely outdo the limited traffic accident of the transport revolution.

—*Paul Virilio,* Open Sky

METAPHORIC ROCKS
(FOUNDING TOURISTS)

Cognitive Jurisdiction

The first step in deconsulting is to challenge the assumptions about cognitive jurisdiction, about what knowledge is relevant to which problems (cancer belongs to medicine, terrorism to law or the military, tourism to public relations). "'Certain words are sort of owned by certain departments,' said Stephen Hallam, dean of Akron's College of Business Administration," addressing the question of ethics education in Business Schools in the wake of the Enron/World Com scandals. "One of the words that is sort of owned by the philosophy department in lots of universities is the word 'ethics'" (Paul Singer, *Gainesville Sun*, August 25, 2002). The fact is that when it is a matter of invention, history shows that innovation almost always comes from outside a specialization. One definition of invention could be "a process by which the status of an idea is transformed from irrelevant to relevant." The EmerAgency is not competing with advertising agencies or consulting firms (let alone Hollywood) for public

*Figure 2. Tourist rhizome: Tyson
Ulmer at Mount Rushmore, 1992.*

relations jobs; it offers a different image expertise, which until now has not been
applied to tourism except in the negative mode of critique. Arts and letters disciplines have said a great deal against tourism, as well as against exclusive reliance on instrumental reason or utilitarian values; the challenge is to design an
improved tourism. The EmerAgency approach is to intervene in tourism at the
level of practice, and to propose not more promotion of what already exists but
to produce a new kind of tourist destination (destiny) and behavior, around
which might form an electrate civic sphere.

The EmerAgency consultation is a hybrid in that the goal is radical tourism, understood in Thomas Kuhn's distinction between revolutionary and
normal science. The aspect of our analogy (tourism) that we wish to radical-
ize is the attraction for tourists of sites of community problems and disasters, an example of which is the Murder, Mystery, and Mayhem Tour in Miami
that takes visitors to famous and not-so-famous crime scenes, including the
home of Gianni Versace, gunned down as he entered his vacation villa in July
1997. Opposing this drive within tourism, the company that recovered arti-
facts from the *Titanic*, RMS Titanic Inc., sought a court order to prevent Deep
Ocean Expeditions from taking sixty people in a submersible vessel to visit the
shipwreck site (a ticket cost $32,500). In contrast, the Russians have taken two
tourists to the orbiting space station and have contracted with a third, 'N Sync

singer Lance Bass (the ticket costs $20 million). The memorial site in Lower Manhattan readily and deliberately enters the tourist spectacle.

Excursions
No Beaches Allowed

Most people go on vacation to get away from reality, not to confront it. But that's exactly what hundreds are paying to do on dozens of "reality tours" organized by Global Exchange, a nonprofit human-rights group based in San Francisco (where else?). For between $135 and $3,600 you can book a trip to visit toxic dumps in California, to survey slums and sweatshops in Mexico or to check out prisons in Belfast. If there's a cause without a tour, an itinerary can be created to address the need. "These trips are experiments in education," says tour coordinator Malia Everette. "It's about meeting people you normally wouldn't." Not everyone praises the experience. Critics claim the politically correct excursions capitalize on those who simply get off on feeling guilty. (Lucy Howard and Ablyn Torias Gajilan, *Newsweek,* April 20, 1998)

Theoria

The EmerAgency could be construed as a vanguard consultancy. Its model comes from a significant point of historical contact between the arts and tourism. The exemplar is Solon, one of the wisest of the ancient Greeks, who is said to be both the first theorist and the first tourist, with the institution combining these practices known as "theoria." Travel was an essential element of archaic theoria. Herodotus noted that theoria was the reason for Solon's visit to the ruler of Lydia. "Originally theoria meant seeing the sights, seeing for yourself, and getting a world view," E. V. Walter commented. "The first theorists were 'tourists'—the wise men who traveled to inspect the obvious world. Solon, the Greek sage whose political reforms around 590 BC renewed the city of Athens, is the first 'theorist' in Western history." This theoria "did not mean the kind of vision that is restricted to the sense of sight. The term implied a complex but organic mode of active observation—a perceptual system that included asking questions, listening to stories and local myths, and feeling as well as hearing and seeing. It encouraged an open reception to every kind of emotional, cognitive, symbolic, imaginative, and sensory experience" (Walter 1988, 3–4).

Nor was the travel of a *theoros* always a response to an event; it could also be a probe. The visit included consultations with the local oracles. The motive for Solon's visit to Lydia, where he went "to see what could be seen," was curiosity. In one of the founding works in the history of method, the *Timaeus,* Plato told the story that is the origin of the legend of Atlantis. On his visit to Egypt, Solon learned from an Egyptian priest that the original Athenians had defeated the empire of Atlantis in its attempt to conquer all the Greeks. The story had been lost when Athens was destroyed in the same cataclysm that sunk Atlantis, and it is retold in *Timaeus* as part of Plato's effort to understand how to put into practice the principles of a just state outlined in the *Republic*. This common source of Solon and chora in *Timaeus* is one motivation for connecting choragraphy with theoria (theory tourism). Plato introduced "chora" as a third metaphysical entity, as the space or region in which being and becoming interacted. This way of conceiving the world is still at work in Leibniz's baroque philosophy. "How can the Many become the One? A great screen has to be placed in between them. Like a formless elastic membrane, an electromagnetic field, or the receptacle of the *Timaeus,* the screen makes something issue from chaos, and even if this something differs only slightly. . . . But the screen only allows compossibles— and only the best combination of compossibles—to be sifted through" (Deleuze 1993, 76). Neither intelligible nor perceptible, chora is relationship as such, sorting chaos into order. Theoria undertakes tours of chora.

The Lost Guide

The MEmorial begins in this shifting on the axis of the metaphor of the travelogue in dialectical essays. Where the two practices part company is on the matter of clarity. Perhaps ideas may be made clear and distinct, but the MEmorial pushes beyond idea into mood, feeling, desire. Acting as theoria, as part of its consultation, the Florida Research Ensemble (FRE) visited the site of the 9/11 disaster and its environs with the assumption that this scene made manifest a choral zone of (dis)order. How could a tour of Lower Manhattan and Ground Zero be put into an image category, to make the event thinkable in electrate terms? To consult in a new way requires first a new apparatus. The larger goal of egents is to become electrate.

There is a connection between tourism and the literate essay that opens a path for this transition. In their analysis of the classic model of the essay, Francis-Noel Thomas and Mark Turner described how the effect of clarity was achieved within literacy. The classic stylist pretended not to argue, but only to present or describe, creating the illusion of an alignment between language and truth. Any style, they proposed, is derived from the conceptual stand of the author—the attitude (perspective) toward truth. The classic stylist believed that truth can be known and recognized. Using conversation as an interface metaphor, the classic essay put the reader in the writer's position or standpoint, and described how things (whether material or abstract) look from there, as if looking out a window to observe a visible scene. "Prose is a window. In the classic attitude, writing serves to present something else: its subject. The subject is conceived of as a 'thing' distinct from the writing, something that exists in the world and is independent of any presentation. Clarity is the central virtue of classic prose because the classic writer's defining task is to present something he has previously perceived. Self-evident truths, Madame de Chevreuse's character, the power of well-ordered thoughts, the food of France are conceived as 'things' with their proper characteristics, existing 'in the world' and completely independent of their presentation" (Thomas and Turner 1994, 36).

"Things" are entities whose articulation, delineation, definition became possible within the conceptual category formation of literacy (Aristotle is credited with the invention of the "thing"—the practice of grouping entities into sets based on definitions of essential versus accidental attributes). The image and relay for classic prose clarity is the tourist guidebook.

> Classic guidebooks are a natural place to begin. They form a large and universal genre in which actual scenes and casts are almost identical to the model scene and cast of classic style. . . . The Michelin Green Guide Series: Places include all the regions of France; many European countries, including Greece and Italy; and several metropolitan regions, including Paris, Rome, London, and Washington, D.C. Classic guidebooks include guides and descriptions of historical sites and monuments, for example, Branislav Brankovic's *Les vitraux de la cathédrale de Saint-Denis,* a pamphlet by the curator of the former abbey church, meant to be used by visitors. Works of art history from a period before documentary photography became routine have a close affinity to guidebooks and are sometimes presented as guides to past mentalities. Emile Male's foundation work on medieval Christian iconography, *L'art religieux au XIII siecle en France* (1898), is a prominent example. . . . Sophisticated classic guidebooks often take the form of travel writing and the literature of places, including the political geography of the historic past and descriptions of imaginary places. (Thomas and Turner 1994, 199)

As opposed to the classic style of the essay still taught in most schools (understandably, since school is an institutionalization of literacy), the MEmorial guide must bring into composition the qualities of modern (electrate) space, which was generated in part by demolishing the perspectivist window and all its extensions as a metaphor for thought.

> This is the outcome of an epoch-making event so generally ignored that we have to be reminded of it at every moment. The fact is that around 1910 a certain space was shattered. It was the space of common sense, of knowledge (savoir), of social practice, of political power, a space thitherto enshrined in everyday discourse, just as in abstract thought, as the environment of and channel for communications; the space, too, of classical perspective and geometry, developed from the Renaissance onwards on the basis of the Greek

tradition (Euclid, logic) and bodied forth in Western art and philosophy, as in the form of the city and town. Such were the shocks and onslaughts suffered by this space that today it retains but a feeble pedagogical reality, and then only with great difficulty, within a conservative educational system. Euclidean and perspectivist space have disappeared as systems of reference, along with other former "commonplaces" such as the town, history, paternity, the tonal system in music, traditional morality, and so forth. (Lefebvre 1991, 25)

That to which a MEmorial bears witness is neither clear nor distinct.

Target Practice

The digital era is beginning in the same way as the era of print, with a religious war in which the status of icons is a central issue. The destruction of the World Trade Center brought tourism and revolution into direct confrontation. Tourist destinations and terrorist targets become synonymous, and tourist guidebooks become espionage databases.

> Large or small, every city, town or village on the map of America believes it has targets that could be a bull's-eye for a terrorist attack. In response, local officials and emergency management experts are taking worried looks at symbols of economic renown and civic pride, major sporting events that draw immense crowds, bridges, dams, nuclear power plants, state capitol buildings and city halls. Suddenly, symbols are being seen as possible risks, from the Seattle Space Needle to the St. Louis Arch; from the Beaverton, Ore., headquarters of Nike Inc., to the Sears Tower in Chicago, to the Daytona Beach International Speedway, where as many as 300,000 spectators gather for auto races. "Every small town should be thinking: What is our town famous for? That could be a target," said John Buckman, president of the International Association of Fire Chiefs. (Miles Benson and Jose Alfredo Flores, *Gainesville Sun,* October 7, 2001)

The propaganda war associated with the Protestant Reformation influenced the institutionalization of print. The conflict of images associated with globalization is likely to influence the institutionalization of electracy. This context raises the stakes of Florida's recurring crisis of image and tourism and clarifies the urgency of coming to terms with electronic monumentality. The FRE began working on these questions in the years leading up to the Columbus quincentenary. The local tourism boards formed in Florida in response to the legislative initiatives of the early 1990s were most concerned with "how and when to advertise and how to get the attention we need." This tendency to treat the question exclusively as a matter of promotion continues through each crisis.

Whether it is murdered tourists, election snafus, or anthrax attacks, Florida protects its image by means of boosterism.

MEmorialization is not tourism, but tourism is an analogy for how the EmerAgency uses the information superhighway to participate in public problem solving. Florida's concern with its public image antedates the debacle of the 2000 election and the ties of the state to every aspect of 9/11, from flight schools where the hijackers received pilot training, to the anthrax attack. Debilitated by recession, embarrassed by its fluctuating rankings on the list of most livable states in America (as low as forty-third one year, based on categories such as income, crime rate, graduation rate, suicide, and taxes; as high as number one in another year, on a different list), Florida's government gave renewed attention to the state's leading industry—tourism. The 1991 legislature created the Florida Tourism Commission and charged it with devising a strategy for promoting tourism. One of the first acts of the commission was to hire the New York consulting firm of Penn & Schoen, which, for a fee of $250,000, assessed what role the state should play in tourism promotion.

In the wake of 9/11, and the need to win the hearts and minds of the Islamic people in the propaganda war between "Jihad and McWorld" (Barber 1995), the U.S. government made a similar move. "President Bush has decided to transform the administration's temporary wartime communications effort into a permanent office of global diplomacy to spread a positive image of the United States around the world and combat anti-Americanism. . . . Officials said the new office would be entirely separate from a proposed Office of Strategic Influence at the Pentagon, which would use the media, the Internet and a range of covert operations to try to influence public opinion and government policy abroad, including in friendly nations" (Elizabeth Becker and James Dao, *Gainesville Sun,* February 20, 2002, 6A).

This situation of state and national government involvement in image management offered a good test for the new consultancy. The Florida image crisis, for example, was a cultural, media-related problem, but the political leadership did not ask the experts in culture in the universities for advice. It turned instead to public relations firms, thus supporting Walter Benjamin's observation that "the time of criticism has passed," to be replaced by advertising. The problem of "how to improve tourism," or "how to communicate with the Islamic public," was framed exclusively as a matter of advertising. Similarly, the CIA officially invited Hollywood entertainers to advise them on brainstorming worst-case scenarios of terrorist attacks, feeling themselves to be imaginatively challenged. These choices are not only understandable but are a recognition of electracy, to the extent that it is within entertainment discourse that electrate reason is emerging. Part of the EmerAgency project is to extract from entertainment forms those features most useful for electrate logic, while dropping those aspects that are peculiar to the institutionalization of new media within a capitalist economy of production (profit motive, competition, mass appeal). It is the task of the EmerAgency to give a voice to education in the war of the spectacle.

Booster Inventions

Group Considers Lures for Tourists
Alachua County Tries to Find Its Niche

Disney World. The Florida Keys. Beaches. Palm trees. That is what usually comes to mind for tourists considering Florida as a vacation destination. But how will Alachua county promote itself to potential tourists? Members from the Alachua County Visitors and Convention Bureau, administrators from surrounding towns, hotel managers and representatives from the arts association and the historical commission in Gainesville met Wednesday to discuss a new vision for area tourism. The idea is to find ways to promote Gainesville more aggressively and successfully. The symposium, hosted by Elaine McLaughlin, principal with Destination Consulting Group, was designed to foster partnerships with leaders from the area's tourism industries. McLaughlin said the county needs to find ways to sell the area's "tourism products," or what the county can pitch to visitors as reasons for coming to the area. The county's strengths, according to McLaughlin, are the unique towns and university atmosphere that make the area different from the rest of Florida. Beginning Saturday, Gainesville will have a front-page feature in *Connections* magazine, which will be in seat backs on all Atlantic Southeast Airlines flights for two months. (Andrew Thompson, *Gainesville SUN,* June 29, 2000)

Theoria foregrounds the heuretic element that has always been at work in tourism, as may be seen in the contribution that tourism has made to the invention of the "United States of America," to the creation of the symbolic capital that carries the value resources of our society. A nation is an idea—an idea with a history. There was a time before nations (the nation-states arose during the era of print literacy), and there may come a time that is without nations (in an electrate apparatus). Tourism has already played an important role in the creation of representations that shaped American national identity. A review of the history of two of the most important embodiments of American identity shows why the Florida Tourism Commission turned to a public relations firm for advice, since PR authored these symbolic inventions. Both originated with booster groups as ways to increase and improve tourism in a specific place.

The first vacation spots in America were spas where people went to "take the waters." This custom, borrowed from Europe, led eventually to the discovery of sea bathing as a leisure activity (an example of a new, invented behavior). Atlantic City, New Jersey, is one of the sites where this new recreation evolved. There were only seven houses there when the railroad arrived in the 1850s (Sutton 1980). By 1900 over $10 million had been invested in hotels. In 1920, looking for a way to keep tourists at the beach through Labor Day, the Business Men's League decided to sponsor a Fall Frolic, which in 1921 introduced a beauty pageant. The first such contest had been held at Rehoboth Beach, Delaware, in the 1880s, but was not repeated. Herb Test, a reporter hired to handle publicity for the Atlantic City version, decided to call the winner "Miss America." "It was decided in committee that newspapers in the Atlantic City trading area would be approached with the suggestion that they use the beauty contest at Atlantic City as a gimmick to increase circulation" (Deford 1971). The association with national identity was established from the beginning, with the first winner (a fifteen-year-old named Margaret Gorman) setting the pattern of a preference for the "civic beauty" of the "amateur" over the "brazen femininity" of professional models and actresses. It may be worth noting that the early pageants were presided over by the figure of King Neptune, the god who was the protector of Atlantis.

Mount Rushmore, also known as the "shrine of democracy," offers a second example of booster inventiveness serving national identity. If Miss America was meant to be the embodiment of our national ideal of womanhood, the Rushmore monument signifies the "achievements of the United States . . . personified by four great national leaders. Washington represents the founding principles of the Union; Jefferson, the Declaration of Independence and the Louisiana Purchase; Lincoln, the preservation of the country during the Civil War; and [Teddy] Roosevelt, the expansion of the country . . . and the conservation of [its] natural resources" (*Tour Book: North Central,* American Automobile Association, 2005). In the early 1920s, Doane Robinson, state historian for South Dakota, began thinking of ways to lure tourists to his state.

Having read of the work of Guzton Borglum (carving a monument to the Confederacy on the face of Stone Mountain, Georgia), it struck Robinson that a monument could be carved in the granite of the Black Hills. He proposed the idea on the spot to a tourist promotion group, suggesting that the principal figure be Chief Red Cloud, supported by other heroes of the Old West such as General Custer (Smith 1985). Booster clubs in the area were enthusiastic, although they considered the idea impossible. Borglum was recruited to the project and changed its theme to the Founding Fathers, to better realize his aim of "a monument dedicated to the meaning of America." After some twenty years the carving was completed, and today it attracts over two million visitors annually.

The Monument as Rhizome

The EmerAgency consultancy concerns not just the design of a "magnet of attraction" for a tourist destiny, but the axis of attraction-repulsion constituting the sacred dimension of experience still active in modern life. The immediate lesson of Atlantic City and Mount Rushmore is that there exists a monumental tourism—an activity whose motivation mixes the economic with the symbolic, involving a visit to a place marked by a thing or an event that represents a collective value. It might be helpful to generalize from these examples in order to discover their relevance to our own situation. The goal of the FRE in the 1990s was to propose a monument—an electrate commemoration—that would attract tourists to Alachua County (Gainesville), Florida, as an initial site for the implementation of a tourism of invention. The purpose of electrate monuments is to raise the awareness of tourists about the creative, productive dimension of their behavior. In the aftermath of 9/11, the government encouraged citizens to return to their consumer behavior as an act of patriotism and even of defiance. In principle, this appeal made citizens aware of the symbolic dimension of their quotidian activities. The MEmorial project builds on this attitude, to use the Internet as a way to open tourist invention to citizens, especially through the public schools. A wedding of the Internet and tourism promises the formation of an international civic sphere.

Rushmore and Miss America are products of what Gilles Deleuze and Félix Guattari called an "abstract machine"—a generative or inventive idea. To convey how such machines operate, the theorists use the metaphor of the rhizome; one of their favorite examples is the relationship between the wasp and the orchid. The relationship that plants form with insects, animals, people, the wind, in order to propagate, is a rhizome. Joseph Beuys used a similar example to express his understanding of creative thinking, stating that people make thought the way bees make honey. Tourism is rhizomatic—it makes collective identity the way bees make honey, that is, tourism offers a possible point of access to a group subjectivity.

> Make a map, not a tracing. The orchid does not reproduce a tracing of the wasp; it forms a map with the wasp, in a rhizome. What distinguishes the map from the tracing is that it is entirely oriented toward an experimentation in contact with the real. The map does not reproduce an unconscious closed in upon itself; it constructs the unconscious. . . . The map is open and connectable in all of its dimensions; it is detachable, reversible, susceptible to constant modification. It can be torn, reversed, adapted to any kind of mounting, reworked by an individual, group, or social formation. It can be drawn on a wall, conceived of as a work of art, constructed as a political action or as a meditation. Perhaps one of the most important characteristics of the rhizome is that it always has multiple entryways. (Deleuze and Guattari 1987, 12)

Florida Rushmore

How to formulate an utterance in the collective discourse of tourism? It is possible to formulate a specific proposal for the Florida Tourist Commission, based on the above discussion. (Here is a heuristic rule: produce your invention in relation to a specific institution and an explicit public policy issue.) The proposal includes the following steps of reasoning:

1. The state desires not only to promote tourism, but to improve it.
2. Monumental practices (including events and celebrations as well as memorials) are magnets attracting tourists to specific sites.
3. Tourism and monuments form a rhizome that in practice "constructs the political unconscious" of a culture.
4. An important public policy issue after 1992 concerns the revision of American national identity in the new postcolonial era of multiculturalism.
5. Theoria names a forgotten function for tourism, in which the process of cultural invention through sightseeing becomes self-conscious, reflexive, and hence potentially intelligent.
6. Critical tourism allows citizens to participate directly in the continuing invention of "America," at a time when "America" is part of global symbolic capital.
7. Conclusion: the EmerAgency deconsulting practice may be tested by designing a new kind of monument, specifically created to support the transition of a literate nation into electracy.

The FRE proposal (made to the county economic planning council in the early 1990s) was to build an electronic version of Mount Rushmore in Florida, a version that revises and supplements the original. The theoretical rationale for this choice is based on the psychological function of monuments known as "mourning." The rhizomatic nature of tourism and monuments is due to the reciprocal relationship between the formation of individual and collective identity. The entry points to the network of American identity are marked by monuments. There is a reason why revolutionaries, when they come to power, destroy the monuments of their predecessors, not to mention those of their foreign enemies.

Mourning

In psychoanalytic terms, "mourning" refers to the process by which the person is constituted as a distinctly separate self, yet part of the larger whole of society. The loss of unity with the mother's body is mourned by internalizing (introjecting) an image of the parents in the unconscious (and eventually other figures with whom the self identifies, forming what is known as the superego). The loss is compensated for by the symbolizing power (language) associated with such introjections. Collective entities such as nations maintain their identity through a similar process of symbolization, mourning the loss of one genera- tion of citizens after the other, back to the Founding Fathers. Monuments are to a nation what the superego is to an individual. "We recall Freud's suggestion that the superego is made up of the 'illustrious dead,' a sort of cultural reservoir, or rather cemetery, in which one may also inter one's renounced love-objects, and in which the ruling monument is the internalized figure of the father" (Sacks 1985).

An electronic Rushmore, however, produces a mourning identification that is flexible and diverse rather than one that is carved in stone. An electronic monument is one in which there is a mapping between the individual and the collective, such that the memorializing reveals to the citizens the rhizome that gives rise to the condition in which "Problems B Us" (the EmerAgency slogan).

> The unconscious is that chapter of my history which is marked by a blank
> or occupied by a falsehood: it is the censored chapter. But the Truth can be
> found again; it is most often already written down elsewhere. That is to say:
> - in monuments: this is my body . . .
> - in archival documents also: these are my childhood memories . . .
> - in semantic evolution: this corresponds to the stock of words and
>   acceptations of my own particular vocabulary, as it does to my style
>   of life and to my character;
> - in traditions as well, but also in the legends which, in a heroicized
>   form, transport my history;
> - and lastly, in the traces which are inevitably preserved by the distor-
>   tions necessitated by the linking of the adulterated chapter to the
>   chapters surrounding it. (Lacan 1968, 21)

The terms (monument, archive, vocabulary, tradition, legend) apply to the collective as well as to the individual versions: the citizens find their missing chapter precisely in the collective, extant, external records of the civilization (their identity as citizens is "extimate" in Lacan's terms: at once inside and out- side of the border of "self"). Guattari says something similar in exploring the nature of the group subject:

> I am not going to try to produce a theory basing the intrinsic interlinking
> of historical processes on the demands of the unconscious. To me that is too
> obvious to need demonstrating. The whole fabric of my inmost existence is
> made up of the events of contemporary history—at least in so far as they have
> affected me in various ways. My phantasies have been molded by the "1936

complex," by that wonderful book of Trotsky's, *My Life,* by all the extraordinary rhetoric of the Liberation, especially those of the youth hostelling
movement, anarchist groups, the UJRF, Trotskyist groups and the Yugoslav
brigades . . . The Algerian war, the War in Vietnam, the left wing of the
U.N.E.F., and so on and so on. (1984, 26–27)

In articulating the peculiar nature of the group subject mediating between
individual selves and the collective processes of society, Guattari takes as his
prototype the American street gang. In terms of the mystory, the gang embodies the mode of power specific to the street as one of the emerging institutions
of the popcycle.

> To achieve any understanding of social groups, one must get rid of one kind
> of rationalist-positivist vision of the individual (and of history). One must be
> capable of grasping the unities underlying historical phenomena, the modes
> of symbolic communication proper to groups (where there is often no mode
> of spoken contract), the systems that enable individuals not to lose them-
> selves in interpersonal relationships, and so on. To me it is all reminiscent of
> a flock of migrating birds: it has its own structure, the shape it makes in the
> air, its function, its direction—and all determined without benefit of a single
> central committee meeting, or elaboration of a correct line. . . . The gang of
> young men that forms spontaneously in a section of town does not recruit
> members or charge a subscription; it is a matter of recognition and internal
> organization. Organizing such a collective depends not only on the words
> that are said, but on the formation of images underlying the constitution of
> any group, and these seem to me something fundamental—the support upon
> which all their other aims and objects rest. I do not think one can fully grasp
> the acts, attitudes or inner life of any group without grasping the thematics
> and functions of its "acting out" of phantasies. (35)

Guattari has confidence in the creativity of the mass of people, but also
warns against the fascist potential inherent within this process of image formation. That is, there is a natural tendency for the group to identify with the
established institution or its leaders. "The institution never sets out to face the
problem of the institutional object, though it is obsessed by it; just as the church
has its God and has no wish to change him, so a dominant class has power and
does not consider whether it might not be better to give that power to anyone
else!" (39). The danger of sovereignty, in Bataille's terms, is when a group reifies
its power (its energy or "effervescence"), projected onto a leader. His description of Hitler has special resonance today:

> Until our times, there had only been a single historical example of the sudden
> formation of a total power, namely, the Islamic Khalifat. While both military

and religious, it was principally royal, relaying upon no prior foundation. Islam, a form comparable to fascism in its meager human wealth, did not even have recourse to an established nation, much less a constituted State. But it must be recognized that, for fascist movements, the existing State has first been something to conquer, then a means of a frame, and that the integration of the nation does not change the schema of their formation. Just like early Islam, fascism represents the constitution of a total heterogeneous power whose manifest origin is to be found in the prevailing effervescence. (1985, 153)

In the case of the "town hall meeting" sponsored by the Lower Manhattan Development Corporation (LMDC), the majority of the more than five thousand people in attendance disapproved of the six plans presented to them, plans severely restricted by the program required by the Port Authority leaseholder whose primary interest was commercial. Is this recalcitrance a sign of group effervescence? Mathew Higgins, a spokesman for the LMDC, was quoted after the meeting as saying, "Now that we've received public input we have to evaluate how to refine the plans to better reflect what people hope to see in Lower Manhattan" (*Gainesville Sun,* July 22, 2002). The EmerAgency MEmorial is intended to expand this public participation in monumentality into a permanent Internet deconsultancy, to adapt the invention of tourist destinations as an analogy for authoring the images that underlie the group subject, and to make them available as sites of possible collective education.

A Holographic Monument

According to the theory in our generative CATTt, a human being circulates around a "hole"; in Lacan's phrase, "truth makes a hole in science." Goedel's last theorem showed that "there is a hole in the field of science that prevents its rational unification. On the other hand, in the field of conjectural sciences, the function of the hole is taken up by the unconscious; the two incompletenesses become figures of one another" (Leupin 1991, 7). In Guattari's terms, there are two kinds of logic: the discursive logic used by instrumental problem solvers, and pathic logic, which is the sort operating in group subjects (1995, 28). The EmerAgency supplements conventional consulting with an inventional exploration of the pathic dimension of problems. Monuments mark, suture, and cover the hole in the civic sphere, as in the project under way in Lower Manhattan. The MEmorial deconsultation supplements this conventional (necessary) monumentality with a reminder of the irreparability of the hole: the hole in the city manifested, if only temporarily, the hole in the real that is the fundamental limit of human existence, and the hole in the subject marking the trauma of individuation.

To evoke the relationship between the collective and personal registers of the hole (the monument and the symptom), Florida Rushmore proposed to use the technology of holography and computers to create a continuously changing image of a face, projected in 3-D at the same scale as the Rushmore heads (sixty feet high). "Holography is a method of lensless photography in which the wave field of light scattered by an object is recorded on a plate as an interference pattern. When the photographic record—the hologram—is placed in a coherent light beam like a laser, the original wave pattern is regenerated. A three-dimensional image appears. Because there is no focusing lens, the plate appears as a meaningless pattern of swirls. Any piece of the hologram will reconstruct the entire image" (Wilber 1982).

Nancy Burson's computer-generated portraits are the model for the faces represented in Florida Rushmore. Burson extended the technique of composite photography, invented by Francis Galton in 1877, to the medium of digital computer graphics. Using software developed by Richard Carling and David Kramlich, Burson essentially reinvented photography. Her technique of amalgamating and manipulating images has been used by the FBI to update photographs of missing children and by *People* magazine to project the effect of age on celebrities. Composites of everything from a lion/lamb through the heads of state of the nuclear powers to an Asian/Caucasian/black (with features weighted according to current world population statistics) are said to explore themes as universal as sexuality and race and concerns as common as beauty, celebrity, and political power.

This compositing is at once practical and memorial, as exemplified in the practice in recent years of including several composites of missing children in the tax form booklets distributed by the Internal Revenue Service. One "Jeremy Grice," for example, "male, born: 5/12/81; Ht: 3'8, 40 lbs; Hazel eyes; Blonde hair," is pictured in two photos: as he was at the time of his disappearance and also as "age-progressed to 18 years. He was last seen by a neighbor at about 8:45 a.m. He was standing near a mailbox, wearing no shoes. Child was last seen on 11/22/85 and is missing from North Augusta, SC." The public service ad is the work of a partnership between the IRS and the National Center for Missing and Exploited Children (1-800-THE-LOST, http://www.missingkids.com). The "age-progressed" photo is a composite produced by updating the child's features with those taken from photos of relatives.

That Burson's technique is especially suited to theoria has to do with the historical affinity between psychoanalysis and photography. Walter Benjamin said that photography is to the visible world what psychoanalysis is to the mind—producing thus the "optical unconscious." Freud himself drew on Galton's composite technique to describe the logic of dreams:

What I did was to adopt the procedure by means of which Galton produced family portraits, namely by projecting two images on to a single plate, so that certain features common to both are emphasized, while those which fail to fit in with one another cancel one another out and are indistinct in the picture. In my dream about my uncle the fair beard emerged prominently from a face which belonged to two people and which was consequently blurred; incidentally, the beard further involved an allusion to my father and myself through the intermediate idea of growing gray. (1965, 328)

Ludwig Wittgenstein extended the relevance of the composite family photo from the unconscious to conscious reason or category formation by suggesting that concepts gathered discrete units of information together based on a kind of family resemblance among the units. Working with this same association between human and logical classification, Bataille took the side of the remainder, of the features eliminated in the composite. "Thus twenty mediocre faces constitute a beautiful face, and one obtains without difficulty faces whose proportions are very nearly those of the Hermes of Praxiteles. The composite image would thus give a kind of reality to the necessarily beautiful Platonic idea. At the same time, beauty would be at the mercy of a definition as classical as that of the common measure. But each individual form escapes this common measure and is, to a certain degree, a monster" (Bataille 1985, 55).

The MEmorial experiments with the Internet as a prosthesis of the (political) unconscious by mapping the features that fall within and outside the lines of the group subject. In principle the group subject may become aware of itself in this composite way as an emergent effect of a distributed monument. In practice this means that the force that Freud describes as the superego is externalized, visualized, and potentially rendered scriptable. For the individual this means that part of making a MEmorial involves locating and distinguishing the experience of superego effects. For the community the collective nature of these effects may be registered and coordinated. An assumption is that while there is relatively good awareness of the operations of a collective libido in entertainment discourse, there is less appreciation of the work of superego (to use these psychoanalytic terms as shorthand for the complex collective process of the human struggle with animal existence). The riddle we are unpacking is given another version by Deleuze and Guattari:

There is no longer even a need for a transcendent center of power; power is instead immanent and melds with the "real," operating through normalization. A strange invention: as if in one form the doubled subject were the cause of the statements of which, in its other form, it itself is a part. This is the paradox of the legislator-subject replacing the signifying despot: the more you obey the statements of the dominant reality, the more in command you are as subject of enunciation in mental reality, for in the end you are only obeying yourself! (1987, 130)

The Popcycle

Tourists visiting Florida Rushmore have an opportunity to fill out a questionnaire designed to elicit information indicative of the figures with whom they identify in each of the popcycle institutions—figures that represent their personalized or internal Rushmore. Mystory as allegory helps individuals map what Guattari calls a "transversalist subjectivity, one which permits us to understand both its idiosyncratic territorialised couplings (Existential Territories) and its opening onto value systems (Incorporeal Universes) with their social and cultural implications" (1995, 4).

> Should we keep the semiotic productions of the mass media informatics, telematics and robotics separate from psychological subjectivity? I don't think so. Just as social machines can be grouped under the general title of Collective Equipment, technological machines of information and communication operate at the heart of human subjectivity, not only within its memory and intelligence, but within its sensibility, affects and unconscious fantasms. Recognition of these machinic dimensions of subjectivation leads us to insist, in our attempt at redefinition, on the heterogeneity of the components leading to the production of subjectivity. Thus one finds in it: 1. Signifying semiological components which appear in the family, education, the environment, religion, art, sport . . . 2. Elements constructed by the media industry, the cinema, etc. 3. A-signifying semiological dimensions that trigger informational sign machines, and that function in parallel or independently of the fact that they produce and convey significations and denotations, and thus escape from strictly linguistic axiomatics. (ibid.)

To make a mystory an egent is to map the path of connections that traverse these heterogeneous discourses, to locate the "existential refrain" that brings into alignment or attunement the institutions of family, entertainment, school, and discipline (career specialization). Entertainment as an institution is understood in the broadest terms, as one of the core discourses of the popcycle—the matrix of languages and administrative orders that every citizen learns, and that serves to interpellate (hail) or socialize people into the cultural order of their community (the nation-state within literacy). The popcycle is so named to reflect the circulation of ideas or memes through all the institutions, with any of the discourses being a potential source for materials used in any of the other discourses.

Family

The discourse of family operates by means of:

    natural language
    oral forms (anecdote, proverb, joke)
    commonsense reasoning
    self-evident proof

Through family experience a person comes to embody a specific version
of the ideological categories of identity formation (race, ethnicity, religion,
gender, sexuality, class, nationality).

Entertainment

The discourse of entertainment operates by means of:

    pop culture
    media forms (ad, sitcom, news, documentary)
    mytho-logic
    fashion as proof

Through experience of entertainment a person internalizes a set of norms
(VALS—values and lifestyles) reflecting the preferred choices among all the
possibilities available within the ideological identity categories (the hegemony in the United States of white, Anglo-Saxon, Protestant, masculine,
heterosexual, bourgeois, American . . .). These stories bridge the gap between
the official ideals and values authorized by school and the actual experience
of life in the family.

School

The discourse of school operates by means of:

    official history
    textbooks
    cultural literacy
    proof by authority

The institution of school instills the practices of literacy through training
in analytical reason in general, and indoctrination in the version of history
approved by the local and national community.

Career

The discourse of career operates by means of:

    disciplinary knowledge
    treatise
    (formal) logic
    proof by argumentation

Through the institution of career one becomes an expert in a specialized field of knowledge. The method of the field embraces (or simulates) the scientific state of mind—objectivity and systematic doubt—without acknowledging that the dynamics of the "entry into language" that operate in the other discourses by means of identification and introjection (internalization of tutor figures as imagoes) also occurs in this discourse.

For some people, two other institutions—church and street—play significant roles in the popcycle as well. One way to understand the Euthyphro paradox is in terms of the popcycle. Every educated citizen is native to most if not all of these institutions, and the circulation of information, ideas, and values through these different logics constitutes an economy of creativity in the modern world. The history of invention shows that the greatest problem solvers are those who somehow intuitively learned how to think with the whole popcycle. Or, to use Guattari's terms, creativity involves thinking with a group subjectivity. This multitasking thought may be described as bringing to bear on discipline puzzles or enigmas the resources of problem solving figured imaginatively in the researchers' experience of the discourses supposedly irrelevant to the disciplinary paradigm. Inventors have had to be their own Champollions, discovering how in each case to decipher the Rosetta Stone of their popcycle—how to translate across the different languages and logics internalized through interpellation to form their cognitive maps, their psychogeography. At the same time, the popcycle articulates the sources of *ATH,* those circumstances already in place and into which we are thrown at birth, providing the default moods enforcing in us the institutional construction of identity.

Thus one thing researchers have to do to participate in the EmerAgency is to construct their personal Rosetta Stone as a backstory for the MEmorial. The mystory is a cognitive map locating the maker's position in each of the popcycle institutions. A goal of the mystory is, in Nietzsche's phrase, *to find that secret point at which the aphorism of thought intersects with the anecdote of life.* Such a crossroads exists in virtually every person's biography, marking the border or destiny of identity. Mapping this intersection is one way of providing testimony as a witness in the creation of public policy. The mystory helps the egents experience the truth of the EmerAgency slogan: Problems B Us.

A Mystorical Survey

Visitors to Florida Rushmore fill out a questionnaire whose purpose is to locate the tourist's internal monument. The questionnaire uses the formula of mystory, that is, a discursive equivalent of a composite photograph. A mystory condenses/displaces into one account information from the four core discourses used by Americans: family anecdotes, school history textbooks, popular media, and disciplinary expertise. The computer uses the tourist's responses to the questions to identify four figures—one from each discourse area (family history, public history, entertainment, and career field)—as a representation of the individual's superego.

The computer collects in its memory the composite face of each tourist's personal Rushmore, randomly selecting a new one every fifteen minutes to be projected as the face of Florida Rushmore. As Andy Warhol said, in media America, everyone will be famous for fifteen minutes. Thus the Rushmore of an electronic, postcolonial America will be as diverse as the population of the nation itself. The tourist may purchase a graphic printout of his/her composite as a souvenir. A tourist whose superego is projected as the national monument is awarded a commemorative hologram. Burson's work has been praised for creating utterly believable faces, "like the faces in our dreams, struck from life but recast by our concerns. It is an instrumental imagination, manifesting human inner vision" (Burson et al. 1986, 21). Florida Rushmore puts this imagination to work on the task of representing the continuing dream of a democratic, free America. Part of its purpose is to remind citizens that "America" is precisely a dream. A nation, like an individual, can come to know itself better by learning how to remember and tell its dreams. The externalization of the psychological process of identification (mourning) demonstrated in the monument makes Florida Rushmore the founding site of tourism as theoria.

The challenge of the programmers is the expression on this face, which must convey the very nature of faciality as a machine of white walls and black holes, in Deleuze and Guattari's terms. They place this machine of power in a grammatological context of literacy as apparatus. Certain social formations (we would say literate social formations) need face and also landscape.

> It is these assemblages, these despotic or authoritarian formations that give the new semiotic system the means of its imperialism, in other words, the means both to crush the other semiotics and protect itself against any threat from outside. A concerted effort is made to do away with the body and corporeal coordinates through which the multidimensional or polyvocal semiotics operated. Bodies are disciplined, corporeality dismantled, becomings-animal hounded out, deterritorialization pushed to a new threshold—a jump is made from the organic strata to the strata of signifiance and subjectification. A single substance of expression is produced. The white wall/black hole system is constructed, or rather the abstract machine is triggered that must allow and ensure the almightiness of the signifier as well as the autonomy of the subject. You will be pinned to the white wall and stuffed in the black hole.

This machine is called the faciality machine because it is the social production of face, because it performs the facialization of the entire body and all its surroundings and objects, and the landscapification of all worlds and milieus. (Deleuze and Guattari 1987, 181)

Location: The Devil's Millhopper Sinkhole

Doane Robinson's idea for a monument on Mount Rushmore was inspired in part by his love for the landscape of the Black Hills, especially the granite cliffs protruding above the forested hills. The geology of South Dakota, in fact, was suited to the fixed concept of the nation common in the America of Robinson's era. But the psychogeography of America has changed in the postmodern era, for which the limestone acquifer of Florida is a better metaphor than is the bedrock of the plains and foothills of the North. As children sometimes write in their social studies reports, "We should not take our freedom for *granite*." The best location for Florida Rushmore is the sinkhole known as the Devil's Millhopper, where the flux of the electronic portraits and the instability of the land figure together the fragility of the digitally imagined community (the porous character of the land corresponds to the porosity of baroque space).

Two miles northwest of Gainesville is the state geological site (the only one in Florida), the Devil's Millhopper, exemplifying one of the most unusual features of the Florida landscape—the sinkhole. Formed nearly twenty thousand years ago, the sink is nearly 120 feet deep and 500 feet across at the top. Since 1976 a 221-step wooden stairway takes the visitor to the bottom of the hole. "The sink got its name after fossilized bones and teeth were found there, and visitors termed the hole the lair of the devil" (Marth and Marth 1992). "In general, sinkholes are the result of the action of water on the porous limestone substrate underlying northern Florida, which is characterized by countryside riddled with shallow, interweaving networks of caves. When the ceiling of an underground cave has worn too thin from dissolution, it simply cannot support its own weight and collapses" (Stubbs 1972). Sinkhole formation continues today, accelerated by human activity such as the heavy pumping of ground water. In the Gulf Coast city of Dunedin, just since 1990 more than 172 homeowners reported structural damage because of sinkholes, causing an insurance company to discontinue homeowner insurance for the entire city. In 1981 a hole opened in Winter Park, Florida, developing within a few hours into the size of a football field and as deep as an eight-story building, causing two million dollars in damages to swallowed and sunken property. Within days the hole ranked as a major tourist attraction, and many people were seen wearing "Sinkhole 1981" T-shirts.

A sinkhole is just one of several features of karst topography, which includes poljes, dolines, caverns, lapies, and the variety of plants, animals, and human habitation associated with such formations. The term "karst" originated as the proper name of the northwestern part of Yugoslavia, including Croatia, and was then generalized to refer to any area similarly rich in soluble limestone rock. The ethnic warfare under way in that region since the collapse of the Soviet Union represents a warning, of which karst may serve as a reminder, of one possible alternative to national identity. The value of locating Florida Rushmore at a sinkhole is that the karst geology may serve as a figure in a psychogeographical allegory—the underground movement of water, following the line of least resistance (greatest permeability) through fractures and cavities, creates the surface features of the landscape, analogous to the way the workings of the unconscious are manifested in symptoms. Symptoms, in turn, are said to be personal monuments to forgotten traumas.

The geology itself, in other words, is an allegory of our social and psychological processes. Freud used landscape as an explanation of his "structural" model of the psyche—divided into ego, superego, and id.

> Let me give you an analogy; analogies, it is true, decide nothing but they can make one feel more at home. I am imagining a country with a landscape of varying configuration—hill-country, plains, and chains of lakes—, and with a mixed population: it is inhabited by Germans, Magyars, and Slovaks, who carry on different activities. . . . A few things are naturally as you expected, for fish cannot be caught in the mountains and wine does not grow in the water. Indeed, the picture of the region that you brought with you may on the whole fit the facts; but you will have to put up with deviations in the details. (Freud, in Erdelyi 1985)

The analogy is picked up in Deleuze and Guattari's notion of faciality, having to do with the effects of power in the relationship of a state to its citizens. In terms of signification—as an abstract machine—a face is a system created by the relationship of black holes to white walls. Power circulates in this system through such facial rhizomes as the mother/child, two lovers, the celebrity/fan, the politician/voter. What the face is to the body, the landscape is to the environment (a system of surfaces and holes organized into significance, expressing relations of power).

Although the original plans for Mount Rushmore called for the sculpting of the whole bodies of the figures, the final embodiment of the idea in the four heads relates the monument to the talking heads of the electronic era (anticipated by the close-up shot in cinema). The face is produced only when the head ceases to be a part of the body, when it ceases to be coded by the body. That is, identification with this face makes one not the member of a family, but the subject of a state. The karst topography of Florida, with its multitude of flooded sinks, is a setting ideally suited to teaching (and deconstructing) the facial implications of landscape.

Emblematic Rocks

In our electronic monument Freud's analogy is modified: let Florida represent the American psyche. It remains to be worked out how to fit the tenor to the vehicle in this metaphor, how to assign the divisions of the population (Caucasian, Hispanic, African-American, Arab-American, Native American) and the economic activities (agriculture, mining, tourism) to the divisions of the structural model of the mind. But as Freud said, there is a certain disorderly mixing among all these components, whether as nation or psyche.

We begin with the old bones found at Millhopper that could be associated with the themes of mourning (the bones found in a grave or tomb). For tourists, to perform theoria does not require full awareness of the method of metaphors from which are composed the myths holding together a nation. They do not need to be experts or linguists of national identity in order to become monumentally inventive. Indeed, as one commentator on nation-building noted, what a society really wants to remember it puts into the bodies of its members. At the level of behavior, monumentality is a kind of writing whose school is tourism: its "thought" is its performance. The matrix of geology, technology, and culture existing in the Millhopper landscape makes it an ideal location for bringing this symbolic practice (written mourning) into reflexive visibility. Tourist behavior is the "parole," so to speak, of this monumental "langue."

> The realm of signification, as the correlate of subjective individuation, is abandoned in favor of that of the machinic plane of consistency, which allows of the conjunction of meaning and matter by bringing into play abstract machines that are ever more de-territorialized and more closely in contact with material fluxes of all kinds. Signification proceeded from the movement of consciousness returning upon itself, form a turning inwards to representative images from a rupture with machinic conjunctions. A collective apparatus of utterance may remain meaningless to particular people, and yet draw its meaning (its historical or poetic meaning, for instance) from a direct creative conjunction with the fluxes. . . . In short the equation "signified + signifier = signification" arises from the individuation of phantasies and from subjugated groups, whereas the equation "collective force of utterance = machinic sense/nonsense" arises from group phantasy, and the group as subject. (Guattari 1984, 96)

It is not what tourists say but what they do that counts. The "fluxes" refer to the flows of energy and material circulating through a region in the form of electricity, finance, traffic, and the like. A tourist destination has always functioned as a means to attract and harness such flows to a particular location.

Freud compared psychoanalysis to archaeology, with the analyst sifting through the products of the unconscious the way an archaeologist penetrated the surface of the landscape to reconstruct the facts of a buried city, like Schleimann at Troy. Contemporary archaeology includes the use of satellites and remote sensing technology, as in the discovery of the city of Ubar, "a major hub of the frankincense trade that vanished beneath the desert sands of southern Oman two millennia ago." The city perished in a disaster around AD 100. "Evidence at the Oman site indicates that much of the settlement fell into a sinkhole created by the collapse of an underground limestone cavern" (Bower 1992). Indeed, Florida is in the same latitudinal belt as great deserts such as the Sahara and the Arabian Desert, but being a peninsula and the proximity of warm ocean currents make it one of the nation's wettest states.

The sinkhole is "cartographic," in Guattari's terms, constituting an image passage between diverse times, places, activities. The link between Florida and Ubar rests on more than the shared karst topography. Researchers found the city by tracing ancient desert roads detected beneath the sand in pictures taken by the radar and optical cameras carried by the space shuttle *Challenger* in 1984. The shuttles, of course, are launched from Florida (including the spectacular, catastrophic explosion of *Challenger* in 1986). This link suggests that the Astronaut Memorial located at Spaceport USA, Cape Canaveral, would be a good anchoring site for an electronic monument. Lawrence of Arabia referred to Ubar as "the Atlantis of the Sands," thus associating the destruction of Atlantis with a sinkhole collapse. As the part of the continent to emerge most recently from the ocean, Florida might be thought of as a natural Atlantis (which was expected to rise again). Some of the early maps of the New World, in any case, identified the place Columbus discovered as "Atlantis." This allusion returns us to Solon, who told the story of Atlantis in Plato's *Timaeus*. In other words, the simulation of an individual's superego as a postcolonial Rushmore shows how chora mediates individual/collective identities. Chora names the way in which a specific geographical region provides a mnemonic space for collective invention.

Plato used a karst feature—a cave—as the setting for his famous allegory of enlightenment. A prisoner escapes from a cave where all the citizens are held captive, permitted to see only the shadows cast on a wall by a fire behind them, where their captors carry all manner of objects whose reflections are accepted as reality. The escape allows the prisoner to see how the shadows have been produced (the world of belief). He leaves the cave and enters the sunlight (the world of forms). He then feels obligated to return to the cave to tell the others about the truth he has discovered. Many commentators on this allegory have observed that if Plato were writing today, he would use the popular institutions of cinema and television instead of the fire and shadows to represent the world of the cave. In Florida this allegory may be associated with the Sunshine Law, which requires public access to government documents and proceedings, thus mapping a matrix of public access to information, sunbathing, and the representative of the Good in the physical world (old Sol).

Social Sculpture

The immediate goal of the deconsultation is to introduce tourists to their participation in theoria. This introduction includes suggestions for inventive activities. To accommodate this need, a Museum of Cultural Inventions is established at the site of the electronic monument with displays tracing the contribution of arts and letters to American traditions, such as Washington Irving's invention of the myth of Columbus, or Owen Wister, Teddy Roosevelt, and Frederick Remington's invention of the cowboy. The museum sponsors exhibits from the history of the liberal and fine arts that might serve as models showing theoria groups how to become inventors of the kind of images that support group subjects.

A series of projects by the German performance artist Joseph Beuys exemplifies the nature of such exhibits. Beuys developed the strategy of a politically therapeutic "social sculpture" in environmental works such as *Show Your Wound,* in which he set up an installation in an ugly, dangerous place—the underground pedestrian area in Munich. "Beuys assembled one of his most tragic environments, *Show Your Wound,* in the underground pedestrian area between Maximilianstrasse and Altstadtring in Munich. The concrete desolation of such a place gave it the connotation of a sick spot in the urban environment, a wound inflicted by the abstraction of modern planning. Individual and collective sickness is taken as symptomatic of the profound alienation of the contemporary human condition" (Tisdall 1979).

In *Tallow* Beuys selected a similar site in Munster, which he used as a cast for a giant sculpture using twenty tons of mutton and beef fat. This line of work led to his proposal for a Free International University (FIU) to be established in Belfast to function as an arts consultancy for resolving the dilemma of Ireland. "It is typical of Beuys to seek out a wound, a sore spot, which is also a very concrete representation of the wider context of social failure. It is equally typical that the artist does not simply use this sore spot for a denunciation, but applies to it his own kind of dialectic. He attempts to heal the place" (Laszlo Gloser, in Tisdall 1979). Beuys's FIU is one of the inspirations for the EmerAgency. The choral principle involved is that the outer sore spots figure an inner wound inherent in individual subject formation (identity is irreparably traumatic). Problems B Us. The sore spots of the community may be grasped pathically as features of identity.

According to the theory guiding our CATTt, human identity (individual and collective) is formed through a figural operation (the unconscious is structured like a language). The three registers ("exigencies") in Lacan's account of the psyche—the Real, the Symbolic, and the Imaginary—are held together by a fourth register—the Symptom. "The symptom is a signifier: more precisely, a metaphor, unthinkable outside a rhetoric of the unconscious, which produces the individual as a unique combination of the three exigencies: 'The symptom is the peculiar notation of the human dimension.' It is clear that the three exigencies are bound only by a hole in their center: the void is therefore the possibility of linkage itself, repeating in each exigency the lack of the master signifier, the phallus" (Leupin 1991, 15). The hole at Ground Zero is a collective symptom, and this is its positive function in the growth and change of the spirit of America.

The "symptom" is sometimes written in the archaic version, *sinthome,* to distinguish this specialized meaning. *Sinthome* names the trait, the signifier without signified, whose insistence transforms nonsense into a plane of consistency (Lacan's analogy is with the way style informs an artist's oeuvre with a unique identity). Guattari's name for this non-sense trait is "existential refrain," thus calling attention to its musical quality. "Like Bakhtin, I would say that the refrain is not based on elements of form, material or ordinary signification, but on the detachment of an existential 'motif' (or leitmotiv) which installs itself like an 'attractor' within a sensible and significational chaos. The different components conserve their heterogeneity, but are nevertheless captured by a refrain which couples them to the existential Territory of my self" (Guattari 1995, 17). An implication for electrate identity is that a unique refrain, a singularity, may be the clasp that holds together a collectivity (that the nation, so to speak, "hangs by a thread"). Or, in a different version, the electrate collectivity is *heterogeneous* and does not even know itself as "whole."

The lesson for mystory is that an apparatus must be able to coordinate in one discourse all the registers of human experience. In the medieval world this correspondence was represented in allegory, with anagogy in the form of Christian cosmology providing the coherence. In postmodernity we returned to allegory, but the coherence principle organizing the disparate orders of experience comes now from the singular trait marking an individual's style of thought, expression, being—the *sinthome.* Mystory is a version of this postmodern allegory, exchanging Lacan's four exigencies for the discourses of the popcycle. A MEmorial visualizes at least a part of this formation of coherence, in which electrate society is held together not by a master narrative but by collections of meaningless signifiers (the material embodiment of the *sinthome*). Here is the challenge of the MEmorial: to test the possibility of a monumental *sinthome* or symptom. In the same way that Florida Rushmore is not any one superego composite, but the continuous display of different superegos, so too is the deconsulting practice a way to focus the multiplicity of MEmorials into a civic sphere. The prognosis of the apparatus, however, is that even if the MEmorial project works, it is only a transition, useful in the emergency of the transvaluation of values whose ultimate outcome will be the declining relevance of nation-states and the experience of selfhood to the coming global order/chaos.

Problem Tours

A goal of the EmerAgency, through theoria as an Internet school practice, is to conjoin the activities of tourism and consulting to create an electrate civic sphere. We are talking about introducing a new behavior into public life, associated with the commemoration of 9/11, the way the Pledge of Allegiance was introduced to mark the opening of the Columbian Exposition in 1893. We have to remember that there was a time when sea bathing, for example, especially in mixed company, was unimaginable, yet now it is one of the chief attractions of Florida. Travel experts report that overseas visitors, for example, who have been coming to the United States in record numbers, are beginning to seek out places off the beaten track. Perhaps this curiosity about America, expanded to include the whole of American experience, could be channeled into psychogeography. Or perhaps these sore spots are the material for a new dimension entirely—the tourist "repulsion."

> The more a place is set apart for free play, the more it influences people's behavior and the greater is its force of attraction. This is demonstrated by the immense prestige of Monaco and Las Vegas—although they are mere gambling places. Our first experimental city would live largely off tolerated and controlled tourism. Future avant-garde activities and productions would naturally tend to gravitate there. In a few years it would become the intellectual capital of the world and would be universally recognized as such. (Chtcheglov 1981)

The situationist inventors of psychogeography wanted a chance to play a part in the creation of situations, as the "tourist" wandered aimlessly or drifted through the urban landscape. One experimenter in this vein used a map of London to explore an area of Germany with which he was unfamiliar. In conventional tourism, getting lost is at best inconvenient and at worst dangerous. The Museum of Cultural Invention built on the grounds of Florida Rushmore has a Tourist Hall of Fame commemorating tourist sacrifices to chance, such as the Dutch tourist who happened to be in Paris when the Commune took over the city at the end of the Franco-Prussian war. Because of his resemblance to one of the leaders of the rebellion, this tourist was executed on suspicion of being a communard (Mercer 1964).

This incident shows that the opposition between tourism and revolution is grounded in history, with a continuing pattern into the present, as in the case of the Norwegian Hans Christian Ostro. Muslim separatists in Kashmir (once India's greatest tourist attraction, after the Taj Mahal), took Ostro and several other tourists hostage. To show they meant business, the separatists executed Ostro and carved the initials of their terrorist organization on his abdomen. More recently, in the Philippines, Muslim rebels stormed a resort and took a group of eighteen tourists hostage. The Abu Sayyaf rebels beheaded several people, including an American, Guillermo Sobero. They released everyone else, except an American couple, Martin and Grace Burnham, whom they held for ransom. The Burnhams were celebrating their eighteenth wedding anniversary at the Dos Palmas resort hotel when they were seized (*Gainesville Sun*, November 27, 2001). Martin Burnham was killed in June 2002, during a gun battle between the rebels and Filipino soldiers sent to rescue him. Perhaps the assassination of Israel's minister of tourism is not in the same category as the murder of private citizens. Meanwhile, carpet dealers in Afghanistan have set up shop on Chicken Street in Kabul, counting on the return of tourists to their country. And in certain Islamic countries, designers have introduced a full bodysuit that allows women to mix the Western pleasure of going to the beach with the modesties of their faith.

Witnessing

When tourists add theoria to their itinerary, they expose a problematic dimension of the environment to a new kind of attention whose function would not be spectacle but revelation. By analogy, the task of the EmerAgency is to produce an electrate practice capable of focusing this attention on our collective behavior in the way that tragedy was a literate way of focusing the attention of the classical Greeks. Grounded on a physical site (Devil's Millhopper Sinkhole) and extended through the Internet, the information highway, theoria does not rely only on chance to bring tourists to sore spots (repulsions). Communities often provide maps, such as the one suggested by an Alachua County commissioner (Gainesville, Florida), "alerting residents to crime-ridden areas that need to be avoided." The commissioner explained her proposal, motivated by the recovery of a murder victim's body in Gainesville, "that certain wooded areas are havens for prostitution, selling drugs and other criminal activity." Ordinary citizens use these same woods "to walk and meditate." Such maps, and any other available information and documentation of intractable public problems, provide material for a MEmorial.

The point is that such wounds—all the forgotten, denied, troubled places, the leftovers (the unconscious), as well as the more public and famous places

Figure 3. Florida Rushmore composite: blended portraits of Walter Ulmer, George Custer, Gary Cooper, and Jacques Derrida.

such as Ground Zero—emblematize the (w)hole of our condition. They render visible chora, the sorting operation producing the borders of a society. To map and visit these psychogeographic scenes transform the landscape into a rhizome for national self-knowledge. We already have a place in Florida that advertises itself as "an adventure without risk," designed by "imagineers." Theoria is an alternative to, a supplement of, this normal tourism, and those who tour wounds such as the woods in Gainesville are working more in the tradition of adventurers who accepted the risks of travel into the unknown. What might be the effect of this gaze or of the circulation of this testimony preserved in home videos, snapshots, and anecdotes?

The EmerAgency is not tourism, but tourism is a "relay," an analogy (in a CATTt generator) for an Internet-deconstructed consultancy—in particular that inventive aspect of tourism that produces some of the emblems of our collective identity. Egents as theoria know something about the karstification of culture. They learn how a visit to Florida may show that the idea of America is not granite (not igneous, however ingenious) but limestone (not metamorphic but metaphoric), soluble in water, and with the rains becoming more acidic every year. Our imagined community has something in common with Atlantis and Ubar, one legendary, one historical—cities that fell into sinkholes. Engineers can deal with geological karst, but who knows what to do with sinkholes of spirit?

┌─────┐
│ 2 │
└─────┘

THE TRAFFIC SPHERE
(A MEMORIAL PROTOTYPE)

Prospectus

A MEmorial begins in the form and style of the *proposal*. It has a certain "as if" quality of speculation. The design is described and contextualized in a rationale such that it does not depend on the acceptance of the plan in order for the idea to influence its intended audience—those who select public problems and the policies formulated to deal with them. This prototype for an electrate monument (a MEmorial) is addressed to the combined agencies of the National Aeronautics and Space Administration and Mothers Against Drunk Driving (MADD). The proposal is part of a deconsultation on the problem, stated by theorists of architecture (among others), that entertainment media in general, and television in particular, bear responsibility for the decline of the public sphere mediating the relationship of private citizens with the state. Monumental architecture played a large role in maintaining this public sphere, having to do with the forming and preserving of a community. But is it really the case that the electronic excludes monumentality?

The purpose of the proposed experiment is to explore the possibilities of the monumental electronic, to help invent a role for digital technology in general, and the Internet in particular, in a counter-public sphere, applied to community formation and identity. The focus is the memorial aspect of monumentality, concerned with the way the rituals of mourning contribute to the formation of a community. Societies from ancient Egypt to contemporary America have embodied their experience of death, loss, and separation in built constructions, landmarks that provide a referent of unity linking the passing generations to one another. Memory, both collective and individual, is reorganized in an electronic apparatus (electracy). The challenge is to adapt the possibilities of this apparatus to the cultural function of monumentality, productive of both individual and collective identity.

Regional Context

The Gainesville community recently commemorated the anniversary of one of the worst crimes in its history. During the last week of August 1990, five students, in Gainesville for the start of the fall semester at the University of Florida, were murdered in their apartments. First, two women were found stabbed and mutilated. Rumors spread that there were still more bodies. The police denied it. The next day another victim was found, a "petite brunette" like the first two. More rumors, and more denials. The third day, two more victims—a man and a woman this time. Panic. Parents came to take their children out of school; others packed up and left on their own. Ironically, the students who fled Gainesville in their cars to avoid becoming victims of the mad slasher were at greater risk of death on the highway, statistically, than if they had stayed at home, taking appropriate precautions by propping shut their sliding glass doors with broom handles.

The front section of the newspaper during the following weeks was devoted equally to the investigation into the murders and the crisis in the Persian Gulf—the invasion of Kuwait (the first Gulf War). The two stories were united by the same theme, a shared myth-history (mythistory). The murderer (whose identity had not yet been established at the time) and Saddam Hussein were characterized in similar terms, as being at once crazy and calculating. Although the events were described as the work of these respective individuals, journalists explained that the instability in the Gulf region and the insecurity of local apartment complexes would remain unchanged even if the two villains were eliminated.

The second shared element of the mythistory was the declaration that this time of crisis was the finest hour of the respective communities: that the nations of the world and the people of Gainesville had come together in a qualitatively new way in response to the dangerous situation. Phil Donahue brought his TV show to Gainesville in this spirit, he said, to help the community carry out the mourning process (and not to exploit or sensationalize the mutilation murders of co-eds). The local and global stories were the same. The new cooperation of the Eastern and Western nations, united in ostracizing Iraq, was repeated locally in the way friends formed groups for mutual protection and comfort and in the joining together of the city and the university in the rituals of mourning. The relationship between disaster and community formation was clearly manifested during those weeks, a condition demonstrated again in the case of 9/11.

A related pattern manifested again in 9/11 is the acausal coincidence of a domestic and international crime, with the latter constituting a comment on the former. In 9/11 the coincidence is between the collapse of the skyscrapers (the physical location in principle of our financial center) and the white-collar crime and corruption exposed in numerous corporations and accounting firms. The fall of the towers in a certain narrative could be described as an act of God in more ways than one. The towers' collapse acted out in the real the corruption rotting the core of American business.

How to do something, knowing how to repeat a performance, is a kind of memory, a kind of thinking that takes place in the collective conduct of a ritual. How to stop making mistakes? How to reduce error and eliminate accidents? These are the goals of a certain scientific method incapable of thinking wreckage as sacrificial ceremony, as the foundation of a national identity. To think of car wrecks as mistakes, as errors, as not knowing how to drive, for example, reflects the Enlightenment's contempt for dreams. Individuals may not want to wreck their cars, but nations do.

Problem Accident

Public discussion remained fixed on the events, rarely reflecting on the frame of the events, never raising the structural questions that might help grasp the cause and function of private and public death. Nonetheless, a certain awareness persisted of the relationship of the events to our demand for freedom—that a lifestyle of independence in terms of private cars and apartments carries a price: a price we are in fact willing to pay. How much do we actually know about this commitment or contract?

Why does the community insist on treating public and private crises on a case-by-case, individualized basis? Is it possible to grasp the frame, bring into perceptibility, make recognizable for a public consciousness the cumulative significance of a quantity of dispersed, private acts? Georges Bataille pointed out the difficulty of this level of consciousness in his discussion of the General

Economy of the movement of energy (fluxes) on the planet. "Man's disregard for the material basis of his life still causes him to err in a serious way. Humanity exploits given material resources, but by restricting them as it does to a resolution of the immediate difficulties it encounters, it assigns to the forces it employs an end which they cannot have. Beyond our immediate ends, man's activity in fact pursues the useless and infinite fulfillment of the universe" (1988, 21).

The example Bataille gave for such an unexamined productivity was the manufacture of automobiles in America. Bataille's theory of General Economy offers an insight into the link between the Gainesville murders and the Gulf crisis, which may be understood as reflecting the possibilities of energy use: available energy must be spent. "If the excess cannot be completely absorbed in [the system's] growth, it must necessarily be lost without profit." In these terms, the large, anonymous apartment complexes, with each unit supplemented by a mobile room parked in the parking lot, may be seen as the utilitarian side of an energy use whose alternative is a war in the Gulf: the quantity of oil that it would take the mobile rooms to burn in decades may be consumed in a matter of days in a Gulf war. The possibility of consuming a major part of the world's oil reserves all at once is a monumental prospect, whose prospectus was expressed in the oil fields left burning in the wake of the Iraqi retreat from Kuwait.

Automobile production is normally considered within what Bataille called the Restricted Economy—the conventional capitalist understanding of profit, productivity, expansion, accumulation. In this context it is possible to understand the difference between inventional and conventional consultants: egents consult from the perspective of the General Economy, while consultants work within the Restricted Economy. In terms of the rhetoric and logic of electracy, egents transfer the methods of advertising and boosterism learned in the Restricted Economy to the dynamics of the General Economy. As Paul Virilio pointed out, every invention brings into the world its own form of accident. "The accident is an inverted miracle, a secular miracle, a revelation. When you invent the ship, you also invent the shipwreck; when you invent the plane, you invent the plane crash; and when you invent electricity, you invent electrocution. . . . Every technology carries its own negativity, which is invented at the same time as technical progress" (1999, 89).

The premise of the General Economy is that the negative side of invention also has an important function and is not merely a remainder. Automobile accidents, in our example, are a link between two options, or crises (between murder and war), according to electrate cognition. That is, the car crash may serve as the material basis of an electronic monumentality precisely because of its status as accident. This monumentality performs a certain lap-dissolve shot marking the historical moment in our civilization in which the windshield gives way to the monitor screen as the glass mediating our experience of time and space.

We are going to witness the accident of accidents, the accident of time. It is no longer the accident of a particular time in history like Auschwitz or Hiroshima. Like time, any trajectory also has three dimensions: past, present and future; departure, voyage and arrival. No one can be deprived of these three dimensions, either with respect to time or trajectory, which means that I go toward the other, that I go to far away places. However, the hyperconcentration of real time reduces all trajectories to nothing: the temporal trajectory becomes a permanent present, and travel—from here to there, from one to another—a mere "being there." (81–82)

The value of the tourist analogy for the EmerAgency is its relevance to this convergence of time and travel. The MEmorial is a consultation on the possibility of the accident of accidents. We must learn to reason at the speed of light. Thought at light speed glimmers.

History

World War I, the Eastern front. A soldier in the Austrian army named Ludwig Wittgenstein is sitting in a trench. The austerity of the trench suits his mood. Two problems compete in his mind for attention: the nature of the significant proposition; the need for paper to use in the latrine. He has with him a magazine to use as toilet paper. Leafing through it he comes on a schematic picture illustrating the possible sequence of events in an automobile accident. The metaphor of the car crash as war does not occur to him. Instead, he realizes, in a flush of ecstasy, that the analogy supporting the function of the diagram—the correspondence between the parts of the picture and the event in reality—could be reversed: "that a proposition serves as a picture, by virtue of a similar correspondence between its parts and the world. The way in which the parts of the proposition are combined—the structure of the proposition—depicts a possible combination of elements in reality, a possible state of affairs" (Malcolm 1958, 7–8). This insight allows Wittgenstein to complete the manuscript of his *Tractatus Logico-Philosophicus.* This invention, bringing together car wrecks, war, and language philosophy, shows an idea (*eidos,* shape) without speaking of it directly.

How to read the patterns made of wreckage? Wreckwork is the materialization of dreamwork in public ceremony—a paradoxical manner of thinking that is at once memory and forgetting. The place of the wreck is cleared, the scene erased, leaving the event to dissipate, dissolve, fade, decay into an outline, a pattern that is learned then all the more easily. The wreck lives on, survives as this abstraction, a transparency consulted ceaselessly by bodies negotiating cultural traffic. Here is the scene of mourning. The curve of a two-lane blacktop highway, narrow shouldered, with tall prairie grasses nearly obscuring two metal crosses posted just beyond the embankment. Along the fence line is posted a series of signs, red with white lettering, faded but still legible:

> *Around the curve*
> *Lickety split*
> *Beautiful car*
> *Wasn't it.*
> *Burma Shave.*

Principle (sic) Investigator

I took only one class in architecture. In a general education class at the University of Montana in 1964 I became interested in philosophy after reading something by Heidegger. I went to an academic advisor, a man wearing a hearing aid that seemed to give him considerable trouble. It functioned less as a prosthesis and more as a sign—deaf. "I'm interested in the notion of Dasein," I told him. "Could you recommend a class I might take that would deal with Dasein in more detail?" He sent me to a course in architecture, an introduction to design.

> Heidegger says, "'It' calls *('Es' ruft),* against our expectations and even against our will. On the other hand the call does not come from someone else who is with me in the world. The call comes from me and yet from beyond me." The following paragraphs reject the concept of conscience as the "voice of God" ("an alien power by which Dasein is dominated") and continue Heidegger's implicit argument against the psychoanalytical notion of the superego. But when Heidegger seeks to fix the call of conscience as something both immanent to the subject and yet beyond him, the psychoanalyst is free to read *"Es ruft"* as "It speaks" in the sense that Lacan employs the phrase. The reader will remember that in Lacanian and Freudian psychology the "true subject" is the barred subject ($), and that Lacan constantly plays on the homophony of "$" and "Es." Dasein calls itself, concludes Heidegger, but: "The caller is unfamiliar to the everyday they-self; it is something like an alien voice." (Wilden 1968, 181)

I have never been able to decide whether or not the advice was a mistake. For one thing, we pronounced the word "design" incorrectly as "duh-zein," as in "I'm interested in duh-zein. What kinda jobs do duh-zeiners get?" More significantly, the instructor in the architecture class devised design problems based on readings of philosophers. "Draw Kierkegaard's laugh and integrate it into the model of Nietzsche's eternal return that you constructed out of cardboard last week." In fact, I didn't notice the possible error until years later, while reading Roland Barthes's *S/Z* (his poststructural text on Balzac's short story "Sarrasine").

SarraSine: customary French onomastics would lead us to expect SarraZine. On its way to the subject's patronymic, the Z has encountered some pitfall. Z is the letter of mutilation: phonetically, Z stings like a chastising lash, an avenging insect; graphically, cast slantwise by the hand, it cuts, slashes. This Z is the letter of deviation: S and Z are in a relation of graphological inversion: the same letter seen from the other side of the mirror: Sarrasine contemplates in La Zambinella [the castrato whom he has mistaken for a beautiful woman] his own castration. Hence the slash (/) confronting the S of SarraSine and the Z of Zambinella has a panic function: it is the slash of censure, the surface of the mirror, the wall [le mur] of hallucination, the verge of antithesis, the abstraction of limit, the obliquity of the signifier, the index of the paradigm, hence of meaning. (Barthes 1974, 106–7, translation modified)

The same things could be said of the word and concept "design," spelled "S" but pronounced "Z." In electracy the concept is restated as de-sign: architecture is de-signed, without the Z. But against the de-signers will be ranged the deS/Zigners, with unforeseeable consequences. Or the S/Z might be written as the barred "S" ($), occupying by default the same keyboard letter as the dollar sign, hence condensing in one shape general and restricted economies. An egent is a deS/Zigner (a de$igner). An image category must be de$igned.

Theory

Traffic Sphere is a work of chora, as elaborated by Jacques Derrida, concerning the three categories of being and discourse: mythos, logos, and genos. Chora, associated with genos, replaces topos as the concept of place in electrate memory. "The chora seems to be alien to the order of the 'paradigm,' that intelligible and immutable model. And yet, 'invisible' and without sensible form, it 'participates' in the intelligible in a very troublesome and indeed aporetic way" (Derrida 1987, 265–66). Chora is about the crossing of chance and necessity, whose nature may only be discerned indirectly in the names generated by a puncept rather than as a concept (or paradigm), including the qualities associated with "core" terms: chorus, choreography, chord, cord, corral, coral.

The MEmorial project suggests the necessity of adding to this series the term "coroner." This consultation is conducted in the spirit of the musical sense of chora: music associated with the muses and hence with general (economy) education, as it was for the ancient Greeks (the significance of the patterns and rhythms absorbed unawares through the musical experience by the young were to be made explicit later by means of philosophy). "Chora"—signifying a space that is sacred in classical Greek—was used by Plato in *Timaeus* to name the order of genos within which being and becoming could interact. This dialogue transmitted the Pythagorean notion of the music of the spheres—the meta-physics of cosmological correspondences—to the Christian Middle Ages. The function of chora in this metaphysics is to sort chaos into order (the elements or principles of earth, air, fire, water). As reactivated in contemporary theory, chora names a secularized, personalized sacred: it maps a relationship between an individual and those places that reveal the categories (classifying system, metaphysics) of a society.

The musical or formal order of the car crash is noted in the remarks of a traveling salesman, quoted in a newspaper account of a chain reaction crash caused by a morning fog covering Interstate 75 over the Hiwassee River, Tennessee, in which fifteen people were killed and fifty-one more were injured. The salesman pulled off when he noticed the traffic slowing down. "I started hearing bangs and booms from everywhere. Immediately after that there was a truck on fire from across the road. We started hearing them banging and booming from over there. Then all of a sudden you started hearing booms from everywhere." Booms in the fog.

The wreck is not the "thing itself" in the same way that the dream is the "royal road to the unconscious." The road is clear, free of wreckage, and punctuated with crosses. Sacrifice is not the thing itself but a mediation, bringing into relation a people with its god. Perhaps the car wreck is to sacrifice what shopping malls are to Christmas—a secular support for a sacred practice. Wreckwork brings into existence a space for thought, an interface within which people and machines may communicate. This opportunity is lost if we only think about eliminating the interface rather than accessing its memory. What might be recalled by means of wreckage? The least advanced, most neglected area of electronic culture is interface design. Thinking in this area works only with the economy of savings, conceiving of those who use computers in the way that Buckminster Fuller thought of drivers: they will never learn to drive safely, so roads must be built on which it is impossible to get hurt. But what of the economy of expenditure? Do thoughts need the same protections to which bodies must submit? Should navigation through a database be restricted by the habits of highway safety?

Method

The compatibility of the ideas of two French poststructuralist theories has been confirmed in the real. Actually, the compatibility exists at the level of metaphor—the key metaphors used in two important theoretical texts. The metaphors model the concept of dissemination or distribution of ideas. Jacques Derrida in *The Post Card* developed the image of mail delivery and the whole history of the post as a model for a theory of signification. Gilles Deleuze and Félix Guattari introduced in *A Thousand Plateaus* the image of a rhizome as a kind of spreading growth (weeds, crabgrass) that offered an alternative way to think about how ideas spread through cultures and history.

What is the relationship between these two conceptual images? The answer may be found in an article in *Natural History* magazine, describing how some of America's most troublesome weeds were dispersed through the mail by means of the mail-order seed business. In the late 1840s, when postal rates became affordable, "the mail quickly became an efficient dispenser of plants," such as Johnson grass, sold across the country. "The high forage production of this grass came at a steep price for the farmer. In the course of its vigorous growth, Johnson grass forms tenacious tangles of rhizomes, among which few other plants can grow" (Mack 1990, 51). From the old seed catalogs the author draws the following lessons: "how good intentions can go amiss"; never disseminate any wild plant until "we have firm evidence that it is unlikely to become weedy" (52). Ironically (at least for someone who remembers the Cold War), one of the icons of the American frontier—the tumbleweed (also the product of unwanted seeds distributed through the mails)—originated in Russia.

Sacrifice

Georges Bataille pointed out that, despite all the discussion over the ages, "there is nothing that permits one to define what is useful to man" (1988, 116). The problem is that individuals, and human societies, can have "an interest in considerable losses, in catastrophes that, while conforming to well-defined needs, provoke tumultuous depressions, crises of dread, and in the final analysis, a certain orgiastic state" (117). Bataille distinguished between the normal practices of production/consumption and unproductive expenditure—"luxury, mourning, war, cults, the construction of sumptuary monuments, games, spectacles, arts, perverse sexual activity"—activities, that is, with "no end beyond themselves"; not a balanced economy, but one in which the "loss must be as great as possible in order for that activity to take on its true meaning" (118).

Expenditure works openly in a community organized around the practices of sacrifice. Sacrifice is one of those concepts, such as taboo and fetish, translated from the practices of "primitive" civilizations to the theoretical systems of the human sciences. Bataille extended the concept as a way to understand his own society, considering war as that which makes social life what it is. The purpose of sacrifice in primitive societies, according to Bataille's sources, was to reveal the continuity through death of discontinuous beings (the monumental function). Through their survival, the survivors who witnessed the sacrifice experienced continuity (death took place and left them still alive).

If I am to find an answer to the enigma of sacrifice, I must be deliberate and shrewd. But I know and have never for an instant doubted that an enigma as dangerous as this one lies outside the scope of academic method; the sacred mysteries must be approached with craft, with a show of boldness and transgression. The enigma's answer must be formulated on a level equal to that of its celebrants' performance. It is my wish that it become part of the history of sacrifice, not of science. This general wish may account for my proposing to solve the enigma—in laughter. (Bataille 1986, 68)

These are the things that happen to thought in dreamwork, rendering it incoherent: condensation or compression. Every situation in a dream seems to be put together out of two or more impressions or experiences. The dreamwork then proceeds just as Francis Galton did in constructing his family photographs. The photographs of the victims remain in the possession of those who remember them. It superimposes the different components upon one another. The components, as it were, collide. The most convenient way of bringing together two dream-thoughts that have nothing in common to start with is to alter the verbal form of one of them and thus bring it halfway to meet the other, which may be similarly clothed in a new form of words. A parallel process is involved in hammering out a rhyme. How to listen to the hammering out in the rhythm of wrecking?

Proposal

A substantial sacrifice is performed annually in the private sphere in America, occurring at an individual level, unperceived or, if perceived statistically, not experienced and certainly not understood. That sacrifice is the death of over forty thousand people each year in automobile crashes (MADD) in the United States. Death is necessary, Bataille reminded us, and it seems obvious that highway fatalities are an expenditure of fundamental importance to the community's identity. The premise of the MEmorial is that traffic fatalities are not an anomaly in an otherwise rational order, as normal consultants would have it. Buckminster Fuller remained within the model of individual responsibility for one's actions when he declared drivers to be ineducable, leading to his proposal for the four-lane divided highway, intended to eliminate most collisions.

Even Marxist or social-constructionist critics who shift the frame from ethics to politics to point out that the corporate demand for profits overrides all other considerations in a capitalist culture still remain within the terms of the restricted economy. The de$ign premise, following Bataille, is that traffic fatalities are fundamentally "abject," meaning that they are a sacrifice on behalf of some "value" that is more important to the society than the annual loss of motorists. This value is not an ideal that may be named in a concept (justice, virtue, freedom), but remains inarticulate within the bodies and behaviors of individuals in the private sphere, untransformed, nontranscendent, untransposed, unredeemed (what Bataille called "formless"). Call it an "abject." What memorials are to ideals, MEmorials are to abjects. Is it the case that every ideal is shadowed by an abject? The place to look for formless values is not in social narratives but in the habitus of behaviors. The traffic accident is a short circuit bringing into direct contact an abstract machine and the fluxes of matter, productive of group subjectivity. Perhaps this is what Virilio had in mind when he said that accidents could serve as revelations. Bataille proposes the *me* as monster or remainder that refuses to be distracted by the glorious body of the ideal:

> Blind, but tranquil and strangely despising his obscure baseness, a given person, ready to call to mind the grandeur of human history, as when his glance ascends a monument testifying to the grandeur of his nation, is stopped in mid-flight by an atrocious pain in his big toe because, though the most noble of animals, he nevertheless has corns on his feet; in other words, he has feet, and these feet independently lead an ignoble life. . . . Since by its physical attitude the human race distances itself as much as it can from terrestrial mud—whereas a spasmodic laugh carries joy to its summit each time its purest flight lands man's own arrogance spread-eagle in the mud—one can imagine that a toe, always more or less damaged and humiliating, is psychologically analogous to the brutal fall of a man—in other words, to death. (1985, 25)

It may be acceptable for conventional monumentality to neglect the dimension of repulsion, of base materialism, that Bataille associates with the big toe (also spit and spiders), but not for inventional MEmorials intended to bring tourism to self-consciousness as a point of departure for a virtual public sphere.

Visualization

The goal of Traffic Sphere is to make highway fatalities perceptible, thinkable, recognizable as *sacrifice*—to shift them from the private sphere of one-at-a-time individual, personal loss to the public sphere of collective values. Americans: *we-who-die-behind-the-wheel.*

> Scientific visualization is concerned with exploring data and information graphically—as a means of gaining understanding and insight into the data. Scientific visualization is graphical process analogous to numerical analysis, and is often referred to as visual data analysis. Scientific visualization systems are combinations of hardware and software systems and techniques. By displaying multi-dimensional data in an easily understandable form on

a 2D screen, it enables insights into 3D and higher-dimensional data and data
sets that were not formerly possible. Often data sets are very large, and this
gives rise to problems of scale and of finding correlations and relationships
between different parts of the data. Visualization is also a means of gaining
a quick understanding of processes. (Earnshaw and Wiseman 1992, 5)

The MEmorial is a form of humanities visualization of data sets, giving insight into large-scale complex processes and events within an arts and letters
frame of reference. The traffic proposal is to launch a satellite—a giant ear in
the sky, equivalent to the eye-in-the-sky weather satellites. In the same way
that citizens catch a glimpse of the earth each evening during the weather report on the local news, graphically enhanced to show the activities of clouds,
rain, and wind, so too does the ear in the sky make it possible to focus on the
sounds significant to our culture. With its sensitive recording capacities, the
ear satellite is programmed to coordinate feeds from microphones distributed
along the nation's roadways, to remember the noise made by car crashes all over
the country. With computer enhancement, the recorded crashes are replayed at
various speeds, compressed in various ways, similar to time-lapse photography,
in order to discern the rhythm of the crashes. Beat or pulse is one of the four
operations of heterology, the logic of formless that finds its point of application
in electracy and image reason, which is an alternative to the literate mode of
categorizing what is by means of concepts and related binary structures.

> To practice sacrifice and dismemberment requires some kind of organization
> (no one was more methodical than Sade, whose "use value" Bataille wanted
> to recover; and, as we have noted, the supreme disorder of the *Documents*
> dictionary camouflages a carefully premeditated strategy). The works in the
> exhibition *Formless: A User's Guide* were grouped according to four differ-
> ent vectors within which we discover, starting from Bataille, the mark of the
> formless. This division into four operations (which for purposes of brevity
> will be termed "horizontality," "base materialism," "pulse," and "entropy")
> presupposes a type of classification, but this classification is porous. (Bois and
> Krauss 1997, 21)

Instrumentation

Pulse or pulsation "attacks the modernist exclusions of temporality from the
visual field," and "involves an endless beat that punctures the disembodied
self-closure of pure visuality and incites an irruption of the carnal" (Bois and
Krauss 1997, 32). Here is another kind of instrumental reason. It is possible
that the accidents produce a specific beat. While this beat should be analyzed
scientifically for any patterns that might provide an insight into the enigma of

sacrifice, it could also be adapted to performative ends, including the invention of a new musical knowledge. Following the lead of those composers who mix documentary sound with instrumentation, and exploiting the technology of sampling, the crash rhythms become danceable. Such a record may lead to better forecasting of crash rates, of the sort already provided before holiday weekends. Such rhythms may be sources of transversal creativity, in Guattari's terms, detached fragments functioning as attractors to hold together disparate fields of meaning. "Thus it is not only in the context of music and poetry that we see the work of such fragments detached from content, fragments which I place in the category of 'existential refrains.' The polyphony of modes of subjectivation actually corresponds to a multiplicity of ways of 'keeping time.' Other rhythmics are thus led to crystallise existential assemblages which they embody and singularise" (Guattari 1995, 15).

Reported in their own spot on the evening news, automobile deaths take on their proper significance for our society, making clearer than is now possible why we are willing to go to war for Arabian oil. Adding the abject to the ideal makes hypocrisy unnecessary. A new national ritual is to be introduced, consisting of a moment not of silence but of noise—that unmistakable sequence of screeching tires preceding the collision, collapsing metal, and an automobile horn blasting—played at the end of each school day, as the teenagers prepare to drive home. In this way the disproportionate number of teen lives sacrificed for the car is recognized. Such a recognition, giving these victims their due, contributes to the mourning process, making available for the first time an appreciation of the value for which the loved ones gave their lives. The title for the person assigned to organize this service is choroner. Simonides, it should be remembered, invented artificial memory by being able to identify the bodies of those killed when a roof collapsed on a party (he remembered where each person was seated). The relationship between catastrophe and memory must be reorganized once again for an electronic apparatus, which continues the mnemonic tradition in its own way.

To imagine the future of Traffic Sphere as an institution, compare its current embodiment—the video arcades—with the beginnings of cinema, similarly organized originally as a sideshow for the circus or carnival. The games of road racing (and the inevitable crash) and war making that tend to dominate the arcades provide a technological and social location for grafting onto current practices the monumental function of the Traffic Sphere. The new behavior known as road rage in this context may be seen for what it is: untransposed (base) patriotism. There is a reason why NASCAR oversees the most popular "sport" in America. Like golf, whose popularity on television is explained by the fact that so many amateurs play the game throughout their lives, the automobile crash is not confined to well-paid experts on professional racetracks, but is engaged in by amateurs at every stage of life.

Psychoanalysis and automobiles were invented at about the same time. In condensation, two strangers traveling at high speed enter one another's vehicles through a mutual windshield. The parts of the vehicles in contact have something in common, forming a composite idea, while indistinct subordinate details correspond to the parts that are scattered about the roadway. If displacement takes place in addition to condensation, what is constructed is an "intermediate common entity," which stands in a relation to the two different cars similar to that in which the resultant in a parallelogram of forces stands to its components. At least two wreckers are needed in such a case, if not the jaws of life, for the idea to complete its shape.

Peripheral

The ear in the sky is a long-range proposal, perhaps only conceptual in nature (it does not need to be built for its effect to circulate as information). The rapid evolution of wireless connectivity and broadband speeds in any case make the Internet the more likely support for monitoring the general auto wreck. Meanwhile, the MEmorial is initiated in a more immediately practical way by means of a peripheral monument. Peripheral monuments, like their computer counterparts, add functionality to an established memorial. The peripheral is a transitional device, relating literate monumentality to its electrate counterpart. Another sense of "peripheral" relates the device to propaganda, or at least rhetoric (persuasion). Researchers have described two routes to persuasion: the central and the peripheral (corresponding to the use of strong or weak argumentation).

> In many ways we are cognitive misers—we are forever trying to conserve our cognitive energy. Given our finite ability to process information, we often adopt the strategies of the peripheral route for simplifying complex problems; we mindlessly accept a conclusion or proposition—not for any good reason but because it is accompanied by a simplistic persuasion device. Modern propaganda promotes the use of the peripheral route to persuasion and is designed to take advantage of the limited processing capabilities of the cognitive miser. . . . We have a state of affairs that may be called *the essential dilemma of modern democracy.* On the one hand, we, as a society, value persuasion; our government is based on the belief that free speech and discussion and exchange of ideas can lead to fairer and better decision making. On the other hand, as cognitive misers we often do not participate fully in this discussion, relying instead not on careful thought and scrutiny of a message, but on simplistic persuasion devices and limited reasoning. (Pratkanis and Aronson 1991, 31)

Advertising uses the peripheral route, which is synonymous with image cognition. Thought moves along this route at light speed, the kind of thought required for our virtual civic sphere in order to resist the Internet accident. A goal of the EmerAgency is to contextualize the peripheral route within electracy. The Internet virtual civic sphere will not be literate but electrate, although literacy and orality both have an important, if subordinate, role to play. The propaganda problem is due not to the weakness of imaging, but to its relative newness as an apparatus. The challenge to democracy is to educate an electrate citizenry.

How does a memorial peripheral work? A memorial proper, such as the Vietnam Wall on the Mall in Washington, DC, honors a sacrifice for an acknowledged community value. The peripheral establishes a connection between this acknowledged value and the unacknowledged but lived value of the loss in the private sphere—in this case traffic fatalities. Peripheral memorialization already occurs both officially and unofficially. In the case of 9/11, the many wall posters for missing persons papered around the neighborhood of Ground Zero represented an unofficial or spontaneous peripheral memorial; the twin towers of light (two powerful searchlights), installed temporarily in a vacant lot next to the trade center complex, represented an official peripheral. The juxtaposition of the peripheral and the proper memorials creates an analogy for visitors that adds to their tourist practice the status of theoria (witness). The most inspired peripheral to date is the quilt appropriated for the NAMES project (the AIDS Memorial Quilt), which helped shift AIDS-related deaths from individual loss to collective sacrifice. The achievement is especially important as a relay for electronic monumentality since many of the victims were associated with behaviors that the mainstream society experienced as abject (homosexuality, drug abuse). The quilt, in the context of the society as a whole, began not as an "attraction" but as a "repulsion."

AIDS Quilt Relocates to Atlanta

SAN FRANCISCO—The AIDS Memorial Quilt dedicated to 80,000 victims of the disease left San Francisco on Friday with a tearful send-off from the city where the first of its 40,000 panels were stitched together 14 years ago. The NAMES project Foundation is moving its AIDS memorial quilt to Atlanta, hoping it will have a greater impact in the South, where HIV among blacks is rampant. The 54-ton memorial will be housed in a climate-controlled warehouse.

"By being in Atlanta, we are going to be able to make sure that this quilt is as useful and as powerful and as important to the African-American community and its struggle against this terrible disease as it was to us in the Bay

Area and in the gay and lesbian communities," said Cleve Jones, who stitched the first panel in 1987 to remember his best friend. . . .

AIDS officials in Atlanta awaited its arrival. "Here in the South, we feel that the church is a perfect vehicle for reaching the young black community. The quilt is a safe way of getting the message into the community," said Chris Parsons, acting deputy director of AID Atlanta, the largest AIDS service organization in the Southeast. "I hope that we can do San Francisco proudly by handling it as well as you did out there."

The foundation also is moving its offices from San Francisco to Washington. The origin of the quilt can be traced to a 1985 candlelight memorial march for former San Francisco Mayor George Moscone and openly gay city supervisor Harvey Milk. The two politicians were gunned down by former supervisor Dan White in 1978. Jones handed out cardboard squares and markers to those attending the memorial, urging them to jot down something about a loved one lost to AIDS. The crowd then pasted cardboard panels on the outer wall of a health services building. Jones mentioned to a friend that the panels looked like a quilt. Over the years, the quilt was taken across the country and around the world, but always came back home to San Francisco. (*Gainesville SUN,* March 31, 2001)

Abject Genre

The genre of a MEmorial includes the following elements (with the response of the Traffic Sphere in parentheses):

- Select an existing monument, memorial, celebration to which to attach the peripheral (Vietnam Memorial).
- Select an organization, agency, or other administrative unit that has some responsibility for policy formation in relation to the disaster, to be the nominal recipient of the consultation (Mothers Against Drunk Driving).
- Select a theory as the source of the rationale informing the consultation (Bataille 1988).
- Place an (electronic) device at the site, designed to link symbolically the established sacrifice with the unacknowledged sacrifice (computer printout listing traffic fatalities as they occur).
- Represent the above features on an Internet Web site, including links to Web representatives of the relevant sites and organizations and a simulation of the peripheral.

The exemplarity of this case, juxtaposing traffic victims with war dead, is due in part to the controversy surrounding Maya Lin's design for the Wall, which before it was built was widely denounced as the "black gash of shame" and as such unsuitable for paying respects to American soldiers. The winning design for the Trade Center memorial—"Reflecting Absence" by Michael Arad—has also been criticized as inadequate. An editorial published in the *National Review* during the controversy over Maya Lin's design, prior to the building of the Wall, argued that this black wall listing the names of dead soldiers dishonored their sacrifice for the nation: they might as well have been traffic accidents, the editorialist complained. The car crash is abject in being a degraded, disavowed, repressed sacrifice. Most deaths in America are assigned to such categories as natural causes, accidents, disease, murder, suicide, to which the MEmorial would add sacrifice. The soldiers died for the ideal of freedom; they did their duty, in the official story of the nation.

And the automobile operators and passengers? They died for a formless value (an abject)—the behavior that performs freedom: *To drive wherever I want, whenever I want, for whatever purpose, in whatever manner I choose, so help me God.* To focus on this behavior initiates the formless operation of base materialism—the desublimation of all ideals. For Bataille, the value of the loss need not be explained in terms of any benefit other than the waste of resources as such, since his theory of General Economy indicated that civilizations like individuals required a balance of accumulation and destruction of energy. Here is the context for Virilio's Internet accident—the necessity of wreckage in the General Economy. The middle-class focus on accumulation and the repression of expenditure made war inevitable (in order to release the accumulated energy). The accounting gimmicks of counting expenditures as profits, which apparently became nearly standard practice in the 1990s (as used by Arthur Andersen et al.), are symptoms not only of individual greed but of this collective antipathy for waste (expense)—a group fantasy. "The lesson from corporate America seems to be there is nothing wrong with your checkbook that black-ink magic cannot fix. For several years, AOL counted the free-trial subscription disks it sends pell-mell through the mail as assets, regulators said, as if some recipients were already signed up and paying. . . . Shenanigans have gotten so out of hand that the Securities and Exchange Commission is requiring hundreds of companies reporting on their finances to swear they really, really mean it" (*Gainesville Sun*, July 22, 2002).

One of the clearest examples of the emergence of untransposed values in contemporary America is the National Rifle Association promotion of gun ownership as a constitutional right. They retain the appeal to the ideal (the principle of innate rights), but they insist on the material behavior (as in Charlton Heston's slogan, uttered while holding aloft a musket: "from my cold dead hands"). There is direct contact with the material register, with the economic flow of weapons and ammunition. The value is not constitutional liberty but the firearms themselves.

Or rather, the thing *is* the principle. It was reported that one of the best places for al-Qaeda training outside of Afghanistan was the United States itself, since our gun laws are among the most lax in the world. For many motorists the NRA slogan might be equally applicable, should their right to drive be threatened. The gun and the car and their related behaviors are icons supporting a group subject. In some cultures public events are marked by firing automatic weapons into the sky; the expended bullets fall to earth they know not where. In Japan there may be somewhere a shrine honoring expended bullets and collapsed stocks.

Cost-Benefit

Cynics might denigrate the claim of freedom as a mask for a less lofty purpose such as imperialism, colonialism, capitalist exploitation of global natural resources and markets, and in these terms the juxtaposition of the Vietnam Wall and Traffic Sphere has a critical effect. From the point of view of electracy and the desire to educate the collective Euthyphro or group subject, the masking is not cynical but cognitive: the ideal prevents the collective from understanding itself as such (as a w/hole). Formless values, that is, untransposed, abject investments that have not seemed worthy of public recognition except in the category of anomaly, error, accident—are made reflexive in the MEmorial. These abject values are often not embraced as such by individuals, but are emergent features of the collective and function without being thought as such. We depart from our landfills the way a cat departs from its litterbox—tentatively taking a few sniffs, shaking one or the other foot, and forgetting about it. Collectively, we are willing to expend a certain number of lives and a certain amount of money in exchange for the freedom of the road. We know exactly the expenditure charged to traffic accidents. The National Highway Traffic Safety Adminstration reported that in 2000 the 41,821 people killed, 5.3 million injured, and 27.6 million damaged vehicles cost the country $230.6 billion, or an average of $820 for every American (*Gainesville Sun,* May 10, 2002). Such statistics, reflecting discursive knowledge, fail to address the pathic knowledge of the group subject. The dollar sign evokes the barred subject at work in the events measured by these figures. The catharsis of abject de$ign.

The MEmorial does not advocate or condemn the social commitment to the automobile, but only makes it recognizable as a specific kind of value, belief, commitment, with the purpose of helping the public understand itself in its collective identity. The proposed traffic peripheral makes a good prototype since it literally is a computer peripheral device—a printer. *A computer is set up at the Vietnam memorial to print out the names of victims of crashes as they occur.* The total number of Americans killed in Vietnam (more than 58,000) establishes a threshold for the acceptable annual automobile death rate. Should this number be exceeded, the computer triggers a mechanism in the ear-in-the-sky satellites (or on the Internet) that causes all monitors nationwide to blink uncontrollably. The satellites at the same time take over traffic lights nationwide, setting all signals to red. No driving is permitted from that moment on, until the new year, when the meter returns to zero and the lottery begins again. Meanwhile, citizens visiting the Wall to touch or make rubbings of the names of loved ones lost in the war may at the same time get a copy of the page listing the name or names of loved ones killed in traffic.

Wreckwork

The manifest content of wrecks consists for the most part in pictorial situations; and the wreck-thoughts must accordingly be submitted to a treatment that will make them suitable for a representation of this kind. The material is submitted to a pressure that condenses it greatly, to an internal fragmentation and displacement that, as it were, creates new surfaces, and to a selective operation in favor of those portions of it that are the most appropriate for the construction of situations. Dreamwork builds with the forces of wreckage a rhetoric governed by the five forces of stress:

- Compression is the direct expression of gravity pulling everything to the center of the earth.
- Tension is the opposite of compression; where there is one there must be the other. The other three forms of stress are based on these two pure forms.
- Shear is a complex stress. When two forces are thrusting in opposite directions but offset and slide past each other, shear is present.
- Bending: in structural concerns, shear and bending are found between the pulling of tension and the pushing of compression.
- Torsion is a result of all four of the other forces. Torsion is twist. The dreamers' hands turn the steering wheel, exerting a twisting force that is transferred to the dream-thoughts. Torsion is actually a specialized bending, a circular bending. With these forces in both harmony and discord, the living and the inanimate face the perils of dreaming.

What happens to cars happens to thoughts. The forces of compression, tension, shear, bending, and torsion work on bodies and minds in the manner of stress, works on logic in the warped space ME of MEmorial. There is a mapping between the physics and metaphysics of stress. Here is the feeling not felt, meaning not recognized as such, as a mood, an attunement to the world. The wreckage—these designs we are reading—presents us with a wish in a coded form. It is interesting to observe that the popular belief that car wrecks foretell the future is confirmed. Actually, the future that the wreck shows us is not the one that will occur but the one that we should like to occur (do you notice the ventriloquism?). The popular mind is behaving here as it usually does: what it wishes, it believes. What is the spirit of America, as a state of mind, an attunement? Any wrecked automobile supplies an emblem for it. The topology of folds.

References

The Web site dimension of the MEmorial serves in part as a support for a meditation on the material signifiers of the sacrificial behavior. This meditation composes an image category, gathering into a temporary set cultural examples associated with the scene.

Jean-Luc Godard, "Weekend"

Loud music over a shot of wrecked cars blazing on either side of a road. There are bright orange flames, clouds of black smoke; the wrecks crackle and bang as their petrol tanks explode. Camera cranes up as ROLAND and CORINNE limp into view in the background. Roland addressing a corpse lying in the road: "Hey, you, where's the nearest garage?" (1972, 54)

Jim Dine, "The Car Crash"

Traffic sounds (crash) for approx 2 min. Spot on wringer. Car cranks out *help*, Pat is saying help softly, one white person is banging softly, other is passing out help signs. Pat gets louder, keeps saying help in a drone. Car begins to stutter and draw cars and erase them. Two white people stand and cough, gag, stammer and stutter. (1966, 190)

Peter Greenaway, A Zed and Two Noughts

The film begins with a car crash. Outside a zoo, a Mute Swan smashed into the windscreen of a white Ford Mercury, registration number NID 26 B/W, driven by a woman wearing white feathers called Alba Bewick. An accident? "Five thousand accidents happen every day—bizarre, tragic, farcical. They are Acts of God, fit only to amaze the survivors and irritate the Insurance Company." This one is different for God's sake. Or Darwin's. (1986, 13)

J. G. Ballard, Crash

In his vision of a car-crash with the actress, Vaughan was obsessed by many wounds and impacts—by the dying chromium and collapsing bulkheads of their two cars meeting head-on in complex collisions end-lessly repeated in slow-motion films, by the identical wounds inflicted on their bodies, by the image of windshield glass frosting around her face as she broke its tinted surface like a death-born Aphrodite, by the compound fractures of their thighs impacted against their handbrake mountings, and above all by the wounds to their genitalia, her uterus pierced by the heraldic beak of the manufacturer's medallion, his semen emptying across the luminescent dials that registered forever the last temperature and fuel levels of the engine. (1985, 8)

Equipment

Communication satellites are microwave relay links in space. Generally, there are (four) types of satellites: weather and observational satellites, communica-tion satellites, space probes (and sacrifice frames). Since the late 1970s, four geostationary satellites have been in orbit for U.S. weather observation. Their viewing areas take in the north and south poles. One satellite covers the area from the Mississippi west to New Zealand; the other, from about five hundred miles off the California coast east to the western coast of Africa. The other two are parked in reserve orbit. The daily task of the satellite service station is the collection and distribution of images. The satellite spins on its axis, and every time the camera comes around facing the earth, it takes one scan line (Marsh 1982, 79–88).

A similar arrangement is feasible for a sky ear, using geostationary or syn-chronous satellites fixed over a particular spot on earth. The orbits for the sky ears, however, would have to be somewhat lower than those for the eyes in the sky. Three designers—Williams, Rosen, and Hudspeth—working for Hughes Aircraft, invented the geostationary satellite in 1962 (Winston 1986, 261). Enough progress has been made in surveillance technology to permit low-orbit listening transmission, including relays from ground stations placed at regu-lar intervals relative to the interstate highway system. The advances in global-positioning networks and handheld devices of the sort used by the military in Afghanistan may support this additional service.

The ceremony of the car includes the design process. Designed for safety more than sacrifice since the challenge to Detroit by Japan, cars are built now as impact cushions, collapsing and folding on contact, so that even modest fender benders produce spectacular wreckage. The car as ruin is anticipated in its creation. What of these post-crash designs? The ones we are reading as architecture? Are these the first to rectify the balance of design, mountains of drawings in the production process, and none coming after the catastrophe? The latter lift from the wreck the memories it contains, showing us the writing of the event. It is not so much writing, but a score. It is music to be played.

Dawn Gregerson told her story in an ad for Volvo. "We were laughing because on this desert highway, in the middle of nowhere, in the middle of the road, there was a man painting yellow lines on the road. We never saw it coming. He came out of nowhere. One second we were joking, the next we were flying through space, tumbling and tumbling." Each year there are thirty-six million traffic accidents in this country, the ad continues. An accident every second. An injury due to traffic accidents every six seconds. A death every twelve minutes. When Dawn Gregerson opened her eyes after the accident, she felt like she had been sleeping for a hundred years. Volvo has been able to develop crumple zones that absorb impact energy, steel-reinforced passenger cages, and a side-impact protection system, the ad declares, so that Dawn did not become a statistic. She just had a bad dream.

> Thus the glorious body of advertising has become the mask behind which the fragile, slight human body continues its precarious existence, and the geometrical splendor of the "girls" covers over the long lines of the naked, anonymous bodies led to their death in the *Lagers* (camps), or the thousands of corpses mangled in the daily slaughter on the highways. To appropriate the historic transformations of human nature that capitalism wants to limit to the spectacle, to link together image and body in a space where they can no longer be separated, and thus to forge the whatever body, whose *physis* is resemblance—this is the good that humanity must learn how to wrest from commodities in their decline. Advertising and pornography, which escort the commodity to the grave like hired mourners, are the unknowing midwives of this new body of humanity. (Agamben 1993, 50)

The task of the EmerAgency is to bring this peripheral route of thought—the *defile* of commodities and pornography—into the realm of public discourse, to refunction it on behalf of an intelligent group subject.

Part II

Make It New(s)

A searing pain in me is only the prolongation of a series that led me into it, even if I did not notice it, and now it is continued in the series of my pain. There is a prolongation or continuation of convergent series, one into the other.
—*Gilles Deleuze,* The Fold

3

THE CALL
(ABJECT MONUMENTS)

THIS SECTION OF THE BOOK extrapolates from the prototype and its rationale to the context of the MEmorial in art and popular culture. A MEmorial consists of two parts: a *peripheral* (proposal for an electronic device to be placed at the site of an existing monument associating it with an abject sacrifice) and a *testimonial* (a Web site representing a meditation on the abject sacrifice). Keeping in mind the status of the EmerAgency as a "fifth estate" of the public sphere, deconsulting begins by monitoring the agenda-setting performance of the daily news (journalism). The kind of news event that may provoke an egent into action often may be something local, given the MEmorial function of calling attention to abject (unacknowledged) sacrifices. An exemplary scene of provocation is central to the film *About Schmidt,* directed by Alexander Payne (2002). Warren Schmidt (Jack Nicholson), just retiring from a career as an insurance actuary, starts a search for something meaningful in his life. In this state of mind he is moved by a TV solicitation to sponsor for twenty-two dollars a month a six-year-old Tanzanian orphan named Ndugu

57

Figure 4. Railroad bridge monument, Miles City, Montana.

Umbo. That Schmidt, inured to all normal life emotions, would respond to the appeal for charity is credible in that child sponsorships for African famine relief are one of the most successful philanthropic campaigns ever conceived (Moeller 1999, 9). To be touched from a distance in this way is the beginning of the consultancy.

Reasoneon

What is the experience of image reasoning? It is the experience of a neon sign, a metonym for the city as such, evoking the mood of an urban setting with its nightlife and street atmosphere. The electric energy powering the sign joins the actual and virtual cities and evokes the evolving technology whose present manifestation is the Internet. The EmerAgency began its existence as a neon sign or, rather, a representation of a neon sign made in Photoshop® and posted on the World Wide Web. A passage from Walter Benjamin, the theorist who proposed that history was most accessible through an image, is one of the motivations for the name of the consultancy:

> The tradition of the oppressed teaches us that the "state of emergency" in
> which we live is not the exception but the rule. We must attain to a concep-
> tion of history that is in keeping with this insight. Then we shall clearly
> realize that it is our task to bring about a real state of emergency, and this

will improve our position in the struggle against Fascism. One reason why Fascism has a chance is that in the name of progress its opponents treat it as a historical norm. The current amazement that the things we are experiencing are "still" possible in the twentieth century is not philosophical. This amazement is not the beginning of knowledge—unless it is the knowledge that the view of history which gives rise to it is untenable. (1969)

Are we amazed that the things we are experiencing are still possible even in the twenty-first century? The choice of name for the agency suggests an affirmative answer to this question. Some of the purposes of the consultancy are suggested at once in this portmanteau word: figuring out what such an organization might accomplish involves extracting the terms condensed in this name—merge, emerge, emergence, emergency, urgency, urge. The very nature of the name indicates an important feature of method—analytical and creative exploration of language. A first reading might be: it is an agency (an organization that provides some service) that addresses contemporary conditions within this frame of "the state of emergency." This word "agency," unfortunately, is not stable and has to do with the shifting site of responsibility for actions taken.

Part of the difficulty of this name is its calligraphy: its shape—with the capital "A" rising above the lowercase letters—creates a silhouette that is part drawing. This "A" inserted into "emergency" is a heraldic device whose associations remain to be unpacked as the project evolves. The consulting methods of egents derive from the practices gathered together by this "A." A short list of practices evoked by the "A" includes Brecht's Alienation effect, Derrida's "differance," Lacan's "Autre" or other (big and little "a"), Levinas's "Autrui," Cixous's ladder of writing (an open stepladder viewed in profile resembles an "A"). What is so urgent? The philosopher says: *justice cannot wait.* And yet, law and justice are not the same thing, and their inevitable conflict in previous eras was the stuff of tragedy. Today it is the stuff of consulting. The EmerAgency considers policy formation from a poststructural frame of reference. "The transcendence of the law was an image, a photo of the highest places; but justice is more like a sound (the statement) that never stops taking flight. *The transcendence of the law was an abstract machine, but the law exists only in the immanence of the machinic assemblage of justice. The Trial* is the dismantling of all transcendental justification. There is nothing to judge vis-à-vis desire; the judge himself is completely shaped by desire. Justice is no more than the immanent process of desire. The process is itself a continuum, but a continuum made up of contiguities" (Deleuze and Guattari 1986, 51; italics in original). The clarity or even the intelligibility of theoretical statements such as this one by Deleuze and Guattari is not the issue in reasoneon, but the evocative power motivating inquiry. *Justice is no more than the immanent process of desire?* This and similar statements throughout these chapters are intended as creative stimulants, as much explained by the MEmorial as explaining.

The EmerAgency proposes to apply an electrate mode of knowledge to the dilemmas of contemporary (in)justice. Walter Benjamin explained in *One-Way Street* why the sign has to be neon:

> Fools lament the decay of criticism. For its day is long past. Criticism is a matter of correct distancing. It was at home in a world where perspectives and prospects counted and where it was still possible to take a standpoint. Now things press too closely on human society. The unclouded, innocent eye has become a lie, perhaps the whole naive mode of expression sheer incompetence. Today the most real, the mercantile gaze into the heart of things is the advertisement. It abolishes the space where contemplation moved and all but hits us between the eyes with things as a car, growing to gigantic proportions, careens at us out of a film screen. And just as the film does not present furniture and facades in completed forms for critical inspection, their insistent, jerky nearness alone being sensational, the genuine advertisement hurtles things at us with the tempo of a good film. . . . What, in the end, makes advertisements so superior to criticism? Not what the moving red neon sign says—but the fiery pool reflecting it in the asphalt. (1978, 85–86)

Benjamin would agree with the commonplace observation that advertising sells not the steak but the sizzle. Benjamin differs from most critics with his view that critique is best served not by opposing the neon effect but by learning how to appropriate it. It is not that the neon effect replaces critical reason for the EmerAgency, but that reason and neon merge in a hybrid modality: neither reasoning nor neon, but *reasoneon*.

The significance of the neon effect noted by Benjamin was further elaborated in the writings of Jacques Lacan. Lacan was one of those French theorists present at the conference, held at Johns Hopkins University in 1967, that is said to mark the beginning of the poststructuralist movement in America:

> When I prepared this little talk for you, it was early in the morning. I could see Baltimore through the window and it was a very interesting moment because it was not quite daylight and a neon sign indicated to me every minute the change of time, and naturally there was heavy traffic, and I remarked to myself that exactly all that I could see, except for some trees in the distance, was the result of thoughts, actively thinking thoughts, where the function played by the subjects was not completely obvious. In any case the so-called "Dasein," as a definition of the subject, was there in this rather intermittent or fading spectator. The best image to sum up the unconscious is Baltimore in the early morning. (Lacan 1970)

A commentator explained the fit between the material and the theoretical information, between the neon tube and the concept of the "subject" in Lacanian theory:

> In his L-schema Lacan represented the unconscious as a four-sided relation in which the flow from the Other to the Subject is modulated by the ego-other relation. He used the image of a triode vacuum tube to clarify this movement: the flow of electrons from cathode (o) to anode (s) is modulated by the third electrode (e-o, the imaginary relation) which can either interrupt the current or amplify it depending on its charge. As with any electrical circuit, the current will flow only when the circuit is closed, and in alternating current, a system of feedback is set up such that the flow in one direction reverses the charge and thus automatically opens the circuit, inducing it to flow in the opposite direction. Moreover, if the tube is filled with a gas such as neon, it will light up only when the flow of the electric current is interrupted and forced to move back onto itself. The point of his little electronic parable, is that the interruption of the flow, transference as resistance, is necessary for the lighting up, transference as the relation to the Other. (Chaitin 1996, 163)

"Transference" refers to any experience from the past reactivated in the present relationship between analyst and analysand during psychoanalytic treatment. Lacan observed that as soon as there is a subject who is supposed to know (the Other), there is transference (Evans 1996, 212). A consultant is such a one. In short, the neon sign forms an emblem that anticipates the consulting practice that remains to be invented: the egent "conducts" an inquiry into the unending disaster.

The Auratic Axes

How does one write a disaster? What clarity is to literate truth, aura is to electrate truth. This parallel has the double function of noting the connection between style and knowledge in electracy, and acknowledging the fact that truth is an effect specific to an apparatus. The intersection of the axes of the pop-cycle pun on the ax blow of the punctum that the EmerAgency mobilizes as the unit of electrate inference against the defensive repressions of the spectacle. The assumption of the MEmorial is that the event to be commemorated was not experienced directly by the egents, but was mediated by the spectacle in an image. One paradox of the spectacular image noted by many commentators is "compassion fatigue": We know more about worldwide catastrophes than ever before, and care less. Or rather, we are unable to conjoin our intellectual understanding and our emotions, and this disjunction of discursive and pathic knowledge is systematic, structural, and seemingly irreducible. Part of the paradox marking the difficulty of the transition from literacy to electracy is that the very pathetic sentimental emotional "fallacies" of propaganda against which critical reason constructed an entire logical defense become in electracy a point of departure for a new mode of reason (the categorical image).

The methodological strategy of the categorical (thinking) image comes from Roland Barthes's idea of a third meaning in a photograph, distinct from the denotation or connotation of the image (most fully developed in his book *Camera Lucida*). The third meaning is obtuse, indirect, based on an involuntary memory or association triggered by the scene. Some detail of the photograph stings or pricks the viewer (the punctum), which is to say that in viewing certain images (but certainly not all images) I have an experience in my body, an emotional, pathic response, and it is at this point of the *me* that the discursive abstract information and my unique existence intersect. This experience of memory is precisely the feature of organic human thought that is taken up by the prosthesis of the image apparatus and raised to the power of science (so to speak). Commemoration thus in electracy becomes intelligence not confined to mourning, but extended to personal and public reasoning about all matters whatsoever. Mary Carruthers helps us understand how a personal association with an image operates as a mode of reasoning in an educational practice when she associates the "aura" of an image or place with the medieval mnemonic practices in which a word or image was said to "glow" with associated meanings (1998, 45):

> I want to focus first on a trope that brings together, as a rhetorical "common place," the physiology of *memoria* and its requirement of strong emotion. This trope clusters on Latin *pung-o, punc-tus,* literally meaning "to pierce, puncture," and thus "wound" some surface. This word quickly came as well to mean emotional vexation, anxiety, grief, and so on, and its close relative, *compunctus,* had much the same range of meanings, both the sense of piercing a surface and the emotional sense of goading and vexing the feelings. In medieval Latin, *punctus* came to be used also as the word for the dot or point pricked into the parchment surface, which helped to mark up and "divide" a written text for comprehension in reading, and so to "punctuate" it, in our modern sense. . . . So we have here a chain *(catena),* mnemonically associated through the key syllable *punct-,* which attaches physical puncture-wounds, with (page) punctuations, with affective compunc-tion of heart—and so from heart to memory, via a dual meaning of Latin *cor(d).* . . .
>
> The "wounding" of a page in punctuation and the wounding of memory in *compunctio cordis* are symbiotic processes, each a requirement for human cognition to occur at all. Several scholars working on *memoria* in medieval culture have noted how violence seems to be a recurring preoccupation, almost a mnemotechnical principle. . . .

I am well aware that current psychoanalytical theory has emphasized the role of trauma in memory making. I do not wish to be thought to believe that analysis based on these psychoanalytic constructs has no role to play in our perception of medieval cultures. But medieval people did not construe themselves in this way, and I have noticed that scholars who use psychoanalytic language to talk about the importance of "trauma" in the undoubtedly violent lives of medieval people can neglect the more social, rhetorical roles such violence played, at least in their art and their pedagogy. So instead of talking about psychic trauma, I will concentrate on the rhetorical figure of puncture wounds. (100–101)

The combined tasks of the MEmorial (peripheral and testimonial) are to show how a consultation on a social issue articulated in a news report cohere around the rhetorical sense of trauma. The testimony is already incipiently present in my response to the news event (for example, a famine in Africa), when the event is "remembered"—establishing a map positioning me in the pathic field of my world. Here is the basic method of witnessing, intended to counter the effect of the spectacle that frames all events within the commercial order of entertainment. The news is an abstract machine whose order words determine the behavior of employee-journalists, whatever their individual conscience or consciousness might be. The news as discourse was stuck for months on one group image (the disappearance of the Washington, DC, intern Chandra Levy), and then switched to 9/11. The disproportionate nature of the two events, each given similarly obsessive treatment, reveals the operation of the machine. Individuals acting independently on the Internet, for example, or radio talk shows and the like, have no more power to alter the functioning of this machine or disturb its field (the plane of consistency that it maintains) than do individual professional journalists within the institution. The EmerAgency is designed as a corporate or collective entity, appropriating features of consulting and tourism, to construct another abstract machine capable of intervening at the same level of the group subject addressed by the spectacle.

The potential of news reports to open wounds, rather than to cue defensive attitudes of invulnerability (the spectacle), is demonstrated by Hélène Cixous. Although she is talking about the reception of literary texts, the point of departure for her discussion is an example of a literary work initiated by a newspaper story. One instruction from this example is that the MEmorial as a form translates the event into an emblem. The formula is: news + art = testimonial.

The initial story, the starting shot from which [Dostoyevsky's] *The Idiot* arose was—anecdotally or unanecdotally—a news item: a young sixteen-year-old girl, Umetskaia, had killed her entire family after having been victimized. She is there throughout *The Notebooks,* she is constantly transformed, sometimes she's a man, sometimes a woman, sometimes young, sometimes old. She will end up dividing herself between Nastasia Philipovna and Rogojine. Dostoyevsky was prey to this character's mystery: what causes a young woman to bloody the entire house. She is a monster who isn't a monster. I could be her. I who am also you. . . .

Here is what Kafka wrote in 1904 to his friend Pollak: "I think we ought to only read the kind of books that wound and stab us. If the book we are reading doesn't wake us up with a blow on the head, what are we reading it for? But we need the books that affect us like a disaster. A book must be the axe for the frozen sea inside us.". . .

That is what I believe [too] but it also saddens me because very few books are axes, very few books hurt us, very few books break the frozen sea. Those books that do break the frozen sea and kill us are the books that give us joy. Why are such books so rare? Because those who write the books that hurt us also suffer, also undergo a sort of suicide, also get lost in forests—and this is frightening. (1993, 15, 18)

This passage proposes a connection between disasters and books: disasters that stimulate creativity; books that affect us like disasters. Here is a warning and an instruction: watch for the ax blow of recognition ("I could be her"). The MEmorial process begins as a collection of scenes (fragments) that return our gaze, that resonate for us due to some glint of recognition. It is easy to find public relays for these personal, idiosyncratic connections. Perhaps the best example is the way the site of a significant event becomes sacralized through the process of becoming a tourist attraction. The site itself might be without any intrinsic interest until a piece of information is added that connects the place with a story. Thus, a Midwestern cornfield, a motel balcony in the South, or an anonymous intersection in the urban sprawl of Los Angeles are transformed by the knowledge that these are the sites of the police ambush that killed Bonnie and Clyde, the assassination of Martin Luther King Jr., and the beating of Rodney King respectively.

A photograph of these sites, supplemented by a caption, almost never fails to create interest on the part of a viewer in a scene that otherwise would be dismissed or ignored. Joel Sternfeld, for example, produced a collection of fifty photographs of sites of newsworthy violence, accompanied by brief, descriptive captions. A photograph of a few seats in a movie theater, one of them with the seat down, is labeled "Aisle 2, Row 3, Seat 5, Texas Theatre, 232 West Jefferson Boulevard, Dallas, Texas." The caption informs us that "Lee Harvey Oswald was sitting in this seat when he was arrested by Dallas police at 1:50 P.M., November 22, 1963. The double feature playing that day was *Cry of Battle* and *War is Hell*" (Sternfeld 1996). The theater seat shown in the photograph is indistinguishable from all the others pictured, and from all the ones we have ever seen, for that matter. But the caption gives it aura, so that it becomes an emblem pointing to something more and different from itself. It is a metonym for a disaster.

Aura is a sign of recognition. Warren Schmidt recognized Ndugu Umbo as an image of his own spiritual famine. The MEmorial becomes testimonial when the egent designs it as an image, figure, parable, emblem, using some feature of the news event as an objective correlative for the witness's state of mind, mood, attunement to the world. Using aesthetic means, basic devices of literary language and art design, the egent generalizes the event into an image of what the world is like, how things stand with the witness *(I am starving for love)*. Former employees of Enron, for example, whose jobs, life savings, and retirement have all been wiped out due to corporate fraud, might (involuntarily) recognize in the fall of the twin towers the collapse of their personal sense of reality.

The insight guiding this sequence is that the news story that stings me does so because of its aura. The story is somehow not new but a reminder of something I already know or should know. It is fundamentally uncanny. The arts include many works that explore a connection between incidents reported in the news and personal experience. A principle of the EmerAgency is the application of arts methods to consulting. While it is true that the spectacle is aesthetic, it is a particular exploitation of the aesthetic within the institutions of entertainment and capitalism. Art practices are a homeopathic cure for the aestheticizing of politics. The following examples are only a sample showing the basic device of EmerAgency consulting: the mapping of connections across the popcycle (what Guattari called transversality) to create an effect of testimony linking one to the call (the egent's life to the found news event). A MEmorial begins with a response to news. This chapter focuses on some exemplary responses by artists to the call of news that we may use as relays, conducting us to our own designs.

ASSIGNMENT

Monitor the daily news until you find a report or story that troubles you or stings you in some way. Document the story and do some research on the background of the problem and the policy issues related to it.

- There is no need to analyze or interpret the incident or situation at this point. Instead, gather details or further document the problem.
- The feeling aroused by this story constitutes the call to a consultation on behalf of the EmerAgency.
- In your Web site make links to Internet sites relevant to the policy issues raised by the news story.

Getting the News

A "relay" is a "weak" model: it is not a template for our own work, but it orients us in the right way, demonstrating some of the possibilities of the form and style that may be adapted to the needs of our project. The examples included in this chapter contribute to a MEmorial tradition and offer some insight into the larger poetics of EmerAgency consulting. It is important to realize that the MEmorial is not new but is the extension into an educational setting of a poetics invented within avant-garde production. To testify as a witness for an Internet consultation on a public policy issue, I must realize that I am inside the field of the gaze, not outside with the privileged overview of the "objective" expert. Justice is immanent, not transcendent. The disaster outside looks at me, catches my eye or my body, and I recognize it (acknowledge its recognition of me). I get it. Not every disaster affects me in this way; to be an egent is to learn to notice this effect of correspondence in which the environmental event happens in me—"extimacy," the moebius topology of intersubjectivity explored by the modernist poets at least since the time of Baudelaire.

Ben Shahn, "The Biography of a Painting"

Shahn describes the genesis of a painting entitled *Allegory*—"The central image of the painting was a huge Chimera-like beast, its head wreathed in flames, its body arched across the figure of four recumbent children. These latter were dressed in very commonplace clothes, perhaps not entirely contemporary, but rather as I could draw them and their details form my own memory" (1957, 30).

> The immediate source of the painting of the red beast was a Chicago fire in which a colored man had lost his four children. John Bartlow Martin had written a concise reportorial account of the event—one of those stories which, told in detail, without any emotionalism being present in the writing itself, manages to produce a far greater emotional impact than would a highly colored account. . . .
>
> I examined a great deal of factual visual material, and then I discarded all of it. It seemed to me that the implications of this event transcended the immediate story; there was a universality about man's dread of fire, and his sufferings from fire. There was a universality in the pity which such a disaster invokes. Even racial injustice, which had played its part in this event, had its overtones. And the relentless poverty which had pursued this man, and which dominated the story, had its own kind of universality.
>
> I now began to devise symbols of an almost abstract nature, to work in terms of such symbols. Then I rejected that approach too. For in the abstracting of an idea one may lose the very intimate humanity of it, and this

deep and common tragedy was above all things human. I returned then to the small family contacts, to the familiar experiences of all of us, to the furniture, the clothes, the look of ordinary people, and on that level made my bid for universality and for the compassion that I hoped and believed the narrative would arouse. . . .

Of all the symbols which I had begun to develop, I retained only one in my illustrations—a highly formalized wreath of flames with which I crowned the plain shape of the house which had burned. . . .

I had some curious sense of responsibility about it, a sort of personal involvement. I had still not fully expressed my sense of the enormity of the Hickman fire; I had not formulated it in its full proportions; perhaps it was that I felt that I owed something more to the victim himself. . . .

The narrative of the fire had aroused in me a chain of personal memories. There were two great fires in my own childhood, one only colorful, the other disastrous and unforgettable. Of the first, I remember only that the little Russian village in which my grandfather lived burned, and I was there. I remember the excitement, the flames breaking out everywhere, the lines of men passing buckets to and from the river which ran through the town, the mad-woman who had escaped from someone's house during the confusion, and whose face I saw, dead-white in all the reflected color.

The other fire left its mark upon me and all my family, and left its scars on my fathers' hands and face, for he had clambered up a drainpipe and taken each of my brothers and sisters and me out of the house one by one, burning himself painfully in the process. Meanwhile our house and all our belongings were consumed, and my parents stricken beyond their power to recover. . . .

The image that I sought to create was not one of a disaster; that somehow doesn't interest me. I wanted instead to create the emotional tone that surrounds disaster; you might call it the inner disaster. (32–33, 35, 37)

Stephen Yenser on James Merrill, "18 West 11th Street"

In Robert Altman's *The Player* there is a scene in which a writer demonstrates in a meeting with staff of a Hollywood studio how to translate any newspaper report into a narrative story line for a movie. Poetry as well as fiction takes its cues from what the French call *faits divers*. Cornelius Eady, in *Brutal Imagination*, wrote a cycle of poems narrated by the imaginary black kidnapper invented by Susan Smith to cover up her murder of her two small sons. "When called, I come. My job is to get things done" (Eady 2001, 5). Sometimes the anecdote of life and the aphorism of thought (the secret point that Nietzsche said could be found in every career) intersect literally, and not only figuratively, as in the case of Merrill's poem.

The narrative actually comprises two strands, one of which splices bits of the history of the Greenwich Village townhouse that used to stand at the address given in the title and that was Merrill's family's New York residence from before his birth until some five years later. In March 1970, almost exactly forty-four years after he was born, the townhouse was blown up when members of the militant radical faction of Students for a Democratic Society known as the Weathermen accidentally set off some dynamite in the building's basement, which, police later determined, had been serving as a bomb factory. Three of the five young people in the building at the time were killed. Two women—Kathy Boudin and Cathlyn Wilkerson, the latter the daughter of the townhouse's owner—escaped the tremendous blast with cuts and bruises, borrowed clothes from a neighbor, and fled the scene (neither to appear again in public until they turned themselves in separately after more than ten years spent underground).

The second narrative strand is a recollection of a love affair with a woman the speaker calls B. B broke off the affair in the winter of 1969–70, had an affair with another man, then tried to patch things up in June, when it was too late. In addition to these two sketchy plots, which cross paths to suggest that in the destruction of the building Merrill sees a parallel to the fate of the relationship, the poem's structure involves occasional indirect observations on its composition.

The first of the poem's five sections (eight tercets each) begins in the past perfect tense as though it were to be about the Weathermen, breaks off in relief at sunset, then drops into the present tense and ruminates on the poem's raw material and the immediate setting. The second section consists mostly of the poet's memories of the house's music room and the player piano. The third begins with recollections of the house and then calls up the days after the explosion, when the speaker, laid up with a cold and abandoned by B, reads the newspaper accounts. The love affair dominates the fourth section, which also alludes to the poet's sympathy for the other man, and then taking things in reverse chronological order, recalls his feelings of anger and grief on the night B left him. The last section, making a marvelous transition, continues the film "run backwards," except that now it is a newsreel of the explosion. It takes us from the billowing smoke back through the coiling—no, the recoiling of the hoses, the unswearing in of a city commissioner, the thinning of the crowd as it once more nears the point at which it began to gather, and then back through the emergence from the wreckage of one of the women, through her disappearance and the explosion itself, to this vision of the street before the blast and the townhouse as it would have looked when first put on the market. (Yenser 1987, 195–96)

On Christian Boltanski, *Detective*

Detective is part of a series called *Lessons of Darkness,* by the French artist Christian Boltanski (Ulmer 1994b). It is a kind of archive, consisting of four crudely constructed wooden shelves holding cardboard boxes and twelve framed collages of photographs with clamp-on lamps. In other versions the photographs are taped to the fronts of the boxes, or the cardboard boxes are replaced by biscuit tins. The photographs are appropriated from a French crime magazine called *Detective*: he used every photograph from all the issues published in 1972 and 1973. The photos, acquired by the magazine from the family albums of victims and criminals alike, were used to illustrate the tabloid prose describing the crimes:

> Now it's impossible to know who is the victim and who is the murderer, because half are murderers and half are victims. And in the boxes you have the stories of these people, but you can't open the boxes. If you opened the cardboard box you wouldn't understand anything anyway because the stories and the faces are mixed up. When you see a face on the box, it's not that person's story that's inside, it's another story. The idea of the work is that perhaps we're all both murderer and victim. (Boltanski 1988a, 26)

Boltanski was interested in the family photo album for some time, making a variety of works based on such albums, and also on other vernacular sources of photographs such as school yearbooks. He always reworks the found materials into simulations or "docufictions." *Research and Presentation of Everything That Remains of My Childhood, 1944–50* is described typically as an "archeological inquiry into the deepest reaches of my memory" (following his practice of couching his simulations in scientific forms, especially imitating the displays found in museums of natural history). It is a book of photocopied snapshots of objects from his childhood (most of which actually belonged to his nephew). His goal in such works, he said, is not to represent his autobiography, but to explore and evoke familiar cultural types, archetypal gestures, to create an archive or model images of generic normal or collective life.

The ultimate referent for these pictures, based on an association of the photograph with death, as memorial, is the Holocaust, with the mass of snapshots, as in *Detective,* suggesting the mass of anonymous victims of the camps. Boltanski need not make any explicit reference to the camps because, given his textual mode of composition, he counts on the ubiquitous presence of the Holocaust in our collective memory, in our cultural code, to provide inevitably that association, to show the relationship between the public and private spheres. "I work with the idea of collective memory. The idea is that a piece of art is always made by the person looking at that art. I send a stimulus so that each person sees

something different. If we look at a photograph of a boy on a beach you and I see
something different; while I see a beach in France, you see a beach in England.
I try to send an open message so that everyone can reconstruct a private story"
(Boltanski 1988b, 48).

John S. Weber on Gerhard Richter, "18. Oktober 1977"

As the artist has noted, many of his photo-based paintings have a "kind of
fate or tragedy to them," and this is nowhere more evident than in his series of fifteen paintings on the Baader-Meinhof Group, titled "18. Oktober
1977." Painted in 1988, the imagery in this cycle of blurry monochrome
canvases is taken from documentary photographs of the capture, impris-
onment, death, and funeral of West Germany's most notorious left-wing
terrorists, who ostensibly committed suicide in Stammheim prison on
October 18, 1977. Beyond their eerie, somber beauty, the value of these
pictures lies in the precision with which they interrogate the use of both
paintings and photographs to convey information of historical significance today.

For viewers unfamiliar with the Red Army Fraction (RAF), as Andreas
Baader and Ulrike Meinhof's urban guerrilla group called itself, some
background information will help clarify the ambivalent stance that
Richter took in these paintings. Beginning as an activist group opposed to
the Vietnam War, the RAF became West Germany's most infamous and
widespread terrorist organization. In the mid-1970s, the RAF was thought
to have as many as three hundred underground members and up to three
thousand active adherents. Through acts of political violence such as as-
sassinations, armed attacks, and propaganda they sought to destabilize the
West German state, demonstrate its oppressive nature, and provoke a class
war. The government's response was harsh and ultimately effective. West
German civil liberties were curtailed to punish potential sympathizers, police rights of search and seizure were expanded, and a new, ultrasecurity
prison, Stuttgart-Stammheim, was built. The leading members of the RAF
were captured and held there. On October 18, 1977, the government reported that Baader, Jan-Carl Raspe, and Gudrun Ensslin had jointly committed
suicide during the previous night, following the failure of repeated attempts
by RAF "commandos" and sympathizers to obtain their release by armed
abductions and the hijacking of a commercial jetliner. The government released a series of photographs to buttress its claim, but many West Germans
still claimed that the "suicide" was in fact a state execution. The same skepticism had earlier greeted Meinhof's prison suicide in 1976. . . .

By failing to take sides with or against Baader, Meinhof, and their com-
rades, Richter forces his audience to judge for itself their actions and their

fate: did they truly die by their own hands or by those of the state? In either case, were their deaths an example of the just rule of democratic law, or a tragic case of misguided martyrdom? . . .

Discussing the Baader-Meinhof cycle, Richter has said that it expresses "compassion for the illusion that it is possible to change the world." Yet in speaking of his ambitions for his own work, he has also said, "I know for a fact that painting is not ineffectual. I would only like it to accomplish more." In fact, there are few subjects which get to the heart of the political and moral challenges faced by modern Germany more quickly than the short, violent rise and fall of the Baader-Meinhof Group. (Weber 1994, 89–90)

ASSIGNMENT

Start an archive of pictures and text found on the Internet that could serve as a vocabulary of stock representations of your news event as a scene.

- In all of these examples the artists appropriated historical or actual happenings for purposes of personal expression as well as for general reflection. In some of Boltanski's work he takes this technique one step further by using found materials (photographs, personal anecdotes, toys, and other objects) to stand in for the actual sights and details of his personal life. The technique has a theoretical point concerning the disappearance of selfhood as the predominant experience of identity in the society of the spectacle. On the design side, the point is that the Internet is a collage engine. The emotional effectiveness of Boltanski's work shows that a substitute image (picture or text) works just as well as the actual one, since the point is generative, to trigger or cue the atmosphere or mood, not the empirical reproduction of a past reality.
- Review the examples and do an inventory of their methods and features. Write a set of instructions based on these features that could be used to produce your own version of such a work connecting a news event with a personal experience or situation.

Countermonuments

The set of readings above indicate how artists think about specific news events within their medium and style, manifesting a movement contrary to the appropriation of the image of disaster into the spectacle (of propaganda and pornography). The next step in the relay is to consider an arts approach to monumentality (as distinct from the officially sanctioned process of proposals and competitions such as those under way for Lower Manhattan). Egents write the disaster in the middle voice (neither active nor passive). It is significant in our context that the textbook example illustrating the grammar of voice in linguistic theory is "to sacrifice."

> A linguistic notion may give us the key: that of diathesis or, as the grammar books put it, "voice" (active, passive, middle). Diathesis designates the way in which the subject of the verb is affected by the action; this is obvious for the passive; and yet linguists tell us that, in Indo-European at least, the diathetical opposition is not between active and passive but between active and middle. According to the classic example given by Meillet and Benveniste, the verb *to sacrifice* (ritually) is active if the priest sacrifices the victim in my place and for me, and it is middle voice if, taking the knife from the priest's hands, I make the sacrifice for my own sake; in the case of the active voice, the action is performed outside the subject, for although the priest makes the sacrifice, he is not affected by it; in the case of the middle voice, on the contrary, by acting, the subject affects himself, he always remains inside the action, even if that action involves an object. Hence, the middle voice does not exclude transitivity. Thus defined, the middle voice corresponds exactly to the modern state of the verb to write: to write is today to make oneself the center of the action of speech, it is to effect writing by affecting oneself, to make action and affection coincide, to leave the scriptor inside the writing— not as a psychological subject, but as agent of the action. (Barthes 1986, 18)

The MEmorial or minor monumentality supplements official monumentality with commemoration in the middle voice, in which egents experience the disaster precisely as sacrifice through the act of memorializing it. Another citation from Bataille reminds us of the dimension of reality accessed by modern chora (sacred space):

> If one followed these associations, the use of the sacrificial mechanism for various ends, such as propitiation or expiation, would be seen as secondary, and one would only retain the elementary fact of the radical alteration of the person which can be indefinitely associated with any other alteration that suddenly arises in collective life: for example, the death of a relative, initiation, the consumption of the new harvest. . . . Such an action would be characterized by the fact that it would have the power to liberate heterogeneous elements and to break the habitual homogeneity of the individual, in the same way that vomiting would be opposed to its opposite, the communal eating of food. . . . Repugnance is only one of the forms of stupor caused by a horrifying eruption, by the disgorging of a force that threatens to consume.

The one who sacrifices is free—free to indulge in a similar disgorging, free, continuously identifying with the victim, to vomit his own being just as he has vomited a piece of himself or a bull, in other words free to throw himself suddenly outside of himself, like a gall or an aissaouah. (1985, 70)

A question that addresses a paradox of radical tourism concerns the revolutionary potential of monumentality. Mullah Mohammed Khaqzar, once a powerful member of the Taliban movement (one of the sixty clerics who met at a mosque in 1994 to form the Taliban religious army), did not flee Kabul when the Taliban abandoned the city, an act that marked his rejection of the movement. "For Khaqzar, the Taliban's decision to destroy two sandstone statues of Buddha, hewn from a cliff face near Bamiyan in the 3rd and 5th centuries, was a breaking point. He said he argued in vain in the Taliban council for saving the statues" (*Gainesville Sun*, December 9, 2001). There is a third position possible, between booster statues and their total destruction. The references to terrorists in Richter's and Merrill's works resonate in the context of 9/11, but the German case exists in a context of antimonumentality that followed World War II and the abuse of monumental practices by the Nazi state. Postwar German artists have developed a countermonumentality.

At home in an era of earthworks, conceptual and self-destructive art, these young artists explore both the necessity of memory and their incapacity to recall events they never experienced directly. To their minds, neither literal nor figurative references suggesting anything more than their own abstract link to the Holocaust will suffice. Instead of seeking to capture the memory of events, therefore, they remember only their own relationship to events, the great gulf of time between themselves and the Holocaust.

For German artists and sculptors like Jochen Gerz, Norbert Radermacher, and Horst Hoheisel, the possibility that memory of events so grave might be reduced to exhibitions of public craftsmanship or cheap pathos remains intolerable. They contemptuously reject the traditional forms and reasons for public memorial art, those spaces that either console viewers or redeem such tragic events, or indulge in a facile kind of Wiedergutmachung or purport to mend the memory of a murdered people. Instead of searing memory into public consciousness, they fear, conventional memorials seal memory off from awareness altogether. For these artists, such an evasion would be the ultimate abuse of art, whose primary function to their minds is to jar viewers from complacency, to challenge and denaturalize the viewers' assumptions. (Young 1993, 27–28)

While it is a deconstruction of conventional monumentality, the MEmorial differs from the German countermonuments in democratizing monumental memory rather than rejecting it altogether. MEmorials are not only reflexive—

Florida Rushmore as a critique of Mount Rushmore—but also transitive, intended as interventions in public policy formation. Their purpose finally is not only monumentality as such, but also consulting. Their memory work is not only abstract, serving to mark an event or issue in order to bring it into representation and make it thinkable, but also practical in addressing the relationship between behaviors and beliefs or values. Traffic fatalities, for example, cannot be treated exclusively as an issue of product safety, driver training, law enforcement, and the like. MEmorials are intended to bring out this extra dimension, the human question, the disaster as a collective self-portrait. The portrait is not taken as a given, but as a glimpse of a process in progress (the past-future of Deleuze and Guattari's "becoming" that replaces metaphysical concern with "being").

The following relays represent the potential of countermonumentality to contribute to a deconsultancy on public policy, including a critique of values and beliefs.

Graeme Gilloch on Walter Benjamin's Countermonumentality

The meeting-house where Benjamin and the other members of the radical wing of the Youth Movement met was also the place where the bodies of Heinle and Seligson were found after their joint suicide in 1914. This constitutes nothing less than a holy place for Benjamin. It is a shrine not only to the young lovers, but also to Benjamin's own youthful aspirations of cultural renaissance. It is a monument to a betrayed generation. . . .

There are other shrines: his grandmother's house in Blumenshof and the surrounding neighborhood have become "an Elysium, an indefinite realm of the shades of deceased but immortal grandmothers." This is a half-affectionate, half-scornful monument to the previous bourgeois generation that locked itself away in gloomy interiors crowded with obsolete commodities. Blumeshof comes to be a memorial to the misguided bourgeois sense of security, to its misplaced notion of comfort and well-being, to the folly of dismal, claustrophobic lives spent accumulating now outdated, ridiculous objects. Benjamin also refers to Luise von Landau, a girl in his class at school who died in childhood. It is to her, not the imperious Queen Luise, that Benjamin offers his love among the statues of the Tiergarten.

Benjamin sets up a series of personal counter-monuments: to the Siegessaule (the glorification of war), he contrasts the meeting-house (the horror of war); to the Tiergarten statues of Friedrich-Wilhelm and Queen Luise (the self-adoration and immortality of the bourgeoisie), he counterpoises the house of his grandmother (the dingy bourgeois junk-room, its precious objects obsolete) and that of Luise von Landau (frailty and transience). For Benjamin, each building, each space in the city, has its own half-forgotten tale to tell. The city is the "discovery site of the personal past." For the urban physiognomist, the city is a series of monuments. Like the *memoire involontaire*, it interweaves forgetting and remembering. The cityscape stimulates recollection; it serves as a mnemonic device. For the physiognomist, as for the archaeologist, such personal monuments, fleetingly recognized by the remembering adult, reveal the modern metropolis as the sprawling agglomeration of the multitudinous houses of the dead. (Gilloch 1996, 76)

Barbara Rose on Claes Oldenburg

Oldenburg's monuments had their genesis within his imagination during the summer he spent in Provincetown, in 1960. The daily sight of the Pilgrim Memorial there set him thinking about America's historical past and uncertain future, and comparing the ideals on which the country had been founded with the degeneration of its goals.... The sources for Oldenburg's monuments are many: illustrations in children's books; the gigantic balloons in Macy's Thanksgiving Day parades, which he never misses; the whole tradition of architectural fantasies, including the work of the visionary architects of the late eighteenth century, Boullee, Ledoux, and Lequeu, whose drawings Oldenburg had studied while working in the library at Cooper Union; as well as the popular tradition of structures built in the shape of animals....

The message of Oldenburg's monuments is the same as that of his sculpture: humor is the only weapon for survival. For example, he conceived a monument for the suicides of the 1929 crash—a structure between the buildings of Wall Street, with figures falling off it. Unlike Surrealist fantasies, Oldenburg's monuments always refer to specific places, and often to specific times. They are grotesque caricatures of some realities of contemporary culture that we would perhaps prefer not to face. "Is a monument always a memory of something?" Oldenburg asks. "No, it's not. A monument can be anything. Why isn't this hamburger a monument? Isn't it big enough? A monument is a symbol. I think of a monument as being symbolic and for the people and therefore rhetorical, not honest, not personal." ...

The choice of objects for specific sites is made on the basis of Oldenburg's analysis of the dominant mood or spirit of a place, and his attempt to find the appropriate image to summarize that quality. London, for example, seemed to him a "leggy" city, so he invented *Colossal Monument: Knees for Thames Estuary*. To replace the Washington obelisk, his proposal was a colossal *Scissors in Motion*, set like its prototype near a reflecting pool....

The monuments are meant to be taken seriously, in that they are true symbols of our age and reveal the choices open to society; but they are also meant, by their extravagant exaggeration, to shock people into consciousness of what is really happening. The possibility that his projects will be taken literally no doubt fills Oldenburg with certain misgivings. (Research was done by some Cornell students on the feasibility of erecting the *Colossal Block of Concrete Inscribed with Names of War Heroes* that he proposed for the intersection of Canal Street and Broadway—the spot where experts have calculated that a dropped A-Bomb would do the most damage—but the costs proved prohibitively high.) The point is, of course, that it is no more ridiculous to erect an Oldenburg monument than to build a giant skyscraper on top of Grand Central Terminal or put up a travesty of the Campidoglio at Lincoln Center. In this sense, Oldenburg's projects are monuments to the negative as well as to the positive power of human imagination—its power to "think the unthinkable." (Rose 1970, 103, 107–8, 110)

Robert Smithson, from "A Tour of the Monuments of Passaic, New Jersey"

On Saturday, September 30, 1967, I went to the Port Authority Building on 41st Street and 8th Avenue. I bought a copy of the *New York Times* and a Signet paperback called *Earthworks* by Brain W. Aldiss. Next I went to ticket booth 21 and purchased a one-way ticket to Passaic. After that I went up to the upper bus level (platform 173) and boarded the number 30 bus of the Inter-City Transportation Co.

I sat down and opened the *Times*. . . . On page 29 was John Canaday's column. He was writing on *Themes and the Usual Variations*. I looked at a blurry reproduction of Samuel F. B. Morse's *Allegorical Landscape* at the top of Canaday's column; the sky was a subtle newsprint grey, and the clouds resembled sensitive stains of sweat reminiscent of a famous Yugoslav watercolorist whose name I have forgotten. A little statue with right arm held high faced a pond (or was it the sea?). "Gothic" buildings in the allegory had a faded look, while an unnecessary tree (or was it a cloud of smoke?) seemed to puff up on the left side of the landscape. Canaday referred to the picture as "standing confidently along with other allegorical representatives of the arts, sciences, and high ideals that universities foster." . . .

The bus passed over the first monument. I pulled the buzzer-cord and got off at the corner of Union Avenue and River Drive. The monument was a bridge over the Passaic River that connected Bergen county with Passaic county. Noon-day sunshine cinema-ized the site, turning the bridge and the river into an over-exposed picture. Photographing it with my Instamatic 400 was like photographing a photograph. The sun became a monstrous light-bulb that projected a detached series of "stills" through my Instamatic into my eye. When I walked on the bridge, it was as though I was walking on an enormous photograph that was made of wood and steel, and underneath the river existed as an enormous movie film that showed nothing but a continuous blank.

The steel road that passed over the water was in part an open grating flanked by wooden sidewalks, held up by a heavy set of beams, while above, a ramshackle network hung in the air. . . . I was completely controlled by the Instamatic (or what the rationalists call a camera). The glassy air of New Jersey defined the structural parts of the monument as I took snapshot after snapshot. A barge seemed fixed to the surface of the water as it came toward the bridge, and caused the bridgekeeper to close the gates. From the banks of Passaic I watched the bridge rotate on a central axis in order to allow an inert rectangular shape to pass with its unknown cargo. The Passaic (West) end of the bridge rotated south, while the Rutherford (East) end of the bridge rotated north; such rotations suggested the limited movements of an outmoded world. "North" and "South" hung over the static river in a bi-polar manner. One could refer to this bridge as the "Monument of Dislocated Directions." (Smithson 1979, 52–54)

Krzysztof Wodiczko, "The Homeless Projection: A Proposal for the City of New York" (1986)

Architecture

What has been called architecture is no longer merely a collection of buildings with "stable forms" and "permanent structures." Architecture must be recognized today as a social system: a new economic condition and a psycho-political experience. . . . What has been defined as architecture is really merciless real estate system embodied in a continuous and frightening mass-scale *event*, the most disturbingly public and central operations of which are economic terror, physical eviction, and the exodus of the poorest groups of city inhabitants from the buildings' interiors to the outdoors.

The New Monument

Such forced exteriorization of their estranged bodies transforms the homeless into permanently displayed outdoor "structures," symbolic architectural forms, new types of city monuments: *The Homeless.*

The surfaces of *The Homeless*—over- or underdressed, unwashed, cracked from permanent outdoor exposure, and posing in their frozen, "classic" gestures—weather and resemble the official monuments of the city. *The Homeless* appear more dramatic than even the most colossal and expressive urban sculptures, memorials, or public buildings, however, for there is nothing more disruptive and astonishing in a monument than a sign of life. To the observer the slightest sign of life in THE HOMELESS is a living sign of the possibility of the death of the homeless from homelessness.

The homeless must display themselves in symbolically strategic and popular city "accents." To secure their starvation wages (donations), the homeless must appear as the "real homeless" (their "performance" must conform to the popular *myth of the homeless*): the homeless must become *The Homeless*.

Adorned with the "refuse" of city "architecture" and with the physical fragments of the cycles of change, the homeless become the nomadic "buildings," the mobile "monuments" of the city. However, fixed in the absolute lowest economic and social positions and bound to their physical environment, *The Homeless* achieve a symbolic stability, while the official city buildings and monuments lose their stable character as they continuously undergo their real estate change.

Unable to live without the dramatic presence of *The Homeless* (since their contrast helps produce "value"—social, economic, cultural) and denying the homeless as its own social consequence, "architecture" must continuously repress the monumental condition of the homeless deeper into its (political) unconscious.

Projection

If the homeless must "wear" the building (become a new, mobile building) and are forced to live through the monumental problem of Architecture, the aim of *The Homeless Projection* is to impose this condition back on the Architecture and to force its surfaces to reveal what they deny:

- To magnify the scale of the homeless to the scale of the building!
- To astonish the street public with the familiarity of the image and to make the homeless laugh!
- To employ the slide psychodrama method to teach the BUILDING to play the role of *The Homeless*!
- To liberate the problem of the homeless from the unconscious of the "architecture"!
- To juxtapose the fake architectural real estate theater with the real survival theater of the homeless! (Wodiczko 1996, 426–27)

Revolutionary Monuments

The CATTt contrast introduced between tourism and revolution becomes a convergence in the context of monuments and countermonumentality. Just one example will have to suffice to represent this alternative between the boosterism of the conventional monument and the critique of the countermonument.

Nikolai Punin, from "The Monument to the Third International"

In 1919 the Department of Fine Arts within the People's Commissariat for Enlightenment commissioned the artist V. E. Tatlin to develop a design for a monument to the third International. The artist Tatlin immediately set to work and produced a design. . . .

The main idea of the monument is based on an organic synthesis of the principles of architecture, sculpture and painting and was intended to produce a new type of monumental structure, uniting in itself a purely creative form with a utilitarian form. In accordance with this idea, the design of the monument consists of three large glass structures, erected by means of a complex system of vertical struts and spirals. These structures are arranged one above the other and are contained within different, harmoniously related forms. . . .

A social revolution by itself does not change artistic forms, but it does provide a basis for their gradual transformation. The idea of monumental propaganda has not changed sculpture or sculptors, but it has struck at the very principle of plastic appearance which prevails in the bourgeois world. Renaissance traditions in the plastic arts appear modern only while the feudal and bourgeois roots of capitalist states remain undestroyed. The Renaissance burned out, but only now is the charred ruin of Europe being purged.

It is true that Communist governments for a certain time will use, as a means of monumental propaganda, figurative monuments in the style of Greek and Italian classicism, but this is only because these governments are forced to use them in the same way as they are compelled to use specialists of the pre-revolutionary school. Figurative monuments (Greek and Italian) are at variance with contemporary reality in two respects. They cultivate individual heroism and conflict with history: torsos and heads of heroes (and gods) do not correspond to the modern interpretation of history. Their forms are too private for places where there are ten versts of proletarians in rows. At best they express the character, feelings and thoughts of the hero, but who expresses the tension of the emotions and the thoughts of the collective thousand? A type? But a type concretizes, limits and levels the mass. The mass is richer, more alive, more complicated and more organic.

But even if a type is portrayed, figurative monuments contradict actuality even more through the limitation of their expressive means, their static quality. The agitational action of such monuments is extraordinarily weak amidst the noise, movement and dimensions of the streets. Thinkers on granite plinths perhaps see many, but few see them. They are constrained by the form which evolved when sailing ships, transport by mule and stone cannon balls flourished. . . .

One of the most complex cultural problems is solved before our very eyes [by Tatlin's design]: a utilitarian form appears as a purely creative form. Once again a new classicism becomes possible, not as a renaissance but as an invention. The theorists of the international workers' movement have long sought a classical content for socialist culture. Here it is. We maintain that the present project is the first revolutionary artistic work, and one which we can send to Europe. (Punin 1992, 311, 313)

Electronic and Soviet constructivist monumentality share an interest in appropriating the memorial genre for the purposes of mass education, collective identity formation, and liberation (however that is understood) by combining pure creative process with utilitarian concerns. That aspect of Tatlin's famous design that "flees from the earth," however, distinguishes the revolutionary ideal from the MEmorial focus on the abject or formless dimension of value immanent within actual behavior. In addition, the Internet as a living monument supports the shift away from the Leninist vanguard of monuments *for* the people.

The EmerAgency proposes monuments *by* the people. Some of the formal and practical dilemmas still present in Tatlin's monument—such as the problematic relationship between the individual and the collective—are resolved by the nature of the electronic apparatus. The interlinked proliferation of individually authored MEmorials on the Internet, coordinated and focused through the EmerAgency interface metaphor of consultant tourists (theoria), externalizes and shows citizens the "cognitive map" tracing the collective reality of individual actions. The gap between a singular event and general statistics is bridged through the linked testimony of the egents, enacting the slogan "Problems B Us." Might the EmerAgency learn from Lenin how to write a group subject? Lenin's slogan—"All power to the Soviets"—is the prototype of the "order word" that is the essence of language, according to Deleuze and Guattari. "The abstract machine is always singular, designated by the proper name of a group or individual, while the assemblage of enunciation is always collective, in the individual as in the group. The Lenin abstract machine, and the Bolshevik collective assemblage. . . . The abstract machine does not exist independently of the assemblage, anymore than the assemblage functions independently of the machine" (Deleuze and Guattari 1987, 100).

"Problems B Us" works only through the collective of the EmerAgency. And its purpose is not to impose one virtue-vice, but to open sloganeering to the fifth estate of egent pupils. "For the question was not how to elude the order-word but how to elude the death sentence it envelops, how to develop its power of escape, how to prevent escape from veering into the imaginary or falling into a black hole, how to maintain or draw out the revolutionary potentiality of the order-word. . . . A single thing or word undoubtedly has this twofold nature: it is necessary to extract one from the other—to transform the compositions of order into components of passage" (110). Here is a task for the EmerAgency.

4

Transversal
(Into Cyberspace)

WHETHER ENCOUNTERED IN PRINT OR ON TELEVISION, news is a feature of the institution of entertainment, meaning that the information is structured as a commodity, governed by the profit motive. Deconsulting must make itself heard and felt within and across the frame of this institutional arrangement. The emergence of tabloid journalism into "legitimacy" in the past decade simply makes explicit what is implicit in the principle of the spectacle—news is part of entertainment; it has to sell (sizzle, glow). A consultation influences policy through the spectacle. The spectacle names a condition in which actuality and images merge and become indistinguishable, leading, it is argued, to the destruction of civic life and the related benefits and responsibilities of a free, democratic society. Critics argue that this effect is due not only to the commodity form, which replaces critical reflection with maximized desire, but to the limitations of the human sensorium, vastly augmented and extended by media technology. This sensorium is designed not only to receive and process external stimuli, but also to filter and exclude stimuli, to protect the organism from being overwhelmed. The argument is that the spectacle effect is a necessary collective *defense mechanism,* making it possible to deal with the immense amount of information that a postmodern citizen receives every day. We want to be on a spiritual no-call list.

The forms and practices of entertainment discourse are designed to filter as much as to convey information. It is not just a matter of compassion fatigue, but of the very design of our information in entertainment forms that ensures that we know more but care less about what happens. Nonetheless, a news item still has the power to sting, to irritate, to provoke me with a feeling of justice or injustice. This feeling is what Roland Barthes called the "punctum," the third meaning, the obtuse or indirect significance of an image or scene. The obtuse dimension of information opens a network of personal associations and memories, a rhizome connecting the citizen to the event in a peculiar, unforeseeable, unprogrammable way. The obtuse associations map the singular body of formless reason. One purpose of the MEmorial is to develop a pedagogy adequate to the data stream of the spectacle by putting the obtuse network into a writing/design practice.

The point of intervention of EmerAgency consulting on public policy is through the group subject, mediating the formation of identity at the individual and collective levels. Many of the effects of the spectacle characterize the transitional conditions of literate identity within an electrate apparatus. This chapter provides some context for the MEmorial project by documenting a case that shows the potential for arts and entertainment practices to produce a methodology capable of grasping a situation holistically in an image. This holistic reach of image categories is necessary for the success of the MEmorial, whose purpose is to make intelligible the collective status of a multitude of individual behaviors, and ultimately to become a means of writing images for group subjects. In Guattari's term, the goal is to implement an abstract machine. "Machine" in this approach replaces the notion of "structure":

> When we speak of abstract machines, by "abstract" we can also understand "extract" in the sense of extracting. They are montages capable of relating all the heterogeneous levels that they traverse and that we have just enumerated. The abstract machine is transversal to them, and it is this abstract machine that will or will not give these levels an existence, an efficiency, a power of ontological auto-affirmation. The different components are swept up and reshaped by a sort of dynamism. Such a functional ensemble will hereafter be described as a machinic assemblage. The term "assemblage" does not imply any notion of bond, passage, or anastomosis between its components. It is an assemblage of possible fields, of virtual as much as constituted elements, without any notion of generic or species' relation. In this context, utensils, instruments, the most basic tools and the least structured pieces of a machine acquire the status of a proto-machine. (Guattari 1995, 35)

Simulacrum

A term related to the transversal assemblage of abstract machines is "simulacrum," in a usage that is less commonly noted. In the spectacle original and copy merge, rendering moot most models of literate truth—hence the importance of reasone-on. The categorical images activated in a MEmorial are simulacra, emerging from a series of repetitions, without reference to or grounding in some origin.

> For what constitutes the simulacrum as a form—its undecidable relation
> to its origins and to the various ties and spaces it traverses through its
> repetitions—can neither be presented in nor represented by the image as such,
> but only alluded to by its absences or excesses. Its effect is inseparable from a
> series that cannot be definitively rendered manifest in an individual image,
> nor exhausted by any preexisting code. It can only be recreated by the work-
> ings of memory and imagination, which retrospectively and prospectively
> weave between its various avatars relations of identity or difference, priority
> or secondariness, regularity or variation, being or becoming. The simula-
> crum is at once removed from and infinitely proximate to its point of origin;
> as such, it is essentially displaced, elsewhere than itself. But, as the ambigu-
> ous "return" of a model that it at once renders visible and withholds it is also
> fundamentally untimely: nonsynchronous with and becoming other than
> itself. (Durham 1998, 17)

We are speaking of a mode of peripheral inference that elsewhere I have called "conduction." One of the examples Durham gives for such a serial movement evoking a virtual model is the writings of Jean Genet. "The simulacrum often appears in Genet as a means of mapping the relation between distinct spheres of discursive and social practice, each of which 'repeats' the image differently, as a function of its own forms of expression and its own relations of power and desire. So it is in Genet's prison novels, where he emphasizes the variation in the image of the criminal, as it passes from the domain of the journalists and judges to the underworld of the pimps and *tantes,* from the cell of the imprisoned nar-rator to the private spaces occupied by his readers" (1998, 24).

Egents must learn this style of mapping (choragraphy) as a support for a group subject. The challenge is to locate and engage with the hole that neces-sarily opens onto the outside of every whole. This hole is a wormhole if you like, a logical shortcut. The paradox of modern knowledge circulates around the in-completeness theorem postulating the paradox that no system is able rigorously to account for itself. There is a blind spot at the very core of clarity, whose effects it is the task of the MEmorial to document.

> An event can be coded politically by sending troops to fulfill a particular
> mission in a delimited region of the world. Economically, that "same" event

can be coded in terms of oil prices and adjustments in one's stock portfolio. Legally, it can be determined that the losers of the military confrontation were "war criminals" and thus were vanquished "justly." The "event" in question, however, does not exist for society outside of these coded representations. Even the mere physical description of what occurred is just that, a physical *description,* communicated (morally, journalistically, ecologically) according to well-established, if flexible, codes. Each description increases the complexity of the event and thereby the complexity of the social world that these communications reproduce. (Rasch 2002, 23)

These are descriptions of the operations of group *até.*

The strategy that suggests itself for engaging positively with the paradoxes of incompleteness and the simulacrum is that of the distributed observer.

As Luhmann says, the observer, as the distinction, is the excluded middle or blind spot of observation. As the eye that remains outside the field of vision, the observer excludes itself from its own operations; yet, as one of the many observers (distinctions) operating in the world, it is made visible by other distinctions, other observations. . . . In Hegelian terms, we are faced with a bad infinity, a network of observations that never fully closes the circle, a structure of latency that never achieves complete transparency. In Nietzschean terms, we are immersed in a radically incommensurable perspectivism with no hope of an overarching coordination of viewpoints. In quantum terms, the talk is of a "complementarity" of observations, in which "every observation introduces a new uncontrollable element," such that "an independent reality in the ordinary physical sense can neither be ascribed to the phenomena nor to the agencies of observation." (Rasch 2002, 25)

This fundamental inhibition of totalization limits control for better and for worse. In this epistemological setting the EmerAgency proposes a practice capable of appropriating surveillance technologies on behalf of group self-consciousness as a counterweight to the specter of panoptic totalitarianism. To appreciate the anxieties surrounding surveillance, we should imagine that we are witnessing the equivalent for the group subject of Socrates questioning Euthyphro about the meaning of "impiety," revealing in the process a new force in reality: the contradiction.

A Machinic Assemblage

This following set of documents suggests some of the features of an image category, its transversal, simulacral effect of virtuality, emerging as an effect of a series. These readings begin with a newspaper story about a transsexual, as an example of the kind of story about someone's life problem that might trigger the punctum or its alternative, a disavowal (defense). It is an extreme case of a problem originating in the family discourse, of not fitting the norms of the identity (ideology) categories. The subsequent readings track the issue as it circulates into Hollywood cinema, an art installation, and theory, thus manifesting the dynamics of the popcycle as a circulation of signifiers through the different discourse institutions. Part of our interest in this set is the way transsexuality becomes a fragment that crosses through different territories or kinds of order to become a refrain holding together heterogeneous elements in a way that demonstrates how images mediate individual and collective experience in electracy.

"Mr. Gordon isn't Mr. Gordon anymore."

The Associated Press, Eastchester, N.Y.—When last seen by students at Eastchester High School, art teacher Randy Gordon was a man. When they return to class in September, that no longer will be the case. "Mr. Gordon isn't Mr. Gordon anymore," said the 52-year-old teacher who underwent a sex-change operation last month. "But it's still me. The parents and the kids who knew me as a man, they'll accept me. The person hasn't changed. I'm the same crazy, humorous person I was before."

Many people who undertook sex changes—there are an estimated 1,000 annually in the United States—decide to start a new life with a new identity. But Gordon, who has taught in the New York City suburb for 10 years, is one of a small number of transsexual teachers across the country who are returning to the classroom. . . .

It doesn't always work that way. Dana Rivers, a teacher in Sacramento, Calif., was fired in 1999 after becoming a woman. The school board said parents complained Rivers had talked to students about the decision. Rivers denied that and sued; she received a $150,000 settlement and resigned. . . .

To prepare for Gordon's return to the 600-student high school, the district invited students and parents to what turned out to be a lively meeting that covered everything from privacy rights to bathroom use. (She said she plans to use the unisex faculty bathroom in the school's art wing).

"There was a lot of confusion, and people had questions," Superintendent Bob Siebert said. "Most people were supportive. We told them everything we could about what had happened and we assured them that Randy was going to have to be responsible, like any other teacher, about what she says to the students. We also told them Randy had rights that have to be protected."

Ellie Giotas, who has a daughter at the high school, has doubts. "They're trying to justify something in the name of freedom, in the name of the law," Giotas said. "I would tell this guy, why don't you get the hell out and start your new life somewhere else? Why do you have to impose this on us, upon our children."

Still, some students seem untroubled. "He's not a killer, he's not a child molester," senior Zack Sciarabba told The Journal News of White Plains. "He's a person who wants to live his life. He was a great guy, and there's no doubt he'll be a great woman." (*Gainesville Sun,* July 26, 2001, 2A)

Frank Pierson, *Dog Day Afternoon*

Frank Pierson, involved as a writer, director, or producer with such television successes as *Have Gun, Will Travel* and *Man from U.N.C.L.E.,* and author of scripts for *The Ballad of Cat Ballou* and *Cool Hand Luke,* describes in this excerpt how he started with a newspaper story and built the character of Sonny in his script for the film *Dog Day Afternoon:*

> For me, *Dog Day Afternoon* began with a huge pile of clippings, news and magazine reports of a bank robbery motivated by the need of the homosexual wife of the robber for a sex-change operation. I also had a huge pile of transcripts of tape recorded interviews with all of the various people involved, the hostages the robber held in the bank, the various cops and FBI people who eventually captured him and shot and killed his partner, with the robber's family and friends, his homosexual wife, and his heterosexual wife. It was overwhelming. . . .
>
> The first problem in dramatizing this event was to identify what it was that was so fascinating. It was tempting to believe that the public event was the interesting aspect, a television first, as it were. But his is the stuff of documentaries; . . . The problem lay in the character of the hero. . . . I knew the bare bones of his history, where he'd gone to school, that he'd been a rather conservative young man who'd been a Goldwater delegate at a Republican convention, that he had a wife and two children, who loved him, that he once worked in a bank and so knew how banks worked and where things were kept. I knew his height and weight and that he looked a lot like Al Pacino. I knew he'd married a man (Ernie) in a Catholic church ceremony, without getting a divorce from his female wife. I knew he'd been unable to keep a job regularly as his life grew more and more chaotic. I knew his homosexual wife grew exasperated with him as he was sexually demanding and jealous. I knew his heterosexual wife was exasperated with him for all kinds of reasons. I knew he'd gone into the bank to steal money because he thought a sex-change operation as a birthday present would make his homosexual wife happy.
>
> His behavior in his life and in the bank was riddled with contradictions, quixotic gestures of kindness alternated with raging defiance, noisy

outbursts of anger with sudden quiet. . . . I knew what was wrong. I could not find in this character anything I could understand and identify with, that would let me find the way he felt and understand why he did the things he did. It was impossible to imagine the things I would have to make up to create the story. . . .

Then it struck me that Sonny conceived of himself as a magician with the power to make dreams come true, to fulfill hopes and ambitions. He loved the needy and unfulfilled, and he went through life trying to fulfill their dreams of themselves, to make them whole. And once they were whole, they could give back to him the love he had given to them. But this was an impossible dream. All he was able to do was fan their hopes. He was a convincing dreamer because he believed the dream was real. And when the eventual disaster materialized, he was blamed for letting them down. Instead of love, he got back from everyone waves of anger and resentment. (Pierson 1988, 139–41)

Daniel Birnbaum on Pierre Huyghe's *The Third Memory*

In the news story that Frank Pierson turned into a screenplay, the transsexual is a "ficelle," a secondary character or supporting role in a drama about a bank robbery. His focus is on recasting the event into an entertainment (fictional) narrative. The French artist Pierre Huyghe picked up the narrative and recast it again into the form of a fine arts installation piece.

In the end, John Wojtowicz's story was too good to recount just once. Its first telling came in 1975, via the Sidney Lumet–directed movie *Dog Day Afternoon,* starring Al Pacino as Wojtowicz, the gay bank robber whose heist "should have taken ten minutes," in the words of the Warner Brother's advertisement, but "four hours later, the bank was like a circus sideshow. Eight hours later, it was the hottest thing on TV. Twelve hours later, it was history." ("And it's all true," concluded the ad, breathlessly.) The film depicts Wojtowicz's 1972 attempt to rob a New York City bank to pay for his lover's sex-change operation, and as such could be read as offering a vivid parable of what Guy Debord must have meant by life in the society of the spectacle (and accounts in part for the film's cult status). Wojtowicz and his accomplice, Sal, were media superstars not for fifteen minutes, but for at least fifteen hours. . . .

This was all too much for French artist Pierre Huyghe to resist. A filmmaker known for his metacinematic experimenting, Huyghe decided to invite Wojtowicz, paroled in 1979, to tell his "real story" in front of a camera. The result is *The Third Memory, 2000,* an installation on view in Montreal at the Musee d'Art Contemporain until early next year that consists of two projections, each showing reconstructions from different angles of the robbery and hostage-taking in the Brooklyn bank. Wojtowicz, now a rather heavy man in his late fifties, is shown walking around the set, built to look like the scene of the crime, brandishing a rifle, instructing a group of extras where to stand, how to move, and how to act. "OK, this is a stickup," he says. "OK, girls, raise your hands, take a giant step back. Raise your hands slowly. Anyone touch the alarms and I'll blow your brains out."

Those who have seen and remember *Dog Day Afternoon* will automatically make comparisons between the two films, a process that Huyghe facilitates by providing fragments from the Hollywood version in one of the two projections. But how much is Wojtowicz himself influenced by the film? Of course he thinks he is reconstructing hard facts, but when he refers to what really happened as "the real movie," as he does in *The Third Memory,* one has reason to get suspicious. The situation is complicated: Not only were Wojtowicz's looks compared to Pacino's in the press at the time of the robbery, but it was Pacino, along with Marlon Brando, who provided a fictional model for how to be a crook; the robbers watched *The Godfather* for inspiration the very afternoon of their crime. (In another twist, the same actor who played Fredo in *The Godfather,* John Cazale, played Sal in *Dog Day Afternoon.*) Now the "real" Wojtowicz, who was brought to tears by Pacino's performance when he first saw the film in prison, paces the set, reconstructing the "real" event. (Birnbaum 2000, 131–32)

Fredric Jameson on *Dog Day Afternoon* as Cognitive Map

The interest of this story is that it explicitly engages the conditions of the image as spectacle. A MEmorial is one way to accomplish what the Marxist critic Fredric Jameson calls "cognitive mapping," which is needed to help citizens grasp their position within a historical field. His essay on *Dog Day Afternoon* locates a dimension in this film that makes thinkable the disjunction between the apparatuses of literacy and electracy, or, in his terms, the "radical incompatibility between the possibilities of an older national language or culture (which is still the framework in which literature is being produced today) and the transnational worldwide organization of the economic infrastructure of contemporary capitalism."

> The result of this contradiction is a situation in which the truth of our society as a whole—in Lukacs's terms, as a totality—is increasingly irreconcilable with the possibilities of aesthetic expression or articulation available to us; a situation about which it can be asserted that if we can make a work of art from our experience, if we can give experience the form of a story that can be told, then it is no longer true, even as individual experi-

ence; and if we can grasp the truth about our world as a totality, then we may find it some purely conceptual expression but we will no longer be able to maintain an imaginative relationship to it. In current psychoanalytic terminology, we will thus be unable to insert ourselves, as individual subjects, into an ever more massive and impersonal or transpersonal reality outside ourselves. This is the perspective into which it becomes a matter of more than mere intellectual curiosity to interrogate the artistic production of our own time for signs of some new, so far dimly conceivable, collective forms which may be expected to replace the older individualistic ones (those either of conventional realism or of a now conventionalized modernism); and it is also the perspective in which an indecisive aesthetic and cultural phenomenon like *Dog Day Afternoon* takes on the values of a revealing symptom. (Jameson 1985, 732–33)

Against the modernist alienation of first-world cultures, with its absolute split between the private and public spheres, Jameson looks to the literatures and popular culture of third world nations to find examples of works that, by means of allegory, overcome the disjunction. "Third-world texts, even those which are seemingly private and invested with a properly libidinal dynamic— necessarily project a political dimension in the form of national allegory: the story of the private individual destiny is always an allegory of the embattled situation of the public third-world culture and society" (Jameson 2000, 320). His reading of *Dog Day Afternoon* shows where to look for this allegorical collective (popcycle) dimension in an entertainment narrative. His method applies Freud's notion of "figurability" (an element of dreamwork by which something latent and repressed finds its way into the manifest content of the dream), and also Sartre's "analogon" or "analogue," coordinating a complex interaction of intra- and extra-aesthetic relationships, "that structural nexus in our reading or viewing experience, in our operations of decoding or aesthetic reception, which can then do double duty and stand as the substitute and the representative within the aesthetic object of a phenomenon on the outside which cannot in the very nature of things be 'rendered' directly" (731).

Figure

In the first half of the article Jameson dismisses what most observers took to be the best part of the film—the brilliant performance of Al Pacino in the role of Sonny. Jameson attends instead to the background, setting, or place of the drama, and the way the film transforms this site into a figure of an otherwise unthinkable transformation of the world by transnational capitalism. His reading depends on undoing the work of the screenplay, with its focus on Sonny's

motivation, "and to relinquish those older narrative habits that program us to
follow the individual experiences of a hero or an anti-hero."

If we can do this—and we have begun to do so when we are willing to reverse the robbery itself, and read Sonny's role as that of a mere pretext for
the revelation of that colonized space which is the branch bank, with its
peripheralised or marginalised workforce—then what slowly comes to occupy the film's centre of gravity is the action outside the bank itself, and in
particular the struggle for precedence between the local police and the FBI
officials. Now there are various ways of explaining this shift of focus, none
of them wrong: for one thing, we can observe that once Sonny has been
effectively barricaded inside the bank, he can no longer initiate events, the
centre of gravity of the narrative as such then passing to the outside. More
pertinently still, since the operative paradox of the film—underscored by
Al Pacino's acting—is the fundamental likability of Sonny, this external
displacement of the acting can be understood as the narrative attempt to
generate an authority figure who can deal directly with him without suc-
cumbing to his charm. But this is not just a matter of narrative machinery;
properly interrogated, we can understand it as an ideological problem as
well, as part of the internal needs of present day legitimation, as a narrative
answer to the fundamental question: how to imagine authority today, how
to conceive imaginatively—that is in non-abstract, non-conceptual form—
of a principle of authority that can express the essential impersonality and
post-individualistic structure of the power structure of our society while
still operating among real people, in the tangible necessities of daily life
and individual situations of repression? . . .

The police lieutenant thus comes to incarnate the very helplessness
and impotent agitation of the local power structure, and with this inflection of our reading, with this interpretive operation, the whole allegorical structure of *Dog Day Afternoon* suddenly emerges in the light of
day. The FBI agent—now that we have succeeded in identifying what he
supersedes—comes to occupy the place of that immense and decentral-
ized power network which marks the present multinational state of mo-
nopoly capitalism. The very absence in his features becomes a sign and an
expression of the presence/absence of corporate power in our daily lives,
all-shaping and omnipotent and yet rarely accessible in figurable terms,
that is to say, in the representable forms of individual actors or agents.
The FBI man is thus the structural opposite of the secretarial staff of the
branch bank: the latter present in all their existential individuality, but
inessential and utterly marginalised, the former so depersonalized as to
be little more than a marker—in the empirical world of everyday life, of

faits divers and newspaper articles—of the place of ultimate power and
control. (Jameson 1985, 727–29)

ASSIGNMENT

Locate the argument that emerges in the relationship among these four
readings. What are the implications for EmerAgency consulting and the
possibilities of a virtual civic sphere of the displacement from the problems
of transsexuals themselves, such as Ms. Gordon, through the notoriety of
the bank robber John Wojtowicz and the character motivation of "Sonny"
in the Hollywood film, to the indirect glimpse of transnational corporate
power in the figure of the FBI agent?

1. Analyze the story/incident you selected from the news (in the
   previous chapter) in terms of the sliding displacement noted
   above. Compose a treatment for a new kind of account that
   would drop the melodramatic narrative (Sonny's story) and
   instead focus on the narrative fragment identified by Jameson.
   Keep in mind that the fragment figured the truth of a specific
   setting. "The hero becomes a simple pretext for the emergence and new visibility of something more fundamental in
   what might otherwise simply seem the background itself. This
   more fundamental thing is the sociological equivalent of that
   wholesale liquidation of older ideological values by consumer
   society on which we have already commented: but here it takes
   the more tangible form of the ghettoization of the older urban
   neighborhoods. . . . We want to remember how vividly *Dog Day
   Afternoon* explores the space which is the result of these historical changes, the ghettoized neighborhood with its decaying
   small businesses gradually being replaced by parking lots or
   chain stores. It is no accident indeed that the principal circuit
   of communication of the film passes between the mom-and-
   pop store in which the police have set up their headquarters,
   and the branch bank—the real-life original was appropriately
   enough a branch of Chase Manhattan—in which Sonny is
   holding his hostages. Thus it is possible for the truth of recent
   urban history to be expressed within the framework of the
   bank scenes themselves" (Jameson 1985, 725–26). Borrowing
   a phrase from Bertolt Brecht, one that summarizes the position
   of the protesters and rioters at international meetings of the
   World Trade Organization, Jameson concludes: "What kind of

a crime is the robbing of a bank, compared to the founding of
a bank?" (724).

2. Apply the interests and criteria of emphasis observed in
Pierson, Huyghe, and Jameson to your news story. Is it possible
to give equal treatment to all three "takes" or aspects in one
Web site?

3. Treat your news story as an image (a scene). Apply Barthes's
method of reading photographs in terms of punctum and studium.
Relate your findings to the readings.

ASSIGNMENT

Extract from the assemblage a set of instructions for how to transpose
a life situation into a system of meaning (cognitive map). Apply this map
to your own situation.

1. We don't know if Mr. Gordon had anyone like John Wojtowicz
in his situation. The readings together demonstrate how a life
situation acquires shape (*eidos,* the Greek term for idea, originally meant "shape") that makes it intelligible, generalizable.
The strategy is to allegorize the particulars of the situation, to
promote them to personifications of the forces or powers that
they embody or represent, such as in Jameson's posing of binary
oppositions, pairing off the local police chief and the FBI agent,
or the treatment of the branch bank setting as an emblem of the
dynamics of capitalism.

2. Pierson's script translated Wojtowicz's life into dramatic coherence. Think about your own life in these terms. Do for your own
experience what Pierson did for Wojtowicz (locate and foreground that narratable unifying thread). Your life is less dramatic
(hopefully) than those portrayed in the case study. But from the
point of view of our project, it is just as important to find or compose the shape of the egent's situation in order to move from the
MEmorial to testimony, in keeping with the EmerAgency motto:
Problems B Us.

Cyberspace Testimony

The call of transsexuality is due in part to its special relevance to subject formation in the electrate apparatus. To give testimony as an egent is to design a
structural self-portrait using a proportional ratio: A is to B as C is to D. It is not

that one resembles the figure in the news, but that the position one occupies in one's own scene may be figured by the news event. The news event serves as a metaphor evoking the feeling of what it is like to be in my situation (Warren Schmidt:Ndugu Umbo). For now, working at this general level, we can say that Mr. Gordon's literal circumstances provide a figure for what is happening to electrate people as they become image. The riddle of identity mutation away from "self" (identity as natural essence), expressed in the category of sexuality, is generalizable to every ideological category. Identity is as much a part of the apparatus as technology and institutions. Technological change is driven as much by human desire, fantasy, ideology, and metaphysics as it is by influences intrinsic to equipment and practical necessities. The efforts to produce virtual reality (VR)—an inhabitable image, a lucid dreaming as the interface that accesses universal information—does not begin with digital technologies, but originates in an ancient desire for transcendence of the body. As the commentators note, this transcendence separates the image of the body from the material body. If shamanism is the oldest application of this dream to practice, the most recent is cyberspace, named by William Gibson and dramatized in his cyberpunk novels.

Neuromancer has been described as a science-fictionalized sexual fantasy of the adolescent male that nonetheless has motivated serious scientific inquiry (just as the story of the invention of the atom bomb passes through science fiction). The agenda-setting power of popular culture is based on its ability to transform science and history into a set of images and narratives that constitute the mythology of our society.

> As the political struggles of the twentieth century intensified, the genres of mass culture became crucial as a common site in which Americans could imagine (or observe others imagining) the basis for a new (or renewed) cultural consensus on the meaning and direction of American society. In the fictive or mythic "space" defined by the genres of mass culture, the primary contradictions of value and belief embodied in the ideological styles of progressives and populists were continuously "entertained"—imaginatively played out in story-forms that either tested ideological propositions against the traditional values embodied in myth or invited the projection of utopian visions of a "possible" or "alternative" outcome to the nation's historical travail. (Slotkin 1993, 24)

The EmerAgency deconsultations address policy formation at this level of mythology. As Slotkin points out, there is a direct relationship between the way an ideological program is narrativized in our fictions and the discourses of real-world politics (157). The spectacle is commemorative. "As the links to the past attentuated they were replaced by the accumulation of movie images purporting to represent American history and the West—vivid, 'authenticated,' and above all *memorable*" (237). "Film and event 'speak' to each other—even lending political resonance to the fiction, the fiction providing mythological justification for particular scenarios of real-world action. They did so in the first instance (1950 *[Rio Grande]*), not because one necessarily caused or influenced the other, but because the conceptual categories which shaped the scenarios developed by both movie-makers and policy-makers were drawn from the same cultural lexicon, the same set of mythological models" (365).

Our civilization is engineering (imagineering) cyberspace. The notion of cyberspace is relevant to us to the extent that it provides some insight into the transformation of human experience in electracy and the era of the spectacle. The frontier allusion as well as the sexual innuendo are deliberate in the description of the "console cowboy" Case "jacking in" to cyberspace, which includes the possibility of entering the sensorium of cyborgs, digitally enhanced humans such as the beautiful kung fu warrior Molly, with whom Case is collaborating. The point for us is that multiple border zones (frontiers)—including the borders of categorization itself—are opened up or put in question in electracy. What is at stake in this polysemic reorganization of frontiers/classification is the mythology of heroic action (emblematized in the star persona of John Wayne) that provided "the functional terms in public discourse and symbols of the correct or heroic response to the challenges of the Cold War" (365).

Richard Slotkin on the Border Zone

> The geography of the Frontier represented in Western movies is that of a world divided by significant and signifying borders, usually marked by some strong visual sign: the palisade of the desert fort; a mountain pass or a river, especially one whose name is recognized as a boundary marker, like the Rio Grande; the white empty street of the town. Finally the hero must leave a good woman and place of safety, enter that street, and confront the enemy who advances from the opposite end. Through persistent association, these border signs have come to symbolize a range of fundamental ideological differences. The most basic of these is that between the natural and the human or social realms, "wilderness vs. civilization." This opposition is given depth and complexity by metaphors that liken it to social and ideological divisions: between white civilization and Red-skin savagery; between a corrupt metropolitan "east" and a rough but virtuous "west"; between tyrannical old proprietors (big ranchers) and new, progressive entrepreneurs (small ranchers, homesteaders); between the engorged wealth of industrial monopolies (railroads) and the hard-earned property of the citizen (farmers); between old technologies

(stagecoaches) and new (railroads); between the undisciplined rapacity of frontier criminals and the lawman's determination to establish order. The borderline may also be construed as the moral opposition between the violent culture of men and the Christian culture associated with women. It is nearly always understood as a border between an "old world" which is seen as known, oppressive, and limiting, and a "new world" which is rich in potential or mystery, liberating and full of opportunity. The action of the narrative requires that these borders be crossed by a hero (or group) whose character is so mixed that he (or they) can operate effectively on both sides of the line. (351)

William Gibson, *Neuromancer*

Egents attempting to write the disaster online need to keep in mind the persistence of all these "frontiers" and "frontier" as such that are transposed into the new space of electracy.

> Cyberspace slid into existence from the cardinal points. Smooth, he thought, but not smooth enough. Have to work on it . . .
>
> Then he keyed the new switch.
>
> The abrupt jolt into other flesh. Matrix gone, a wave of sound and color . . . She was moving through a crowded street, past stalls vending discount software, prices feltpenned on sheets of plastic, fragments of music from countless speakers. Smells of urine, free monomers, perfume, patties of frying krill. For a few frightened seconds he fought helplessly to control her body. Then he willed himself into passivity, became the passenger behind her eyes.
>
> The glasses didn't seem to cut down the sunlight at all. He wondered if the built-in amps compensated automatically. Blue alphanumerics winked the time, low in her left peripheral field. Showing off, he thought.
>
> Her body language was disorienting, her style foreign. She seemed continually on the verge of colliding with someone, but people melted out of her way, stepped sideways, made room.
>
> "How you doing, Case?" He heard the words and felt her form them. She slid a hand into her jacket, a fingertip circling a nipple under warm silk. The sensation made him catch his breath. She laughed. But the link was one-way. He had no way to reply. . . .
>
> The transition to cyberspace, when he hit the switch, was instantaneous. He punched himself down a wall of primitive ice belonging to the New York Public Library, automatically counting potential windows. Keying back into her sensorium, into the sinuous flow of muscle, senses sharp and bright. (Gibson 1984, 56)

Sandy Stone on Cyborg Envy

The computer expert and transsexual, Allucquere Rosanne (Sandy) Stone, speaks with the insight of Tiresias into the evolving identity experience evoked in the vision of cyberspace:

> In psychoanalytic terms, for the young male, unlimited power first suggests the mother. The experience of unlimited power is both gendered, and, for the male, fraught with the need for control, producing an unresolvable need for reconciliation with an always absent structure of personality. An "absent structure of personality" is also another way of describing the peculiarly seductive character of the computer that Turkle characterizes as the "second self." . . .
>
> I find that reality hackers experience a sense of longing for an embodied conceptual space like that which cyberspace suggests. This sense, which seems to accompany the desire to cross the human/machine boundary, to penetrate and merge, which is part of the evocation of cyberspace, and which shares certain conceptual and affective characteristics with numerous fictional evocations of the inarticulate longing of the male for the female, I characterize as *cyborg envy.* . . .
>
> The act of programming a computer invokes a set of reading practices both in the literary and cultural sense. "Console cowboys" such as the cyberspace warriors of William Gibson's cyberpunk novels proliferate and capture the imagination of large groups of readers. Programming itself involves constant creation, interpretation, and reinterpretation of languages. To enter the discursive space of the program is to enter the space of a set of variables and operators to which the programmer assigns names. To enact naming is simultaneously to possess the power of, and to render harmless, the complex of desire and fear that charge the signifiers in such a discourse; to enact naming within the highly charged world of surfaces that is cyberspace is to appropriate the surfaces, to incorporate the surfaces into one's own. Penetration translates into envelopment. In other words, to enter cyberspace is to physically put on cyberspace. To become the cyborg, to *put on* the seductive and dangerous cybernetic space like a garment, is to put on the *female.* . . .
>
> In all, the unitary, bounded, safely warranted body constituted within the frame of bourgeois modernity is undergoing a gradual process of translation to the refigured and reinscribed embodiments of the cyberspace community. Sex in the age of the coding metaphor—absent bodies, absent reproduction, perhaps related to desire, but desire itself refigured in terms of bandwidth and internal difference—may mean something quite unexpected. Dying in the age of the coding metaphor—in selectably in-

habitable structures of signification, absent warrantability—gives new and disturbing meaning to the title of Steven Levine's book about the process, *Who Dies?* (Stone 1991, 108–9)

Becoming Image

The gender and sexual identity confusion or blurring associated with cyberspace may be generalized in virtual reality to identity experience as such, putting all borders, boundaries, and categories in question—not to eliminate categories but to renegotiate them. The importance of this possibility for the consultancy is that categories equal metaphysics: what is real, and hence what constitutes problems and solutions, are relative to the apparatus. Or, as Thomas Kuhn said about paradigm shifts, a new paradigm does not solve the problems of the old paradigm, it just makes those problems irrelevant. The history of writing shows that the experience of reading a text to oneself produced an experience of self-awareness that eventually produced the behavior and identity formation of self. In the era of recording technologies that capture the look and sound of the body in action, a new experience of identity is emerging. The vanguard of this experience of becoming image are the celebrities, whose images are appropriated and augmented by entertainment discourse in the spectacle. Mariah Carey was quoted as saying, in response to tabloid reports about her love life that had no basis in fact, "My image is having more fun than I am!" This sense of disjunction between one's self and one's image, along with the power of the image to affect the behavior and situation of the actual person, appears in an extreme version in the life and death of Princess Diana.

Princess Di demonstrates the extent to which celebrity—image identity—forces the organic body to conform to the virtual one. The public type and fantasy of "princess" established the body measure that Diana first attempted to meet with bulimia, and then with a personal trainer. The depth of character within literacy is brought back to the surface to become an electrate interface. What happened to Diana is overtaking to some degree every person in electracy. The technology of becoming-image is still evolving, from the invention of photography in the nineteenth century to contemporary attempts to build a functioning virtual reality, defined as environments "in which the user feels present, yet where things have no physical form and are composed of electronic data bits and particles of light" (Hillis 1999, 1). This sense of presence includes the metaphysical ideal of a perfect self-presence (being present to and for oneself). But every invention has unforeseen consequences, and the spectacle is not an exception to this rule.

In the context of the EmerAgency, in this respect, we note the correspondence between descriptions of the effects produced when virtual realities are made visible and accessible in virtual environments (VE), and social-psychological accounts of fetish, gaze, and aura. The point is that the kind of identity experience supported by imaging is as different from the instrumental utilitarian rationality of the literate scientific state of mind as that state of mind is different from the experience of religious spirituality. We should keep in mind throughout this series that becoming-image is happening to us here and now.

Commemoration in the public sphere is dominated so far by the spectacle, which is to say it is a collective process that sanctions certain images and not others, around which group subjects form. The EmerAgency MEmorial is designed to intervene in this process, to democratize the process of the making, selecting, and sanctioning of the icons that condense and distribute the mythologies of national identity.

Marita Sturken on the Film as Memorial

The Vietnam War films are forms of memory that function to provide collective rememberings, to construct history, and to subsume within them the experience of the veterans. As docudramas, they move from personal memory into cultural memory and finally into history. They are memorials in a certain sense, telling what is often as singular a narrative as Frederick Hart's statue, occasionally an ambivalent tale more analogous to the wall of the Vietnam Veterans Memorial. A film like *Platoon* which is considered to have told the "real" story of the war, offers a particular kind of closure and allows viewers to feel they have access to that "site of truth" represented by the veteran. In subsuming and reenacting documentary images, such films eclipse the iconic images of the war. The personal memories of Vietnam veterans are merged with the cultural memories produced by documentary images of the war and then reinscribed in narrative cinematic representations that make claims to history. When William Adams writes that, painfully, "what 'really' happened is now so thoroughly mixed up in my mind with what has been said about what happened that the pure experience is no longer there," he is referring to this allegiance of image and memory. (Sturken 1997, 120–21)

Ken Hillis on Telepresence

In this model of cyberspace telepresence, the subject's eye remains linked but detached from his or her body. This state of affairs may be imagined as facilitated by the eye's extension along what I will metaphorically term a coaxial cable that may be imagined as a flexible sight line operating within a full six degrees of freedom. As in an out-of-body experience, this cable connects the subject-self who remains grounded in subjective and embodied reality across or behind the interface/frontier/dialectic of the screen with the emergent imperium of cyberspace. This "coaxialized" extension of self-identity into virtuality might seem to offer the illusion of an emotionally satisfying alternative to the inability of the visually conceived unitary subject to join with its dialectical "other."

Virtual points of view B3 and B4 suggest how it might also be possible for separate images, or avatars, of the self to face each other as seemingly discrete entities, and also for that part of the self remaining on this side of the interface to watch both, as in "I see myself seeing myself." This relationship may also occur in "real" space and is shown by A1 gazing at A2. Virtual self B2 suggests the potential for the disembodied point of view to turn back and gaze upon its body (A2), which may appear to it as an "other" or as a shell. For the self, whose spatial coordinates now are split, these relationships beg the question of "where" its identity is located. Identity begins to exist and situate within a schizophrenic dialectic operating, as it were, unto itself, ironic or incoherent as this might first appear. (Hillis 1999, 106)

Chorography may be used to map the field of the gaze (to educate the collective Euthyphro). Hillis uses the term "gaze" advisedly. The identity situation supported by VR/VE (cyberspace) is the equipmental equivalent of poststructural theories of subject experience based on fetishism and related notions theorized in relation to cinema. The theory explains interpellation or the construction of identity in the popcycle institutions in terms of a psychological experience of feeling scrutinized. Krips distinguishes his use of Lacan's psychoanalysis from the use made of it in film theory: "According to Screen theory, in addition to functioning as a vehicle for meanings, the filmic image operates as the site of a 'gaze,' meaning a place where viewers experience themselves as under scrutiny. The gaze is the mechanism through which the image imposes its meanings and thus creates constitutive effects. As in the case of Foucault's panopticon, the scrutiny characteristic of the gaze appears to come from outside the subject but in fact is *a mediated form of self-scrutiny.* Screen theory identifies the mechanism of the gaze with the form of self-(mis)-recognition described in Lacan's account of the mirror stage" (Krips 1999, 98). To write the disaster in the middle voice foregrounds the I-I (or "H") function of language as self-knowledge, as distinct from the I-S/He circuit of communication. "In what follows," as Yuri Lotman said in his study of the semiosphere, "we shall try to demonstrate that the place of autocommunication in the system of culture is far more significant than is commonly supposed" (Lotman 2000, 21).

The key point to keep in mind is that this self-scrutiny of the gaze, however disorienting it might be for the individual, is the basis within electracy for the emerging group (corporate) subject. The MEmorial as a mode of autocommunication made possible by the Internet is central to the politics and ethics of deconsulting. The connection between the experience of VR/VE and the psychology of the gaze is relevant to the EmerAgency assumption that the Internet is a prosthesis of the *unconscious* (intersubjective) mind. The nature of the unconscious is based on the notion of the split subject (located, for example, in grammar in the difference between the "I" of the subject of a sentence and the "me" of the predicate). In the mental (mindbody) enhancement of the digital Internet computing, this split is made consciously accessible. Who or what is scrutinizing me? The superego: the introjected imagoes from each popcycle institution play the role of the panel of judges flashing the scorecard of my life. That is, the unconscious includes the superego as well as the libido. The mystory maps the superego, showing the maker's internal Mount Rushmore—one figure from each discourse with whom the subject identifies. The feeling not felt by anyone is that of the group subject.

Krips wants to locate the gaze effect not in the Imaginary but in the Real. The effects of self-scrutiny, rather, occur "in the visual field where the system of perceptual categories falters, a 'rupture between perception and consciousness' where viewers are jolted from their comfortably established habits of viewing by failing to recognize what they perceive" (1999, 99). The difference comes down to a shift of the gaze effect of the image-object from, in Barthes's terms, the studium to the punctum. The new experience of electrate identity moves along a path not of publicly encoded meanings (even if these may be vehicles or conduits), but of unconscious associations peculiar to each individual (107). The relevance to our project is that cyberspace is customizable, which actually enhances the universality of its communicative capacity. Unlike literacy, which was one size fits all, the interface giving access to the electrate datasphere may be specific to each user. Here then is a link between obtuse meaning (the "memoria" of electracy) and the technologies of electracy. The MEmorial enhances and augments the contribution of personal memory (and fantasy) to commemoration, balancing the contribution made by genre conventions and star icons of the spectacle in shaping event into history, history into precedent, precedent into policy formation. The EmerAgency gathers these individual experiences of self-scrutiny in order to produce the reflexivity of a group subject.

Henry Krips on Fetish Gaze as Punctum

The *punctum* challenges the viewer, who feels himself under scrutiny, challenged to make sense of what is seen. As Barthes points out, the paradoxical nature of the punctum spills over onto the viewer, who is left without a sense of how he or she is seen. Thus the experience takes on the paradoxical dimension of being looked at but knowing no one is looking. Barthes illustrates this phenomenon with a story taken from life: "The other day, in a cafe, a young boy came in alone, glanced around the room, and occasionally his eyes rested on me; I then had the certainty that he was looking at me without however being sure that he was *seeing* me; an inconceivable distortion: how can we look without seeing?"

The punctum is closely related to what Lacan calls the gaze, which he illustrates with the story of an experience at sea. A fisherman, Petit-Jean, "pointed out to me something floating on the surface of the waves. It was a small can, a sardine can. It floated there in the sun, a witness to the canning industry, which we, in fact, were supposed to supply. It glittered in the sun. And Petit-Jean said to me—*You see that can? Do you see it? Well, it doesn't see you* ... I was not terribly amused at hearing myself addressed in this humorous, ironical way." Thus the gaze, like the punctum, is a distortion precipitating the viewer into looking back at himself or herself, into interrogating what is seen, "doubling reality" and "making it vacillate" (Barthes).

Walter Benjamin also offers a representative anecdote that points to the phenomenon of the gaze: "Looking at someone carries the implicit expectation that our look will be returned by the object of our gaze. When this expectation is met (which, in the case of thought processes, can apply equally to the eye of the mind and to a glance pure and simple), there is an experience of the aura to the fullest extent." In Benjamin's terms, then, the tin can in Lacan's story takes on an "auratic" quality. Lacan's failure to see Petit-Jean's joke indicates that the tin can is a site not only of aura, but also of that which Benjamin opposes to the auratic, namely, the raw shock of the lived, manifested as signs of anxiety. (Krips 1999, 10–11)

The Optical Unconscious

A MEmorial may not be clear and simple, since, paradoxically, the machinery of mechanical visualization exploded the illusion of the alignment between the standpoint of an observer and the truth. The capacity of the camera to separate itself from the human physical and mental eye, combined with the theories of psychoanalysis, produced the notion of the "optical unconscious" (Benjamin). The attitude toward truth as standpoint in the image apparatus of electracy is that clarity is an *effect of repression,* blindness *(ATH).* In the new (electrate) apparatus, the clear distinction between subject and object disappears, replaced by a psychogeography (choragraphy).

> Space, in those various iterations, has been increasingly defined as a product of subjective projections and introjection, as opposed to a stable container of objects and bodies. From the beginning of the century, the apparently fixed laws of perspective have been transformed, transgressed, and ignored in the search to represent the space of modern identity. Thus the body in pieces,

physiognomy distorted by inner pain, architectural space as claustrophobic, urban space as agoraphobic, all warpings of the normal to express the pathological became the leitmotivs of avant-garde art. The vocabularies of displacement and fracture, torquing and twisting, pressure and release, void and block, *informe* and hyperform that they developed are still active today, deployed in work that seeks to reveal, if not critique, the conditions of a less than settled everyday life. (Vidler 2000, 1)

As Rosalind Krauss explained, applying the poststructural psychoanalysis of Jacques Lacan, the "extimate" inside-outside nature of the human subject installs an opaque obstacle "within the very heart of a diagrammatic clarity that is now a model both of vision's claims and of vision's failure. . . . The graph of an automatist visuality would show how the vaunted cognitive transparency of the 'visual as such' is not an act of consciousness but the effect of what is repressed: the effect, that is, of seriality, repetition, the automaton. Which is to say, it is a function of a caesura in vision, a gap" (1994, 74). This gap is the "hole" traced by the MEmorial as a symptom signaling the location of chora—the sorting system of a society. The choral map brings the hole into the speed-of-light peripheral logic (reasoneon).

The classic standpoint of the literate observer, organized in terms of the subject-object binary, still exists within electracy, but now with the observer displaced from the central position to being just one point within a field network (a matrix) of which s/he is not the master.

Lacan's discussion of vision in *The Four Fundamental Concepts of Psychoanalysis* is centered on a scopic drive structured by the distich, the rupture, the schiz. He calls the opening chapter "The Split between the Eye and the Gaze." But the whole of his account is called "The Gaze as *objet a*," or the gaze as part-object, the object that, because it marks the subject with the individuation of his existence, is most fundamentally the object of desire. Lacan wants to show the dialectic between deictic and distich, between pointing and screen, between this! and absence.

The space of pointing, or of deixis, is the space that Lacan terms "geometral," namely, the space of perspective, a space that Diderot shows in his *Letter on the Blind* is actually a tactile space, a space mastered by the subject as though he were reaching out to grasp it, to palp it, running fingers over its front and sides, manipulating it.

In contrast to the tactile "visuality" is the space of light, which Lacan calls "dazzling, pulsatile": an atmospheric surround that illuminates the viewer from both back and front, so that from the start there is no question of mastery. And in the context of this space of the luminous, the viewer is not the surveyor—standing at a point just outside the pyramid of vision—but, caught within the onrush of light, he is what blocks the light, what interrupts its flow. In this interruption the "viewer" invisible to himself enters the "picture" created by this light as a "stain" or blind spot, as the shadow cast by the light, the trace, its deictic mark. And from this place the subject, in all his exposure to view, can neither see himself nor see the source of the light. His position is one of dependence on an illumination that both marks him (the deictic) and escapes his grasp (the distich). The illumination Lacan calls the "gaze." It is the part-object operating within the instinctual field of vision, forever un-locatable, out of focus, in metamorphosis, pulsing. (Krauss 1994, 87–88)

The only glimpse of this optical unconscious within the empirical view is that offered by optical illusions (137), such as the famous duck-rabbit, through which viewers become aware of their participation in the act of seeing (aspectuality). The literate production of truth that is clear and simple is an epistemic "optical illu-sion." We can agree with Thomas and Turner that writing involves a standpoint. The challenge of the MEmorial as an educational practice is to learn how to write from the standpoint of being a figure within a field of warped space. Papers that are clear and simple as the truth must be integrated with MEmorials that are ob-scure and complex as the real. To resist the Internet accident requires thinking with all my being—with my stupidity (my blindness) as well as with my (in)sight.

Emblematic Disasters

We may return in this context to the initial framework of an electrate assign-ment. The transformation of the analytical essay into the MEmorial brings peda-gogy into alignment with the poststructural critique of Western metaphysics. In grammatological terms "metaphysics" refers to the system of categorization native to a given apparatus. The shift from literacy to electracy necessarily in-cludes the invention of a classification or category formation that is the image equivalent of the concept. Descartes with his neat formulation of the subject as *cogito* and his methodological insistence on clear and distinct ideas has provided the touchstone contrast for most attempts to think beyond the literate category of the concept. The baroque period as manifested in the philosophy of Leibniz provided Gilles Deleuze with a convenient reference point for theorizing this new kind of category and the related formal structure needed to represent it.

Plato is credited as the inventor of philosophy, which includes, among other things, the invention of the first formally defined concept—justice. From Plato to Deleuze, the work of philosophy has been the invention of concepts. Leibniz's critique of Descartes condenses the entire history of the concept from Aristotle's topics to Descartes's ideas. Leibniz's shift from object to event as the means for organizing reality offers the opening Deleuze needed to propose an alternative category formation. Distributed through Deleuze's reading is a list of contrasts, using Descartes's classicism as a convenient checklist of features for which the postliterate category (in our terms) must have an equivalent. Deleuze proposes Leibniz as *the* philosopher of the baroque worldview, whose defining trait is the fold. The baroque invention of the text-image form, the emblem (the Italian *concetto*), provides a name and form for the new category (in English, "conceit" names a verbal emblem).

> The Baroque is widely known to be typified by the "concetto," but only insofar as the Baroque concetto can be opposed to the classical concept. It is also widely held that Leibniz brings a new conception to the concept, with which he transforms philosophy. But we have to wonder about the composition of this new, Leibnizian conception. That it is opposed to the "classical" conception of the concept—in the way that Descartes had invented it—is best shown in Leibniz's correspondence with De Volder, a Cartesian. First of all, the concept is not a simple logical being, but a metaphysical being; it is not a generality or a universality, but an individual; it is not defined by an attribute, but by predicate-as-events. (Deleuze 1993, 42)

A table distinguishing Leibniz's concetto from Descartes's concept would include at least the following distinctions (which are not posed as opposites):

Descartes	Leibniz
classic	baroque
ease	disquiet
to be	to follow
essence	manner
attribute	event
solid	fluid
abstraction	series
part/whole	singularity/differential
parts	requisites
clarity	chiaroscuro
distinct	remarkable
collection	distribution
state (condition)	change
subject/object	superject/objectile
subject	point of view
painting/window	tabulation
window/countryside	information/city
woven cloth	felt
necessary	contingent

The most useful feature of the concetto as category is that it provides a form with which to compose the image-text (seeing-reading). With an explicit acknowledgment of Benjamin's study of the baroque emblem as allegory, Deleuze summarizes the components of the emblem form, which he finds at work within Leibniz's methodology of "scenographies-definitions-points of view." "Devices or emblems have three elements that help us understand the basis of allegory: images or figurations, inscriptions or maxims, and personal signatures or proper names of owners. Seeing, reading, dedicating (or signing)" (Deleuze 1993, 125).

> First, basic images tend to break their frames, form a continuous fresco, and join broader cycles (either of other aspects of the same animal, or aspects of other animals) because the pictured form—an animal or whatever—is never an essence or an attribute, as in a symbol, but an event, which is thus related to a history or to a series. Even in the worst of representations, "Fidelity Crowns Love," we find the charm of allegory, the presence of the event that makes an appeal to an antecedent and a sequel. Second, inscriptions, which have to keep a shrouded relation with images, are themselves propositions akin to simple and irreducible acts, which tend toward an inner concept, a truly propositional concept. A judgment is not broken down into a subject and an attribute; rather, the whole proposition is a predicate, as in "From near and afar." Finally, the many inscriptions or propositions—that is, the propositional concept itself—is related to an individual subject who envelops it, and who allows himself or herself to be determined as the owner: allegory offers us Virtues, but these are not virtues in general. They belong to Cardinal Mazarin and figure among his effects. Even the elements are put forth as belongings pertaining to Louis XIV or to someone else. (126)

What makes a concept a concetto, Deleuze stresses, is the folding of the concept into the individual. "Although practicians and theorists of concettism had rarely been philosophers, they developed rich materials for a new theory of the concept reconciled with the individual" (126). Although the Italian term "concetto" is useful to call attention to its equivalence with concept, Deleuze's emphasis indicates that he had in mind specifically the variant known as the "impresa." Peter Daly comments that it is difficult to distinguish between the emblem and impresa formally:

> The basic difference is one of purpose. The *impresa* represents the "principle of individuation"; it was used by one person only "as the expression of a personal aim." The word itself comes from the Italian for "undertaking," which underlines the functional purpose of the *impresa*. The emblem, on the other hand, is addressed to a larger audience; its message is general; and it fulfills a didactic, decorative, or entertaining function, or any combination of these.

One example may illustrate the difference. The motif of the phoenix was associated with such concepts as "uniqueness," "regeneration," and "indestructibility." The motif becomes an *impresa* when an individual chooses this motif and one of these concepts to express a personal intention. Paradin's *Devises heroiques* (Lyons, 1557) contains the *impresa* of Eleanor of Austria, Dowager Queen of France, who chose the motto "Unica semper avis" to stand above the picture of a phoenix surrounded by fire. (1998, 29)

In practical terms, as a relay for the MEmorial, the impresa/emblem indicates how the egent testifies with respect to the disaster. The egent is "undertaker" of the disaster (the "me" in memorial). The emblem continued a tradition of drawing moral or prudential truths from historical events, ancient myths, fables, and the natural sciences (among other sources) that dates back to the classical historians.

[Hercules's] story was much allegorized and interpreted for its typification of the struggles of the moral life. No episode in it was better known than that, found first in Xenophon's *Cyropaedia,* in which Hercules has to choose between two women, one of whom offers him Pleasure while the other indicates the apparently contradictory path of Virtue; eventually he finds the way to reconcile them, and wins immortality. The moment of his choice, as well as his person, is a common emblem subject, frequently used or alluded to in mythological or allegorical paintings and tapestry, precisely because it could not only call up a whole moral process but could also be made to value and apply to a multiplicity of present issues and dilemmas. (Moseley 1989, 4)

Transvaluation of Virtue

This moralizing of events continues into the present day, as may be seen in the editorial pages of newspapers. Pat Robertson's interpretation of 9/11 as God's judgment on America is in this tradition, and echoes some of the sermonizing that made use of the sinking of the *Titanic* as a way to evaluate the moral ills of the early twentieth century. The allegorizing of the *Titanic* disaster shows some differences between modern conceits and the tradition. In the traditional practice the meaning of events was determined anagogically by the Christian worldview. This determinism continued in the *Titanic* story to some extent, along with the virtues expressing the ideological commitments of the hegemonic powers (white Anglo-Saxon Protestant capitalist heterosexual men). The narrative of the disaster was made to fit the assumptions of the society about the heroic character of the upper classes. "Part Christian conversion narrative and part knightly adventure story, the conventional version of the disaster provided closure by showing how the ruling class redeemed itself when put to the test and, more broadly, how modernity was traditional after all. 'When the twentieth century is called material, commonplace, sordid,' said the Reverend R. L. McCready of Louisville, 'we only have to point to the decks of the sinking *Titanic* and, behold, all the ages of the past have never surpassed its achievements of heroism and chivalry'" (Biel 1996, 83).

As Deleuze remarked in distinguishing modern neo-baroque from Leibniz's version, the purpose of theodicy (Leibniz as God's attorney) was gone. A new element also apparent in the *Titanic* stories was a reversal of explanatory direction, the dissolution of the anagogical dimension of the allegory, so that the disaster became the source rather than the target of explanation.

> Beyond shock and grief, the disaster produced a contest over meaning that connected the sinking of an ocean liner in a remote part of the North Atlantic with some of the most important and troubling problems, tensions, and conflicts of the time. . . . The disaster was neither catalyst nor cause, but it did expose and come to represent anxieties about modernity—about deeper changes that were occurring regardless of whether an ocean liner struck an iceberg and sank in the spring of 1912. If not a transformative event, it was nonetheless a highly dramatic moment—a kind of "social drama" in which conflicts were played out and American culture in effect thought out loud about itself. (Biel 1996, 8)

Nietzsche's project of the transvaluation of values made explicit the shift in public morality at the turn of the nineteenth century away from the frame of the "virtues and vices" toward a new understanding of the role of power and invention in the conduct admired by a society (Himmelfarb 1995, 10). William J. Bennett's *Book of Virtues* may be seen in this context as a nostalgic attempt to return to a pre-Nietzschean vision of social mores.

The MEmorial, performing the EmerAgency motto (Problems B Us), treats the disaster as a source for understanding contemporary values, specifically as a mode of self-knowledge, rather than attempting to impose on the disaster a predetermined meaning. A crucial point in this regard is to understand how concetti form categories, how they gather the diversity of the world's materiality into intelligible sets. Rather than working analytically in the way of the concept, a concetto accumulates items into a scene that, taken as a whole, produces a certain feeling, atmosphere, or mood. The example Deleuze takes from Leibniz is the circumstances of a household in which a man beats his dog:

> Can we say that a pain is spontaneous in the soul of a dog that is flogged while it eats its meal, or in that of Caesar the baby when stung by a wasp while sucking at his mother's breast? But the soul is not flogged or stung. Instead of sticking to abstractions, we have to restore the series. The movement of the

rod does not begin with the blow: carrying his stick, a man has tiptoed up to
the dog from behind, then he has raised the instrument in order then to strike
it upon the dog's body.

Just as this complex movement has an inner unity so also, in the soul
of the dog, the complex change has an active unity: pain has not abruptly
followed pleasure, but has been prepared by a thousand minute perceptions—
the pitter-patter of feet, the hostile man's odor, the impression of the stick
being raised up, in short, an entire, imperceptible "anxiousness" from which
pain will issue "sua sponte," as if through a natural force integrating the preceding modifications. If Leibniz attaches so much importance to the question
of the souls of animals, it is because he knows how to diagnose the universal
anxiety of the animals watching out for danger. . . . That is the second aspect
of Mannerism without which the first would remain empty. The first is the
spontaneity of manners that is opposed to the essentiality of the attribute.
The second is the omnipresence of the dark depths which is opposed to the
clarity of form, and without which manners would have no place to surge
forth from. (Deleuze 1993, 56)

The anxiousness of the dog is a way of remarking the mood of the epoch,
disquiet, *Unruhe* (69). The monad (individual soul) "expresses the entire world,
but obscurely," and in the fog of microperceptions unfolding in the dark depths,
"the monad's spontaneity resembles that of agitated sleepers who twist and turn
on their mattresses" (86). "The animal that anxiously looks about, or the soul
that watches out, signifies that there exist minute perceptions that are not integrated into present perception" (87). To reason with events rather than concepts involves holistic "prehension," Deleuze explains, in noting the three great
moments in which this mode was theorized—the Stoics, Leibniz, Whitehead.
"The subjective form is the way by which the datum is expressed in the subject,
or by which the subject actively prehends the datum (emotion, evaluation, project, conscience . . .). It is the form in which the datum is folded in the subject,
a 'feeling' or manner" (78).

We have been following a transversal series, exploring the conductive inference logic of electracy. The point of transition away from classic prose, taken
as an expression of the ideology of literacy as an apparatus, is the reference in
Thomas and Turner to the era in which "documentary photography became
routine" (1994), thus undermining the persuasiveness of the argumentative
window. The emergence of electracy is dated from the invention of photography, just as the epoch of literacy dates from the invention of the alphabet. The
paradox of photography is that it technologizes perspective at the same time
that it subverts the worldview in which perspective was invented. The practical point for the MEmorial is that photography, in whatever technical form,

foregrounds the need for a poetics of using the visible to write the invisible (the outside to render an inside).

The theory of the apparatus assumes that digital imaging is a social machine—that the desire that created it is distinguishable from the history of technology. The proper context for the invention of photography in any case is not (only) the natural science of light, but the dream of a perfect language, capable of universal communication across all natural languages and cultures. This dream motivated the intense interest in Egyptian hieroglyphics and Chinese ideograms, both thought to be image discourses allowing direct authoring with nature itself (that is, to be able to write as well as read nature as the Book of God) (Eco 1995, 165, 175). The desire for universal peace and harmony motivating the immense scholarship and creativity invested in the hermetic arts, however mistaken or misplaced, accounts for a family resemblance among its aesthetic spin-offs—the baroque emblem, the modernist ideogram, psychoanalytic dreamwork, and contemporary cinema. The MEmorial continues this tradition.

Part III

The Categorical Disaster

I have been assured by a very knowing American of my acquaintance in London, that a young healthy child well nursed is at a year old a most delicious, nourishing, and wholesome food, whether stewed, roasted, baked, or broiled; and I make no doubt that it will equally serve in a fricassee or a ragout.

—*Jonathan Swift, "A Modest Proposal"*

5

FORMLESS EMBLEMS
(TESTIMONIAL)

Event

Electronic monumentality addresses the responsibility of revising and register-
ing within the digital apparatus the borders and boundaries of an American
national identity. At issue is the kind of identity experience—the group subject,
between individual and collective—emerging within electracy. This experience
is likely to be as different from self and nation as these are different from the oral
experiences of spirit and tribe. The question is: what is inside and what is outside
(of anything)? The goal is a recalibration of this kind of distinction at every level
of being—logical, psychological, ethical, and political categories. Within the electrate apparatus a new category is emerging, supported by imaging. As an institution of the image, the Internet is the prosthetic unconscious of a virtual America
becoming global, and in this capacity it constitutes a living, dynamic, thinking,
and feeling monument. To consult on a public policy issue for the EmerAgency is
as much an act of commemoration as is the construction of a tourist destination.

pcu KIII SUI

n 50 miles ordered the state's child
th her new welfare agency to return the
ardy, and baby, who has been in foster
care since the
t be a good day after he
e opportu- was born.
ead detec- "This may
h says she be one o
another those rar
cases where a
on, a mur- parent ha
haill of the been able t
epartment. progress from
to end up Bradley a point of tota
McGee inability t
are agency parent an
Hardy not protect a chil
oy. Martha to a point of competence," Rus
s chief of sell wrote in his decision.

*Figure 5. Bradley McGee
(newspaper clipping).*

Here is one of the more difficult challenges that electracy poses to the institution of schooling. There is a reason (and an unacknowledged reasoneon) why the academic curriculum holds on to the belief in clear and distinct ideas long after the epistemology that supported it has been superseded. There is, of course, the illusion of the teachability of clarity, within a utilitarian ideology. Beyond that is the difficulty of anamorphic thought, which includes the complete libidinal axis: not only attraction but also repulsion. The desiring machine, in Deleuze and Guattari's terms, puts in motion two heads (trajectories)—fetishistic attraction and paranoiac repulsion (1977, 326). The MEmorial attempts to reduce the resistance by supplementing (merely) the literate tourist experience (as if looking at an objective scene through a window) with the electrate image designed to expose one's own presence as shadow or blind spot in a collective field of value. It does not proclaim "You are blind!" but only discovers in each case the maker's relation to *ATH*. The electrate student does not (only) argue a public issue in a paper but designs a concetto for a MEmorial.

The project uses formless operations (Bataille's *informe*) to displace the conversational perspective of literate observation and to record the collapse of the ideal into the immanent, the obliteration of the gap separating ought and is. These operations will be noted and discussed as the account of the MEmorial unfolds. The MEmorial as theoria (theory tourism) does not use the verticality of the classic window as the interface metaphor for the Internet screen, but Bataille's horizontality ("lowering from the vertical to the horizontal," "horizontalization"). Puns supply the digital jumps between semantic domains, connecting computer "screen" with the "screening" or blocking effect of the gaze. MEmorial tracks the gaze within the observation: the desire that operates within the analytical inspection of problems.

> Man is proud of being erect (and of having thus emerged from the animal state, the biological mouth-anus axis of which is horizontal), but this pride is founded on a repression. . . . Another modernist version of this opposition singles out human symbolic practices; it is this version of the vertical-horizontal opposition that Bataille's operation reveals to be repressive. On the heels of the impressionists' exaltation of "pure vision," a crisis, traditionally pin-pointed in the work of Paul Cezanne, shocks the visual arts. It suddenly became clear that the strict demarcation between the realms of the "purely visible" (the verticality of the visual field) and the carnal (the space that our bodies occupy)—a demarcation theorized since the Renaissance by means of the conception of painting as a "window opened onto the world"—was a fiction. In Cezanne's work—for example *Still Life with Plaster Cupid* (c. 1892) in the Courtauld, where the floor plane is verticalized outrageously, the objects are ready to slide from their position, to dislodge themselves and roll onto our feet: the line of demarcation between the wall and the ground is erased.
> [Marcel Duchamp] immediately put his finger on this semiological repression. His *Three Standard Stoppages* knocks one of the most arbitrary systems of the sign there is (the metric system) off its pedestal to show that once submitted to gravity, once lowered into the contingent world of things and bodies, the sign does not hold water: it dissolves as an (iterable) sign and regresses toward singularity. (Bois and Krauss 1997, 26–27, 28)

The egents use mystory to generate the parts of an emblem—locating the obtuse meaning, the personal sting of the disaster as image—to register the arbitrary and singular body that constitutes, in its obstinacy, the shadow blocking the light of empirical instrumental consulting on public policy issues. The MEmorial undertaking uses the outside disaster to discover and map this inner condition of the egent *(I am this event)*. The EmerAgency retains the guidebook as interface metaphor for learning electracy, but in a deconstructed version within the larger analogy used to generate an Internet civic practice—the inhabitable monument. In touring the chora of America the de$igner of a MEmorial discovers what Benjamin had in mind when he suggested that the tourist souvenir is to the modern city what the corpse was to the baroque tragedy. Why emphasize the "me" in MEmorial?

> Me, I exist—suspended in a realized void—suspended from my own dread— different from all other being and such that the various events that can reach all other being and not *me* cruelly throw this *me* out of a total existence. . . .
> The empirical knowledge of the structure this *me* has in common with the

other *mes* has become an absurdity in this void where my dominion manifests itself, for the very essence of the *me* that I am consists in the fact that no other conceivable existence can replace it; the total improbability of my coming into the world poses, in an imperative mode, a total heterogeneity. (Bataille 1985, 131)

This heterogeneous standpoint is at the core of the methodology of the MEmorial, taking up the paradox of group subjectivity in electracy. Electrate space is not geometric but warped (wrecked). "The aesthetics of the appearance of objects or people standing out against the *apparent horizon* of classical perspective's unity of time and place is then taken over by the aesthetics of the disappearance of far-off characters looming up against the lack of horizon of a cathode screen where unity of time wins out over the unity of the place of encounter. The *real-time perspective* of large-scale optics once and for all outstrips the small-scale optics of *the perspective of real space,* the vanishing point of focusing light rays surrendering its primacy to the vanishing of all the points (pixels) of the televised image" (Virilio 1997, 36).

A consultancy that applies heterogeneous (un)knowing to problem solving may be a self-refuting enterprise, since Bataille defines the heterogeneous as the remainder excluded from science. For now, the justification for our experiment is the unique relation of this ME to death. "It is only at the boundary of death that laceration, which constitutes the very nature of the immensely free *me,* transcending 'that which exists,' is revealed with violence. In the coming of death, there appears a structure of the *me* that is entirely different from the 'abstract me' . . . also from the moments of personal existence, locked away due to practical activity and neutralized in the logical appearances of 'that which exists.' The *me* accedes to its specificity and to its integral transcendence only in the form of the 'me that dies'" (Bataille 1985, 132, 133). The EmerAgency helps the community notice the death's head, the *vanitas,* smeared across the consultants' reports on how to solve the problems of 9/11 and beyond.

Addressing this question of borders and categories, the process of MEmorializing begins with a sting (punctum) received from a news item, a story from the daily dose of information circulated by journalism. This sting signals the activation of a border zone. Something about the story is irritating, troubling, and ultimately memorable. I find myself still thinking about it. Such an incident is *the report of the murder of Bradley McGee, in Lakeland, Florida, July 28, 1989.* The initial facts are that Sheryl Coe, the mother, stood by smoking a cigarette while her husband, Thomas Coe, "repeatedly rammed the boy's head into the toilet like a plunger, angered that the toddler had soiled his pants" (Associated Press, *Gainesville Sun,* November 24, 2001). Bradley was two years old.

I will bear witness to this mediated scene by filling out the sting, expanding it into a chain of associations, gathering information from various discourses (news, theory, art, history), in order to map the degrees of separation between me and Bradley McGee. I am not seeing this event through a window, oriented by perspective. Such testimonials, forming a temporary (transversal) category around the event, may be mounted as part of the Web site supplement to the electronic monument (the peripheral). The form of the meditation is that of a collage or assemblage, a series of associated fragments, connected by the repetition of certain signifiers and themes. The series is interpolated into a rationale and explanation of method intended to bring out the larger implications of the experiment and make this example generalizable for others to use as a relay for their own MEmorials. The testimonial thus treats the event both as idea and as atmosphere or mood (emotion), leading up to a proposal for the materialization of the monument in a peripheral. I am meditating now on the murder of a child.

Gift (Concetto)

Thomas Coe—who was convicted of first degree murder and is serving a life sentence—admitted ramming the boy's head into the toilet. Sheryl [Coe] Hardy said she lit a cigarette and watched, then joined Coe when he beat the boy with couch cushions until Bradley collapsed. He died the next day of head injuries. Sheryl Hardy told police Coe had tormented the boy almost as soon as he arrived. She insists Coe was responsible for the worst of the abuse but said she played a part, too: cleaning Bradley with a garden hose when he soiled his pants, shaking him and running a fork over his mouth with feces on it. "I know it was gross," Hardy told the Chicago Tribune in a recent interview. *"I know it was harsh. That's something I see when I close my eyes."* (Gainesville Sun, *November 24, 2001*)

In a chapter titled "You *Should* Give a Shit," Žižek discusses the "anal object," unfolding the problematic of attraction-repulsion in relation to the formation of borders and boundaries:

> The small child who gives his shit as a present is in a way giving the immediate
> equivalent of his Inner Self. Freud's well-known identification of excrement as
> the primordial form of gift, of an innermost object that the small child gives
> to its parents, is thus not as naive as it may appear. The often-overlooked point
> is that this piece of myself offered to the Other radically oscillates between
> the Sublime and—not the Ridiculous, but, precisely—the excremental. This is
> the reason why, for Lacan, one of the features which distinguishes man from
> animals is that, with humans, the disposal of shit becomes a problem: not
> because it has a bad smell, but because it came out from our innermost selves.
> We are ashamed of shit because, in it, we expose/externalize our innermost
> intimacy. (2001, 59)

The EmerAgency is applying electrate reason to the question of what is inside and what is outside "America," which is another way of asking about shame (or its absence). A consultation on the death of Bradley McGee tests the possibilities of imaging to support an inquiry. The revision of "sign" that becomes especially useful in the formation of a MEmorial, taking up Deleuze's advice to extend concept into concetto, comes from Lacan's modification of Saussure's discussion of signifier-signified (his addition of the unconscious to the equation). A sign *means* not by reference to reality, but by a relationship between its parts—a material element (sound or letter) and a concept. The grammatological point of leverage on this structure is the fact that "concept" is specifically the category formation of literacy. In electracy chora replaces topos (topic, element, principle) as the mode of organization and classification. A topos collects entities into universal homogeneous sets based on shared essences, necessary attributes; chora gathers singular ephemeral sets of heterogeneous items based on associations of accidental details. Yet chora paradoxically becomes categorical (general) through the aesthetic evocation of an atmosphere by means of these details. Chora is a flash category, a shortcut through the encyclopedia, an inferential immanent trajectory of signifiers.

Saussure illustrated the sign relationship with the word "tree" and a drawing of a tree, separated by a horizontal line. Lacan replaced Saussure's example with his own—a pair of words ("ladies" and "gentlemen") above, and an outline drawing of a pair of doors below (above and below separated by a line or bar), supplemented by an explanation that the public life of Western man, like that of the great majority of primitive communities, "is subjected to the laws of urinary segregation" (Lacan 1977, 151). The illustration includes a "hypericon" (a paradigmatic anecdote condensing in an image or scene the essence of a theory) (Mitchell 1994), based on "a memory of childhood." The anecdote is well-known, concerning a little boy and girl seated opposite one another looking out the window of a train as it arrived at a station. "'Look' says the brother, 'we're at Ladies!'; 'Idiot!' replies his sister, 'Can't you see we're at Gentlemen.' . . . For these children, Ladies and Gentlemen will be henceforth two countries towards which each of their souls will strive on divergent wings, and between which a truce will be the more impossible since they are actually the same country and neither can compromise on its own superiority without detracting from the glory of the other" (Lacan 1977, 152).

A woman who served nine years in prison for the 1989 potty-training death of her 2-year-old son has won custody of her infant son in Illinois. A judge in Jerseyville County, Ill., on Friday ordered the Illinois Department of Children and Family Services to immediately return the infant to his mother. Sheryl Hardy, formerly Sheryl Coe. The 9-month-old baby was taken at birth by Illinois social workers.

Foster parents, children's advocates, and lawmakers used the Bradley McGee case to bring about major changes in how state social services workers handled child abuse cases. Following his death, state legislators ordered changes in the Department of Health and Rehabilitative Services. The agency was later dismantled and reorganized as the Department of Children and Families, and child welfare was put ahead of family reunification. Sheryl Coe left prison July 7, 1999, under an early release program. She moved to Illinois, remarried and had another child. (Gainesville Sun, *November 11, 2001)*

The basic unit of signification in Lacan's theory is not the sign, but the emblem, given that his counterexample has the tripartite structure of this genre (slogan + picture + commentary). Bradley McGee's death is not clear and simple as the truth, but obscure and complex as the real. Instructions: de$ign a concetto.

Peter Daly on the Emblem Form

The emblem is, properly speaking, a mixed form comprising a motto, a picture and an epigram. The motto introduces the emblem and usually indicates the theme, which is embodied symbolically in the picture that depicts one or more objects, persons, or events. Beneath the picture is printed an epigram or short prose statement that interprets the picture and elucidates the theme. Alciato's emblem is a typical example. The emblem begins with an abstract statement in the motto "Fortuna virtutem superans" [Fortune overcoming virtue]. The picture shows Brutus about to fall on his sword. The epigram relates briefly that Brutus had been overcome by Octavian's forces, and that he had seen the river Pharsalia flowing with the blood of his fellow citizens. There upon he committed suicide. The significance of the action is summarized in Brutus's own words, lamenting that Virtue follows Fortuna, i.e., fortune and not virtue rules the world.

The Brutus emblem is characteristic of the genre insofar as a general message or moral is enunciated in the motto, embodied in the picture through the particular fate of Brutus, which in turn is elucidated in the epigram. The function of the emblem is didactic in the broadest sense: it was intended to convey knowledge and truth in a brief and compelling form that will persuade the reader and impress itself upon memory. In this process the choice of picture symbol is essential, since it encapsulates visually the meaning of the emblem. . . . Not unlike the Renaissance emblem, modern advertising is an exercise in communication and persuasion, and like the emblem much symbolic advertising may be considered a form of exemplary discourse. (Daly 1988, 350)

Daly goes on to explain the effect of the emblem as that of creating an enigma in the relation between the motto and the picture, which is then resolved by the epigram (351). The epigram, which could be in either prose or verse, often quoted learned sources. The success of the emblem or ad depends on the use of codes shared by the audience. E. D. Hirsch called these shared codes "cultural literacy"—a superficial knowledge of an encyclopedia of information that, he said, it was the job of the public schools to teach. Emblems assumed a knowledge of the classical tradition, for example, including an awareness of stock images selected from the tradition and fixed into iconic poses and gestures. The historical literary stories are miniaturized in the emblem into one pose that expresses the fundamental significance, and atmosphere, of the narrative.

Jurors were seated Wednesday night in the trial of a man accused of fatally beating his daughter, despite earlier concerns attorneys would be unable to find an impartial panel because of pretrial publicity. Richard Adams, 26, confessed to hitting Kayla McKean with a paddle and throwing her against a wall after the 6-year-old girl soiled herself the day before Thanksgiving Day 1998. Kayla's death resulted in sweeping changes in the Florida child welfare system. Defense attorney Candace Hawthorne asked prospective jurors whether they had ever spanked or hit their children to discipline them or if they were averse to viewing graphic photos. "Have your children ever pushed your patience to the extreme?" Hawthorne said. (Gainesville Sun, *May 4, 2000*)

The audience had to be familiar with this context, associating certain figures with specific virtues or values in order to read the emblem. "Such figures stand paradigmatically for abstract notions: Ulysses for prudence, Brutus for virtue vanquished, and David for the healing power of music. In every case the emblem writer refers to a personage well known to his readers, who are persuaded by the argument of exemplary instance. The emblem seeks to persuade by referring to symbolic figures who are beyond doubt and question" (358). Advertisers similarly use "famous contemporary personages who endorse a range of products and services," with the assignment of celebrities or other icons to products carefully restricted according to "appropriateness," to maintain credibility (359). A typical Marlboro ad is readily described as an emblem.

- The *motto* (slogan, caption, *inscriptio*) reads, "Come to where the flavor is. Come to Marlboro Country." It is inscribed in the lower right-hand corner of the frame.
- The *picture* is a photograph of a cowboy: a rugged-looking man with a mustache, visible from the waist up, wearing a white cowboy hat low over his eyes, head at three-quarters face, eyes squinting into the distance, leaning forward, elbows resting on the pommel of his saddle, the horse only suggested in the darkness at the bottom of the frame.

The motto and picture together compose an enigma, which is resolved by the epigram.

• The epigram *(subscriptio)* includes the following material: a small inset picture of two cigarette packages in two sizes, with three filtered cigarettes protruding from the top of the smaller pack. Beneath the packs some small print reads, "Marlboro Red or Longhorn 100s. You get a lot to like." The surgeon general's warning is superimposed as a label with a white background on the lower left-hand border of the frame.

A foster father is charged with murder after wrapping a 3-year-old boy with cerebral palsy in a blanket tight enough to torture him for soiling his pants, police said. James Theodore Curtis, 25, was arrested Friday on a first-degree murder charge in the death of Alex Charles Boucher. New Port Richey Cpl. Jackie Pehote said Curtis admitted to wrapping the blanket so tightly around the child's body that it pinned his arms to his sides, then pulling the blanket up just under Alex's bottom lip to keep him from crying. Curtis returned to the bedroom about 30 minutes later to free the child because his wife, Jennifer, was due home from the store, Pehote said, but Alex was unresponsive. (Gainesville Sun, *October 1, 2001*)

Scholars of emblematics have shown that modern advertising uses the emblem structure.

Judith Williamson on Ad Structure

Catherine Deneuve's face and the Chanel bottle are not linked by any narrative, simply by juxtaposition: but there is not supposed to be any need to link them directly, they are as it were in apposition in the grammar of the ad, placed together in terms of an *assumption* that they have the same meaning, although the connection is really a random one . . . ; the link is in terms of what Catherine Deneuve's face means to us, for this is what Chanel No. 5 is trying to mean to us, too. . . . The ad is using another already existing mythological language or sign system, and appropriating a relationship that exists in that system between signifier (Catherine Deneuve) and signified (glamour, beauty) to speak of its product in terms of the same relationship; so that the perfume can be substituted for Catherine Deneuve's face and can also be made to signify glamour and beauty.

Using the structure of one system in order to give structure to another, or to translate the structure of another, is a process which must involve an intermediate structure, a system of systems or "meta-system" at the point where the translation takes place: this is the advertisement. Advertisements are constantly translating between systems of meaning, and therefore constitute a vast meta-system where values from different areas of our lives are made interchangeable. . . .

Only the form and structure of the referent system are appropriated by the advertisement system; it is the relationship and distinction between parts, rather than the parts themselves that make an already-structured external system so valuable to advertising. The links made between elements from a referent system and products rise from the place these elements have in the whole system rather than from their inherent qualities. Thus Catherine Deneuve has significance only in that she is not, for example, Margaux Hemingway. (Williamson 1978, 25–26)

An 18-year-old woman whose boyfriend is charged in her baby's death told state child care workers three weeks earlier there was a history of domestic violence at home. Juan Ferrer is charged with first degree murder and aggravated child abuse in the death of 3-week-old Yarine Yasmine Ferrer-Saez. Police say he hurled the infant against a dresser after she vomited on his shoulder as he burped her. (Gainesville Sun, *July 29, 2001*)

The emblem is a specific device used within the allegorical mode. In the baroque era the compositions were guided by the religious worldview of the time or by the anagogical level in terms of the allegory form. As Walter Benjamin pointed out in his study of baroque drama, the modernist image secularizes the mode. The appropriation of allegory in mystory replaces the traditional Christian cosmology with the personal sacred. The mystorian may not construct the emblem in the same way as the allegorist, who knows the moral in advance, for which a suitable image must be found. The mystory testimonial inverts this process, beginning with the mapping of the event, locating a repeating pattern across the discourses, and isolating the signifiers found in this pattern. A MEmorial emblem may then be composed by means of these signifiers in order to discover the metaphysics and morality they evoke. Formally or compositionally, however, the allegorical and mystorical emblems are similar.

In our project, the most useful feature of the emblem-ad operation is the translation of values across cultural domains. The MEmorial brings into representation and thought an event as an emblem of a value. In the same way that an ad-emblem for perfume testifies to its value by the juxtaposition with a movie star, the MEmorial juxtaposes abject values with social ideals. The murder of Bradley McGee replaces the anecdote of the siblings arriving at the train station in my example. The focus on urinary segregation as the embodiment of the bar or separating slash of language in Lacan's iconic story is opened up to include the toilet as strange attractor, or as metonym evoking "toilet work" as a way to understand the formation and maintenance of identity borders in civilization. The sacred operates in the real through dirt. We are tracking an abject category.

The body of an unidentified child was discovered Monday afternoon in a trash bin located behind a local gas station after station employees notified police of a strange odor. The body is believed to be that of a black female between the ages of 3 and 7, and police suspect foul play. "The ASO detectives searched the dumpster because employees said they smelled something and after some investigating they found what appeared to be the body of a young girl," Wallace said. "If she is a girl 3 to 7, she can't get into the Dumpster by herself. There were circumstances around the body that make it appear that there may be foul play involved." (Independent Florida Alligator, *May 22, 2001)*

The Personal Sacred

The interest of Lacan's emblem is that it shows a way to make the literate sign (semiotics) something electrate. It is not that concept is eliminated but that the literate pair signifier-signified (or sound/mark-concept) is extended to include chora. The gift of shit mapped here is not a topos but a chora. The electrate unit of "signifierness" ("signifiance") is signifier-signified-chora (sound/mark-concept-image). The emblem embodies the abstractive power of writing in a specific social rule and place—the bathroom (in Lacan's example), thus preventing the sign from collapsing when it is brought down to earth. Sign does not refer but operates within and between institutions. "Chora" names the memory or memorial operation of sorting or ordering of that which remains undifferentiated. The choral emblem situates meaning generation materially within the practices of an institution. In principle, any socialized place may supply the materials of the sign. For Bataille the bedroom localized the modern sacred:

> The darkness of the sacred place, which contains the real presence, is no more oppressive than that of the bedroom where lovers have locked themselves; the knowledge to be gleaned is no less foreign to the science of laboratories in the sacred place than it is in the lovers' hideaway. In the sacred place, human existence meets the figure of destiny fixed by the caprice of chance: the determining laws that science defines are the opposite of this play of fantasy constituting life. (1985, 232)

The bathroom is another such place, guiding this theorization of MEmorial design. "The sense of border which emerges in infancy is not an innate sense but a consequence of relating to others and becoming a part of a culture. Thus, the boundary between the inner (pure) self and the outer (defiled) self, which is initially manifest in a distaste for bodily residues but then assumes a much wider cultural significance, derives from parents and other adults who are, by definition, socialized and acculturated" (Sibley 1995, 7).

Michel Leiris identified the bathroom as a primary site of the sacred in modernity. In the secularized conditions of modernity (and these are the conditions of chora as sacred place in electracy), it was easier to understand the sacred at a personal level ("those objects, places, or occasions that awake in me that mixture of fear and attachment, that ambiguous attitude caused by the approach of something simultaneously attractive and dangerous, prestigious and outcast" [1988, 24]). To locate the sacred in one's own experience, Leiris looked to memories of childhood, the earlier the better. His family home was organized by a sacred polarity on a right-left axis of parental bedroom and the bathroom. The bathroom served not only its designated function but also doubled as a secret clubhouse where he and his brother collaborated on the composition of fantastic narratives.

> There was something more or less forbidden in what we were doing, which, moreover, brought us scoldings when we stayed shut up in there too long. As if in a "men's house" of some island in Oceania—the place where the initiates gather and where from mouth to mouth and from generation to generation, secrets and myths are passed on, we endlessly elaborated our mythology in this room, our clubhouse, and never tired of seeking answers to the various sexual riddles that obsessed us. Seated on the throne like an initiate of higher rank was my brother; I, the youngest, sat on an ordinary chamber pot that served as the neophyte's stool. The flushing mechanism and the hole were, in themselves, mysterious things, and even actually dangerous. (26)

In elimination, it is clearly experienced that I push something out that was me, and make it non-me. With this action the problem of what is me, and what is not—or the delimitation of self verses nonself—is clearly presented to the child. My guess is, because it entails for the first time both a consciously goal-directed action and a great deal of physical doing: the pushing out of feces. Therefore as a conscious process it very much provides the experiences: "I can eliminate exactly when and where I wish," and this can add greatly to the sense of autonomy, of self. But this is true only if the time and place for eliminating is based on the child's decision and if the whole thing begins in a context of mutuality. . . . Unfortunately, this gaining of a heightened self-esteem is too often interfered with in the toilet training of children, because they are told that if they want to enjoy the experience they must conform to parental conditions. The warning that stools are dirty can further detract from the pleasure. Then the child does not think, "I wish to go to the bathroom because I feel a pressure in my body that I want to relieve," but "I have to go so I won't get a licking, or get criticized for soiling my pants." The result is that whatever the child does—whether he goes to the toilet or soils—he will not feel any pleasurable relief. (Bettelheim 1967, 36)

Such humble, elemental experiences are overlooked by conventional consultants following the rules of sufficient reason, but manifest nonetheless that gesture expressing the social function of sacrifice, understood as abjection, "the necessity of throwing oneself or something of oneself out of oneself" (Bataille 1985, 67). In a time of emergency, however, that Leiris shared with Benjamin (they both participated in the College of Sociology conference held in Paris just before the beginning of World War II), a moment when the repressed sacred seemed to have erupted once again directly into political life, it was necessary to take a more inclusive approach to experience in order to understand what was going wrong. Georges Bataille's base materialism is an operation for attending to the real, to untransposed conduct, immanent action. Borders are formed in the toilet.

Alfredo [Montes's] body, wrapped in a bedspread with figures of Disney's "101 Dalmatians" on it, was spotted late Thursday by a passing motorist 30 feet off the edge of Interstate 275 in West Central Florida. Chouquer, 23, is charged with first-degree murder and aggravated child abuse in the boy's death. Lawrence, 22, is charged as an accessory after the fact. Police said Chouquer told investigators in Utah he was disciplining Alfredo after the boy soiled his pants, hitting him at least five times in the face. Police said he told them the boy never got discipline. (Gainesville Sun, *July 14, 2002*)

The Safety Patrol

The relevance of Lacan's sign-emblem to electronic monumentality presented itself through the circumstances of my own encounter with this hypericonic scene. To function as witness—to offer my testimonial—I relate the disaster to my own case. The context was the fifth-grade trip to Washington, DC, for which I was one of the chaperones, accompanying my son. The trip was a reward for those students who had served in the safety patrol during the year. Safety is a primary value, underlying Homeland Security and its heritage of *Heimat*.

Such trips have become part of an annual ritual at schools all over the country, whose official purpose is that of a pilgrimage to the shrines of American democracy, inculcating in the younger generation a connection with the monuments representing the founding beliefs of the nation. The unofficial or actual experience of the trip itself is somewhat different from the ideal (here is the gap measuring the abjectness of values). Our group took the train from Gainesville, Florida, to the nation's capital—a long, overnight ride. It soon became clear that our destination was a matter of symbolic importance only, relevant to the educators and the institution of schooling, but of little importance to the children. Or rather, they experienced the tour in a distracted manner. Their focus was never on the monuments or any part of the object of the tour, and always on their interactions with each other.

A toilet bowl on board a British Rail train traveling from London to Brighton was converted into a camera. First, a specially designed aluminum "insert" was fitted into the recess of the toilet bowl. This device housed both lens and shutter device as well as a pneumatic seal which, when inflated with a bicycle pump, held the contraption firmly in place whilst also sealing out unwanted light. The operator then removed his trousers in order to "load" the photographic paper, placing his arms down the trouser legs in the manner of a changing bag. After being "exposed," the toilet was flushed (taking care to avoid flushing while at a station), and developer was simultaneously injected into the toilet cistern pipe at the rear of the bowl. This operation was then repeated for the fixer after which the toilet was flushed again to wash the print of any residue chemicals. The print was then retrieved. (Pippin 1995, 184)

The children paid almost no heed to the adults (only when forced to) and instead acted out a sorting and resorting (choral) process that was at once biological and metaphysical. Lacan observed, regarding his anecdote, that "the rails in this story materialize the bar in the Saussurian algorithm" (1977, 152). Here is a key to the allegory, to the emblematic register of behavior. The bar is the division of articulation that operates in every dimension of the human world. In my scene the bar was materialized not only by the train tracks but also by the belt that the safety patrol wore while performing their duties before and after school—the belt, colored Day-Glo (emergency) orange, that included a diagonal strap crossing over the shoulder from the front to the back of the waistband. This diagonal belt emblazoned the bar or slash, the division, split, separation productive of meaning in language as such, sorting tenor and vehicle in figuration, metaphor, and metonymy, and representing the repressive operation of the unconscious that permitted the sliding of the signified under the signifier through displacement and condensation.

It also echoed the shape of Lacan's L-schema, so named for its resemblance to the uppercase Greek letter lambda, later simplified into a Z shape. "The main point of the schema is to demonstrate that the symbolic relation (between the Other and the subject) is always blocked to a certain extent by the imaginary axis (between the ego and the specular image). Because it has to pass through the imaginary 'wall of language,' the discourse of the Other reaches the subject in an interrupted and inverted form" (Evans 1996, 169). The schema maps intersubjective relations in society, and the intrasubjective structure of the psyche, with the "subject" encompassing the entire field of positions. Related to the mirror stage of identity formation, in which the infant is alienated through her (mis)recognition of her reflection in the mirror as "me," the L-schema shows the outside-inside or extimate nature of subject formation as alienation. The MEmorial reveals to its makers the location of the border that passes through them (through me). It is composed/performed in the middle voice.

Two behaviors dominated the social interactions manifesting the filtering of the signifier into the signified that was part of Lacan's emblem. Within each sex a cruel, pitiless (from the standpoint of an adult) sorting took place between those included and those excluded, those considered cool and those judged to be dorks. Adult interventions in this polarizing were futile, since any rearrangements imposed at the official level dissolved as soon as supervision relaxed. Across the sexes, meanwhile, an opposite behavior developed, concentrated around the rather large bathroom with which each car of the train was equipped. There was only one bathroom in the car. Small mixed groups of boys and girls continually attempted to slip into the bathroom together and lock the door. Further symmetry was created by the fact that the boys and girls trying to get into the same bathroom belonged to their respective "cool" groups. Indeed, a willingness to transgress the official codes played a part in determining the coolness of a person. The dork children did not attempt to mix genders, but paired up with a peer. My duty became that of sitting in the seat next to the bathroom to enforce the rule of urinary segregation. Far from preventing their pleasure, according to the theory, my position (my value) kept the game going.

> The chaperone illustrates the structure of the *objet a*. Often represented as an aged female relative, she is not paradigmatically an object of desire but instead stands in the way of what the suitor wants: the beloved. Nevertheless, the chaperone is covertly instrumental in producing a certain desire or even the contemplation of such attainment but rather from engaging with the chaperone, in particular from successfully allaying her suspicions and evading her scrutiny. That is, as in the *Fort-Da* game, she is the object around which the subject moves to produce pleasure, the cause of desire rather than its object. (Krips 1999, 23)

It concerns the fact that even written matter can also be conceived of as excretion; as an example he quotes the stock metaphor which describes the book as a first difficult or even abortive birth; he mentions the vulgar expression this or that author cannot hold his ink; he refers to the case of the writer who first of all takes something in, then digests it and finally spews out the work; lastly even the famous fouler of his own nest mostly goes about his business in a literary way. In fact it is conceivable that the alliance between literature and excrement has been consolidated since the former began to identify itself more and more with the violation of a system. The origins of this association are older and more simple. He knows examples of the closest and most primitive psychological coupling: cases where the author attempts to read from his feces, as if they were coffee grounds,

the literary work he is going to produce next day, and even its specific quality. It
is no use denying that there is something slightly unappetizing about the occupa-
tion. This has nothing to do with the occasional choice of an offensive theme, but
as in the case of bodily excretion with the uncertainty of it belonging to the person
who produces it, and the shamelessness not only of abandoning it but even of ex-
posing it publicly. "I'll let down my trousers and shit stories on them, stories . . ."
(Samuel Beckett, "The Unnamable"). (Enzensberger 1972, 34–35)

Mourning

Commemorative consulting supports the public-private circuit of mourning
by taking into account the various embodiments of the bar line in the hypericon of the sign. The purpose of a MEmorial peripheral to an existing monument is to open to further thought the relation between private and public
experience, individual and collective actions, events, behaviors. The premise
of a conventional memorial is that the loss it commemorates is recognized
as a sacrifice on behalf of a public, collective value. The prototypical memorial is a war monument such as the Vietnam Wall. The value may be stated
abstractly—"freedom," for example, or "duty," "valor"—but it is understood
that certain actions and behaviors in daily life embody and perform the belief.
A monument condenses an inferential sequence, in other words, moving in
either direction along a chain of reasoning that might be spelled out as behavior, cost-benefit, belief, value, public recognition, ideal, sacrifice, memorial,
ritual, forgetting. Within the apparatus of literacy it has been difficult to sustain an awareness of this entire sequence, especially its sublimating, sanitiz-
ing operation (monumental enthymeme). The point that usually is forgotten is
the specific behaviors bought by the sacrifice. Here is the problematic issue of
the abject, its multivalent status as at once structure and matter (similar to the
multiple meanings of "value").

Words, boy, they're too much. Forget it. Let's see. I started in show business in
'50. I won the Arthur Godfrey Show, then I went to the Strand in New York, then,
about ten years ago, I went right into the toilet, Bong! But at this time I did Arthur
Godfrey and His Friends Show, and the comment of the day was: "Lenny, you're
gonna go a long way, because you're—you're not like those other comics, you
don't have to resort to filthy toilet jokes. Anybody can get a laugh on toilet jokes,
but you're clever . . ." And I started thinking about that. I was proud, but then I
started thinking, "How dirty is my toilet?" Yeah. That's sort of strange, that I have
to resort to it, or even protest against it, or my bedroom—toilet jokes, bedroom
jokes. Then I would just lay in bed, and I wouldn't even say that word at that time,
you know, I'd just think it, you know, then I'd thunder out of the bedroom and

dash open the door and "Look at you, you dirty, dopey, Commie toilet, you! And the tub and the hamper—you should know better." (Bruce 1967, 223–24)

The purpose of the peripheral is to make a case for losses of life (or other kinds of expenditure) whose public, collective relevance as sacrifice are not recognized. Victims of child abuse, like traffic fatalities, are not recognized as a public, collective sacrifice in the monumental sense. Part of the consultancy is to inquire into this question of why some losses are recognized as sacrifices on behalf of the community while other, often much greater losses, are not granted collective status, so that their cumulative totals never register in the record of group identity as a price paid for the maintenance of a certain lifeworld. The challenge for the EmerAgency is to show that tourism is capable of influencing public policy through bearing witness to base sacrifice. The full significance of using the verb "to sacrifice" to illustrate the middle voice may be seen in Bataille's comments:

> I have acquired over what happens to me a power that overwhelms me; since everything that follows refers to the traditional practice of "sacrifice," I do not hesitate to write, even though in relation to me it is painfully comical, that it is a power analogous to that of a priest who slashes the throat of a cow. . . . The practice of sacrifice has today fallen into disuse and yet it has been, due to its universality, a human action more significant than any other. Independently of each other, different peoples invented different forms of sacrifice, with the goal of answering a need as inevitable as hunger. It is therefore not astonishing that the necessity of satisfying such a need, under the conditions of present-day life, leads an isolated man into disconnected and even stupid behavior. (1985, 73)

A hill on which there was something like an open-air closet: a very long seat with a large hole at the end of it. Its back edge was thickly covered with small heaps of feces of all sizes and degrees of freshness. There were bushes behind the seat. I micturated on the seat; a long stream of urine washed everything clean; the lumps of feces came away easily and fell into the opening. It was as though at the end there was still some left. Why did I feel no disgust during this dream? Because as the analysis showed, the most agreeable and satisfying thoughts contributed to bringing the dream about. What at once occurred to me in the analysis were the Augean stables which were cleansed by Hercules. This Hercules was I. The hill and bushes came from Aussee, where my children were stopping at the time. I had discovered the infantile aetiology of the neuroses and had thus saved my own children from falling ill. The seat (except, of course, for the hole) was an exact copy of a piece of furniture which had been given to me as a present by a grateful woman patient. It thus reminded me of how much my patients honored me. Indeed, even

*the museum of human excrement could be given an interpretation to rejoice my
heart. However much I might be disgusted by it in reality, in the dream it was a
reminiscence of the fair land of Italy where, as we all know, the W.C.s in the small
towns are furnished in precisely this way. (Freud 1965, 506)*

Formless Value

The modernist aesthetic most relevant to the MEmorial is the set of operations called "formless," derived from the writings of Georges Bataille and the
Documents group. Bataille called for a relationship to events that resists all
"transposition" (sublimation, idealization). "Base materialism" includes the
ability to look "without transposition and to the point of screaming, eyes open
wide; opening them wide, then, before a big toe" (Bois and Krauss 1997, 50). If
man is a "blob of spit," it has nothing to do with resemblance, even if the experience of disgust or loathing in the repulsion from the excremental is another
name for the sacred.

> Bataille will drive in the nail of desublimation: there is nothing more human
> than this blob of spit that man despises; man . . . is this blob of spit. Whence,
> as well, the heuristic implication of human sacrifice, which does not differ
> all that much from the spectacle of the slaughterhouse: if one considers as
> secondary "the use of the sacrificial mechanism for various ends, such as
> propitiation or expiation," one is driven to retain "the elementary fact of the
> radical alteration of the person" and to see that "the victim struck down in
> a pool of blood, the torn-off finger, eye, or ear, do not appreciably differ from
> vomited food." (Ibid.)

The formless operations (base materialism, horizontality, pulse, entropy)
bring abject experiences into discourse without uplifting them into beauty or
significance. Formless gives access to the abandoned, neglected modern sacred,
and the MEmorial follows up by articulating the unacknowledged values to be
found at this level of experience. In the same way that the electrate logic of conduction does without the abstractions of concepts, electrate ethics does without
the transcendences of ideals. Bataille's heterogeneous formless, as an explicit
counter to the categorical work of literate concepts in science, opens the way to
the image categories of electracy.

> The collecting of anthropological documents is abandoned in favor of an in-
> tervention of a different sort. At the very moment that science, in the name of
> the neither-high-nor-low, claims to appropriate the low, something happens
> to it. Science gets dirtied by its object. Lets itself be contaminated by it. The
> object fails to keep its distance, abandons its reserve, overflows onto the page

which describes it. . . . Something bites into the very page that wanted to appropriate it, something that is not in its place, something heterogeneous. Like the fly on the lecturer's nose. Or like the ego in the metaphysical whole. The appearance of the ego, Bataille says, is utterly shocking. Certainly it was this ego which shocked d'Espezel. "The title you have chosen for this journal is hardly justified except in the sense that it gives us 'documents' on your state of mind." (Hollier 1995, 142)

In the collective expression, the miserables, the conscience of affliction already veers from its purely negative direction and begins to pose itself as a threat. All the same, in principle no positive attitude nor any active leaning justifies the exclusion which ejects the victims of misery outside the moral community. In other words, misery does not engage the will and disgusts of both those who experience it and those who avoid it; it is lived exclusively as impotence and does not leave any possibility of affirmation whatsoever. Thus imperative existence and social abjection also compose each other as active and passive, as will and suffering. The abjection of a human being is even negative in the formal meaning of the word, because it has at its origin an absence: it is simply the inability to assume with sufficient force the imperative act of excluding abject things (which constitutes the foundation of collective existence). Filth, rot and vermin are enough to render an infant vile; his personal nature is not responsible for it, only the negligence or helplessness of those raising it. General abjection is of the same nature as the child; wreaked by impotence under given social conditions: it is formally distinct from sexual perversions in which abject things are cultivated and which derives from subversion. The social process of segmentation which separates nobles from miserables is then not a simple one. (Bataille n.d., 9–10)

Here is a name for that inexperience that the concetto attempts to bring into an image category—"general abjection." Formless has its own method, in addition to introducing the "me" (the sting) into definition, which is to find or open a hole in a concept or literate classification, to make concepts leak and stain one another and mix (Ffrench 1999, 129). The poetic/logic operation is most dramatically demonstrated in "The Story of the Eye." Roland Barthes analyzed the device:

The eye seems the matrix of a new trajectory of objects which are in a sense the different "stations" of the ocular metaphor. The first variation is that of eye and egg; this is a double variation, both of form and of content (although absolutely discrepant, both objects are globular and white). Once posited as invariant elements, whiteness and rotundity permit new metaphorical extensions: that of the cat's milk dish, for instance, which functions in the first erotic exchange between Simone and the narrator; and when this whiteness becomes nacreous (like that of a dead, rolled-up eye), it introduces a new development of the metaphor—sanctioned by current French usage which calls the testicles of certain animals *eggs*. (1972, 241)

Image categories, to the extent that they share this formless quality of not resembling anything, gather disparate items not by essential properties but by accidental features. Roland Barthes went to Japan to learn from haiku culture how to write without resemblance or mimesis, without argumentative logic or narrative description. In *The Empire of Signs* he simulates haiku reason by writing impressions, pure designations of scenes of daily life (the use of chopsticks, a theatrical performance). A logic not of resemblance but of connections is what Deleuze and Guattari call "becoming" (extracted from a "schizophrenic cogito"):

> The wolf, as the instantaneous apprehension of a multiplicity in a given region, is not a representative, a substitute, but an *I feel*. I feel myself becoming a wolf. . . . It is not a question of representation: don't think for a minute that it has to do with believing oneself a wolf, representing oneself as a wolf. The wolf, wolves, are intensities, speeds, temperatures, nondecomposable variable distances. A swarming, a wolfing. Who could even believe that the anal machine bears no relation to the wolf machine, or that the two are only linked by an Oedipal apparatus, by the all-too-human figure of the Father? For in the end the anus also expresses an intensity. . . . The jaw descends to the anus. Hold onto those wolves by your jaw and your anus. The jaw is not a wolf jaw, it's not that simple; jaw and wolf form a multiplicity that is transformed into eye and wolf, anus and wolf, as a function of other distances, at other speeds, with other multiplicities, between thresholds. Lines of flight or of deterritorialization, becoming-wolf, becoming inhuman, deterritorialized intensities: that is what multiplicity is. To become wolf or to become hole is to deterritorialize oneself following distinct but entangled lines. (1987, 32)

"Kindertotenlieder"

A first step in the design of a MEmorial is to notice an abject loss that the community acknowledges is a problem but that is not accepted as a sacrifice on behalf of a belief or value structuring a group subject. This use of "abject" is related to Julia Kristeva's sense of the term. The MEmorial addresses abjection in both individual and national identity, having to do with a lack of fit, a certain disparity between the two sides of what is compared in an identity condition. Toilet work demonstrates the genesis of an abject category.

> While the body ego, formed at the time of the mirror stage, signifies a unified, phantasmatic gestalt of a newly formed subject's body, the stability of

this image is continually threatened from within by traces of abjection, such as corporeal wastes (excrement, urine, blood, breast milk, vomit, pus, and spit) that are jettisoned or leaked from the body. These traces of abjection represent both "me" and "not me," referring back to the child's "physiological natal prematuration" and the traumatic and liminal separation of self and other. Furthermore, the ideal bodily imago is also threatened from without, in a "society of control" which disperses bodies into desiring machines and part-objects. Observing the early modern workplace, Georg Lukacs noted that, "the fragmentation of the object of production necessarily entails the fragmentation of its subject." This slicing and portioning of the body finds its corollary in abjection. (Taylor 1993, 60)

A premise of the MEmorial is that the affect of abjection is felt collectively as well as individually. John Caputo described the feeling in his account of a poetics of obligation, in which something shocks me, some event or condition has a hold on me (1993, 30). He suggests a starting point not with the best but with the worst of our world, such as the case of a child dying of AIDS. The example resonates with the mission of the "safety patrol."

There is no *principium* or standard of Good behind the child or beyond the child, watching over the child and making the child safe. The child is not safe. The child is a disaster. There is no sure principle that is implicitly at work that renders possible the recognition of the disaster that besets the child. We cannot begin at the beginning, with a *principium,* but only where we are, with the child. We can only begin by responding to the child, who is a disaster, by coming under the singularity of the claim she makes upon us, and by making damaged lives our business. That is where we are. (39)

The MEmorial concerns just such disasters as this, whose modality is "impossibility," according to Caputo, since they are "without why." A MEmorial then exists in the same modality as the poetry of Paul Celan. "The poem happens not as a meaning-giving event but as an event of commemoration, as a way of keeping a record, of recording the date of a disaster. The poem is a recording, *im Herzen,* in the heart, of a disaster. It does not bestow beauty on the event (aesthetics), or sense (theology). . . . Divested of both *Kehre* and *Resultat* the poem simply re-cords the event, writes it down—or lets the disaster do the writing—as a gesture of mourning and commemoration. . . . There is no suggestion that we can put a stop to it, only that we can watch out for it or provide an idiom for its record" (Caputo 1993, 183). Paul Celan wrote about Auschwitz in terms not of communication but of commemoration. He gave testimony. Caputo in several books has established an abject domain joining the obscenity of attempting to give reasons why the Holocaust took place (imposing the order

"Here There Is No Why" that Claude Lanzmann took as the title of a manifesto for his Shoah project) (LaCapra 1998, 100), with the ethics of the Mystic Rose of Angelus Silesius and Meister Eckhard ("the rose is without why; it blooms because it blooms. It cares not for itself; asks not if it is seen") (Caputo 1978, 9). The connection between these domains is Heidegger.

What would it be to think "abjection" apart from the objects of disgust—the filth, the rot, the vermin, the corpses—that Bataille himself enumerates, after all, in his own treatment of the subject? Well, as Bataille also shows us, it would be a matter of thinking the concept operationally, as a process of "alteration," in which there are no essentialized or fixed terms, but only energies within a force field, energies that, for example, operate on the very words that mark the poles of that field in such a way as to make them incapable of holding fast the terms of any opposition. So that, just as the word sacer *already undermines the place of the sacred by revealing the damned within the very term for the holy, the designation for that part of the social field that has sunk into abjection—the word* miserables—*had started off as a term of pity ("the wretched"), but then, caught up in a rage of revulsion, became a curse ("wretched!"). Bataille is interested in this splitting apart of meaning from within, since, as we know, all acts of fission produce wastes—the sun's very brightness, for example, piling up an unassimilable, excremental slag. And it is the inevitable waste of the meaning system, the stuff that is no longer recyclable by the great processes of assimilation, whether intellectual (as in science or philosophy) or social (as in the operations of the state), that Bataille wants to explore by means of his own procedure, which he names "theoretical heterology." . . . In describing the heterogenous product as "excremental," Bataille leads us to imagine that heterology will concentrate—as one of its related terms, scatology, would indicate—on what is untouchably low. And yet Bataille will also point out that, if the lowest parts of society have become untouchable (abject) through wretchedness, the very summit of that same society is also separated out as untouchable, as kings and popes are precipitated out of the top of the homogeneous structure to form that very exception of which the rule is the product, but from which the sovereign himself is exempt. (Bois and Krauss 1997, 245–46)*

Sublime Abuse

The purpose of a MEmorial is to witness and testify regarding the event of a public problem, to shift it from the private, individual status of one at a time, each case in isolation, to a cumulative public status of sacrifice on behalf of an unrepresented national value. A MEmorial attempts to bring such abject losses to the attention of the public without transposing them into abstractions or ideals. The public problem addressed in my testimony is child abuse. What could be the *value* of which this abuse is a symptom, such that it is sustained despite the cost in loss of life? The abuse is the behavior we want to deny or forget and that in fact is impossible to recognize, or at least impossible to place in the chain or put on the rails of the tracks leading from event to principle (the emblematic shot of *Shoah*—the train tracks leading into Auschwitz). This revulsion is the mark of the sacred. A MEmorial often turns out to be a tourist "repulsion."

It must be remembered that the abuse is not itself the value but the sacrifice necessary to maintain a value. Not every child is abused, any more than is every soldier killed in action. It takes only a certain number annually to pay the debt so that we may have our way of life (the ritual lottery of winners and losers). The MEmorial witnesses this commitment and makes it visible, even monumentally evident. What does it mean to say that abuse-value precedes and makes possible use- and exchange-value? Is it really necessary to try to add child abuse to the choral series of this term? In so doing I take up Caputo's suggestion, since the occasion that holds me and obliges me (a feeling of recognition) is the story of Bradley McGee (the event reported in the local newspaper). Here is the event of sacrifice, a secular, private equivalent of the rituals conducted on the stone altars of Mayan temples. Unrecognized, it is an abject sacrifice. This event begins to fill out the *signifiance* of Lacan's emblem. What is to be done?

The community is outraged by Bradley's murder, but it does not recognize it as a sacrifice, that is, as a necessary consequence of the way of life we currently embrace as a civilization and hence fundamental to American national identity, at least as it is presently constituted. As this death and similar ones are reported day after day in the paper, leaders, pundits, spokespersons, sermonize against the disaster, invest public money to hire conventional consultants in order to find ways to ameliorate if not eliminate such events. These leaders lack an idiom that would help them and us grasp what is happening *(ATH)*. Their commitment to the principle of sufficient reason prevents them from taking into account the unconscious. Slavoj Žižek referred to such circumstances as "the sublime object of ideology," noting this need to treat as exceptions and anomalies (remainders, inassimilable wastes) those matters that are in fact essential features of a way of life (Žižek 1989).

Testimonial (mystory applied to a public policy issue) dramatizes this blindness. The "sublime" names a feeling that the MEmorial exposes, externalizes, articulates—morality as the internalization of a Reign of Terror.

> The logic at work in the experience of the dynamical sublime is therefore
> as follows: true, I may be powerless in face of the raging forces of nature,
> a tiny particle of dust thrown around by wind and sea, yet all this fury of
> nature pales in comparison with the absolute pressure exerted on me by
> the superego, which humiliates me and compels me to act contrary to my

fundamental interests! (What we encounter here is the basic paradox of the Kantian autonomy: I am a free and autonomous subject, delivered from the constraints of my pathological nature, precisely and only insofar as my feeling of self esteem is crushed down by the humiliating pressure of the moral Law.) . . . The fear of raging nature and of the pain other men can inflict on me converts into sublime peace not simply by my becoming aware of the suprasensible nature in me beyond the reach of the force of nature but by my realizing how the pressure of the moral Law is stronger than even the mightiest of natural forces.

The unavoidable conclusion to be drawn from all this is: if Beauty is the symbol of the Good, the Sublime is the symbol of . . . Here, already, the homology gets stuck. The problem with the sublime object (more precisely: with the object which arouses in us the feeling of the Sublime) is that it fails as a symbol; it evokes its Beyond by the very failure of its symbolic representation. So, if Beauty is the symbol of the Good, the Sublime evokes—what? There is only one answer possible: the nonpathological, ethical, suprasensible dimension, for sure, but the suprasensible, the ethical stance, insofar as it eludes the domain of the Good—in short: radical Evil, Evil as an ethical attitude. (Žižek 1993, 47)

In the consultation, the disaster or public problem replaces in Žižek's formula the raging forces of nature. The event of Bradley McGee's murder included in a MEmorial, through this feeling of the Sublime, augments the initial sting of recognition that motivated its selection and transforms the process of design into an ethical encounter. The Copernican revolution of chorography becomes clearer in this context—the inversion in which I do not explain the problem; it explains me (shows me my group subject). I catch sight of my superego by appropriating an event that I recognize as somehow expressive of a feeling. In this scene I recognize not so much my own history as the nature of existence as I believe it to be (a metaphysical intuition).

Writing the Disaster

We use the emblem to write a disaster that we cannot think (or feel). Electrate writing is not clear and simple as the truth, but obtuse and complex as the real (and these two stands collaborate in the passage from literacy to electracy). One may still look through the window as in the classical stand (whose prototype is the view achieved by a tourist guidebook), but the result is more like the one Blanchot reported as a moment of revelation.

(A primal scene?) You who live later, close to a heart that beats no more, suppose, suppose this: the child—is he seven years old, or eight perhaps?— standing by the window, drawing the curtain and, through the pane, looking.

What he sees: the garden, the wintery tree, the wall of a house. Though he sees, no doubt in a child's way, his play space, he grows weary and slowly looks up toward the ordinary sky, with clouds, grey light—pallid daylight without depth.

What happens then: the sky, the same sky, suddenly open, absolutely black and absolutely empty, revealing (as though the pane had broken) such an absence that all has since always and forevermore been lost therein—so lost that therein is affirmed and dissolved the vertiginous knowledge that nothing is what there is, and first of all nothing beyond. The unexpected aspect of this scene (its interminable feature) is the feeling of happiness that straightaway submerges the child, the ravaging joy to which he can bear witness only by tears, an endless flood of tears. (Blanchot 1986, 72)

The emblem structure discernible in *Writing the Disaster* includes the scene of home, looking out the window on a winter day. The scene is associated with an intuition that may be described as metaphysical in the sense that it evokes Blanchot's (the narrator's) feeling of attunement, *Stimmung,* giving an understanding of how the world is. The mood or feeling opens onto this metaphysical dimension, which in turn is associated with the Holocaust. "Concentration camps, annihilation camps, emblems wherein the invisible has made itself visible forever. All the distinctive features of a civilization are revealed or laid bare ('Work liberates,' 'rehabilitation through work')" (81). The world is: Holocausts. The third element in the emblem is the morality entailed by this attunement: "The ever-suspended question: having died of this 'ability to die' which gives him joy and devastation, did he survive—or rather, what does to survive mean then, if not to be sustained by an assent to refusal, by the exhaustion of feeling, and to live withdrawn from any interest in oneself, disinterested thinned out to a state of utter calmness, expecting nothing?—Consequently, waiting and watching, for suddenly wakened and, knowing this full well henceforth, never wakeful enough" (116). To say that the camps are an emblem means that they may not be explained, but constitute a measure of the real. The emblem is catachrestic. Here is what the egent must write in a deconsultation: *a memory, a disaster, a morality.* Against the disaster Blanchot chose the way of most wisdom traditions, the stand of ataraxy—a decathexis of the world, reduction and elimination of desire. Ascetic serenity.

Pulsation

The dream logic of the phrase "a child is being beaten" (a fantasy analyzed by Freud) has become the iconic scene of an image category—formless (Bois and Krauss 1997, 104). This phrase operates not by a structure but a matrix; it is not a system but a block superimposing simultaneously all possible arrangements of the positions or functions rhetorically available in this phrase, in all modalities and voices. The most important dimension that this logic adds to the empirical account of such scenes is fantasy. *A child is being plunged headfirst into a toilet.* A story of fathers and sons, but neither tragic drama nor scientific analysis are capable of telling it.

The intractability of the problem of child abuse (for example) is intelligible to instrumental consultants to the degree that they admit the link between individual cases and the foundational value of family (to give one name to it). They might accept the notion of sacrifice in rejecting the reductio argument that to eliminate child abuse the state would have to administer child rearing. This level of surveillance being the greater evil, they might say, we must accept a certain amount of abuse, to be ameliorated by parenting classes and the like. We lack what Fredric Jameson called a "cognitive map" that would graph the passage (the *defile*) connecting individual experience with collective historical structure.

Electracy makes it possible to revisit our relationship to disaster, our relationship to events that resist every effort of problem-solution. To write the disaster is to find the group subject in me. What is to be done remains open to invention. A MEmorial is a cartography of *ATH,* tracing the paths joining blindness and calamity. The point is that until the abuse is acknowledged as the symptom of a value (until it is given collective recognition as such) there is no hope of altering the behavior. The goal of cumulative MEmorials is collective self-knowledge. In the testimonial, the maker gives evidence, testifies to the ethical experience, the feeling of duty that abuses me (if it does). My identification with (recognition of) this disaster outside me as a fractal measure of the disaster within makes writable the category of justice, and is the point of departure for an electrate postnational identity.

> "A child is being killed." This is the title which must at last be recalled in all its indecisive force. It is not I who would have to kill and always to kill again the *infans* that I was, so to speak, in the beginning and when I was not yet, but was at least in the dreams, the desires and the imaginary of some, and then of all. There is death and murder (words which I defy anyone seriously to distinguish and which must nonetheless be separated); but there is no designated or designatable dealer of death. It is an impersonal, inactive, and irresponsible "they" that must answer for this death and this murder. And likewise this child is a child, but one who is always undetermined and without relation to anyone at all. A child already dead is dying, of a murderous death—a child of whom we know nothing (even if we characterize him as marvelous, terrifying, tyrannical, or indestructible) except this: that

the possibility of speaking and of life depend on the fictive establishment, through death and murder, of a relation of singularity with a mute past, with a prehistory, with a past, then, which is outside the past and of which the eternal *infans* is the figure at the same time that he is concealed therein. (Blanchot 1986, 71)

Armed with all the certainties acquired over the course of this journey through ethnology, the history of art or of styles, and logical ontology, you finally plunge into your corpus in order to extract a model from it, the embodied proof of your theory, its paradigm. And out of it you pull—indeed, yes—a urinal. This particular one, rebaptized Fountain and signed R. Mutt, although everyone knows that its real author is a famous artist called Marcel Duchamp, is reverently kept in a museum, under the name of work-of-art and as part of their cultural patrimony. Its import seems indeed to have reduced the work of art to being the very symbol of this symbolic value that the word "art" confers on the objects of an exchange, whether linguistic, economic, ritual, or sumptuary. More than any other work of the cultural patrimony, Duchamp's urinal manifests the magic power of the word "art"; testifies to an almost impertinent freedom vis-à-vis the history of styles, which it appears to summarize and complete without owing it anything; and above all, illustrates the undecidability, the openness, and the indeterminacy of the concept of art, or even its entrenchment in solipsism or its expansion into universal tautology. Further, it is just as much the emblem of a theory of art-as-performative-institution. . . . And nothing distinguishes it from just any ordinary urinal, from non-art, except, once again, its name, art. (de Duve 1998, 12–13)

Jacobin States

Thinking about the safety of Bradley McGee as an emblem of the spirit of America brings me into the territory of the Taliban. There is one historical solution ready-made for the vices and failures of our society: terror. Is the choice between the morals of tourists or terrorists? It has been demonstrated often enough that "opposite" is a relative category, culturally specific, as much ideological as logical, and complex in itself (Ogden 1967). The binary pair named by Dean MacCannell in his study of tourism works well for our project: "The central thesis of this book holds the empirical and ideological expansion of modern society to be intimately linked in diverse ways to modern mass leisure, especially to international tourism and sightseeing. Originally, I had planned to study tourism and revolution, which seemed to me to name the two poles of modern consciousness" (MacCannell 1976, 3). MacCannell's opposition clarifies the intertext emerging within our CATTt, in this case in the interaction of analogy and contrast, filled with the domains of tourism and revolution respectively.

We know from contrast the approach to change we do not want—the conceptual field created by the opposition utility/revolution. To take up one extreme of this pair, we inventory the behavior or conduct entailed by revolution, for example, the tactics proposed by Lenin.

Our contrast helps us define an initial restriction on our invention: we will do the opposite of whatever Lenin proposed (our riddle becomes: what is the opposite of terror?). Leninism suggests that one's method should emulate the spirit, mood, atmosphere, ambiance of threat, aggression, attack, polemic, rivalry, domination associated with any vanguard, contemptuous in principle of that which it opposes. "Lenin thought that the workers could not develop by themselves the necessary political consciousness and that they needed an organization through which professional revolutionaries would lead them and be able to exploit a revolutionary situation when it arose" (Bullock and Stallybrass 1977, 345). This desirability of class consciousness: I am saying that the group subject is emerging in electracy willy-nilly. For clarification, the authors of the entry on Leninism in an encyclopedic dictionary prompt the reader to "see Jacobinism." What is Jacobinism (referring to the original "reign of terror" during the French Revolution)? "Contempt for the will of the majority, dictatorship by a determined revolutionary minority, Committees of Public Safety as embryo institutions for implementing terror—these are some of the historically archetypal features of Jacobinism. Underlying it was the idea, derived from Rousseau, that the masses were insufficiently enlightened to carry out a revolution" (325).

The Jacobin mode of vanguard problem solving finally is: *establish Committees of Public Safety in your area of interest.* It is symptomatic that the most powerful ministry in Afghanistan under the Taliban was the Ministry for the Protection of Virtue and the Prevention of Vice (*Gainesville Sun*, December 9, 2001, 12A). Our theory suggests, however, that the difference between "them" and "us" is that "we" in the West (according to Hegel) internalized the terror and called it morality.

> Throughout the entire dialectic of *Bildung,* the appearance of an equivalent exchange between subject (self-consciousness) and substance is thus maintained: in exchange for his increasing alienation, for sacrificing a further substantial part of himself, the subject receives honor, wealth, the language of spirit and insight, the heaven of Faith, the Utility of the Enlightenment. However, when we reach the apogee of this dialectic, "absolute freedom," the exchange between the particular and the universal Will, the subject "gets nothing in exchange for everything." (The historical epoch which stands for this moment of "absolute freedom" is, of course, the Jacobinical Reign of Terror, in which, for no apparent reason, I could be proclaimed traitor and have my head cut off at any moment.) . . . That is to say, what is "subject" if not

the infinite power of absolute negativity/mediation: in contrast to a mere biological life, self-consciousness contains in itself its own negation, it maintains
itself by way of negative self-relating. This way, we pass from absolute freedom
(of the revolutionary *citoyen*) into "the Spirit certain of itself" epitomized by
the Kantian moral subject: the external negativity of the revolutionary Terror
is internalized into the power of moral Law, into the pure Knowledge and
Will qua Universality, which is not something externally opposed to the subject but something which constitutes the very axis of his self-certainty. (Žižek
1993, 23–24)

In Žižek's Lacanian reading of Hegelian history, "the subject who, in the
Jacobinical Terror, had to accept his worthlessness in the eyes of the State,
must now, in his capacity as moral subject, sacrifice what he most cherishes to
a Demon within. Therein consists the Hegelian 'negation of negation': what first
appears as an external obstacle reveals itself to be an inherent hindrance, i.e., an
outside force turns into an inner compulsion" (25). The question is not the guil-
lotine, yes or no, but where to put it: without or within? In our context of education and pedagogy, the Jacobin issue may be translated into the issue of the
balance between safety and risk, applied to the realm of ideas and imagination.
The issue has several levels: to know the difference between virtue and vice, how
to motivate people to behave accordingly, whether or not this classification and
behavior are even relevant to electracy.

The EmerAgency approaches policy problems neither from the perspective
of instrumental engineering nor Jacobin politics. An inventory of these approaches to problem solving provides a negative definition of our contribution.
A preliminary description of EmerAgency consulting is *to find in oneself the
feeling of a Committee of Public Safety*. Virtue is not the given of deconsulting,
but the riddle. "One of the great mysteries of Western thought," the philosopher
Leo Strauss has said, is "how a word which used to mean the manliness of man
has come to mean the chastity of women" (Himmelfarb 1995, 15). We have an
image of Taliban soldiers shaking their weapons at the contrails of U.S. bombers over Afghanistan and challenging them to come down and *fight like men*.

ASSIGNMENT

Write a Disaster

The lesson of writing a disaster is that overcoming compassion fatigue
begins by discovering this circuit connecting my experience of being to
the disaster outside. To test this claim, compose a pastiche of Blanchot's
primal scene, writing your own version of a moment of revelation you may
find in a childhood memory. What were the circumstances of a scene in

which you passed from the immedicacy of daily living into a condition of self-awareness, a recognition of your own apartness and isolation from every other being? The literature suggests that this experience is in fact quite common (that the experience of the sages is repeated commonly in the lives of children everywhere).

Example

A primal scene? The boy is eleven, starting seventh grade. His father explains that it is time to learn the value of work. He has arranged a job for his son with a friend whose name is Cutting and who owns a sheet metal shop. Every Saturday the boy rides his bicycle across town to Cutting's Sheet Metal. The employees are done for the week at noon on Saturday. He has to arrive by noon so the boss can lock up, leaving the boy inside (he is too young to be trusted with a key). The job is to clean the shop—sweep the floor, gather up the tools and align them neatly in their designated places on the work benches, collect the remnants and clippings of the metal sheets scattered everywhere. It takes most of the afternoon to finish the chores. The shop is a cavernous open warehouse, with rows of heavy scarred tables, the walls lined with shelves stacked to the distant ceiling with equipment, tools, metals. It is quiet, the stillness of dust motes swirling in the beams of sunlight filtered through the few windows high up near the roof, carving vectors through deep shadow. The sunlight catches the edges of a museum of blades, a taxonomy of every snipping snap slice chop saw hack rend rip cleave nip or severing machine. Half-shaped tin

Figure 6. Shrine (Institution Formation).

objects stand in rows behind piles of hammers and modeling frames. After so many weeks and months of Saturday noons the boy begins to lose touch with his former friends and companions, who go their separate ways.

What happens then? The light and shadow of the industrial building open all at once onto a black hole and white wall of divided worlds in this little infinite town: The official world of adults (parents, teachers, coaches, ministers, scoutmasters) that until then had constituted reality, and the unofficial world of peers, whose existence he had only just discovered. Two different systems of virtue and vice, success and failure, winning and losing, were enforced in these realms: What earned admiration and respect in one system was inversely judged in the other. Choose! He could not have articulated the revelation so abstractly then. The unexpected aspect of this scene is the sense of isolation that overcomes the child, a spilling out or abjection, an absolute exhaling of substance, followed soon after by the inhaled relief of knowing that it doesn't matter, since everyone and everything dies everywhere the same death.

6

THE AGENCY OF THE IMAGE
(UPSILON ALARM)

I AM THINKING NOT ABOUT BRADLEY MCGEE but with him. What makes writing the disaster reproducible as a practice for egents is the simplicity of the means. I make an allegory, a figure of thought. I juxtapose some documents from two domains (my life, the public problem), and the human sensorium does the rest. If a correspondence exists, the feeling occurs as an event. The uncanny. The device is no less powerful for being a commonplace of the arts. David James, describing the allegorical method of alternative filmmaking (concerned specifically in this example with radical cinema), says, "Each of the special interest groups—students, GIs, the Vietnamese themselves, and indeed everyone conscious of the way his or her experience of capitalism, even at the psychic level of alienation from oneself, recapitulated the situation of third World people—had thus a 'Vietnam' of his or her own, a lived experience of imperialism" (1989, 196). I have an "abuse victim" of my own in this emblem: the chaperone of Bradley McGee's toilet.

Blanchot shows what is at stake in these deaths and in learning to write the

Figure 7. Space Mirror: Ulmer family visiting Kennedy Space Center, 1996.

disaster. What needs to be brought into focus is the smear of *vanitas,* since the commemoration witnesses my own inevitable death. Christopher Fynsk's study comparing Blanchot's revelation with the dream of the burning child (a topos of psychoanalytic theory) explicates a deeper meaning of the allegory: that the death of the child emblematizes the experience of being human, of what it means to enter language and become a speaking being. The recourse to the *infans* (one who does not speak) with the infant sacrifice is a commonplace of emblematics.

> By word and deed God has amassed a number of discreet witticisms which are spelled out by the Church Fathers and then broadcast from the pulpit by lesser, but nevertheless learned divines. One of God's most brilliant conceits was the Incarnation, although it took a saint rather than a literary critic to see what God was lightly hinting at when the Word became flesh, for it was no less a person than St Augustine who detected God's wit in allowing the Word to become speechless *(infans)* in the *infant* Jesus *(Sermones,* cxc). Hinted at by God and authorized by St Augustine, this etymological conceit on *infans* became an approved *concetto predicabile* available to any poet or preacher who aimed at stimulating devotion by exercising wit. So it is that "the Word is dumb" in Southwell's poem on the Nativity; and Lancelot Andrewes, sermonizing on the same topic in a passage T. S. Eliot could not keep his hands off, glosses *Verbum infans* as "the Word without a word, the Eternal Word not able to speak a word." (Ruthven 1969, 46)

In the dream reported by Freud and commented on by Lacan in discussion of the ethical nature of the unconscious, the child, dead from a fever, lying in state in a room accidentally set on fire by a tipped-over candle, says to his father in a dream, "Father, don't you see that I am burning?" In Fynsk's reading, what makes it possible for the father to recognize and hear the voice of the dead child is his own experience of abandonment, which in turn becomes accessible to the father only through this encounter with the other's suffering.

> Must there perhaps be a witness to the child's address for it to come to speech (and could this be part of what Lacan means when he says that "only the father as father—that is to say, no conscious being" can say what the death of a child is)? And does the father perhaps also need the address of the child to say his "own" burning—to present his desire? The address may also be the condition of the father's relation to his "own" experience of conflagration, which is the real object of this dream. Following this argument, we would say that there is, indeed, an address of the other that communicates the "otherness" of the dead child. But the words bearing this address—actually spoken by the child at some point or fantasized by the father—open access to and at the same time represent another "original" relation that involves the father's own "primal scene." The "accident," the catastrophic or traumatic event for the dreaming subject, lies in this access; the address exposes the father to another experience of loss, and this exposure awakens. (Fynsk 2000, 114)

Here is the essence of commemoration as the kind of memory supported and augmented by digital technology and the educational practice of the MEmorial. The dreaming beyond any concept (dreamwork as a logic of a new category formation) witnesses the relationship between language and the real. For one entering language the price of self-consciousness and the freedom it makes possible is the awareness of one's own death. In the Internet prosthesis is it possible for the group subject to awaken, to kill its own dumbness in a revelation of its freedom, that is, its power to choose a course of action other than the one dictated by material nature or ideological habit? The MEmorial has to be an impresa, that is, must take the disaster as a guide to the egent's own experience, to reveal in it this *ATH* already at work. I cannot rely on the archetypes, traditions, stock images, commonplaces if I am to approach the *ATH* of today. This term from a poetics of tragedy alerts us to the ambitions of the consultancy: that the MEmorial may achieve for the group subject an emergent self-consciousness. Fynsk poses the challenge in a theoretical style that we have learned by now how to receive:

> The crucial point is that the death of the *infans,* at the level we are trying to think it, cannot be brought to any representation or figuration—it is an unfigurable figure. And I think we can appreciate better now the full (im)measure of Blanchot's reflection on this death. For we must think the *syncope* of being

that occurs in the writing of the disaster as both (a) an interval that *takes bodily* in throes of dying that are no more than a "silent intensity"; and (b) the fold by which a thought comes to itself in its originary response to what calls it and "spells" its knowledge of the *il y a*. We must think a bodily suffering that is immemorial and perhaps irreducible even to the formal unity of a "subjectivity without subject" together with the perpetuation or the survival of the relation of responsibility that opens as this interruption. We must think, in effect, a structure of exposure—a writing, let us say—that perpetuates exposure both as a reiterated, unsatisfiable exigency, and as the constant presence of an unfigurable material suffering. Perhaps a notion of rhythm could help us think together the body of this interval and the "wave of light" that awakens the body suffering saying. Perhaps rhythm is the true infant figure. But there is no visible or verbal figure that could capture the death of the *infans*. The saying of this death cannot be "said" (or represented) in any mode of signification. Not even a phrase such as "a child is being killed" says this event. Or if it can say it in the mode of a *signifiance* prior to any representation or signification, the phrase itself remains unpronounceable. (2000, 72)

Fynsk deliberately avoids thinking the death of the *infans* in relation to actual deaths of specific children, since he is working the question from the side of knowledge, or "mediation" we might say. And yet he admits an ambivalence about this strategy: "I sometimes feel I'm passing back and forth before the door without recognizing it. And then sometimes I recognize it, and instead of stepping through, I comment just a little more, to be sure of my footing, and then I find it has already closed" (98). I know this feeling, to the extent that I cannot not give one more theoretical citation. The crucial point for learning electracy is that what the *infans* evokes may not be stated nor thought, neither clearly nor simply, which opens it to the simulacrum, the image category that emerges through a transversal passage. The repeated reports of murdered children in the news lend themselves to reasoneon. From the punctum triggered by this policy issue I may unfold a testimonial, with the expectation that from it a simulacrum will emerge. "The repetition of an image does not merely link the various actual worlds in which it is, successively or simultaneously, contemplated or consumed. Nor does it only call up the memory of its tangled history, with all the scenes and variations through which it has passed. It also repeats prospectively the worlds and roles that we, as individual and collective subjects, are not yet capable of thinking or representing, but which nonetheless haunt all our repetitions as what remains unactualized within them" (Durham 1998, 25). What does Bradley McGee say to his father in dreams?

Agency

The consultation on Bradley McGee is not complete until we have a proposal for a peripheral to be attached as an asterisk (disasterisk) to an existing monument. Part of the purpose of this meditation is to consider the modality of de-consulting. What responsibility does an egent have for the disaster? What is the *agency* of the group subject reflexively addressed in a MEmorial? In his reading of Lacan's famous "Agency" article ("The Agency of the Letter in the Unconscious"), Gilbert Chaitin showed that Lacan's revision of Saussure's hypericon of the tree as the paradigm of a sign included not only an anagram ("arbre" = "barre" in French, the slash of emptiness, the nothing that opens the place that makes possible the human subject), but also the letter "Y" ("Y" as idea or *eidos*, shape). To make his point about the associative chain in which the tree was but one link, Lacan ran through most if not all the meanings gathered around "tree" culturally and historically: "Used to stand for the notion of branching, the tree was schematized in the letter Y as the sign of the diverging paths of vice and virtue in a tradition which traced its origin, perhaps mistakenly, to the Pythagoreans" (Chaitin 1996, 18).

Chaitin demystified Lacan's unpacking of the sign "tree" by noting that Lacan's tactic was simply to use every meaning of the term inventoried in the dictionary ("tree" as concept). This tactic is extended by a heuristic rule of choragraphy: not to disambiguate, but to write with all the meanings of a word (the choral word). Not only with the dictionary meanings, but with the puns as well, and with the shapes of things named by the puns. The mapping of the links between experience and structure consists of composite shapes disseminated at the scale of this "Y" or Greek upsilon. MEmorials trace the operations of these letters that "produce meaning effects in the collective beyond intent, without understanding, without individual consciousness" (120). In the prosthesis of electracy (the Internet) this discourse becomes legible, available for reading and writing as an image category.

It turns out that "agency" is caught up within a translation detour passing through "insistence" and "instance" to the Greek "enstasis." Chaitin explained the origin of "enstasis" as a dialectical procedure in Aristotle's logic by which one adduces a counterexample to refute a claim of universality for a rule. The letter in the unconscious moves Lacan to add a modality to the modalities of the proposition available in logical practice, extending the necessary and the possible to an exception that is an exemption from the rule altogether. Chaitin proposes a new translation of the title—"the exception of the letter" (145). Giorgio Agamben revises this modality in a way that shows the memorial logic of choral or sacred space. *Exception.*

The situation created in the exception has the peculiar characteristic that it
cannot be defined either as a situation of fact or as a situation of right, but
instead institutes a paradoxical threshold of indistinction between the two.
It is not a fact, since it is only created through the suspension of the rule. But
for the same reason it is not even a juridical case in point, even if it opens the
possibility of the force of law. This is the ultimate meaning of the paradox
that Schmitt formulates when he writes that the sovereign decision "proves itself not to need law to create law." What is at issue in the sovereign exception
is not so much the control or neutralization of an excess as the creation and
definition of the very space in which the juridico-political order can have validity. In this sense, the sovereign exception is the fundamental localization
(Ortung), which does not limit itself to distinguishing what is inside from
what is outside but instead traces a threshold (the state of exception) between
the two, on the basis of which outside and inside, the normal situation and
chaos, enter into those complex topological relations that make the validity
of the juridical order possible. (Agamben 1998, 18–19)

The manifestation of this zone of indistinction (between chaos and chora)
in the modern social order is the concentration (internment) camp. "One
of the theses of the present inquiry is that in our age, the state of exception
comes more and more to the foreground as the fundamental political structure
and ultimately begins to become the rule. When our age tried to grant the un-
localizable a permanent and visible localization, the result was the concentration camp" (20). While the camp is the extreme instance, zones of indistinction
are distributed throughout daily life in more banal variations. The structure is
found when "an apparently innocuous space (for example, the Hotel Arcades in
Roissy) actually delimits a space in which the normal order is de facto suspend-
ed and in which whether or not atrocities are committed depends not on law
but on the civility and ethical sense of the police who temporarily act as sovereign" (174). The social feature of such zones is a loss of distinction between law
and "bare life," the latter defined as "the life of homo sacer (sacred man), who
may be killed and yet not sacrificed," and whose existence marking the passage between exclusion/inclusion "constitutes the first paradigm of the political
realm of the West" (8–9). Agamben problematizes the meaning of "sacrifice" in
a formless MEmorial with his articulation of bare life.

The wish to lend a sacrificial aura to the extermination of the Jews by means
of the term "Holocaust" was from this perspective, an irresponsible historio-
graphical blindness. . . . The truth—which is difficult for the victims to face,
but which we must have the courage not to cover with sacrificial veils—is that
the Jews were exterminated not in a mad and giant holocaust but exactly as
Hitler had announced, "as lice," which is to say, as bare life. The dimension in

which the extermination took place is neither religion nor law, but biopolitics. If it is true that the figure proposed by our age is that of an unsacrificeable life that has nevertheless become capable of being killed to an unprecedented degree, then the bare life of *homo sacer* concerns us in a special way. Sacredness is a line of flight still present in contemporary politics, a line that is as such moving into zones increasingly vast and dark. (114–15)

The separation of *homo sacer* from sacrificial ideology in our time reflects the profane and banal circumstances of contemporary violence. "Our age is the one in which a holiday weekend produces more victims on Europe's highways than a war campaign, but to speak of a 'sacredness of the highway railing' is obviously only an antiphrastic definition" (114). To speak of the "personal sacred," then, may be a catachresis, to name this continuing evolution of the sacred into electracy. Nonetheless, the call of responsibility originates for Agamben also in the spectacle. "The 'imploring eyes' of the Rwandan child, whose photograph is shown to obtain money but who 'is now becoming more and more difficult to find alive,' may well be the most telling contemporary cipher of the bare life that humanitarian organizations, in perfect symmetry with state power, need" (133). Warren Schmidt and Ndugu find their way into theory, but we need not look so far from home. Bradley McGee and his peers are instances of bare life. *The American home is a zone of indistinction* (my home, your home), a thought not accessible to topics but only to chora (the region wherein topics bleed together).

As for our responsibility, "agency" in individual and collective identity is caught up in this play of modalities, as part of the shift from the metaphysics of literacy to electracy and a different order of categorization based on the image. In chorography there is a short circuit or pun switch crossing between the "mood" of linguistics and the "mood" of state of mind. One does not write the disaster in a literate way, with definitions and concepts (the way of homogeneous science, the expert consultants). Rodolphe Gasche describes how Heidegger used his etymological poetics to show the relation of the two fundamental powers of language. To define a thing *(bestimmen)* is made possible by attunement *(Stimmung)* of state of mind through mood.

> The three essential determinations of *Stimmung*—Dasein's thrownness or facticity, the disclosure of its being-in-the-world as a whole, and the fact that something can "matter" to it—constitute existentially Dasein's openness to the world. In *Stimmung,* in the attunement of a state-of-mind, Dasein, which experiences itself always already factically (knowingly or not), is shown to be capable of being "affected" by the world and of directing itself toward things in a world that in every case has already been disclosed to it. Dasein's being-attuned in a state-of-mind is the existential a priori of all possible linkage, connecting, or relationship. (Gasche 1999, 116)

The MEmorial does not define (analyze) the disaster but discovers its mood. This is the contribution of the EmerAgency in collaboration with expertise. Through attunement the disaster matters to me. Mood in linguistics concerns the attitude speakers take toward their statements (indicative, interrogative, conditional, imperative, subjunctive). To invent the practices of electracy, and enabled by the new digital prosthesis of memory, we may put pressure on our language resources to support an additional modality of voice: the virtual. The mood (linguistic/existential) of an EmerAgency MEmorial is virtual, in the way Deleuze and Guattari use the term to describe an abstract machine such as Kafka's novels. "It consists in prolonging, in accelerating, a whole movement that already is traversing the social field. It operates in a virtuality that is already real without yet being actual (the diabolical powers of the future that for the moment are only brushing up against the door") (Deleuze and Guattari 1986, 48). The egent, like Kafka, is a "bachelor machine," possessed by and articulating the collective multiplicities passing through "me." "When a statement is produced by a bachelor or an artistic singularity it occurs necessarily as a function of a national, political, and social community, even if the objective conditions of this community are not yet given to the moment except in literary enunciation" (83–84).

> We have seen that the world was a unique, infinitely infinite, converging series, and that each monad expressed it in its entirety, even though it clearly expressed only one portion of the series. But, rightly, the clear region of a monad is extended in the clear portion of another, and in a same monad the clear portion is prolonged infinitely into the obscure zones, since each monad expresses the entire world. A searing pain in me is only the prolongation of a series that led me into it, even if I did not notice it, and now it is continued in the series of my pain. *There is a prolongation or continuation of convergent series, one into the other.* (Deleuze 1993, 50)

Headlines after each catastrophe wonder about the mood of the country. The MEmorial is a way to map and participate in mood construction, tracing the series of pain.

The function of the MEmorial within the larger deconsultation of the EmerAgency is to write the new not-yet, the becoming, to break impasses by detaching or deterritorializing the value flows from their dead ends and redirecting, reconnecting with new territories (this is a "cartographic" process—the map constructs the territory). The attitude of the speaker (in the middle voice) is not intended but is discovered, evoked in the manner of an atmosphere created by a poetic figure. The title of an electrate Lacan becomes: "the virtuality of the letter." The term "letter" also must be modified to indicate the new status of the image in chorography. "The virtuality of the figure" indicates that the phonetic reading of the rebus in psychoanalytic theory must be revisited in approaching the Internet as the prosthesis of the (political) unconscious, continuing the fortunate errors that produced the emblem books out of the Renaissance misunderstanding of Egyptian hieroglyphics, and the Vorticist ideogram out of the modernist misunderstanding of Chinese writing (Pound and Fenollosa). The MEmorial probes this new zone of poetic logic by opening a Y within each empirical *why*. The letter-image Y is the dowsing rod generating a transversal gathering of abject values.

Egency

"Egency" refers to an institutional entity created to organize the MEmorial program within a virtual consultancy. The EmerAgency opens the public policy problems identified in the MEmorials to testimony from egents. This testimony is delivered through the cumulative effect of the online MEmorials and the meditative series generated as part of their composition. The Internet as living monument, in other words, delivers or gives the consultation as a collective figure. In a MEmorial the egent writes not the hierarchy of law (or concept) but the field of justice, following the metonymic connectivity, contiguity, the intensities of desire indexed in machinic assemblages. In Kafka's stories the people or animals are indexes of Europe's future: "'The Metamorphosis' forms a complex assemblage in which the index-elements are Gregor-animal and the musical sister; in which the index-objects are the food, the sound, the photo, and the apple; and in which the index configurations are the familial triangle and the bureaucratic triangle. The bent head that straightens up and the sound that latches onto the voice and derails it also function as indexes of this sort in the majority of the stories. There is thus a machinic index each time a machine is being built and is beginning to function, even though one doesn't know how the disparate parts that make it up and make it work actually function" (Deleuze and Guattari 1986, 47). Each MEmorial introduces some set of machinic indexes into the Internet prosthesis, where they may be added to the virtual map forming in the collaborative deconsultation. We must become accustomed to this conductive mode of inference, if not to this terminology, since policies are made as much with neon as with reason.

The transversal movement in our formless inquest into the death of Bradley McGee passes from Lacan's Y to a work of skywriting (we are gathering indices). Transversal is a movement of inference, passing from the known to the unknown, by means of conduction. An image category is forming. In his magazine article about the Space Mirror—the Astronaut Memorial at the Kennedy Space Center—Jerry Adler commented, "It is hard to imagine improving on the spontaneous memorial that appeared in the sky when the space shuttle Challenger blew up in January 1986: the immense twisted Y of the contrails formed by the solid rocket boosters as they diverged, a graphic depiction of vast power gone berserk. Hanging for hours in the clear, still air over the Atlantic Ocean, it was seen by millions and inspired one of them, a Florida architect named Alan Helman, with the idea of a permanent memorial" (1991, 69).

That the *Challenger* wrote a Y in the sky when it exploded gives a clue to the changes that chorography brings to consulting on public policy problems. Nearly every description of a disaster or a foolishness *(ATH)*, whether coming from victims, witnesses, or commentators, poses the question "why?" But as the context of Auschwitz for Celan's poetry would indicate, the kinds of problems engaged by chorography fall into the category of being "without why" (Caputo 1993, 29). "Mosley [the medical examiner] said when someone kills a child, it's very rare that the motive is evident. 'Things like this are inexplicable,' he said. 'One of our natural tendencies when we hear about something like this is to think, 'How could anybody do this' or 'Why would anybody do this?' We just don't know" (A. P. Thompson, *Gainesville Sun,* March 20, 2001). Conventional consulting only takes up those problems considered to be within the domain of "sufficient reason," subject to rational solution. Auschwitz, it must not be forgotten, represents the enframing of "problem" taken to the extreme of madness. The "final solution" to "the Jewish problem," executed using all the formal procedures of a European state, was genocide. From such a catastrophe the Real (the ultimate limit of the Restricted Economy) may be inferred, in the manner of the sublime.

Amelioration and Obstinacy

Certainly there are practical steps that can and have been taken to "solve" the problem of child abuse. After the death of Bradley McGee, and again after the slaying of Kayla McKean, and again after the disappearance of Rilya Wilson, major overhauls of government agencies were undertaken, and certainly not for the last time. A Child Advocacy Center, for example, was established that attempts to coordinate and interlink all the agencies involved in a given case of abuse and neglect, since it often happens that an injured child is assigned to several different counselors, representing different agencies with different responsibilities, each unaware of the other's involvement (Lisa Fisher, *Gainesville Sun,* September 18, 2000). Janet Reno, attorney general during the Clinton administration and gubernatorial candidate in Florida, speaking at an opening ceremony for a Head Start program that treats abused toddlers, called for measures that would break the cycle of violence against children. "As attorney general, Reno approved the $1 million federal grant used to establish the program, which organizers said is the nation's first. Located at an elementary school that's across the street from a public housing project, the Safe Start Initiative will work with 24 toddlers between 12 and 24 months old whom judges determined were abused, neglected or abandoned" (*Gainesville Sun*, November 8, 2001). After each egregious case the Department of Children and Families declares that a sweeping overhaul has been accomplished, only to be embarrassed by the next abused child, and the one after that. A recent editorial, titled "Florida's Shame," calls attention to the persistence of the problem and the troubling inability or unwillingness of government to respond to the issue:

> Society is ultimately judged on how well it cares for its children. By that measure, Floridians should be shamed by the disclosure this week that four out of every five child abuse deaths that occurred in this state over the past two years could have been prevented. Of some 60 cases of death by abuse, 48 should have been preventable with "some reasonable intervention by someone in the system," Nancy Barshter, special counsel with the Attorney General's Office, told the Senate Children and Family Committee this week.
>
> Barshter is a member of the State's Child Abuse Death Review panel, which reviews fatal cases to determine whether timely intervention on behalf of child welfare officials might have, literally, made the difference between life and death. All too often, that panel has found, repeat instances of abuse and neglect are not appropriately addressed due to lack of staffing, inadequate training, poor coordination between child welfare workers and law enforcement, the failure to do criminal background checks, and so on. . . .
>
> Nor is there reason for optimism that things will be turned around any time soon. As Jack Levine, president of the Center for Florida's Children, said at the senate committee meeting this week: "Here they sit in a budget cutting session wondering why we have dead kids. We have pretty much perfected the art of post-mortems . . . but I strive for the day when we perfect the art of prevention. If 80 percent of the cases are preventable," he added, "when are we going to get smart enough or when are we going to get courageous enough to prevent?" That's a good question. How many children have to die to get the Legislature's attention? (*Gainesville Sun*, December 2, 2001)

The MEmorial addresses this gap between the disaster (child abuse in this case) and the ability of public policy to respond. Why were the "preventable" deaths "allowed"? The MEmorial does not offer a reason, but marks this gap or blank in the record (the blank chapter, sign of repression) with a temporary, abject hypothesis concerning the politics of *homo sacer: the deaths are a sacrifice made on behalf of American national identity*. We are confronting not a problem, but an aporia. Conventional consultants try to isolate the aberration as exception, unaware of the logic of bare life. They are unable to conceive of America as we-who-abuse-children.

The McGee MEmorial takes the *Challenger* Y as an idiom with which to form an image category (a map). The idiom is an assemblage linking together a series of disparate items (indexes) on the basis of the letter and shape "Y"—the Y-zone of indistinction (chora).

> Let's say that there exists a definable membrane through which meaning can move when translating from one discipline to another. What I mean by membrane is a thin, pliable layer that connects two things and is, in this case, the middle position of music + architecture. The membrane is similar perhaps to the role of a semi-tone or semi-vowel in the study of phonetics. A semi-tone is a transitional sound heard during articulation linking two phonemically contiguous sounds. Like the *y* sound often heard between the *i* and the *e* of quiet. I am suggesting that something similar occurs, a *y*-condition, in the middle position of music + architecture when translating one to the other. (Martin 1994, 26)

This transversal of a formless category is a digital jump out of the impasse of the "why" that citizens cannot help but ask in the face of disaster, to mark the dimension of blindness, foolishness, that goes unnoticed amid the overwhelming calamity. The pundits bring all their science to bear on the "why" to give a "because" of sufficient reason, but it is never adequate. The O-ring is one answer to the *Challenger* why, for example, referring the query to the administrative bureaucracy of NASA and its decision science. The O shape also points to the hole of the real that "problem" tries to fill without success.

What Does "Y" Spell?

The link between Bradley McGee and Gus Grissom created by the sky Y was confirmed by the appearance of the Y in the details of several stories of children's death reported while this project was in preparation. In one story, a middle-school student named Troy Silcox committed suicide. In the article describing the memorials spontaneously offered by friends and acquaintances, the name of Troy's mother was listed as "Rose Weihe (pronounced like the letter 'Y')" (*Gainesville Sun*, February 25, 1997). The Mystic Rose has a Weihe, but not a why. These spontaneous memorials, springing up all over the country after a disaster (such as the ones in Oklahoma or Colorado or Lower Manhattan) are the vernacular point of departure for the MEmorial. As Bataille noted in his essay on the language of flowers, the conventional meaning of "columbine" is "sadness."

In another story, Sabrina Aisenberg, aged five months, was snatched from her home in the middle of the night while the parents and two older children slept. "Sabrina has an identifying birthmark: a little red 'y' on the back under the right shoulder" (*Gainesville Sun,* January 11, 1998). Sabrina's own parents eventually were arrested for her murder (statistically the most likely possibility anyway). The relevance of the Aisenberg case to electracy is also due to the involvement of surveillance tapes used as evidence to justify the arrest of the parents. When the tapes proved to be largely inaudible, the parents were released and the charges against them dismissed. Nearly four years after Sabrina disappeared, pop star Michael Jackson responded to an appeal from the Aisenbergs for help in finding her, saying he would include a song about missing children on his next album, and put a picture of Sabrina on the inside cover (*Gainesville Sun,* June 28, 2001). O. J. Simpson also went looking for his wife's killer. These searches are $incere.

In the conductive logic of choragraphy, the Y traced by the *Challenger* explosion, the *y* in the name and the birthmark of the missing or dead children, the "why" posed rhetorically in the wake of every disaster (for example, the "WHY" on the cover of *Newsweek,* May 3, 1999, special issue on the "massacre in Colorado") are juxtaposed with the Pythagorean "Y" and its revival in "The Agency of the Letter." The failure of the Wye River accord to bring peace between Israel and the Palestinians continues the transversal in the public realm. This gathering of information by repeated sounds and shapes is how image categories form.

> In classical times the philosophers who called themselves Pythagoreans had come to illustrate the "parting of the ways," or choice, by means of the Greek letter upsilon, the equivalent of the capital Y of the Latin alphabet. The letter Y can be interpreted as a path that divides, and the image is even better if one arm of the Y is made wide and the other narrow. The one is the "broad path" of Vice, comfortable, easy, and without problems but leading toward materialism and perdition. The other is the "narrow path" of Virtue, steep, laborious, thorny, dangerous but at the same time morally the "right path." In European decorative art, ornamentation, and allegorical embellishment of the 16th and 17th centuries the letter Y is also sometimes seen. As a rule it symbolizes the difficult choice between virtue and vice, between good and evil, between the right and the easy path. By extension the Y can stand for the freedom of the will and man's responsibility for his own life. (Achen 1978, 221)

What responsibility does the community have for choices made at the fork in the Y? Terror establishes Jacobin Committees of Public Safety, as in the Taliban Ministry for Protection of Virtue and the Prevention of Vice, relying on the police state apparatus to enforce the right choice. Democracy relies on the ideological state apparatus to instill etiquette if not virtue. Underlying this traditional opposition, Deleuze and Guattari articulate three interacting lines: "a relatively supple line of interlaced codes and territorialities" (primitive societies); "a rigid line, which brings about a dualist organization of segments" (state apparatus); "one or several lines of flight" (war machine) (1987, 222). The theory in our CATTt proposes that every tree structure of literate analysis become a rhizome of electrate feeling; every Y-binary becomes a multiplicity. Every structure becomes a machine. Topics accumulate into chora. Concepts add concetti. The consequence of this switch in the context of Y agency is a different kind of decision diagram—not a series of branching alternatives of the kind traced in the dialectical outline introduced by Peter Ramus as the generator of print composition (the tracery in the facade of the twin towers), but a formless (holistic) tangle of discursive lines. In these terms the Y marks not a parting of the ways but a merging (an interdependence). Electronic monumentality takes up the ethics and politics as well as the logic of tangles: the metaphor of electrate writing is not textile but felt, not weaving but fulling (ibid., 484). It takes a categorical image to map this tangle. That hand gesture, two fingers extended (Nixon in disgrace, turning to face the cameras at the door of the helicopter), is not "V" but "Y," not solution but impasse.

The Wish Switch

Let me negotiate a defile from branch to tangle. The testimonial linked to the peripheral takes the designated public problem as a vehicle, a semantic domain figuring virtually a portrait of my political unconscious (constructed through interpellation into the popcycle institutions). I am mapping the sublime register of child abuse. I simulate my selfhood (not an essence but an ideological construction) in the prosthetic unconscious, as a humanities visualization. The method is to locate personal experiences or attitudes that form a pattern with the public issue, juxtaposed into an emblem that evokes for me and for others a moral group subject. What is the trajectory of the pain through me? The hypothesis is that intractable problems are *sources of explanation* rather than or in addition to being objects of analysis: it is inside me (us) as well as outside in the behavior of others. I don't explain Bradley's abuse; it explains me. Nothing is hidden. I am testifying by mapping the recognition scene.

More power to the conventional consultants as they plan and calculate their solutions. It is not their power but their impotence that is the point of departure for inventional consultants. Why entertain the Y? Because all the conventional efforts are still not enough. We are desperate. We call upon the EmerAgency to find witnesses. Do you *recognize* Bradley McGee? The procedure is fundamentally aesthetic, even lyrical, in that this permeability of the inside-outside border has been mapped by poets at least since the Romantics with phrases such as "negative capability" (Keats), "objective correlative" (Eliot), or "Weltinnenraum" (Rilke). The experience of this fit or correspondence between the public and private worlds was that of an epiphany (Joyce). In an electrate consultancy, art is as important as math and science.

The choral attitude is to consider that the public policy treatment of child abuse (in my example) as a problem to be solved functions in another respect as a shield, defense, or protection ("problema") that covers the unavowable. Chorally speaking, the event that "sticks in my craw," that I cannot swallow, is treated as a fetish. The question "why?" is rhetorical and marks an impasse or aporia that throws the witness into a detour through the personal sacred. To testify with respect to the EmerAgency slogan—Problems B Us—the interrogative "why" is replaced with a quotidian material behavior associated with a different attitude. I suspend concepts and proofs in order to enact something, to discover a formless value in a behavior. "It is too easy to be antifascist on the molar level, and not even see the fascist inside you, the fascist you yourself sustain and nourish and cherish with molecules both personal and collective" (Deleuze and Guattari 1987, 215).

Passing through Customs

For example, following the inferential Y series, I turn to the custom of making a wish using the wishbone of the Thanksgiving turkey (in honor of Kayla McKean, murdered the day before Thanksgiving) as an interface metaphor for a group subject. Let it dry for a time. Hold one end of the inverted Y at the very bottom and a partner holds the other end. Each makes a wish, after which we pull simultaneously until the bone snaps. Whoever holds the larger part gets what was wished for. How widespread is this ritual? For it to be present in a culture requires a population of carnivorous dreamers. The wishbone emblematizes a choral dialogue: I am at one end of the connection, and someone else, whether a stranger or a friend (I tested this with Linda Marie Walker, between Gainesville, Florida, and Adelaide, Australia), perhaps many others at once, is/are at the other end. I can show this end, but I cannot tell the hopes I have for it. It is bad luck to tell my wish. At the same time the proverb comes to mind: Be careful what you wish for.

Choral knowing requires indirection (it is obtuse). To testify I do not ask why Bradley McGee was murdered, nor do I wish that this event never happened. Instead I begin a transversal to map the entanglement of the private and public dimensions of such an event, hoping to come upon a scene of recognition, the uncanny point at which the disaster becomes a self-portrait (to map the topology of extimacy). I look for something in my own experience that might account for the sting, the punctum, the aura that is the obtuse dimension of the image created by the scene of Bradley McGee's toilet work. My point of departure is a memory of how I came to own copies of the sheet music for the first three preludes for guitar by the Brazilian composer Heitor Villa-Lobos. These preludes are the material of my experience of a why within which I look for a wish (a problem shielding a fantasy): "en mi mineur, en mi majeur, en la mineur." The economy of do, re, mi, (and sometimes Y).

Find an Anecdote

The sheet music came from a man named Bob Long. At the memorial service for Bob I told this story about how we met: a telephone call from a complete stranger named Robert Long. In those days the university library did not recall books from faculty members. If the one requesting the overdue book was also a faculty member, the library provided the phone number of the person holding the book. This stranger asked if I had checked out the German edition of Heidegger's book on Nietzsche. I had. Having read this book some years earlier, and hoping to find someone with whom to discuss it, Bob had been monitoring the shelves to see if anyone else would check it out. He did not want to recall the book, but to meet the person reading it.

When the muggers confronted him on his way home from Albertson's, walking with his daughter at 10 p.m., Bob had several different kinds of expertise in his body—mathematics, classical guitar, the marines. I never learned all the details. Did he know the young blacks had a gun? It was silver, his daughter said. Was it because he wanted to protect his daughter? She survived unhurt as the witness. Which of his skills was the most appropriate one for the crisis? Is the archetypal division of human faculties an adequate measure—mathematics for mind, music for heart, marines for guts? The three Ms.

The last time I saw Bob—a few days before he was murdered—he had just come out of the old Book Gallery, a used-book store (no longer in business). I was just on my way in, and he was unlocking his bicycle. We exchanged three or four sentences. Very glad to see one another, but no time to talk. The crime remains on the books, unsolved. Statistics suggest the young men will have paid for their actions in any case, without intervention of the law. Not on purpose the first time, I was in that part of the stacks, Library of Congress, key of B, German philosophy, Heidegger, when I glimpsed a man with a bicycle. Sometimes you see it; students with expensive bicycles take them in the elevator. Heidegger's Nietzsche in German is on the shelf, monitored by this ghost.

The contribution of this example to the MEmorial is the possibility of a subject forming at this basic level of behaviors. There is some event that we wish would happen or had not happened. How many ways are there to make a wish in the world? Is there a culture without whys or wishes? The differences in the practices are as important as what they share. The first rule is not to ask why. The wishbone shape (*eidos,* idea) showed me that the wish could be another way to learn about what the why forecloses: the inverted Y. Do not ask why and do not tell the wish. Instead, I recall the flowers planted in the median of the four-lane boulevard that children must cross to get to Westwood Middle School a few blocks from my home. I do not mean the large beds of flowers tended by city workers. I mean that one plant just at the front corner at the beginning of the turn lane, placed there by the parents of the boy killed by a car on his way to school. Investigators concluded it was the boy's fault; he failed to look behind him when he turned his bicycle out into the road. The car that struck him with the force of the legal limit of forty miles per hour was driven by the boy's own pediatrician, as it happened (such is fate). The boy was not supposed to cross at this spot, but to go all the way down to the intersection overseen by a crossing guard. The last thing his mother said to him as he went out the door was, "Be careful crossing the street."

Hauntology

Deleuze and Guattari speak of the world system of the white wall *(signifiance)* and the black hole (subjectification) that interact in faciality, the monumental visage. "It is not exactly the face that constitutes the wall of the signifier or the hole of subjectivity. The face, at least the concrete face, vaguely begins to take shape on the white wall. It vaguely begins to appear in the black hole. In film the close-up of the face can be said to have two poles: make the face reflect light or, on the contrary, emphasize its shadows to the point of engulfing it 'in pitiless darkness'" (1987, 168). These are the dynamics evoked in the superego holograms of Florida Rushmore and in movie close-ups. The next picture is always of that father (in jail) reading a bedtime story to Bradley. What was the story? A fairy tale. What did Ernst Bloch say in *The Principle of Hope* about the not-yet (the untimely virtual)? About the utopian fairy tale supporting the wish, sustaining that difference, that gap of longing that separates humans from the animal immediacy of the given world? Wishing won't make it so, you say? You forgot about the magic tool.

This transversal of instances constitutes a kind of divination process, shared among all those holding the ends of the virtual wishbone. Together we are like those dowsers who wandered over the grounds of certain premises (geo-logical) holding the fork of the rod in their two hands, the rod pointing downward. A forked stick of hazel was best for finding water, while other woods or even metals were used for finding ore. The Germans referred to it as the wishing rod and used it the same way fortune-tellers use cards or tea leaves. Rhabdomancy, divination by means of little pieces of stick, is an ancient practice. George Dowsing had some skill in the art. Those who attempted to turn this natural phenomenon to the ends of finding treasure consulted Dowsing and other scholars for help. Dowsing managed to raise several spirits in a glass of water, those spirits being no more than an inch long and mistakable for a shadow.

We are reopening the Greek "idea," derived from a term that in the vernacular *(eidos)* meant "shape." Photography extends writing with shapes to all the visible surfaces of the world. The photographic recording reopens conceptual classification to the infinity of accidental (nonessential) properties available to the senses, giving us another reality (another metaphysics). A shape repeats, creating a pattern. This time the Y is upright if I have in mind that letter of the alphabet, that ambivalent vowel (and sometimes why?) of avowal and disavowal. The dowsers were brought to England from the mines of the Harz mountains in Germany. The topology of the heart is in question. The real alchemists always knew the gold was spiritual. The psychoanalytic transposition makes gold not from lead but shit (Bradley's gift). In our values we only want the gold, but formless holds us in the shit. The dowsers held the device by the forks of the why (horns of the dilemma), pointing the stem downward, waiting for this stem to move of its own accord, due to some sympathy between the material of the rod, the body of the dowser, and the treasure below. These shapes—the wishbone or the wishing rod—bear some relationship to the question I am not asking (why?), albeit in an exercise designed to cure me of Q & A. The dowser's story is a parable of EmerAgency consulting.

The Magic Tool

My condition is that of the double bind, the dilemmatic aporia, which perhaps is why deconstruction attracted me. Which came first: my feeling (even if I could not name it) or the theory? The dilemma is structured like the fetish: intellectually I know that nothing I do will improve the world. Emotionally I believe that my actions make a difference for the better ("I know, but still . . ."). Such is not the Jacobin state of mind (to impose virtue through terror). I am operating the materials of the why (of Enlightenment knowledge, of theory and method) as if they were hazel forks or turkey bones. Can I do this? Can I inhabit the theory of narrative as if it were the narrative itself? More than the narrative, as if knowing the theory put the narrative directly into experience? I know that the fairy tale and the wish it expresses are the safe house of the utopian impulse. What may we learn about consulting from narrative? From structuralism we learned about the axes of communication, conflict, and desire. The most important relationship between characters is that between the donor and the hero. The questing hero encounters a being or entity who poses certain tests, especially a test of etiquette, measuring virtue (strength, values). The test implies a promise of gift: the magic tool that enables the protagonist to accomplish the impossible in overcoming obstacles or villains.

The Y-why is the circulating prop that is at once the key to the magic tool the donor gives to the hero, and the empty square that makes signification possible in the logic of sense (and in structuralist linguistics). This mobile empty place that makes language possible (the way empty squares on the game board permit checkers or chess: no play without room to move) corresponds to the hole in me (my incompleteness that activates my desire) and the hole in the world called the Real (inferred from the disaster). As donor it does not matter whether or not I have hope, or if I care at all, or if I even know what I am doing. Education is like the hut of Baba-Jaga, where many are destroyed, but some acquire the magic tool, the wishing why. Buckminster Fuller recommended that society provide free education for everyone, and let them study whatever they want, for as long as they want. He calculated that one person in every one hundred thousand would produce an invention so important that its economic benefits would pay for all the "unproductive" work. Or is this just a bedtime story for educators? Is the inch-long movement in the jar a spirit or a shadow?

Fallacy

This transversal is training in conduction for egents. When teaching informal logic I show that scene from the film *Monty Python and the Holy Grail* that demonstrates the structure of the joke as a form of fallacious reasoning. The knight helps the villagers determine whether a local woman is a witch by seeing if she floats. The script emphasizes the fallacious inference path torturously drawn through the problem. We all laugh. This scene is based on the life of Matthew Hopkins, the most famous witch finder of his day, who traveled the counties of Essex, Sussex, Huntington, and Norfolk, examining females suspected of witchcraft (fetishism). I should have known the Pythons researched their jokes. Hopkins's ultimate test was that of swimming. The hands and feet of the accused were tied together crosswise, after which she was wrapped in a sheet and tossed into a pond. If she sank she was deemed innocent (albeit drowned). If she floated she was deemed guilty and executed. In one year Hopkins oversaw more than sixty deaths by this means. The work of a Committee of Public Safety. Arthur Koestler argued that the experience of getting a joke and of having a creative insight are physically similar.

The Ys have in common this searching, looking—the dowsing rod was also known as the detecting wand. The donor does not seek, but gives the magic tool as a gift to those not destroyed by the tests of worthiness. To whom? Someone then must be seeking in order to need the magic tool? Without the whole story there is no donor and no gift. Someone always misunderstands, turns the method to digging for treasure, and, as happened with those who consulted George Dowsing, becomes vengeful once disillusioned. The first to feel the force of the disappointed treasure hunters are the scholars who showed them shadows in a jar.

The confusion of the material for the spiritual—perhaps it has something to do with which way the why is pointed (earth or sky, the old binaries, as in *The School of Athens*). Behind or coexistent with the donor figure is the sender, mediating between the diegesis (the imaginary space and time of the narrative) and the culture, the society in which the story makes sense. The story could be told in many different ways, and exists as a vehicle for the circulation of a value. Whose story, from what point of view? That photograph of college students watching on television the O. J. Simpson verdict, the African-Americans celebrating, the Euro-Americans confounded. The Confederate flag: badge of heritage or racism? The narrative standpoint determines public policy, told still from within the classic stand, as if looking out a window, or as if reading a tourist guidebook. Here is the challenge in making *ATH* receivable. If it were only a choice between good and evil, the branching Y might suffice.

> In telling their tales, political theorists have tended to ignore, evade, or cover up what A. C. Bradley once called the "essential fact" of tragedy. "It will be agreed," Bradley said, "that in all tragedy there is some sort of conflict— conflict of feelings, modes of thought, desires, wills, purposes; conflict of persons with one another, or with circumstances, or with themselves; one, several, or all of these kinds of conflict as the case may be." The tragedy is that these conflicts are not so much wars of good with evil as they are wars of good with good. At best, political theorists have tended to blink at such contests of values. . . . But as long as our beliefs are contestable or corrigible, as long as we remain bound by the ethical indeterminacy of human life, we will find ourselves confronted by different and contending structures of belief, ways of life, spheres of cultural value, and moral descriptions of our social and political practices. To be forced to choose between two desirable, compelling, and justifiable but incompatible courses of action is an inexorable part of the repertoire of human experience. (Brint 1991, 1–2)

The advance that the MEmorial attempts to make on tragedy and consulting is to provide an image that holistically evokes the tangle of competing stories in a matrix, a block that brings them into a network. The tangle is not a Gordian knot of competing tales, but a quantum field capable in principle of thinking the hole (if not the whole) prior to the decision. But there is no escape from the Y, the decision, the bifurcation threshold.

From Text to Felt

A MEmorial consultation is not a "text" in terms of the textile metaphor of weaving a pattern that structures the meaning of this practice. The fabric that better characterizes the formal operation of a MEmorial is "felt," which coheres as a tangle of interlocking "hooks and eyes" produced in fibers such as hair, fur, wool, when rubbed in conditions of heat and moisture. The matted fibers of felt may be pressed into any shape. The term carries the overtones of emotion, of feeling (I felt the punctum). Deleuze's association with felt as a baroque fabric even includes a reference to the veils of Islamic women:

> The psychiatrist Clerambault's taste for folds of Islamic origin, and his extra-ordinary photographs of veiled women, amounts, despite what has been said, to much more than a simple personal perversion. So does Mallarme's shawl, or the poet's wish to edit a fashion journal. It falls upon formal deduction to straddle many diverse materials and areas. It will have to distinguish: simple and composite Folds; Hems (knots and seams being corollaries of the fold); Drapes, with their proppings. Only then will ensue material Textures and, finally, Agglomerations or Conglomerations (felt made by fulling and not by weaving). We will see to what extent this deduction is properly Baroque or Leibnizian. (Deleuze 1993, 38)

MEmorials are not texts but felts, including the punning overtone of a category that cohere around a feeling or mood. The image category intensifies the "veil" in "surveillance."

Theory shows how a felt structures its material (information) in the exemplary fantasy reported by Freud, "a child is being beaten." Freud noted the positions in the scene—agent (father), victim (child), subject (spectator)—to which he added "drive" (sadistic or masochistic) and "pleasure" (genital excitation). Freud's linguistic analysis showed a transformational operation in the story moving in three stages from active to passive voice. "Now the drive in its regressed form is able to disconnect libidinal pleasure from a genital content and reconstitute it as anal, so that loving and beating combine" (Bois and Krauss 1997, 105–6). Jean-François Lyotard's analysis of the logic of this fantasy is reviewed in Bois and Krauss's study of formless. The move from structure to matrix in their account corresponds to the shift from text to felt:

> A further divergence between the structuralist's system and the unconscious figure—which Lyotard calls the "matrix"—is that while both share the properties of synchrony and invisibility, the invisibility conceived by structuralism is that of a virtual order working within the system to produce its intelligibility: the system as a producer of meaning. But the matrix's invisibility, on the other hand, is a function of the repressive work of mutating everything into its opposite, thereby undermining the productive work of structure. The elements of the matrix, Lyotard argues, do not form a system but a block: "If the matrix is invisible, it is not because it arises from the intelligible, but because it resides in a space that is beyond the intelligible, is in radical rupture with the rules of

opposition; we can already see that this property of unconscious space, which is also that of the libidinal body, is to have many places in one place, and to block together what is logically incompatible. This is the secret of the figural: the transgression of the constitutive intervals of discourse and the transgression of the constitutive distances of representation."

The work of the matrix is then to overlay contradiction and to create the simultaneity of logically incompatible situations. Thus it is at total variance with the transparently self-explanatory structuralist grid. It blocks together active and passive, genital and anal, sadism and masochism, and, in "a child is being beaten," watching and being watched. This, then is the matrix figure's "work," the peculiarities of its "structure"; the statements one can project as layered within it that organize the goal (to beat), the source (the anal zone), and the object (the father) of one sentence are in their turn condensed into a single product formula—"a child is being beaten"—whose apparent coherence allows the psychic life to contain in a single manifold a multiplicity of logically incompatible "sentences." These do not form a system but a block. . . . The destruction of difference, the work here of the matrix figure, is the destruction of form. (Bois and Krauss 1997, 106–7)

The MEmorial felt network embodies this figure in a specific case: the beaten child is Bradley McGee. The consultation situates the fantasy at the collective level of the nation: *Our head is plunging a toilet.* Where is the secret desire, the benefit to the community, in this scene (a pointless question, since no one can determine what ultimately is useful to humanity). How does a mystory form a map? How does commemoration become logic?

One may contrast a *childhood block,* or a *becoming-child,* with the childhood memory: "a" molecular child is produced . . . "a" child coexists with us, in a zone of proximity or a block of becoming, on a line of deterritorialization that carries us both off—as opposed to the child we once were, whom we remember or phantasize, the molar child whose future is the adult. "This will be childhood, but it must not be my childhood," writes Virginia Woolf (*Orlando* already does not operate by memories, but by blocks, blocks of ages, blocks of epochs, blocks of the kingdoms of nature, blocks of sexes, forming so many becomings between things, or so many lines of deterritorialization). Wherever we used the word "memories" in the preceding pages we were wrong to do so; we meant to say "becoming," we were saying becoming. (Deleuze and Guattari 1987, 294)

The disaster is written not by weaving but by fulling (hairs or threads treated so they will mat into a fabric), filling the gap between deaths (composing a felt) by finding the hooks and eyes to form (digital) links. I am pressing McGee and Grissom into a figure (following a feeling). Derrida insists, where there is calculation or divination (planning, control of the future) there is no event, no choice, no decision, no invention, no gift, no promise, no chance. Not calculation OR divination, then, but AS. The question has to be transferred into another moment, for example, 1996 (or 2001), to see the implications of this choice (surprise or safety). In this era of improved global information is there anyone who did not hear the words of the headmaster of the school in Dunblane, Scotland, where a man slaughtered sixteen five- and six-year-old students and their teacher before turning his gun on himself? "Evil visited us yesterday, and we don't know why." No, we don't know: Y. The postcards bearing the single-word question "why," reportedly arriving from around the world, show the phatic function of the question. "Slaughter"—the universal floating signifier. *Matanzas* is inscribed on Florida maps (place of slaughters). It is understood everywhere yet has no meaning. The army alone, said Bataille, has the magical ability to transmute "slaughter" into "glory."

Surprise Safety

If I am safe, may I not be surprised? I am looking at this story as it is laid out in a major news magazine, with a circulation in the millions of readers. It reveals why Wittgenstein, when he saw one of the earliest examples of this kind of magazine representation of an event—in his case a story about a fatal car accident, complete with diagrams—why he experienced the insight that allowed him to complete the writing of his *Tractatus,* stalled precisely by this difficulty concerning the relation of language to event. Propositions are pictures, he said, pictures of states of affairs. It was the diagram of the accident that triggered his eureka; like the diagrams of the murder scene at Dunblane, tracing the path of the "monster," called "Mr. Creepy," through the school, to the spot on which he put himself down. Here is the point of communication between the sender as representative of cultural values and the receiver as character in a narrative diegesis: the monster is to the story what the problem is to society.

Dunblane is a parable about an economy of the gift. The diagram is an allegory. No, not only an allegory but a collective psychological gesture, this man with a gun running amok here, is an atmosphere we produce in our state of affairs. I wonder how things stand with us? I am dunblaned. Consider the luck of Robbie Hurst, the only child in the gymnasium who escaped unharmed. Is he still connected to a star, while we are without the *astre,* without fortune *(des-astre)*? I can imagine that these children already knew about luck. Literacy tells its story from the point of view of luck and finances education with state-run lotteries. Call him Ishmael (the White Whale indexes a border, say the French).

Figure and Tale

The disaster is Y. I am X. Vehicle and tenor. The event is marked in each discourse of the popcycle. In entertainment, Richard Hamilton (the Dunblane murderer) is a monster in a fairy tale (cousin of the Sphinx), a tale to serve as caveat, by the grim brothers. Beware. We prefer those stories in which the plucky little adventurer confounds the ogre and comes through the melodrama by means of the magic tool whose use suddenly becomes obvious at the moment of need. Such is the structure of all our stories. The donor gives away the Y. We forget about the enthymeme of story, implicit, in silhouette—that without the magic tool the adventurer perishes, like those children in the class picture taken the day before the event. I wonder, what is the magic tool, *for me*? This gift is what our civilization believes in and teaches. Only one of you, it says to all who listen, to the group, only one, the one and only you. Each one hears this proposition as if it were addressed personally (the power of hailing, of interpellation, the shifter of identity). Only one. The lucky one, or the chosen one. The rest serve as sacrifices in a Darwinian proof.

These are instructions for felt emblems: to take in the event as a figure of speech, the way an actor forms a psychological gesture to inform a scene of words with spirit and life. It may not be this event in particular, it may not be a disaster at all, but such is the breath of meaning, carrying the movement of thought between particular and general through the popcycle of discourses. The event becomes a scene and moves from public history to private image in me (and back). The unconscious in me is outside, and the EmerAgency's task is to make those operations legible so that they may be included in policy formation. Mr. Creepy fits the type of the mass murderer—a white male loner without hope. Without hope as well as wish or why. Should all tokens of this type be rounded up, *in advance,* in order to be safe (as in the film *Minority Report*)? The difference between Hamilton and me is that I am able to adopt his action as a metaphor: his action, too, is an image of that feeling (the superego, the agency of ethics). If you think Mr. Creepy is havoc, you should meet my superego, my internal Rushmore.

Afterward it all lends itself to a diagram. The experts, the police of knowledge, know exactly the path traced by the monster, in retrospect. We may answer all the journalists' questions save one: who, what, when, where, how are fully documented. If these were vowels we would say, "and sometimes Y"; but never why. Instead, the path becomes legend, from which the wish departs to face into time. Look upstream when you stare into the rushing river; otherwise you might get dizzy and jump in. Does history, like rivers, flow in only one direction (the entropic arrow)? Or is the messianic jump just another Dunblane of why? Another 9 mm state of affairs from his cold dead hand. The proposition of hopelessness. Vertigo, becoming disoriented, not telling past from future, or *Glock* from *Glockenspiel;* turning around, moving through, tracing a path, visiting a site, honoring a memory, sending a postcard, touched from a distance, acting as if, making a gesture, gathering the rosebuds. Always living on December 6, 1941, or September 10, 2001; always surprised by the totally familiar. Afterward reforming the agency, again.

Longing

In electracy will the tourist virtually replace the journalist? The Y gives this figure to contemplate—the newspaper, the magazine, TV, CNN, containing an inventory of modern death. All the old ways of passing on are included, even if carried out by unheard-of tools: Islamic terrorists, genocide in Serbia, homicides motivated by all the known passions, accidents domestic and foreign, natural causes, acts of God, setting the actuarial tables turning. This detour began as a meditation on the obituary of a murder victim, my friend Bob Long. I invoked the mystery of his loss as a new departure in my study of mood—"longing," for example—atmosphere as a structure of thought. Yearning, *Heimweh, saudade* (Brazil), *nostalghia* (Russia), *wabi-sabi* (Japan), *mufarse* (Argentina), *han* (Korea), blues (USA). We live in a time of "total assassination," following from "total war," the term used to describe the extension of warfare to noncombatants. And yet, statistically, there is less crime now than before.

Bob Long was a mathematician interested in philosophy in general, and in Heidegger specifically. Let why = Y, in order to generalize to the event as such. Let his unsolved murder be the event (*Ereignis* in Heidegger). I thought of the Y as a shape, as upsilon—the Greek "i." This Greek "i" could look in several directions. In Greek all initial upsilons were preceded by an "h" sound, or "rough breathing." When Greek terms beginning in Y are anglicized, the "h" is added (HYPERmedia). The H has been waiting before the Y to be noticed once again. The H is the "ladder of writing." In Helene Cixous's poetics, the H is a composite of two "i" letters, I and I, representing the situation of I-I autocommunication, as distinct from I-S/He intercommunication. The MEmorial is self-addressed, first of all, in the middle voice; the action is reflexive, extended through a networked environment to become a group subject.

"To begin (writing, living) we must have death . . . but young, present, ferocious, fresh death, the death of the day, today's death," writes Cixous. Returning to the stacks haunted by the ghost of Long, librarian of Heidegger's Nietzsche volumes, I stood in that pose familiar to all scholars: body parallel to the shelves, head cocked at an angle to read the titles on the spines of the volumes, row upon row (the neck brace I will one day need for the hours passed in this stance should be covered by workman's compensation). Whatever caught my attention would be a statement from this spirit—that was my way of consulting the spirit (divining). The spine that stopped in my Greek eye said, "the mystical element in Heidegger's thought." Upon opening to the title page and seeing the author's name—John D. Caputo—I realized that I had read this book before (copyright 1978). It is a study of the relationship of Heidegger to Meister Eckhart, especially as mediated through the mystical poetry of Angelus Silesius, whose poem Heidegger took as a touchstone for his study of Being. "The rose is without why; it blooms because it blooms / It cares not for itself; asks not if it is seen."

"Warumverbot"

That the rose is without why does not depend on Heidegger's authority. This phrase presented itself before, but I was not prepared to receive it. For the mystic rose the wish is as useless as the why, since the instruction is to let go of the self altogether. Releasement. As Caputo explained, Heidegger turned to the mystic rose as a counterpoint to Leibniz's principle of sufficient reason—itself a stand-in for the entire tradition of method and science in the West. "We have not yet begun to think." It means that in the West reason became captured, enframed, entirely within this history of method (of calculative analysis). Grammatology shows that this capture was a feature of literacy. Heidegger's drive to leap out of or step back from metaphysics figures the goal of the EmerAgency to facilitate the coming of an electrate community. It is never a question of no metaphysics, but of the metaphysics native to an apparatus. Heidegger's leap out of literacy shows the way to electracy. No use to ask Heidegger why.

How does the mystic rose that is without why contribute to a MEmorial? Caputo later challenged his uncritical reading of the mystical dimension in Heidegger with several books exploring an ethics of abjection that does not forget the Jews (or the jews, in Lyotard's generalization of this status) in the way that Heidegger did. The worthy feature concerns the function of the rose from Eckhart through Silesius to Heidegger as a vehicle of poetic reason. Choragraphy may learn something from Heidegger without excluding calculation. Rather, grammatology suggests something more syncretic and less oppositional or dialectical, something part calculative and part lyrical. The mystic and the poet reasoned about the soul by means of the rose, the rose as image, as figure of thought. These incidents of total assassination are this rose too, being also without why, even if they do not bloom unseen. Further, they speak of contemporary spirit, revealing something of the violence that is required for a modern person to relinquish the self. These apparitions of resentment show me what it will take to "die unto myself," to become detached, to give up the will and become open to the event of Being.

The mystic assassination asked if it was seen. The modern feeling has been:

not to be seen is not to exist. Mr. Creepy had a global conversation, whose import was an electronic version of the pyramids in Egypt speaking of immortality. Once the ancient theoria produced the official account of an event, no other version could be uttered on pain of death. This power of theoria to control discourse has expanded in the information age to encompass identity itself. It was forbidden to utter the name of Herostratus (the man who burned the temple at Ephesus in order to acquire the eternity of fame) on pain of death. And yet we know his name. No version of existence other than the one represented is permitted, and that version now is celebrity. Grammatology shows theoretically that selfhood was the form of identity experience in the apparatus of literacy. Collectively and individually will people entering electracy die to themselves as self, let go, let things be, detach from the ideology of individualism, in behaviors that have yet to be invented, or that may be glimpsed in the lives (ironically) of celebrities and, collectively, in the rise and fall of corporations?

The religious (oral) letting go is a relay and not a model for the electrate after-self. Releasement does not conflict with empirical matters; I may still advocate gun control, for example, and continue to be involved with practice, with applied grammatology, with prudence and amelioration. The basic act of MEmorializing is: *accept an event—any event that I recognize (that looks at me)—as the vehicle in a figure whose tenor is soul, subject, spirit. Explore the properties of psyche by means of the inventory of attributes—accidents—available in the vehicle. Learn everything about this event as a provisional container that permits the feeling of Being to come into awareness. Compare these attributes with those produced by others online. Negotiate. Are we enraged today? Is this the spirit of America?*

Upsilon Alarm

As John Caputo observed, on good authority, the best monument is a name and a date, such as JFK, November 22, 1963 (1993, 72). This is also the formula for an abstract machine. The EmerAgency sponsors the creation of MEmorials with their affiliated peripherals and Web site testimonials. I will interrupt this meditation on Y to propose a peripheral for abused children, to acknowledge their suffering and death as a sacrifice on behalf of an abject formless value fundamental to our national behavior, if not to our ideals (the sacredness of the family unit). "The existential question of self-identity is bound up with the fragile nature of the biography which the individual supplies about herself," states Anthony Giddens, in an account that may be extended to collective identity as well. "A person's [nation's] identity is not to be found in behavior, nor—important though this is—in the reactions of others, but in the capacity to keep a particular narrative going" (1991, 54). Giddens may be right about individuals, but the identity of collectivities and groups is found precisely in behavior, or at least that is where to find values that do not speak their name (abject, formless). Benedict Anderson's reminder that a nation is an "imagined community"—an idea—is a clue to how an image overcomes the limits of story: America is an idea as *eidos,* shape. What kind of shape are we in?

A recent column in the newspaper, addressing the case in which a six-year-old boy brought a handgun to class and shot a classmate to death, inventories the persistence of behaviors in our society, many of which apply also to child abuse in general.

> It takes a village to kill a child. It takes a mother who is so strung out on drugs that she abandons her children in a crack house. It takes a father who is married to one woman and "engaged" to another, who has been sued for child support by three women he has never married, and who spends his time in jail rather than with any of his six children. . . .
>
> It takes lawyers and judges who spend their careers extending this procedural due process to every facet of American life in an effort to ensure that individual rights will always and everywhere triumph over the interests of the community. It takes a certain faith in the peculiarly American delusion that legal rights can be adequate substitutes for decent parents, decent schools, decent jobs and decent neighborhoods. It takes a government that registers cars and dogs, and that requires you to get a permit to build a fence in your back yard, but that will not register handguns. It takes an entertainment industry that murders dozens of characters on television every night, and then wonders why our children turn violent fantasies into newspaper headlines. It takes a culture that treats the right to bear children as sacred and inviolate, and then allows utterly unprepared teen-age girls to raise their children without any interference (translation: help) from the so-called community. It takes large doses of that brutal indifference to others we call "tolerance." . . .
>
> It is an electronic village, connected by technologies that make what happened in a first-grade classroom in Michigan part of our lives almost instantly. But the connection is a slender one: After the initial moment of shock, it's just another story on the evening news. The next morning we read the newspaper's account of this almost unimaginable atrocity in our midst—this act that in some sense connects and implicates us all—and then we turn the page. (Paul Compos, *Gainesville Sun,* March 8, 2000)

Compos concludes his column by citing the poem by John Donne whose closing line is "and therefore never send to know for whom the bell tolls; it tolls for thee." Here is my testimony, bearing witness to the sacrifice. *I benefit from the circumstances that make possible the murder of Bradley McGee.* I am a parent; a father of two sons. My right to have children and raise them in my own way was paid for by Bradley McGee (and all the others). Compos has named it: "it takes a culture that treats the right to bear children as sacred and inviolate." That is a value in our behavior important enough apparently to survive a regular recurrence of murdered children (how many? which ones?). Bradley McGee's mother, released from prison for good behavior, remarried and had another child. To each her own. Such is our lifeworld, our zone of indistinction. Recently the worth of a human life, for purposes of cost-benefit analysis, was set at $3 million.

Chora Mirror

The rule of a MEmorial is that my peripheral for abused children must be attached to an extant memorial for acknowledged sacrifice, so that the juxtaposition establishes the public and collective nature of the abject sacrifice. In this case the peripheral is attached to the Space Mirror, the Astronaut Memorial at Kennedy Space Center, Florida. Would Bradley not have wanted to be an astronaut, at some point in his development, had he lived past the age of two? There are fourteen names engraved in the black granite, "42.5 feet high and 50 feet wide, polished to a reflective finish, mounted on a platform that rotates and tilts. As the Earth turns, so does the slab, keeping its back to the sun; the names of the astronauts are carved through the stone so that the letters glow with sunlight, floating in a dark field of reflected sky and clouds" (Adler 1991, 69). Add to these names seven more, the crew of the space shuttle *Columbia*.

The peripheral or add-on feature, associating the death of Bradley McGee with that of Virgil "Gus" Grissom, Christa McAuliffe, and the other heroes, consists of an electronic panel substituted for just one of the ninety-three granite panels of the memorial (the ninety-three panels provide a troubling amount of room for future names, Adler points out). The panel is activated only during an eclipse of the sun, and flashes (one name each second) as many names of children who died from abuse as may fit into the duration of the eclipse while the heroes' names are invisible. This MEmorial is called Upsilon Alarm. How does a MEmorial affect public policy? The egents are motivated to focus attention on the details of the conditions sustaining the abuse by the promise of divination: the problem explains the consultant (the inquiry is conducted in the middle voice). The slogan is: Problems B Us. As in divination, I bring a burning personal question to the inquiry and pose it to the public issue. A side effect is the exposure to public attention of a situation, the configuration of the lifeworld sustained by this sacrifice (regardless of what my personal dilemma might have been).

As an egent I document the record of child abuse in order to understand what it feels like to have internalized the values of my community and passed them on to my sons, a relationship mediated by law. The scene of the disaster opens onto a parable. What is the experience of having the ghost in me *(psyche)*, the superego? In me, in my home, I am three (host, guest, parasite). What is the feeling of attunement? I make an impresa to capture it. It is like having a furious monster use a child as a toilet plunger to dash out his brains on the porcelain of duty. Here is an emblem. Furious. Monster. Child. Toilet. Duty. An engraving by Goya (caprices of war). *Baptism? I will show you "baptism."* Do you have experience of this? What is the spirit of the age (the public mood)? Choler? Rage? In this hybrid humor our bile is yellow, not black; not phlegm. We are not melancholy, not sanguine, we intellectuals, we netizens. In the vocabulary of Vodou, which lwa possess us? Not Rada (the cool divinities, sweet-natured, water loving) but Petwo (angry, bitter, fire-eating). This mood is not in me, I am (we are) in it—which is how an image becomes categorical. I am testifying, not arguing. We are angry now and don't know: Y.

The Upsilon Alarm peripheral is linked to the Florida Rushmore holographic projections. Burson's composites of missing children, originally published on milk cartons, are interpolated into the fifteen-minute cycle of citizen mystories. Every so often the image dissolves and a voice offers, "your face here." Replays of the projections are available in malls, in kiosk-sized milk cartons. In their visit to Florida (virtual or actual) citizens learn that the idea of America cannot be taken for "granite" (not igneous, however ingenious), but limestone, soluble in water, and with the rains becoming more acidic every year. Atlantis, Ubar, Xanadu, the United States of America: such is the composite diegesis, or perhaps a logical sequence of the virtual nation, illuminated by Florida Rushmore. The MEmorial shows us not our fate, but our situation. The Internet is a *living monument.* The EmerAgency offers a practice for a virtual civic sphere that does for the imagination what statistics does for the intellect. If we do not like what we see in the choral mirror, what are we going to do about it?

PART IV

SOFT JUSTICE

If virtue by chance led to fortune, I should have been as
virtuous—or virtuous-seeming—as the next man.
—*Denis Diderot,* Rameau's Nephew

7

Justice Miranda
(A Conceit)

Making Up the Turing Test

If in tragedy *ATH* appeared in the conflict between justice and law *(Antigone)*, what happens in consulting? Since the first literate concept, according to Eric Havelock, was justice, it might be useful to supplement this literate category with an electrate concetto. Egents, in any case, being consultants without port-folios, may help negotiate the passage between justice and law. The combination and collaboration of family and career discourses in one of the defining icons in the history of computing—the Turing test—provide a point of departure for exploring the method of EmerAgency testimonial given in policy disputes. The peculiar features of the Turing test allow us to extend the transversal series traced in previous chapters around the border question ("what am I, man or woman?") into this generation of an emblem of image measure.

The convergence of logic with technology that produced the computer is one of those happy moments in the history of invention. The insight that linked

Figure 8. Carmen Miranda.

the truth table with an electrical switch is to our time what the conjunction of the theology of God as light with the invention of the pointed arch was to the Gothic period (recognized by the Abbot Suger and realized in Chartres Cathedral). In the context of deconsulting, interest in exploiting the creative potential of transversality (finding new connections across different strata of culture and society), the point to keep in mind is the one Raymond Kurzweil makes, tracing the background of this insight from Bertrand Russell's solution to the paradox of the set that is/not a member of itself to the Turing machine. "The Turing machine can execute any plan to solve a cognitive problem. Its success in doing so will be a function of the validity of the plan. We thus come to the same conclusion that we did with the sea of logic. The Turing machine provides us with a simple and elegant model for the hardware of cybernetic (machine-based) cognition, but not the software. To solve a practical problem the Turing machine needs a program, and each different program constitutes a different Turing machine" (1992, 123). Here is an insight into the invention process—the open relationship between hardware and software. The truth table with its technological embodiment in the computer is the culmination of the history of analytical (literate) thinking from Plato to Turing. The Turing test is a point of transition from literacy into electracy.

To demonstrate the image logic (reasoneon) needed for a MEmorial, I will perform a remake, an improvisation (meditation) on the Turing test. This improvisation continues the exploration of virtual identity, the electrate transbordered subject, to suggest that the Turing test models an abstract machine that organizes not just the technology of the electrate apparatus, but the institutional practice and identity formation as well. The transversal mapped in chapter 4 from the transsexual Ms. Gordon into the designer avatars of cyberspace is continued here, following a line of flight leaving in its wake the evocation of a miranda (justice) concetto. What follows is an exploration of iconic writing.

Imitation Game

The uncanny point at which the anecdote of life and the aphorism of thought intersect in Turing's mystory is the famous imitation game he proposed as a thought experiment (although some have taken it literally) to test whether or not a machine could be considered intelligent. The game is a kind of dialogue. "First he described a parlor game of sorts, the imitation game, to be played by a man, a woman, and a judge. The man and woman are hidden from the judge's view but are able to communicate with the judge by teletype; the judge's task is to guess, after a period of questioning each contestant, which interlocutor is the man and which the woman. The man tries to convince the judge he is the woman, and the woman tries to convince the judge of the truth. . . . Now suppose, Turing said, we replace the man or woman with a computer and give the judge the task of determining which is the human being and which is the computer" (Daniel Dennett, in Kurzweil 1992, 48).

The transversal nature of the Turing test is sometimes forgotten—the imitation game, with its origins in family discourse (a parlor game), passing into specialized knowledge (career, discipline) and entertainment (beginning with a televised interview). "If a person failed to distinguish between a man imitating a woman (via teletype) and a computer imitating a man imitating a woman, then the machine succeeded in the Imitation Game" (Schank 1986, 1–2). He imagined a game in which an interrogator would have to decide on the basis of written replies alone which of two people in another room was a man and which a woman. In the BBC television program on the topic of intelligent machines, featuring Alan Turing, most of the questions were couched in the form of "gags," as Turing explained in a letter to his mother. What kind of questions could be asked of the machine? "'Anything,' said Alan, 'and the questions don't really have to be questions, any more than the questions in a law court are really questions. You know the sort of thing, "I put it to you that you are only pretending to be a man," would be quite in order'" (Hodges 1983, 450). For our purposes, to extend the relay and generalize its lesson for the EmerAgency, we will consider the test generalizable to all borders and boundaries.

Advertising Emblems

If the work of philosophy was to invent concepts, the work of choragraphy is to invent concetti (or, to use our vocabulary, to de$ign a MEmorial involves reasoneon about disaster and loss by means of image conceits—Deleuze's neo-baroque impresa). Egents may learn from advertisers everything there is to know about updating the emblem tradition. An emblem for conductive inference was provided by an advertisement that Digital Corporation placed in the *Chronicle of Higher Education*, "announcing a painless way to get the information you need." This ad is typical in its emblematic form, so that part of our interest in it is to learn how to compose emblems ourselves, as part of a consultation. It is a meta-emblem, whose unpacking constitutes a theory of image reason. In addition to this announcement, the ad consisted of a slogan ("Digital, The Open Advantage") and a still from a hard-boiled detective film (film noir) showing three men giving a fourth man what is known as the third degree (an idiom that resonates nicely with its antithesis, Barthes's third meaning). Above the picture is a commentary describing Digital Corporation, punctuated by the company logo. Let's say that the information I need concerns precisely the question of electracy itself (the ad promises that it knows something about this question). I attempt to fill the inferential gap created by the ad between "computing" and "the third degree," testing the premise that advertising is one of the practices most committed to inventing the discourse of electracy.

What is the inferential logic assumed by this ad? The method has been stated by Richard Foreman, "How to write a play (in which i [*sic*] am really telling myself how, but if you are the right one i am telling you how, too)":

> Make a kind of beauty that isn't an *alternative* to a certain environment
> (beauty, adventure, romance, dream, drama all take you out of your real world
> and into their own in the hope you'll return refreshed, wiser, more compas-
> sionate, etc.) but rather make *gaps* in the non-beautiful, or look carefully at the
> structure of the non-beautiful, whatever it is (and remember that structure is
> always a combination of the *thing* and the *perceiving* of it) and see where there
> are small points, gaps, unarticulated or un-mapped places within it (the non-
> beautiful) which un-mapped places must be the very places where beauty *can*
> be planted (Foreman 1976, 84; italics in original).

Almost any ad will do for the experiment, to give us the experience of rea-soning with memory rather than logic (or a logic of memory) as a way to extract the image from its handmaidens (pornography and propaganda). The task is to fill in the gaps, constructing the two series evoked by the juxtaposed semantic fields. The assignment is to find the point of conduction (electrate inference) where the two series cross. Such is the operation of transversality, evoking an emergent simulacrum from an image series. What distinguishes this procedure is not the gap filling, since interrogation also has been described as a gap or hole opened by a question that is then filled by an answer. What is new in the ad is that the inference is a work of images rather than concepts, of associated signifiers rather than arguments. We need some practice with filling gaps between unrelated images, a process that reveals the psychogeography of our cognitive maps, or the path of a flash of spirit through the popcycle network. Egents must reason at light speed, if they are to consult on the general accident.

"It is true that a language is a code which pairs phonetic and semantic representations of sentences. However, there is a gap between the semantic representations of sentences and the thoughts actually communicated by utterances. This gap is filled not by more coding, but by inference" (Sperber and Wilson 1986, 9). Inference does not communicate messages, it orients me in a certain direction by means of evocation. To the deduction and induction of the natural sciences, and the abduction of the cultural sciences, electracy adds conduction, bringing together writing and intuition (including the unconscious). There is no central processor, no fixed set of rules, but a distributed memory, a memory triggered by a cue that spreads through the encyclopedia, the library, the database (connectionism suggests that the hardware itself should be designed to support the spread of memory through an associational network). Conduction is connectionist. We are learning to compose or design (de$ign) with this remembering, moving outside the living body, working a prosthesis, producing the subject experience of electracy that has been called terminal identity (punning on "terminal"), both the end of selfhood as identity and a new cyborg experience of the spectacle in which the border between me and technology begins to blur (Bukatman 1993). In short, the circuit of autocommunication is what electracy adds to literate science.

ASSIGNMENT

Take Foreman's poetic device and translate it into a practical procedure for a mystory, applied to some features of the career and family quarters of the popcycle. Use the procedure as a means to connect any selection of documents from the two discourses.

- Try the exercise first with any ad: locate the gap that it opens and invites you to fill with your cultural literacy or imagination. Then try

to do what Foreman suggests and open a gap yourself in the information you have gathered so far, where one does not already exist.
- The "non-beautiful" may refer simply to any aspect of the world
  not codified by art or aesthetic norms.
- The ad does in an electrate way what interrogative question-and-
  answer does in literacy: opens a gap in signification that may
  produce knowledge.

Justice

While an obtuse meaning is based on a personal memory, the initial feeling produced by the sting of the news story (taking a call from Bradley McGee) may
be named "justice" or perhaps "injustice." The discipline context for the feeling
is Eric Havelock's study of the invention of conceptual thinking by the Greeks.
Analytical thinking in general, and philosophy in particular, emerged in the evolution of thinking about a specific experience and condition—justice—within
the new alphabetic apparatus. Justice was the first concept, the first practice to
pass from the oral mode of representation (dramatized as an event, performed as
the actions of a hero) to a literate mode (abstract definition couched in a logical
syntax). This transformation is one of the touchstones of electracy (repeatedly
invoked), marking a gap that must be filled with the image equivalent of concepts as such and of justice in particular. We may still use the concept of justice
in the EmerAgency, but if we are to intervene in the impasses of 9/11 and beyond,
we must also have access to the new kind of category formation becoming available through imaging.

> Hesiod weaves together the two justices of the *Iliad* and *Odyssey* to compose
> his own story of justice. He does it by making "dike" and "hubris," instead
> of Agamemnon and Achilles and Odysseus, the subjects and objects of his
> discourse. Whereas it would be an easy matter for oral memory to recollect
> what Agamemnon or Achilles did or what happened to them . . . the names
> of "dike" and "hubris" and related terms were buried deep in the oral matrix.
> To rely on oral memory not only to recollect but to collect what happened to
> them would be beyond existing capacity. But place the language of the story
> visibly before the eye, so that the flow is arrestible and the words become
> fixed shapes, and the process of selection and collection can begin. (Havelock
> 1978, 228)

Hesiod discovered in the epics a "field" of meaning that he called "dike."
"The Greek 'dike' and its correlatives perform a diversity of symbolic functions,
which Hesiod is endeavoring to assemble into his 'field of meaning.' The field

had to be prepared for the later growth of a conceptual tree, to the definition and description of which Plato was to devote his most famous treatise" (231). Hesiod built "his own semi-connected discourse out of disconnected bits and pieces contained in oral discourse, either some pieces in which the term 'dike' happened for whatever reason to occur, or others in which incidents occurred that he felt were appropriate to connect with the word. His decision is compositional (rather than ideological), or perhaps we should say re-compositional" (102).

An important link between Hesiod and Plato is Solon, whose law code is more abstract than Hesiod's poetry, but which still treated only the specifics of legal situations. "Solon can earn the title, as far as the record goes, of the first statesman on the European scene, through his program of impartial protection for rich and poor, noble and commoner, powerful and powerless. He describes in a famous passage how he 'stood with my strong shield cast round both parties'" (254–55). The unifying move by Solon—justice as due process protection for all—is completed by Plato, with the invention of conceptual thinking, moving away from dramatization of an event fully into the creation of an abstract topic, in which narrative turns into logic, persons into generalized entities or classes with properties and attributes, in which "to do" is replaced by "to be."

From Topos to Chora

Our goal is to continue this evolution by shifting from topic to chora, just as Plato moved from hero to topic. The experiment involves three registers, following the example of Hesiod. In the same way that alphabetic literacy made conceptual thinking possible, electracy requires another means for arranging diverse particulars into classes, sets, and categories. The new arrangement has to be invented out of the old one, involving a new form and a new style of reasoning. The process of invention cannot occur in general but, as in the passage from the oral to the alphabetic, must evolve in terms of a specific action and topic. Choral thinking, that is, involves learning how an image gathers unrelated items into a meaningful set. A choral category works not with things and attributes but with events.

> Events are produced in a chaos, in a chaotic multiplicity but only under
> the condition that a sort of screen intervenes. Chaos does not exist, it is an
> abstraction because it is inseparable from a screen that makes something—
> something rather than nothing—emerge from it. . . . How can the Many
> become the One? A great screen has to be placed in between them. Like
> a formless elastic membrane, an electromagnetic field, or the receptable of
> the *Timaeus,* the screen makes something issue from chaos, and *even if this
> something differs only slightly* . . . If chaos does not exist, it is because it is

merely the bottom side of the great screen, and because the latter composes infinite series of wholes and parts, which appear chaotic to us (as aleatory developments) only because we are incapable of following them or because of the insufficiency of our own screens. (Deleuze 1993, 76–77; italics in original)

Plato's name for this receptacle/screen was "chora." Just as oral categories (totems) were incapable of noticing contradictions (as Socrates demonstrated), literate categories (concepts) are not able to capture the misty dust of the micro-perceptions that converge in an event. "'There are countless inconspicuous perceptions, which do not stand out enough for one to be aware of or to re-member them.' We have to understand literally—that is, mathematically—that a conscious perception is produced when at least two heterogeneous parts enter into a differential relation that determines a singularity" (Deleuze 1993, 88). What is justice as a singularity? A chora gathers information at the level of images by means of the repetition of signifiers. The accumulation of signifiers expresses a mood. I am exploring the mood of justice, then, in a sense to be un-folded through a series of perceptions. Perhaps it is not so much the invention of justice itself that concerns me, but through it the invention of philosophy, of conceptual thinking, of the form of the treatise, composed of propositions, arguments, definitions, and proofs, arranged in a logical syntax (the discourse of disciplinary learning). What needs to be invented for electracy is not only a thought adequate to the continuing demands of injustice, but an electrate state of mind equivalent to the skepticism that informed the classic stand of philoso-phy. The analogy is: a choral mood is to a conceptual definition what Hesiod's "dike" is to Homer's heroes. "Justice" is the name of an alphabetic category that is as inadequate for the operations of electracy as "Achilles" was for alpha-betic reasoning. In the same way that "dike" replaced "Agamemnon" in Hesiod, so must (something) replace "justice" in chorography. The concept remains in play in chora, folded within a concetto. Leibniz summarized this hybrid as a triad, "scenographies, definitions, points of view" (Deleuze 1993, 126). The con-ceptual practice of definition now serves as the *inscriptio* for an impresa. In a MEmorial all three instances work together: narrative action, conceptual argu-ment, choral image. The sign becomes $ign: concetto. How to fill in the blank of this proportional figure?

A Social Machine

In *Mind over Machine* Stuart Dreyfus explained why he trusted his feelings about how to buy a new car, rather than an algorithm, a "formal car replace-ment model": "hunches and intuitions, and even systematic illusions, are the very core of expert decision-making" (Dreyfus and Dreyfus 1986, 10). It is the "commonsense-knowledge problem." "For a network to be intelligent it must be able to generalize; given sufficient examples of inputs associated with one particular output, it should associate further inputs of the same type with that same output. The question arises, however: What counts as the same type? . . . (All the 'continue this sequence' questions found on intelligence tests really have more than one possible answer, but most humans share a sense of what is simple and reasonable and therefore acceptable)" (xiii). The issue, the challenge to artificial intelligence (AI), and for the EmerAgency as well, with its plan to extend public education into an Internet consultancy, is how to simulate expertise, the way experts, "after years of experience, are able to respond intuitively to situations in a way that defies logic and surprises and awes even the experts themselves" (xiv). The MEmorial testimony is a "continue the sequence" heuristic that draws an outline connecting individual "stupidity" with collective disaster *(ATH)*.

The Digital ad (designed as an information gap) invites me to "continue this sequence." My experiment is to rely on the quotidian intuitive understanding evoked by the ad, to put that quotidian intuition into this prosthesis, and to *write* a disciplinary intuition (a conductive inference). I can do it on paper or on screen (it is a style of reasoning capable of integrating the cognition of all three apparatuses: oral, print, electronic). Stuart Dreyfus did not trust the decision-making algorithm proposed by computer engineers. The problem is that the intuitive judgments he fell back on are equally limited in their own way, as untrustworthy and confining as the decision trees used in expert programs. As Seymour Papert noted in his own efforts to join intuitive to formal practices in his invention of "Turtle Geometry," we need to go beyond the opposition between knowing-how and knowing-that by learning how to "debug" our intuitions (Papert 1980, 144).

In grammatological terms, the opposition between rule-driven symbolic processing and intuition guided by cultural experience is the opposition between literate conceptuality and oral custom described by Havelock in his study of justice. The Dreyfi want a cooperative relationship between analysis and intuition (in grammatological terms, between literacy and orality). And what makes such an "oralysis" possible is precisely the electronic dimension, whose cognitive style (dreamwork forming compromises between primary and secondary process thought) may be grasped by analogy with psychoanalysis. In any case, what Freud was trying to show about the psyche with all his variety of models, all the optical devices, magic slates, and the like (a device able to combine multiple inputs into one system) is readily displayed in the computer (Erdelyi 1985, 124). "Intuition must not be confused with irrational conformity," the Dreyfi note, "the reenactment of childhood trauma, and all the other unconscious and noninferential means by which human beings come to decisions. Those all resist explanation in terms of facts and inferences" (Dreyfus and Dreyfus 1986, 29). This same rejection and suppression (repression) of psychoanalysis may be found in Lakoff and Johnson's *Philosophy in the Flesh*. They might as well have said that unconscious matters resist explanation in terms of literacy. An assumption of electracy is that the Internet is a prosthesis of the unconscious mind, which is what makes it functional as an "inhabitable monument" for a group subject.

The Dreyfi do not deny that part of judgment involves the unconscious, but only that they cannot talk about that part. The task and opportunity of electracy is to learn how to teach dreamwork (giving citizens access to the premises of their judgments) by bringing the previous two cognitive apparatuses into a cooperative relationship—hence this experiment in moving through the popcycle, learning how to write an intuition, that is, how to bring the different discourses of the popcycle into contact with one another for purposes of mutual support and correction through a transversal movement.

Do You Want to Dance?

The Dreyfi propose that intuition writing be thought of as a knowing-how rather than as a knowing-that, in the style of acquiring a skill rather than of solving a problem, a proposal that provides a useful point of departure for electrate deconsulting. "No evidence suggests that we recognize whole situations by applying rules relating salient elements. A boxer seems to begin an attack not by combining by rule various facts about his body position and that of his opponent, but when the whole visual scene in front of him and sensations within him trigger behavior which was successful in an earlier similar situation. We call the ability to intuitively respond to patterns without decomposing them into component features 'holistic discrimination and association'" (Dreyfus and Dreyfus 1986, 28). To write an intuition (involving a hybrid of concept and habit formation) is not to recognize a pattern but to make one. And this pattern formation functions in choragraphy the way concepts functioned in literacy, determining how particulars are gathered into sets for classification and categorization. I will write the pattern that might evoke the thought of justice emerging in electracy, but the experiment could be conducted in terms of any other concept as well. The point, however, is not to adapt concepts to electracy, but to discover the categories native to the new apparatus.

My project to continue the sequence suggested by the Digital ad (in order to remake the Turing test as a concetto) begins by adopting a particular skill as a relay for my pattern. The practice I adopt (and adapt to writing) is not one of those noted by the Dreyfi (riding a bicycle, driving a car, boxing), but by Victor Papert, since his idea extends the promise of the Digital ad from painless acqui-

sition of information to painless education. "I believe that the computer presence will enable us to so modify the learning environment outside the class-
rooms that much if not all the knowledge schools presently try to teach with
such pain and expense and such limited success will be learned, as the child
learns to talk, painlessly, successfully, and without organized instruction. This
obviously implies that schools as we know them today will have no place in the
future" (Papert 1980, 9). The pedagogy of *Mindstorms* is to create a connection
"between personal activity and the creation of formal knowledge" (59), or, in
terms of the popcycle, between the discourses of the family and of entertainment
on the personal (private) side, and school and discipline on the formal (public)
side. "Our strategy is to make visible even to children the fact that learning a
physical skill has much in common with building a scientific theory" (96); to
learn "to transfer habits of exploration from personal lives to the formal domain
of scientific theory construction" (117). Here is a lesson in how to undertake
transversal mapping. The path between the personal and political, between the
private and the collective, passes through the discourses of the popcycle. We are
building this path as we go (mystory).

One of the analogies Papert suggests for this transfer is that of dance.
Learning a new dance step (working with a process—dancing—that is already
familiar to most people in the culture), may then be mapped onto the unfamiliar (the disciplinary material). "The educator as anthropologist must work to
understand which cultural materials are relevant to intellectual development.
Then he or she needs to understand which trends are taking place in the culture.
Meaningful intervention must take the form of working with these trends" (32).
The discipline problem for the EmerAgency is how to educate online, how to be
electrate, which constitutes the unknown in my experiment. An egent's task is
to find an ongoing trend that may be brought into an explanatory relationship
with this unknown. Papert provides an insight into a possible pedagogy:

> Juggling and writing an essay seem to have little in common if one looks at
> the "product." But the processes of learning both skills have much in com-
> mon. By creating an intellectual environment in which the emphasis is on
> process we give people with different skills and interests something to talk
> about. By developing expressive languages for talking about process and by
> recasting old knowledge in these new languages we can hope to make trans-
> parent the barriers separating disciplines. In the schools math is math and
> history is history and juggling is outside the intellectual pale. Time will tell
> whether schools can adapt themselves. What is more important is under-
> standing the recasting of knowledge into new forms. (184)

Papert offers an analogy for the new school institution that is the next step in
the series coordinating the passage from the old paradigm of inquiry (represented

in the ad as a still from a hard-boiled film narrative depicting an interrogation using the method of the third degree) to the new, whose nature is in no way indicated other than to suggest that it is electronic and painless. The analogy for electronic schooling is the Brazilian samba school. "At the core of the famous carnival in Rio de Janeiro is a twelve-hour-long procession of song, dance, and street theater. One troop of players after another presents its piece. Usually the piece is a dramatization through music and dance of a historical event or folk tale" (178). Each troop represents a "social club" that may have thousands of members of all ages and skills, who work together as a kind of community during the year preparing for carnival. "In this book we have considered how mathematics might be learned in settings that resemble the Brazilian samba school, in settings that are real, socially cohesive, and where experts and novices are all learning" (179).

Is choragraphy like dancing the samba? The methodology of an inferential series is to use the semantic domain of the samba as one half of a figure, whose other half must come from the other domain of the ad, in order to produce a field within which to evoke the emerging image category of justice. The transversal has started, the memory is spreading, beginning with the domain of computing, passing through the Dreyfi to Papert, to the analogy of the samba. Conduction is a serial form of inference, whose logic has been described by Gilles Deleuze: "First, the terms of each series are in perpetual relative displacement in relation to those of the other. . . . Second, this disequilibrium must itself be oriented: one of the two series—the one determined as signifying, presents an excess over the other" (1990, 40). Finally, the most important feature is the existence of a paradoxical case shared by both series without being reducible to either one:

> What are the characteristics of this paradoxical entity? It circulates without end in both series and, for this reason, assures their communication. It is a two-sided entity, equally present in the signifying and the signified series. It is the mirror. Thus, it is at once word and thing, name and object, sense and denotatus, expression and designation. It guarantees, therefore, the convergence of the two series which it traverses, but precisely on the condition that it makes them endlessly diverge. . . . As Lacan says, it fails to observe its place. It also fails to observe its own identity, resemblance, equilibrium, and origin. . . . They are strictly simultaneous in relation to the entity by means of which they communicate. They are simultaneous without ever being equal, since the entity has two sides, one of which is always absent from the other. . . . For that which is in excess in the case is nothing but an extremely mobile empty place; and that which is lacking in another case is a rapidly moving object, an occupant without a place, always supernumerary and displaced. (41)

Method Steps

I have two metaphors now, two scenarios, two series producing a gap: In the scenario of literacy, finding out something, doing research, learning the truth, is like giving someone the third degree (putting him or her in the hot seat). In the electrate scenario, learning the truth is like dancing the samba during carnival. But the latter scenario as a means of formal cognition is new, untested, while the former has a history going back several millennia. Even if the product is different, the process of constructing the new scenario might be the same, might follow the same laws of formation as its predecessor, whose nature is worth reviewing.

Page duBois wrote a history of the metaphor of interrogation associating torture with the search for truth in the alphabetic apparatus. Her focus is the Greek term *basanos*. "It means first of all the touchstone used to test gold for purity; the Greeks extended its meaning to denote a test or trial to determine whether something or someone is real or genuine. It then comes to mean also inquiry by torture, 'the question'" (duBois 1991, 7). The semantic field of "basanos" spread by metaphor from the Greek legal system into philosophy, gathering a set of practices and values: of an ordeal demonstrating fidelity, of silence under torture as a virtue (Spartan hardness), of interrogation as figurative "basanizing" ("You give this slave of mine the third degree [basanize]"—*The Frogs,* Aristophanes) (30). The migration of the term into philosophy concerns the Greek idea of truth as something hidden, buried, a secret, a secret at first associated with the slave's body and then with a woman's body, as in the tradition of the Delphic Oracle, or the associations with the earth as feminine, penetrated by the heroes' visits to the underworld.

"Although all this imagery is witty and playful, as often in Plato's texts the joke has its sinister side," duBois notes, referring to *The Sophist*; "logic and dialectic are police arts. Philosophy becomes a method of arrest and discipline; philosophical argument is a dividing, a splitting, a fracturing of the logical body, a process that resembles torture" (113). In the scenes of interrogation performed in the dialogues, the violence is displaced from the body to the abstract arguments of the adversary. "Only relations of force and labor, the coercion through questioning to arrive at the truth, the pushing of the young philosopher to the realm of the metaphysical, the power of the master, can enable the achievement of truth, of the philosophical life. We have for centuries idealized this description of truth seeking. . . . But why should we construct our model of discovery as an allegory of force and pain?" (122). The photograph in the Digital ad, depicting a scene of the third degree, is a metonym for this allegory of truth. It expresses the quality of the Committees of Public Safety that inform every voice that interrogates. The fantasy of literacy is "an idea is being beaten."

The EmerAgency speaks from a different mood or atmosphere, without inter-rogation, and without certainty (it is not expert but tourist). What is this other mood? The samba feeling.

The Enigma Engine

In the same way that oral practices were carried over metaphorically into lit-eracy (truth as ordeal), so too are certain literate practices guiding electronic development. The Turing test, as adapted by computer science, falls within the field of "basanos." It is no wonder that Turing's intelligence test might oper-ate within the tradition of truth as a secret to be found out by police methods, considering his achievement as the leader of a team that cracked the code of the German Enigma machine during World War II. The Enigma machine put mes-sages into code using "electrical wirings to perform automatically a series of alphabetical substitutions" (Hodges 1983, 166). We are following a certain mys-torical pattern in Turing's life, seeking the point—the singularity—at which the anecdote of life intersects the aphorism of thought.

Turing's cryptanalysis treated the problem of decipherment as a mechaniza-tion of a detective's abductive guesses. As a process, the approach offers some lessons for the creation of a semantic field, like that constructed by Hesiod for "dike." It is a lesson in how to recognize and construct a pattern that is not clear and distinct. Since military messages often consisted of stereotyped com-mands, it was possible, using intuition (inference based on cultural literacy), to guess a specific word at its exact location in the scrambled string of letters. The goal was to discover the initial setting of the three (and later, four) rotors in the machine that scrambled the letters. The decipherment technique was to look for patterns of regularity in the message traffic. "Sometimes it would happen that first and fourth letters would actually be 'the same'—or the second and the fifth. This phenomenon was, for no apparent reason, called 'a female.' Thus supposing that TUITUI were indeed enciphered as RYNFYP, that repeated Y would be 'a female'. This fact would then give a small piece of information about the state of the rotors" (173).

Turing's biographer does not link the mystery of this naming to the way the metaphor of female was mechanized, when the work with patterns made use of perforated sheets. "These were simply tables of all the core-positions, in which instead of printing 'has a female' or 'has no female,' there would either be a hole punched, or not" (174). In short, the naming principle was the same one used to identify the plugs on electric cords as female or male, according to the absence or presence of prongs. The procedure was to pile the tables of core positions on top of each other, "staggered in a manner corresponding to the observed relative positions of the females. A 'matching' of the pattern would then show up as a place where light passed through all the sheets." The set of perforated sheets was called a "Bombe." The terminology is a symptom of the fact that the German enigma code was cracked by an intelligence that is also ideologically inflected. The Enigma engine used to encrypt the communications network of the German military is an emblem for the encrypting of the mystory within the popcycle. The mystory finds the pattern (the males and females, the holes, wounds) and reveals the code. At the same time, we have to keep in mind that the Turing test itself is on the side of interrogation, for which electracy must find an alternative. Knowing in electracy is conducted in a different mood, in both the linguistic and psychological senses, a different atmosphere, a different voice, a different stand. To think with the speed of the dromosphere requires finding a Bombe in global information.

Papert and the Dreyfi recommended adopting a practical skill as the model for constructing a theory. I have to keep in mind, however, that police interrogation is itself a skill, according to the handbooks used to teach it. Thinking of the jocular tone used for putting the question in philosophy, I was especially intrigued by one such handbook that began by quoting Groucho Marx: "There's one way to find out if a man is honest—ask him."

> It is appropriate that this book on interview and interrogation begin with a quotation from a comedian. Comedians are perceptive individuals who can see humor and truth in people, two things that sometimes are one and the same. We, as interrogators, are attempting to be as perceptive as comedians— looking for the truth in people. In the following chapters, we are going to follow Groucho Marx's advice and ask suspects whether or not they are telling the truth. The suspects' truthfulness can be evaluated by their verbal and physical behavior as well as by their attitudes toward the interrogator and the investigation. (Zulawski and Wicklander 1992, 1)

Court Appearance

The Turing imitation game also included a judge (the one who must decide which voice writes the truth). The modern art of interrogation has been drastically affected by the heirs of Solon on the Supreme Court of the United States during the activist period of Chief Justice Earl Warren. I am thinking of the famous Miranda decision, which, in our context, has as many implications for philosophers as for policemen.

> Simply described, Miranda could be said to be warnings to a suspect administered during a custodial interrogation. For Miranda to be applicable to an interrogation, it must meet two criteria. First, the setting must be custodial in nature. The court has defined custodial to mean that the suspect's freedom

of action has been curtailed in some significant way. Second, the individual conducting the interrogation must be a law enforcement officer. Should a custody situation arise, the suspect must be advised of the following: his right to an attorney, his right against self-incrimination, and his right to remain silent. If a suspect is taken into custody by police and questioned without advising him of his Miranda rights, his responses cannot be used in evidence against him to establish his guilt. (Zulawski and Wicklander 1992, 36)

This 1966 ruling was one of the most controversial ever handed down by the Court. This notoriety may account for the fact that the ritual scene of reading a suspect his or her rights has become in recent decades one of the most common scenes in television drama. It is a formula that is to TV what "wine-dark sea" is to the ancient epic. The point to be stressed about this ritual scene is that it often shows the police delivering the warnings in the manner of the third degree, that is, with violence. A prototype for such scenes might be the one in a TV movie called *Nails* (1992), starring Dennis Hopper as the cop. At the midpoint of the plot, Hopper confronts a Latino drug dealer in a parking garage, arrests him, and proceeds to beat the man brutally, including a kick to the groin, while shouting the Miranda warnings ("You have the right to remain silent . . ."). A suspect is being beaten.

This scene conveys the extraordinary anger felt in certain parts of the society over the perceived injustice of Miranda, seeming to protect criminals at the expense of victims. Miranda was an indigent Mexican, "a seriously disturbed individual with pronounced sexual fantasies," who after two hours of questioning without benefit of counsel confessed to abducting and raping a white teenage woman (Cushman 1976, 177). The issue was not Miranda's guilt, but how that guilt had been established. Richard Nixon used the issue in the law-and-order theme of his 1968 presidential campaign, and the judges he subsequently appointed to the Court put a stop to the extension of the Miranda "shield" to ever more categories of cases (Witt 1988, 200).

A detail in a police handbook provides a glimpse of how the electronic apparatus is affecting the methodology of interrogation. The authors warn the trainees to avoid performing scenarios made familiar by the media, such as the good cop/bad cop routine. "The exposure this technique has received in television and movies and its having been used in an unprofessional manner has made it largely ineffective against suspects. Additionally, depending on the role of the hard interrogator, it may verge on intimidation and coercion, which could render a suspect's statement unusable" (Zulawski and Wicklander 1992, 2). The handbook adds that, because of TV, people expect interviewers to take notes. To be credible, therefore, one should at least have the props of writing available, unless the situation becomes accusatory, in which case such props should be hidden, so as not to remind the suspects that what is said could be used against them (28). Another handbook avoids such terms as "trickery" and "bluffing," "because of the old mystery story concept of the detective creating a false situation which would entrap the suspect into a dramatic admission of guilt. Such a conception could cause a false impression of this practice as a mainstay of the interrogative art" (Royal and Schutt 1976, 146).

It is worth noting in this context that the pilot for the *Kojak* series (which ran on CBS from 1973 to 1978) was based on one of the four cases grouped under the Miranda decision—the Wylie-Hoffert murders. A black teenager being questioned on an unrelated crime incriminated himself by confessing to the slash murders of two women in Manhattan in 1963. In the episode, fictionalized as "The Marcus Nelson Murders," Telly Savalas plays a hard-boiled detective who fights to keep the teenager from being wrongly convicted, thus putting the tough guy on the side of due process.

Rights

The constitutional question concerns the Fifth Amendment right to protection from self-incrimination. The majority opinion, authored by Chief Justice Warren, first invokes the need for protection from torture: "From extensive factual studies undertaken in the early 1930's including the famous Wickersham Report, it is clear that police violence and the 'third degree' flourished at that time. In a series of cases decided by this Court long after these studies, the police resorted to physical brutality—beatings, hanging, whipping—and to sustained and protracted questioning incommunicado in order to extort confessions" (Cushman 1976, 176).

The more important aspect of the opinion, however, extends the definition of "third degree" to cover psychological violence, citing police handbooks as evidence of prejudicial practices:

A valuable source of information about present police practices may be found in various police manuals and texts which document procedures employed with success in the past, and which recommend various other effective tactics. . . . The setting prescribed by the manuals and observed in practice becomes clear: To be alone with the subject is essential to prevent distraction and to deprive him of any outside support. The aura of confidence in his guilt undermines his will to resist. He merely confirms the preconceived story the police seek to have him describe. Patience and persistence, at times relentless questioning are employed. . . . It is important to keep the subject off balance, for example, by trading on his insecurity about himself or his surroundings. The police then persuade, trick, or cajole him out of exercising his constitutional rights. (176)

The crucial point for choragraphy, looking for an alternative to the third degree, "in all its forms and styles," as the mood of inquiry, is the definition of "interrogation" provided by the Court, to clarify the application of Miranda. "Fourteen years after 'Miranda,' the Court adopted a broad definition of this key word. Interrogation, the Court declared unanimously in 'Rhode Island v. Innis,' means more than just the direct questioning of a suspect by police. It includes other 'techniques of persuasion,' such as staged lineups, intended to evoke statements from a suspect. Indeed, said the Court, interrogation occurs any time police use words or actions that they 'should have known' were reasonably likely to elicit an incriminating response from a suspect" (Witt 1988, 207). In short, Miranda makes rhetoric unconstitutional, at least when it comes to police work.

Samba Time

Alan Turing appears in both series, on both sides of the gap articulating two ways of getting the information I need—painful and painless. Turing is a theorist of the computer whose famous imitation game (one of the legends of computer lore) continues the tradition of the third degree. Thus the two series set in motion by the Digital ad have already crossed, the two series embodied in two scenes, showing the performance of two skills: police interrogation and dancing the samba (the latter posed as the possible figure for an electrate approach to inquiry).

Returning to the samba series now produces the word/thing (the "vinculum" that Deleuze calls for, in *The Fold*) needed to label the set coming into formation in this experiment: Miranda. "Miranda" is the switch word, the "paradoxical entity" conducting information in a short circuit between the two series. The logic of conduction (Deleuze's *logic of sense*, Guattari's transversality) gathers heterogeneous entities, coordinating the parallel series by means of a pun, forming a "puncept." Researching the vehicle of Papert's analogy, I read a book on Brazilian music that noted the important role of Carmen Miranda in introducing the samba into American popular culture:

> The 1940s saw the first export of samba, as songs like Ary Barroso's marvelous "Brazil" reached North America. Ary's tunes were featured in Walt Disney films and covered in other Hollywood productions by a playful, exotic young woman who wore colorful faced skirts, heaps of jewelry, and a veritable orchard atop her head. Her name was Carmen Miranda, and she sang catchy sambas and marchas by many great Brazilian composers in a string of American feature films. . . . For better or worse, she would symbolize Brazil to the world for decades and become a cultural icon in North America and Europe, a symbol of fun and extravagance. (McGowan and Pessanha 1991, 12)

"Carmen Miranda" is a metonym for "samba" in the entertainment discourse of the American popcycle, which qualifies her to serve as guide to this new relationship to information, replacing the search for truth by the third degree as a relay for learning: from third degree to third (obtuse) meanings.

A further switch in this "choral table" confirms the happy chance of "Miranda" as the figure for a demonstration of concetto de$ign. In the memory palace mnemonics of medieval learning, the practice of "miranda" was one in which the rhetor extracted certain key images, scenes, exempla, from the encyclopedia of memorized texts. "Memoria," that is, was not only a means of storage and retrieval of information, but also a means for generating new texts or speeches (invention). "*Memoria rerum*: remembering Scripture for homiletic purposes as a set of summarized plots, within which are embedded a number of gems to be held up individually and admired. The word *miranda* has a distinctive resonance in classical culture as the initial act of philosophical speculation, derived from *mirari*, 'to look with wonder.' These gems are the dark, difficult parts in the text which one can isolate, holding one or two up at a time to the audience for admiration, and proceeding to loosen up its knots and expand its meaning, as one explicates and expounds, composing a homiletic meditation" (Carruthers 1998, 65). The MEmorial functions as *miranda,* selecting certain "gems" from the flood of materials available in each of the popcycle discourses. This improvisation on the imitation game demonstration shows how to locate the gems and string them together into a *catena* (chain, associative series). This chain is felt: it evokes a simulacrum, apprehended through feeling.

It is the question Plato addressed in *Cratylus*—the problem of the motivation of meanings; the relation of the material of language and discourse to the materiality of nature and culture. Is the Miranda decision well-named? The case synthesizes four separate trials, each with its own name. Conduction is based on this tuning of discourse to culture, using these lucky finds as a point of departure for further elaboration and development (a method that has a long history in the mnemonic practices of the manuscript era). Why was "Miranda" the name attached to the "shield" protecting the ignorant or, more significantly, the "illiterate" (in the cases before the court), confirming the precedent established in the first Scottsboro case? A suspect needs "the guiding hand of counsel at every step in the proceedings against him. Without it, though he be not guilty, he faces the danger of conviction because he does not know how to establish his innocence. If that be true of men of intelligence, how much more true is it of the ignorant and illiterate, or those of feeble intellect" (Witt 1988, 205).

In the electronic apparatus, in an era of secondary illiteracy, personification returns to our thinking, with stars and celebrities replacing the gods and goddesses of orality. Miranda intervenes in the history of justice, shielding the illiterate from the third degree and, by extension, shielding everyone from

self-incrimination at the hands of rhetoric. That Carmen Miranda might personi-
fy this event, opening a passage between literacy and electracy, exploits the same
punning procedure that has directed the invention of justice from the beginning.
"The most flagrant of all puns is the one used to indicate that retributive justice
has divine status. 'Dike' is, as it were, defended as the daughter of Zeus on the
basis of her verbal derivation from him ('di-ke': 'di-os'); the pun was 'invented'
by Hesiod, improved on by Aeschylus in the SEVEN" (Havelock 1978, 294). What
Havelock says of "Dike" as goddess applies to Miranda as well: "This piece of
ingenuity, however bizarre, probably indicates an awareness that she has been
placed on Olympus by an act of poetic imagination which needs support" (ibid.).

Brazil

Her full name was Marie do Carmo Miranda da Cunha, born near Lisbon in
1909 (Katz 1979, 813). In her infancy her parents moved to Rio de Janeiro, where
she was educated in a convent. She had to disguise her name to hide her career
as a samba singer from her family, especially from her father, "who believed
entertainers were vile creatures of the lowest social status" (Woll 1983, 114).
The code of her pseudonym is not very difficult to break. Her choice nonetheless evokes a further motivation, recalling an important name in the history of
Latin American independence, second perhaps only to that of Simón Bolívar
himself. Miranda, the Venezuelan general, known as "the great precursor," was
an adventurer committed to the fight for liberty against tyranny, first by serving in the war of American Independence and then in the French revolutionary
army. His name is one of those inscribed on the Arc de Triomphe (Trend 1968,
54). He was the leader of the first attempt at independence by a South American
state. The rebellion failed, partly due to problems with Miranda's leadership, but
also due to bad luck. Many of the towns under his control, including Caracas,
"were destroyed by one of the worst earthquakes in history" (March 26, 1812),
which caused heavy loss of life among Miranda's troops (77). Whatever General
Miranda's shortcomings might have been, no one doubted that his life was devoted to the cause of freedom.

"Miranda" is synonymous with "samba." Or rather, it is a metaphor as well as
a metonym for "samba," in that the "meaning" of samba music is precisely "freedom." The most famous samba of all is "Aquarela do Brasil," by Ary Barroso,
known internationally simply as "Brazil." It is the opening number of *The Gang's
All Here* (1943), perhaps Carmen's best film, directed by Busby Berkeley. "Brazil,
Brazil. For me, for me. Oh! These murmuring fountains where I quench my
thirst and where the moon comes to play." In Terry Gilliam's *Brazil* (1985) "the
song represented a vision of beauty and freedom to the protagonist, trapped in a
futuristic, totalitarian society" (McGowan and Pessanha 1991, 35).

Not that it is possible or even desirable to try to translate samba into a concept. Indeed, its resistance to conceptuality is what recommends "samba" as the relay for an image (untransposed) category based on mood (concetto). The dancing is figurative, a figure of thought. "It is common for Cariocas to say, rather ironically, that everything ends up in samba. If things go wrong there's always samba to lift peoples' spirits. Samba is many things: solace, celebration, escape and abandon, plus philosophy, culture, and tradition" (ibid., 28). The effects of samba are summed up in the word *saudade* ("longing or yearning for something or someone"). "It's a certain poignance, a soulfulness, coming from what Brazilians call 'saudade'—a kind of bittersweet longing, which means, in a way, 'glad to be feeling.' (We have no word in English for this concept)" (Paul Winter, in ibid., 9). One discovery of this series is this feeling, *saudade*, which connects with homesickness, *Heimweh*. Reflecting its origins in the oral traditions of Afro-Brazilians, samba "was an important form of expression for the Carioca lower classes in the early twentieth century. Samba became a voice for those who had been silenced by their socio-economic status, and a source of self-affirmation in society" (32). The Andalusian version of this mood— *duende*—is perhaps more familiar because of its place in the poetics of Garcia Lorca (Hirsch 2002, 11).

Voice. *Stimme. Stimmung.* Miranda moves between two series, two styles of memory and freedom in the Digital ad, two moods, two modalities, attunements, protective on one side (the right to silence) and aggressive on the other (overcoming enforced silence). Electrate citizens need all the mirandas for reasoneon about justice.

Make a Scene

To organize the series generated by the gap between the two paradigms of inquiry (calculative and meditative, interrogative and musical), I need to construct a mnemonic emblem, a secondary elaboration of the dispersed items of information into a coherent pattern. The point of departure for this scene is the Turing test, the imitation game, with Carmen Miranda playing the part of the woman. The neo-baroque concetto, in any case, may be animated. To begin with, I memorize her look, or enter it into the database:

> Her costume was a combination of native Bahian dress and a designer's
> nightmare. With bare legs and midriff, she wore sweeping half-open skirts
> and tons of colorful costume jewelry. She introduced the turban to the
> American scene, and topped it with the fruits of her native Brazil. This exag-
> gerated Latin spectacle appeared atop five inch platform shoes, which she
> claimed to have invented herself. "They come about because I like big men,"

the five-foot-two-inch star explained. "When I dance with big men I can't see over their shoulders. Maybe they flirt with other girl. So I tell shoemaker to build up my shoes." (Woll 1983, 114)

As for her hats, when she was discovered she was working in a department store where she modeled and "created hats." Why the tropical fruit on the hats? Perhaps it was a (mocking) homage to her father, an importer and exporter running a "prosperous wholesale fruit business" (Katz 1979).

They called her the "Brazilian Bombshell," recalling the "Bombe," the "female" (the fragment of information) of the perforated sheets used to break the Enigma machine. "She differed from every movie musical star that Hollywood had yet discovered. Of her debut (singing 'Sous Samerican Why' [Y]) a critic wrote, 'Her face is too heavy to be beautiful, her figure is nothing to write home about, and she sings in a foreign language. Yet she is the biggest theatrical sensation of the year'" (Katz 1979, 115). She died suddenly of a heart attack, at forty-six (in 1955), after a demanding number on a segment of the Jimmy Durante TV show (813).

The key to Carmen's ability to function as a concetto—the personification of the name replacing "dike" in electracy—is her cult status as an icon or fetish, a sign that has separated from the historical person of the 1940s, and from the Hollywood musicals and Brazilian recordings, to live on in popular culture as a myth, a collection of detachable parts. "She inspired legions of Carmen imitators (actor Mickey Rooney was one of the first—in the 1941 film *Babes on Broadway*), and decades later she is still a popular 'character' for costume parties" (McGowan and Pessanha 1981, 12–13). This aspect of Carmen Miranda—her imitability or iterability—is what makes her important for electracy. Giving her the woman's part in the imitation game complicates Turing's test considerably. The fact is that the films of the 1940s reflected the confusion of sex and gender roles in society necessitated by the circumstances of the war, with women taking over from men the jobs vacated by the need for soldiers. It has been observed that film noir (based on hard-boiled detective fiction) reflected the same confusions about gender and sexual identity that marked the musicals. There was much bitterness in the transvestite comedy of the wartime musicals, with one exception:

> Carmen Miranda became the most easily imitated musical star by men and women alike. In such films as *Down Argentine Way, Babes on Broadway*, and *Winged Victory*, both males and females attempted Miranda impressions. The Brazilian's outlandish garb made her an easy mark for her followers. . . .The men in the musicals did not react by attempting to reinforce their traditional roles. Rather, they became confused and disoriented, often turning to transvestite humor as a form of revenge. (Woll 1983, 102)

The qualities that motivated the disparaging references in some encyclope-
dias to Carmen as a "kitsch" figure account also, no doubt, for her "camp" status. Her availability for female impersonation evokes the camp sensibility associated with homosexual subculture. "While camp is now often a joke or pose
among gays, it is not without serious value because it originated as a Masonic
gesture by which homosexuals could make themselves known to each other
during periods when homosexuality was not avowable. Besides being a signal,
camp was and remains the way in which homosexuals and other groups of
people with double lives can find a 'lingua franca'" (Core 1984, 9).

Associating Carmen Miranda with drag queens also evokes their female
counterpart. "Outside New York, 'dyke' and 'fag hag' have not entered journalistic vocabulary as unpejoratively as 'gay' or 'camp.' . . . Yet its strident syllables
perfectly equate the type of woman whose behavior is exaggerated to appeal,
not to lovers, but to male homosexuals" (11). The punning initiated by Hesiod
continues macaronically, then, extending the field of justice, "dike" to "dyke"
(an off-rhyme). Choragraphy continues in this respect the conventions of pre-
print mnemonics. "Even the most apparently pictorial of mnemonic systems
are based on principles governing the nature of signs rather than on iterative
copying. Most require that the 'picture' relate to the word or concept it marks
for recollection via a pun or homophony" (Carruthers 1990, 28). Freud's treatment of the dream as a rebus is consistent with this convention as well. The
slang meaning of "fruit" in this context allows Carmen's hats to serve as a rebus
for this same mnemonic extension of meaning, defiantly, using the tactic of
insult inversion.

Hard-Boiled Eggheads

The role of the man is played in this Turing test improvisation by Ludwig
Wittgenstein. There are several reasons for this casting, not the least being the
fact that Turing's biographer observed that Wittgenstein's work was the closest
to expressing the questions that most interested Turing. Wittgenstein, moreover,
loved American hard-boiled detective fiction. "The ethos of the hard-boiled detective coincides with Wittgenstein's own: they both decry the importance of
the 'science of logic,' exemplified in the one case by *Principia Mathematica* and
in the other by Sherlock Holmes" (Monk 1990, 423).

These adventurer heroes were masters of using the third degree (violence)
on behalf of truth, as in the case of Three Gun Terry (a creation of Carroll John
Daly), the first of many such private eyes. "My life is my own, and the opinions of
others don't interest me; so don't form any, or keep them to yourself. If you want
to sneer at my tactics, why go ahead; but do it behind the pages—you'll find that
healthier. . . . I'm in the center of a triangle; between the crook and the police and

the victim" (Daly 1985, 43). Thugs have kidnapped a woman and are going to torture her to get some information they need. Until Terry Mack intervenes:

> So I push the door very softly, and this Joe waits behind it, all smiles, I guess. Then I suddenly up with my foot and give that door a kick—a real healthy kick. That's the only way to enter a room what you got your doubts on. Bang! Crash! You could hear his head connect with that door in one heavy thud. After that there was nothing to it. I had my flash out and my gun on him, and the door closed and locked before he knew what had happened. It was five minutes before he recovered enough to speak. (59)

Wittgenstein used phrases from pulp sleuths in his conversation and he sometimes used passages from the pulps as points of departure for his classes dealing with "sense data and private experience": "When he quoted from literature, it was not from the great philosophical works, not from the philosophical journal *Mind,* but from Street & Smith's *Detective Story* magazine" (Monk 1990, 355). Despite his interest in the perspective of ordinary life, a friend said of him, "if you had committed a murder, Wittgenstein would be the best man to consult, but that for more ordinary anxieties and fears he could be dangerous" (459).

It is hard to imagine any person who could be more different from Carmen Miranda, more opposed to her sensual style or to what she represents, than Ludwig Wittgenstein. He hated ornament of any kind. His rooms were furnished in the simplest possible way, lacking even books (the only visible reading material was a stack of *Detective Story* magazines) (443). He dressed always the same (wearing a kind of uniform that someone said resembled that of a Boy Scout), and declared that he didn't care what he ate, as long as it was "always the same." He inherited immense wealth, but gave it all away (while Carmen, in her gold digger persona, stated that she knew ten English words: men men men men men and monee monee monee monee monee).

Here is the test, then, the imitation game, the riddle that at first hearing appears so simple—to tell the difference, online, between Carmen Miranda and Ludwig Wittgenstein (which one is the man, and which one is the woman?). The electrate answer may be "both" (a tangle). Or rather, the real lesson of the imitation game for human-machine interface concerns not the hardware or software, but the rhetorical practice of human authors, who must learn the logical equivalent of cross-dressing.

A Muscle Comedy

The purpose of the remake is not to play the imitation game straight, or to leave the Turing test intact, but to devise a replacement, based on something having to do with the samba as the relay for an electrate relationship to information.

To evoke the appropriate state of mind, the performance is not a hard-boiled interrogation, but a musical comedy, to take advantage of the plot structure of musicals, organized around a romance in which the two partners in the couple-to-be begin in a state of diametrical opposition, in a dualism that is harmonized through the course of a courtship. The intent of the remake is not to confirm the myth of marriage, but to find a point of contact between two models of information access, emblematized in the characters of Wittgenstein and Miranda. She has to teach him how to samba. "The basis of the dance is a controlled springy knee action, called the 'Samba Pulse.' Integrated with this up-down movement of the legs is a swaying motion of the upper body—the 'pendulum styling.' The effect of this styling is that of a controlled rocking motion, one partner swaying back as the other sways forward in unison" (Monte 1978, 143). To apply the emblem to method requires us to extrapolate from literal to figurative, using a proportional ratio: physical beating is to research interrogation as samba is to (MEmorial).

Whatever the differences between their personalities, Wittgenstein's favorite actress was Carmen Miranda (along with Betty Hutton). Another favorable factor for my purposes is that Wittgenstein, perhaps for the same reasons as in the case of Miranda (the extremity of manner lending itself to stereotyping), is starting to separate from his historical and textual place and to become available as an icon. Bruce Duffy novelized Wittgenstein's early years as a student of Russell and Moore in *The World As I Found It* (1987), and Terry Eagleton, in *Saints and Scholars,* adapted the philosopher to a political fiction: "This novel is not entirely fantasy. Nikolai Bakhtin, elder brother of the celebrated Russian critic Mikhail Bakhtin, was indeed a close friend of Ludwig Wittgenstein, the foremost English-language philosopher of the century. Wittgenstein did indeed live for a while in a cottage on the west coast of Ireland, although at a later time than suggested here" (Eagleton 1987).

I only need a few scenes, such as one with Wittgenstein rushing to the cinema after one of his classes, as he often did, sitting in the front row, leaning forward, in order to cleanse himself of the disgust he felt when he "said too much." The film is *The Gang's All Here,* opening with the famous samba, "Brazil," which ends with Carmen and the other dancers teaching members of the audience how to dance. In the remake, Carmen gets Ludwig out on the dance floor (abolishing the difference between screen and auditorium, as in Woody Allen's *The Purple Rose of Cairo*). It is not about the literal dance, but the figurative one, changing our cultural style of turning information into knowledge. It is not the dance but what is felt *(saudade, duende).*

Carmen's chances of success with Ludwig are not good (he is not heterosexual), although he changed his mind once before. His *Tractatus Logico Philosophicus* is perhaps the book that marks the closure, if not the end, of the methodology of truth by interrogation in the Western tradition. "It is an important thesis of Wittgenstein that all propositions are truth-functions of elementary proposi-tions and can be built up from them in the following way: Suppose all elementa-ry propositions were given. Each of these could be either true or false. Therefore a proposition containing three elementary propositions 'p,' 'q,' 'r' could have a truth-function T,T,F, or T,F,T, and there would be eight such possible truth-functions" (Magill 1961, 833). This study completed the line of thinking ini-tiated when Wittgenstein first read Russell and Whitehead's *Principia*, whose method of true-or-false logic was shown to have practical application to the de-sign of electrical circuits in Shannon's 1937 thesis, "Symbolic Analysis of Relay and Switching Circuits" (Eames and Eames 1990, 121). The later Wittgenstein turned against his early work, the whole notion of truth tables, and the two-valued logic of the *Principia*. Is it too late for computer hardware to follow Wittgenstein's change of heart? Does the fact that electronic switches have only two choices limit the future of truth in an electronic apparatus, or make it pos-sible? In any case, choragraphy is not a matter of technology (hardware or soft-ware) but of institutional practice.

Musical Space

Freed from the confines of "truth," Wittgenstein does not abandon the idea of logical space, but only the restriction of that notion to the aesthetics of real-ism. In our musical Turing test he revises the representation of concepts along the same lines opened up by Einstein in physics, Gertrude Stein in literature, and Picasso in painting, opening a third possible extrapolation from his work, distinct from both symbolic logic and ordinary language philosophy. This third way is anchored historically in the coincidence of dates, locating the publica-tion of the *Tractatus* (1921) in the same decade as the invention of both the hard-boiled detective story in America ("Three Gun Terry," in *The Black Mask*, 1923), and of the samba school in Brazil (1928). "Technically, samba has a 2/4 meter with its heaviest accent on the second beat, a stanza-and-refrain struc-ture, and many interlocking, syncopated lines in the melody and accompani-ment" (McGowan and Pessanha 1991, 30). The first song officially registered and recorded as a samba was released in 1917, about the time Wittgenstein, despite serving at the front in the Austrian army, started a final draft of the *Tractatus*. Question: what is the logical pattern of the following line—"The commandant of fun told me on the phone to dance with joy"?

The part of the "picture theory" serving as the point of departure for this methodology may be seen in an item in *Prototractatus*: "A gramophone record, the musical idea, the written notes, and the sound-waves, all stand to one an-other in the same internal relation of depicting that holds between language and the world. They are all constructed according to a common logical pattern" (Wittgenstein 1971, 87). Wittgenstein possessed a fine ear for music, even if his tastes were confined to the classics (not counting American musical films). He learned to play the clarinet in his thirties, and in the remake he replaces Benny Goodman playing and singing "Paducah" *(The Gang's All Here)*. He was committed to the idea, in his later work, that understanding philosophy was the same sort of experience as understanding a joke, or music, in which understanding was produced without benefit of concepts. "What is required for understanding here is not the discovery of facts, nor the drawing of logically valid inferences from accepted premises—nor, still less, the construction of 'theories'—but, rather, the right point of view (from which to 'see' the joke, to hear the expression in the music or to see your way out of the philosophical fog)" (Monk 1990, 530).

This "getting a joke" as the aspect from which to revise conceptual thinking is in fact the common ground on which the Wittgenstein-Miranda affair is played out. Wittgenstein was noted for lapsing into the telling of weak sorts of jokes when around women, and his favorite hard-boiled author was Norbert Davis, the distinguishing feature of whose stories was their sense of humor (he created the team of Doan and Carstairs—Doan with the look of a bumpkin but a style crossing Sam Spade and Groucho Marx, and Carstairs, an enormous Great Dane with contempt for his master). The factor mediating the shift from the third degree to the samba (from Jacobin to Malandro) as the atmosphere of learning is Wittgenstein's sense of humor. Carmen Miranda appealed to him, no doubt, because she was herself a great comedian, with a style based partly on her malapropisms and other hashings of English, and on an expressive face and a mouth with an unforgettable curling lip. Carmen asks Ludwig to dance, then, introducing him to the gesture from which "samba" derives its name. "The word 'samba' appears to come from Angola, where the Kimbundu term 'semba' refers to the umbigada navel-touching 'invitation to the dance' that was originally part of many African circle dances" (McGowan and Pessanha 1991, 28). She touches his navel, and says, "Eet rrrimes weeth trooth taable." Ludwig (who has quite an accent of his own) is thunderstruck. He changed his mind once within literacy. Within electracy will he be able to change his body?

Pattern

The key to choragraphy (often confused with choreography) is the recognition and formation of pattern. "Curious though it sounds, proofs in pure mathematics are analogous to the explanations offered in Freudian psychoanalysis. And perhaps the clue to Wittgenstein's shift in concerns, from mathematics to psychology, lies in his finding Freud's 'patterns' more interesting than the 'pictures' of mathematicians. It would, one suspects, have been something of a relief for Wittgenstein to have been able to place the events of his own life into some kind of pattern" (Monk 1990, 442). In my improvisation, this pattern is shown, if not told, as if in a style choreographed by Busby Berkeley. "The Fox film of 1943, *The Gang's All Here,* could be seen as the pinnacle of both the sexual and the abstract urges in his work. The former reaches its apotheosis in 'The lady with the tutti-frutti hat' [Carmen Miranda], where gargantuan bananas carried by chorines plunge rhythmically into strawberry centered patterns made by other girls; the latter in 'the polka dot polka' where the designs, at one point viewed through a kaleidoscope, are no longer erotic, or even human, but momentarily attain total abstraction in a rush of changing patterns akin to the abstract experimental cinema associated with figures like Len Lye and Norman McLaren" (Babington and Evans 1985, 54).

Carmen uses the connection between her hats and her father's fruit business to help Ludwig find the pattern organizing his own career—the connection between the duck-rabbit gestalt switch that illustrated his theory of "aspectuality," and the memory of the duck image that terrified him as a child, projected into the broken plaster of the bathroom. "Of central importance to his whole later work is the idea that there is a kind of seeing that is also a kind of thinking: the seeing of connections. We 'see' a connection in the same sense as we see an aspect, or a 'Gestalt'" (Monk 1990, 537). That this theme is one switch point for crossing the gap between the two sides of the Digital ad is signaled and retained mnemonically in the term "miranda."

Voiced Silence

The name for the specific pattern emerging in this X/Y-logic crossing of two series, tracing an electrate learning style, is "miranda." My prototype miranda has a duck-rabbit pattern, a switch rhythm, an oscillating paradox having to do with silence. In one aspect, the scene displays the famous ending of Wittgenstein's *Tractatus:*

> The correct method in philosophy would really be the following: to say nothing except what can be said, i.e., propositions of natural science. . . . My propositions serve as elucidations in the following way: anyone who understands me eventually recognizes them as nonsensical, when he has used them—as steps—to climb up beyond them. (He must, so to speak, throw away the ladder after he has climbed up it.) He must transcend these propositions, and then he will see the world aright. What we cannot speak about we must pass over in silence. (Wittgenstein 1961, 151)

In electracy, what we may not speak about we must pass over to dance (even if the dance is figurative, de$igned). Adding concetto to concept introduces samba to the scene, identified as *giving voice* to all those condemned to silence by the oppressions of ideological norms (the samba being the discursive "other" of the proposition). Still, there is something of climbing a ladder in both styles: "If you have mastered cakewalking in place," reads one description of the man's part in samba dancing, "swinging your legs under and over each other as if you were climbing an invisible spiral staircase, and pulling up to a sharp halt after sliding sideways very fast with your feet, you are ready to time your performances" (Guillermoprieto 1990, 98). This ladder step reminds us that the concetto reconnects the "chain of being" between the microcosm and macrocosm, the individual and collective dimensions of the world.

In preparing a field in which an electronically evolving thought of justice might emerge (with miranda replacing "dike"—with *duende* replacing interrogation as the mood of method), I compose a scene that might show more than it is able to tell, something about the place of popular culture in the popcycle. The setting is still the same—a cinema, showing Busby Berkeley's *The Gang's All Here*. Cinema is the institutional anchor for this emblem (cinema work, similar to McGee's toilet work). Ludwig is already in the theater. Alan Turing makes his way there as well. "Except for those with eyes to see through the stylized heterosexuality of Fred Astaire and Busby Berkeley, the times favored ever more rigid models of 'masculine' and 'feminine'" (Hodges 1983, 127). Busby Berkeley is camp, serving as a Masonic sign, recalling the status of truth as a secret in the era of the third degree.

A *mise en abyme* is at work, a miniaturization linking the backstage musical (and the courtship between opposite types) to the backstory of the cinema as institution, suggesting the structure of the musical, and all binary dualisms, from Wittgenstein's truth tables and the team of Astaire and Rogers to the switches of computer hardware, are inadequate to the physicality or materiality of existence: the personal sacred, the cinema as institutional place manifesting an invisible social dynamic of sexuality (a cognitive map). These multiple social functions of the public toilet resonate with Lacan's paradigmatic emblem (holistic sign) and Bradley McGee's Upsilon Alarm. The historical context is the conspiracy of silence confronting homosexuals in the era of Wittgenstein and Turing. "This stretch between the urinal and the cinema was where the male homosexual eye was focused—perhaps the same block as trodden by Ludwig Wittgenstein in 1908, such unofficial institutions lasting as long as the respectable kind. Here straggled a motley convoy of souls, and amidst them the odd independent sailing, like Alan Turing" (Hodges 1983, 428).

This life out of bounds bore a family resemblance to that celebrated in the lyrics of many sambas, treating "the lifestyle of the 'malandro,' a type of hustler or layabout that was a romantic bohemian ideal for some in Rio in the thirties and forties. These malandros made their living exploiting women, playing small confidence tricks, gambling. They liked to dress fine" (McGowan and Pessanha 1991, 33). And here the two series show their common origins in the same historical moment of gender relations. Three Gun Terry, despite temptations, would have nothing to do with women, while the early sambistas sang, "may God keep me away from today's women. They despise a man just because of the night life" (31). A crucial aspect of these stories told in samba lyrics is their evocation of the bar scene, the setting of street discourse. What is it to live the malandro's life? Read Jean Genet. For our conceit we do not retain the story in the lyrics, nor the music of the dance, but only the feeling felt.

Investigating by the Book

The switch event in the remake of the imitation game is the suicide of Alan Turing in 1954 (not long after Carmen Miranda's fatal dance on the Jimmy Durante show). His family hired an investigator, perhaps a hard-boiled type, to check into this death. That would be the alphabetic style of cognition, trying to find the truth of it. But what does the miranda pattern show? The facts are the same in both paradigms—that Turing cooperated with the police while refusing to be blackmailed by his lover. It is an interrogation scene—the police questioning Alan Turing, who told them everything.

What does the interrogator's manual say, by way of instructions? Why does anyone confess? "The emotional 'Achilles heel' of the human personality is insecurity. Insecurity exists in all human personalities in varying degrees. . . . Insecurity normal to any personality is a pliant or moveable tool. Correctly adjusted and used, insecurity can produce a condition of oral catharsis that exceeds the potent intestinal effects of castor oil" (Royal and Schutt 1976, 135). And what is the source of greatest insecurity? It is the question noted by Jacques Lacan in his study of the psychotic Judge Schreber, the question that founds human identity: "What am I, a man or a woman?" Perhaps Schreber, and not Earl Warren, should be cast as the judge of the imitation game. For his crime, in lieu of jail, Turing was given court-ordered treatment with estrogen, rendering him impotent and producing breasts (Hodges 1983, 473–74).

I begin to understand how difficult the Turing test is. Could it be a joke, left for future de$igners as a switch point from the third degree into some other model of truth? No one may take the test with any confidence. Or the point of the game is not so much to bring machines into the category of humans, as to put in question this category itself, this border (to expose its uncanniness).

It heralds the coming community of terminal identity. Hodges considers the original imitation game—posed as this attempt to tell the difference between a man and a woman—to be a "red herring, and one of the few passages of the paper ["Computing Machinery and Intelligence"] that was not expressed with perfect lucidity. The whole point of this game was that a successful imitation of a woman's responses by a man would not prove anything. Gender depended on facts which were not reducible to sequences of symbols. In contrast, he wished to argue that such an imitation principle did apply to 'thinking' or 'intelligence'" (415).

What might appear to be a red herring in the aspect of the hard-boiled approach to truth as a secret could be the main clue in samba thinking, showing without benefit of concept a feeling of "miranda." If selfhood puts each subject to the Turing test, perhaps self, truth, and the third degree are all dissolved in felt cognition (not resolved but made irrelevant). In miranda formation, unconscious premises of judgment are included, along with intuition and analysis, to produce conductive inferences. By means of the switch the terror of the third degree becomes *saudade* (glad yearning); the interface becomes the interbody. Two collective cognitive styles or conceptual stands. Two educations. Mr./Ms. Gordon, in me. Concept with concetto.

Hodges wondered why Turing did not remain silent when confronted by the interrogators. There were no Miranda rights to protect him from self-incrimination, from the laws against his sexuality, not in England, and not yet in America either, in 1954 and perhaps not anymore since post-9/11 America has grown tired of such refinements. The biography cites the concluding line of the *Tractatus* as the ending for Turing's story. But it could have added a line from the Miranda warnings, authored by Earl Warren: "The warning of the right to remain silent must be accompanied by the explanation that anything said can and will be used against the individual in court. . . . This warning may serve to make the individual more acutely aware that he is faced with a phase of the adversary system—that he is not in the presence of persons acting solely in his interest" (Cushman 1976, 178).

What about schooling, the family, and the other institutions of society, each with its own zone of indistinction, as adversary systems? In the electrate era of "justice" becoming "miranda" (of topic becoming chora), perhaps every institution will have its own Miranda warnings. Perhaps there will be no tests online, but riddles answered with the rabbit-duck of the unconscious, oscillating between the right to remain silent and the need to testify (between the third degree and *duende*). The slang reference to a stool pigeon takes on new significance ("to sing" meaning "to confess"). No learning without yearning. It is a learning that touches the dream navel, setting the new world order dancing.

ASSIGNMENT

Consultation, 9/11

How to commemorate 9/11? Theoria and revolution gather around the rim of the Real, observing the answer to Rodney King's question (can't we all just get along?).

> Balibar also provides the location of this hole to be filled by the theory of ideology: it concerns social antagonism ("class struggle") as the inherent limit that traverses society and prevents it from constituting itself as a positive, complete, self-enclosed entity. It is at this precise place that psychoanalysis has to intervene (Balibar somewhat enigmatically evokes the concept of the unconscious)—not, of course, in the old Freudo-Marxist manner, as the element destined to fill up the hole of historical materialism and thus to render possible its completion, but, on the contrary, as the theory that enables us to conceptualize this hole of historical materialism as irreducible, because it is constitutive. (Žižek 1994a, 28)

Are we ready for the assignment, a MEmorial for September 11? Here is what we know, in shorthand: de$ign a Bombe (to use Turing's strategy for breaking the code of the Enigma engine). That is to say, align the holes, in a block, matrix, superimposed tangle: the hole in lower Manhattan, Ground Zero; the hole in science; the hole in Being; the hole in me (in you); the empty mobile place in language. Configure the General Economy. Undertake an impresa.

SOFT WISHING Y
(A COLLABORATION)

Genesis

A MEmorial for 9/11 is represented here through a collection of documents (e-mail, Web site files, and planning notes) as well as commentary and description, to show some of the process of my collaboration with the artist Will Pappenheimer (Florida Research Ensemble). Soft Wishing Y applies many of the principles and examples discussed in this book and adds some new elements. A relay rather than a model, these documents form a partial map of a machinic assemblage. This project demonstrates how to use the impresa version of the emblem concetto: consulting by adopting a public problem as a guide for personal action. The method for composing a MEmorial as impresa is a hybrid of mystory and divination. Moreover, the collaborative production leads to an insight into how to organize the accumulated Web MEmorials into an Internet civic sphere. It performs a singular attunement of a group subject, in other words, to measure the mood (the spirit) of place. How might 9/11 look

211

Figure 9. Will Pappenheimer, Y Tour.

when justice includes miranda? The "wishing Y" thread in Upsilon Alarm was the immediate inspiration for Pappenheimer's idea.

The Proposal (Will Pappenheimer)

I had an interesting confluence of ideas last night flying home from CAA in Philadelphia. About a month ago an artist not before known to me, having come upon my Web site, invited me to participate in the project she calls "The Free Biennial" (http://www.freewords.org/biennial/). This will take place in NYC in the fast coming month of April, coinciding of course with the Whitney Biennial, but encouraging "free" citywide works and projects that might exist outside the normal gallery/economic paradigm. This artist, whose name is Sal Randolph, has some very interesting projects online, visible through her Freewords.org site and "Links to Free Culture." Anyway, her interest in the ephemeral nature of my artworks and Web site led through e-mail communications to my entertaining the idea, which has been brewing ever since September 11, of installing some kind of citywide image using the street map of Manhattan and ephemeral mark-ers such as, as has been my long-term interest, fluffy pom-poms.

In addressing the issue of the WTC towers I had thought of encircling Ground Zero with a kind of "healing ring" of tiny blue pom-poms placed along crevices and interesting lines following the appropriate streets. The number of pom-poms was to be designated by some strange kind of calculation/combination of numbers relating to windows in the WTC towers, deaths involved, date, and other numbers yet to be determined. Last night in the airplane magazine I saw that the well-known artist Mary Miss had proposed a blue wall with flowers to surround Ground Zero. This project along with another (light-beamed ghost towers) published on the cover of the New York Times Magazine, *being high profile, are still however awaiting approval by the new mayor's office. My project of course does not have to be approved.*

Discouraged from duplicating the more obvious encircling idea, it occurred to me all of a sudden that perhaps a "Wishbone/Y" from your "Wishing Why" project might be the perfect symbol. This would be a sort of "Soft Wishing Why Monument," performed and pixelated, of course, but large enough to be seen from the sky for a few moments of possibility. Streets forming a Y pattern near Ground Zero would be chosen and the installation would consist of placing a specified number of pom-poms at intervals along these paths to form the symbol/action of the wishbone. The symbol would then bring into play all of the theoretical/conceptual issues that your project of the "Wishing Why" implies in relation to this event (not to mention the issues of "Monumentality"). It would be important to provide a key, perhaps a Web site, that would develop the surrounding theoretical issues.

Choramancy

The larger context for Will's idea that extended the emblem form into new functionality originated in the FRE application of deconsulting to Miami (a project that began in 1995). After monitoring journalistic treatments of Miami over several months, the group focused on the Miami River in the heart of the original city of Miami, overseen by more than thirty-four public agencies with overlapping responsibilities, site of nearly every public policy problem challenging our society. The title of this project is *Miami Miautre,* treated in a forthcoming study, "Miami Virtue: Psychogeography of the Virtual City," that completes the EmerAgency trilogy.

The chief addition to deconsulting beyond Upsilon Alarm that resulted from the Miami experience was the syncretism of poststructural poetics with the Afro-Caribbean epistemology of divination. The formal operations of divination lent themselves well to chorography as sacred space ("chora" in its ancient usage referred specifically to sacred space) applied to cognitive mapping. Divination as an interface for consulting makes mystory intuitively intelligible. A person with an intractable problem consults a diviner, who uses a chance procedure to connect the personal problem with the collective cultural archive, which is also what mystory does (via the popcycle mapping). Mystory generates a cognitive map showing the maker's singular positioning within the popcycle of institutions that construct identity.

Alan Turing's penultimate public act was to consult a fortune-teller. Mystory and divination share the effect of destiny relative to their respective cultural frames of reference. This conflation of two kinds of consulting (scientific and magical) also supplemented the EmerAgency "Problems B Us" with a program of attraction. Our hybrid treated the public policy issue database as the cultural archive, and the mystory practice as the chance procedure used to connect the personal situation with collective wisdom. Here was an answer to the question of exactly how to use the impresa principle of the emblem as a solution to the problem of the civic sphere (compassion fatigue). The disaster adopted as a personal emblem now reciprocates by serving as oracle. The oracular power is an emergent property of the accumulated MEmorials organized into an archive of contemporary wisdom. The Soft Y MEmorial consults (on) 9/11 simultaneously in two senses.

Theoria

A theoria (group) mystory is configured somewhat differently than when a MEmorial is performed by an individual as an act of autocommunication. One member performs as querent on behalf of the group. The policy issue becomes a montage of attractions—is transformed from indifferent circumstances into a "situation"—by posing to it a personal problem formulated as a burning question. The querent includes a memory from the family discourse of the mystorical popcycle. The remaining parts of the popcycle are documented as follows: entertainment = some aspect of popular culture, including tourism; community = details of the policy disaster; career = FRE theory (choragraphy). The chance repetition of signifiers across the popcycle—a simulacrum—produces an answer to the burning question, in the manner of a divination system. The FRE acting as diviner selects the range of the answer, and the querent (the member posing the question) makes the final decision on the answer based on an emotional experience of recognition. The decision to make a hybrid of mystory and divination was motivated by the encounter with Haitian traders and immigrants that was the focus of the Miami consultation. The methodological principle is neither to speak for the "other," nor to turn over discourse responsibility to the "other," but to syncretize the ways of knowing native to the two cultures. The instruction for egents generalized from Miami is to look for the mode of knowledge native to the subjects of the policy problem (as the Haitians were the target of Miami public policy) and to explore the possibility of a hybrid.

I prepared the following summary of the MEmorial context (constituting a summary of the themes of this book), including lessons learned in Miami, to post on Will's Soft Y Web site (http://www.willpap-projects.com).

Summary: MEmorial Consulting

The EmerAgency

The EmerAgency is a deconstructed virtual distributed consultancy, proposed by the Florida Research Ensemble (FRE) as a practice intended to generate a global civic sphere through the Internet. Egents are self-appointed inventional consultants who supplement conventional utilitarian consultancies by applying arts and letters imaging methodologies to public policy issues. Inventional consulting is informed by the following considerations.

Neo-*ATH*

One of the fundamental features of Greek tragedy, *ATH* means "foolishness" when applied to individual actions and "calamity" when applied to collective actions. Tragedies explored the way individual foolishness or blindness produced collective catastrophe. The EmerAgency updates *ATH* from its original medium and mode (theatrical tragedy) to inquire into contemporary *ATH* using Internet consulting. Poststructural theory shows that conventional consultants remain within a middle reality and ignore the macro- and microcosmic dimensions of disaster. Any manifest disaster is a potential map for locating the boundary of possible/impossible in both collective and individual existence: the aporias of the Real (the absolute limits of human power) and the Subject (the irreducible trauma of individual identity formation). An EmerAgency consultation brings into policy formation an awareness of *ATH* today.

Choramancy (Critical Divination)

As a global practice, egent consulting is syncretic, a hybrid combination of contemporary Western arts and letters operations with the wisdom epistemologies of non-Western traditions. "Consulting" thus refers not only to applied expert knowledge but also to divination practices. Divination offers a relay for composing cognitive maps connecting individual existential problems with collective information resources. The switch or pivot between theory and wisdom is the experience and notion of "situation." In Western terms, circumstances transform into a situation through human intention, choice, purpose. In divination, attunement between the individual and the collective is achieved by posing a personal question to the oracle. In either case, the effect of "situation" is the experience of responsibility that makes events in the world personally relevant.

Cyberpidgin

The Ulmer/Linda Marie Walker e-mail correspondence (the origin of the wishbone Y conjecture, published on Mark Amerika's Alt-X Web site) was initiated as an experiment in cyberpidgin: taking Internet English as a postcolonial pidgin discourse, emerging through netizen interactivity. The exchange tests the idea that quotidian folk and popular customs provide a vernacular code of oral wisdom capable of supporting cross-cultural understanding and communication. The custom of making a wish, having many variations, is just one example, a relay for a thesaurus of other customs that may provide a ready-made universal semiotic. The wishbone images a virtual dialogue, with the scene of two wish makers, each one holding an end of a "wishbone," evoking a many-to-many collaboration in global hope and desire. The optimism of the pidgin interface metaphor for the digital apparatus is that pidgin languages mutate into creoles (full-featured languages) for second-generation practitioners.

Conduction

The wishing custom is explicitly invoked as a supplement to empirical problem solving. The wish takes up where practical utility leaves off. The wish does not replace empirical reason, but resonates with the Holocaust imperative of *Warumverbot* ("here there is no 'why,'" said of the concentration camps). As a consultation, the wish draws on the fourth mode of inference—conduction (after abduction, deduction, induction)—the reasoning specific to image. Image inference (transversal simulacrum) moves from the given to the unknown along an associative chain of shapes: In this case, the Y shape of the initial wishbone. Image inference opens a conceptual idea or *eidos* ("shape" as "topos" or topic) to any natural or designed shape, as a possible category or place for gathering heterogeneous bits of information into an order (chora). In this way a concept becomes a concetto (conceit). Thus the wishbone Y traverses other semantic domains such as the Pythagorean Y, dowsing (the Y-shaped dowsing rod), the switch in all its embodiments (from railroad "frogs" to routers), the Y contrails formed by the *Challenger* shuttle when it exploded, bifurcation points in chaos, Vodou "veve" diagrams showing the passage between the dead and the living. The resulting (temporary) *eidos* may be used as an image classification system (a metaphysics) to rearticulate the configuration of problem-solution currently organizing public life. The consulting premise is that

what constitutes a problem (and possible solutions) is determined by
what a category system renders thinkable.

Electracy

The 9/11 Y exemplifies a practice of electronic monumentality,
developed for the study of electracy (the apparatus that is to digital
media what literacy is to print and alphabetic writing). As part of the
EmerAgency response to the warning that a civic sphere is impossible in a society of the spectacle (image apparatus), the EmerAgency
proposed to treat the Internet as a living or inhabitable monument.
Monumentality then becomes the responsibility not (only) of state,
corporate, or collective entities but of individual subjects as well. The
EmerAgency promotes e-monuments especially as a practice for public
schools, to form a quintestate (adding a fifth estate to the three branches
of government and journalism) whose purpose is to testify and provide witnesses for public policy decisions. A complete e-monument
(MEmorial) includes two elements: the peripheral and the testimonial.

Peripheral

Intractable public problems are treated as sacrifices on behalf of an
abject value—a value that is perhaps not recognized as such, but that is
constitutive of a national way of life (and not an anomaly to be repaired
empirically). The MEmorial consists of a peripheral, a commemorative
device attached to an official public memorial or monument, which calls
attention to the disaster ongoing in the private sphere that is equally
worthy of collective recognition as a sacrifice. This term "peripheral"
also alludes to the logical "route" taken by flash reason (reasoneon)
in avoidance of the linear inference paths of literate logic. The formal
structure of the MEmorial as a whole is based loosely on the conventions
of the Baroque emblem in general (the concetto), and the impresa in
particular, which in their iconicity suggest the possibility of a counter-
propagandistic use of peripheral thinking.

Testimonial

Egents look for the third (obtuse) meaning of the disaster or aporia
(problem), taken as an image, that triggers an involuntary memory of
the egents' personal history. Some detail of the public disaster outside
is recognized (appropriated) as a figure for the egents' inner experience (the disaster in me). The pom-pom Y Pappenheimer traced on
the streets near Ground Zero is a peripheral (it adds commemorative
functionality to the official memorial). Will Pappenheimer combines
the placement of the Y with a testimonial, using the chance operations

generated by information related to the site and disaster as divination
zone to which to pose a burning (personal) question. His question
constitutes a strange attractor. The image (tenor and vehicle) resulting
from this consultation gives the surplus value of a cognitive map, an
attunement *(Stimmung)* that temporarily manifests the metaphysical
order of the choral zone at the moment of a wish.

Backstory

Having already begun the process of relocating to New York City a year or so
prior to 9/11, Will volunteered to serve as querent for a group (FRE) consultation on Lower Manhattan. His first step was to test the method of the punctum
(Roland Barthes's third meaning) on the photographic record that Barbara Jo
Revelle (FRE) made in her mapping of the Miami situation, to open a connection between the two zones of trouble. Revelle lived at an inn on the Miami
River for five weeks in the summer of 1998, documenting the site and taping
interviews with many of the people she met during her psychogeographic drifts
through the site (zone). Will recognized a structural self-portrait (his initial
impresa) in the circumstances of the Jamaican, Winston Murdock.

The Burning Boat (Pappenheimer)

I am editing Barbara Jo Revelle's footage of the video Miami Miautre. *It is a secondary virtual experience, but not without resonance to my own. I shuttle back
and forth through the clips in a nonlinear fashion. The temporal order gives way
to a series of images, shifting back and forth like a deck of cards, as if I were sifting through someone else's memories to try and find out what happened. But the
porous question, "what happened," is not quite what I am searching for.*

*Figure 10.
Winston
Murdock,
"Burned Boat,"
Miami River,
Florida.
Photograph
by Barbara Jo
Revelle, 1998.*

"We will project an image of ourselves onto a field of study and recognize our reflection in it." I come to the image of Winston Murdock, standing on the charred deck of a burned boat. He believes it to be the result of sabotage, a multiplicity of possible narratives, leading to this bleak video frame. He conveys his passion for his calling, rebuilding cheaper engines to assist the Haitians. He knows his trade. The camera pans from his sun-drenched body across a thousand successive frames of abstracted destruction, to the murky river below, to the open sea just visible beyond a miniature bridge far away.

My father's family, in an apparent denial of their Jewish heritage, emulated and married the Northeast WASPs. Not just any WASPs, but established families such as the Forbes. The Forbes had a penchant for the sea. Many of them sailed and sometimes in large vessels for recreation. And my parents sailed with them. They loved danger, pitting themselves against the elements. The heroic image of the mariner was often revisited as a behavioral ideal. Since their day-to-day lives remained largely unaffected by financial worries, I figure they needed to simulate adversity, to march into the blizzard, sail stormy seas, and conquer impossible tasks.

But this is not the story of my life. Perhaps I do not hesitate to seek adventure, change, even at this very moment, but not with a sense of enactment, the puritanical gesture. In postmodernity, enactment is understood to represent transgressive activity. But it needs a pinch of reflexivity. Winston Murdock enacts the cultural transgression of American border politics and becomes the target of cultural censure, Bataille's social abject. And yet, from the opposite end of the economic ladder he would have undoubtedly shared my relatives' sympathy for the mariner's life.

This is a scene of shipwreck, in the sense of what I can see in this image, in the sense of what Winston reports, and in the sense of a condition within my own psyche. Heroism of the kind my father envisioned cannot be so easily enacted here. Though Winston will repair his boat, this is a moment of failure, a failure of a particular U.S. immigration system and race relations, of our attempt to reenact family mythologies. This image of shipwreck engenders a set of questions about a network of external and internal conditions.

It is not unlike the scene I view from the makeshift wooden platform overlooking Ground Zero in New York City, March 2, 2002. Standing at this place is a kind of privilege, a witnessing of an abyss left behind by a colossal shipwreck, the attack on the World Trade Center. The vertical space left behind seems unfillable. The cavernous collapsing ground below continues to be excavated. As much as this place has featured the courage and heroism of public servants such as firemen, it is still for this country at this time a place of unspeakable failure and unthinkable disaster.

But what catches my eye is the thin, almost invisible lines of thousands of signatures scrolled across the plywood structure. I notice that every square inch is covered, including the railings. The signature, a metonymic effect of a lifetime's narration, written across the "abyme." Testimony in shorthand. The view of Ground Zero before us, functioning itself as the tourist's postcard, with writing scratched over its backside, the platform, moves "history into private time," as Susan Stewart suggested in On Longing. *The image of the abyss is transformed from "exterior into interior" as there is simultaneously also the reverse process. Just to the side of the down ramp from this spectator platform is an oddly displaced sculpture of workmen sitting on a skyscraper I-beam, the shining symbol of capital and labor in skyscraper production, now also an I-abyme.*

Accumulation, moving toward an endlessly growing archive, is a particular propensity of the contemporary digital electronic system. Hard-drive space doubles each year. Networking multiplies storage to global dimensions, a sea of important or extraneous information, facts, stories, numbers, images, e-mails, and signature effects awaiting retrieval, a megarepository of collective memory. Categorization and recategorization is nearly instantaneous, called up through text, time, numbers, folders within folders, and the mysterious reach of search engines. Some Web sites are simply lists of categories pertinent to the interests of a particular institution and its audience. Searching and sorting are inventive approaches to the data aggregate. Artists Jennifer and Kevin McCoy take the complete '70s sitcom Starsky and Hutch *and reconfigure sequences of every shot with blue in it, every shot with the cast's girlfriends, and every shot with a track out. The resulting works defy the standard literary narrative and analysis.*

The totalizing idea of completion is not necessary to the archive. Nor is the resulting arrangement simply the issue of decontextualization. Each element retains its context, its generative discourses. Information, text, and imagery, understood as input or as prosthesis, are linked to the corporeal, even if through translational systems of representation. The choragraphic site configures place at the mirror intersection of virtual and real, self and other, history and mystory. The shipwreck, whether it is Winston Murdock's vessel, the empty cavern in Lower Manhattan left by the World Trade Center's collapse, or my biographical condition of impasse, calls up a query and a need for divination. Divination, in the fullest sense of its possible interpretations, for the Internet in particular, is our proposal for consultancy. Ulmer's image of the lightning bolt striking through discourse planes becomes electronic metaphor for alignments created by cross-referencing a range of self-contained institution fields, configuring a transversal, one driven by inquiry, by longing on the Web. This story, this answer, accumulates during the course of theoria-travel, virtually, as well as on foot, through landscapes of everything you always wanted to know about.

The Burning Question

Beginning around the fall of 2000 Will began to spend more time in New York as he struggled with the dilemma of his career: the tension between his teaching in Gainesville and the opportunities of the art scene in New York. This dilemma became the source of the burning question he posed to the chora of Lower Manhattan.

Will Pappenheimer, Querent

The question "What is the situation of my art?" arises in a moment of career difficulty and a perceived need to make a choice. The question is connected with a range of issues including occupation, location, lifestyle, practice, and subject matter. To make my artwork, to know the direction I should take in my artwork, what is the situation that will be most conducive? I am confronted with a choice between attempting to stay in my academic position at the University of Florida, which has become difficult due to personality conflicts, or to make a move to New York where I have begun to set up a studio and pursue a new life. In terms of artistic practice the question carries with it the developments arising in my work while at the University of Florida, such as this very project with FRE, exploration with webcams, or pursuing some new unknown form or content of work. The tenor of the moment seems catastrophic, as if efforts to build a life/art/occupation in Florida were being destroyed/blocked. "What is the situation of my art?"

Posing this question transforms the circumstances of 9/11 for Will by including his intention, his purpose (an existential stance). Compassion fatigue is eliminated since Will's own destiny is inscribed within the details of the disaster (the disaster matters). The theoria mix of destiny and tourist destination may be glimpsed in Will's work in the year prior to 9/11. While exploring the possibility of a move to New York, he looked for competitions and grant opportunities. These ideas featured his use of the pom-pom as medium, including two proposals for projects related to the World Trade Towers.

The Medium, before the Disaster (Pappenheimer)

I became interested in using pom-poms to make artwork in 1994. My attraction included the craft, "low" or anti-art nature of these objects, their simplicity, their feminine associations, their qualities of taking on a cathected relationship between the viewer and the fuzzy, their sizes, mostly small, suggested vulnerability, their molecular resemblance as if they were parts of something else, their use as decoration, as ornamental fringe rather than as primary subject, their softness suggesting infantile versus adult usage, the perceived need for comfort or comfort implying trauma, particulate versus collective identity, their ephemeral nature—transience, impermanence, state of becoming.

My surrounding interests included psychology, Freud's notion of the fetish, the Fort/Da stand-in, part-objects, disappearance and return, presence and absence, object-relation theory; Winnicott's transitional objects. Feminist theories, including categories or traits of perceived gender and artwork associated with it. Resignification, appropriation, meaning shift, use-value, ideological and cultural shifts and amalgamations, polysemy and multivalence. Posing the theories about the precision of the image through color theory, Pointillism (from Seurat to Chuck Close), the phenomenology of seeing, the physiology of seeing, new digital image technologies, the pixel image, against the problematics of representation through setting up an image that can't be seen except through a system, or not yet seeable, not really fixable, not objectifiable, not knowable.

Fluffy Pom Pom Flemish Print Redecoration Project, *1997, instructional video, excerpts from the full twelve-minute video. In this instructional video I suggested that old outmoded Dutch prints could be redecorated using different artwork strategies to arrange colorful pom-poms on the prints and then scanning them into the computer to create new and "better" digital works. This is where I developed the idea of using lines of pom-poms to trace or emphasize existing formal elements or to create entirely new overlaid visual imagery. The resulting hybrids imparted a new meaning to the original work.*

In the opening introduction to the video: "Fluffy poms-poms are usually used at the fringe of things like clothing. Even though they are often thought of as decorative or insignificant, they are also very colorful, inescapably cozy, and full of their own kind of life. Pom-poms come in a surprising range of sizes, all the way from 2 inches down to 2 or 3 millimeters. This allows for a wide range of uses as well as different interpretations of what they mean. They are a perfect element to redecorate our eighteenth-century Dutch prints."

Venus Apartment, *9' x 10'. Four thousand one-inch pom-poms, exhibited at the Harn Museum of Art, 2000. Artwork instructions (included in framed plaque next to artwork): "I went to landofvenus.com and Venus wasn't there. She was probably out because it was about 3:30 PM her time. It was another 2:30 minutes till her next show. I copied a still of her apartment and separated it out into 8 colors that matched the colors of pom poms I had. Using a projection of this image I arranged the about 3750 pom poms to match the corresponding colors in a 10 by 7 and a half foot square."*

Lower Manhattan Cultural Council. 5 World Trade Center, Suite 9235. New York, NY 10048. March 7, 2001. Proposals for World Views Studio

Residency Program. *The WTC Fluffy Pom-Pom Window Display Project. This project would involve a performative installation gesture consisting of a giant image placed in the windows of a World Trade Center tower (WTC). The image would be composed of up to 20,000 small multicolored pom-poms positioned as stand-ins for pixels, one in each window of approximately one hundred floors of the WTC. The source image would be derived from a webcam download from a location and subject at great distance from the WTC. The nature of this source image would have to be determined through research and aesthetic considerations. The image dimensions, approximately two hundred wide by one hundred high in pixels or pom-poms, would wrap around the building. It would only be visible conceptually. Pictures of as many pom-poms in situ as possible would be taken and archived on a WWW site in the configuration of the image.*

The LMCC offered yearly artist residences on the ninety-second floor of Tower One. I had visited a friend in the residency there in 1999 and had been considering site-specific ideas for the proposal the previous spring. There were two proposals I submitted, one involving webcams associated with each business in the building and the other to install a huge image made of pom-poms that were to be distributed to each business within the building and displayed in each window. The resulting displays, one colored pom per window, in theory, would create a wraparound image on the entire skyscraper. The image, interestingly enough, was yet to be determined, and my proposal was not accepted.

Through this process there was at some level a kind of emotional investment and bonding I had with both the artist program and the buildings. After September 11 I reflected on this proposal, in particular calculating the number of windows in each building, the haunting psychological image of the windows broken and the pom-poms scattered across the area had I executed my project. I might have been in the buildings when they were hit. (One of the artists accepted, Michael Richards, was in fact killed.) There was also the question of what was the image to be? I suppose this is all part of my burning question.

Mystory

The Miami template indicated that the disaster zone could be made to answer the burning question by a mystorical mapping across the relevant popcycle. The chance procedure required for divination to produce its uncanny effect of recognition involves the repetition of a signifier between the querent's personal memory and the other parts of the popcycle. To compose his divination engine, Will generated a preliminary mystory.

The Pappenheimer Popcycle

Family.

My first instrument/my father's instrument: the cello
Family music mythologies:
  - *Discipline/Impulse*
  - *Science/Music*
  - *Masculine/Feminine*
  - *Father/Mother*
  - *Rational/Emotional*
  - *Controlled/Uncontrollable*
  - *Skill/Talent*

The renaissance man, the humanist as the ultimate persona bringing all aspects of man as "artifice" and the scientific as "real" under controlled creativity, achievement, and fulfillment. Tuning fork: hard, precise.
  - *I learn classical music/I taught myself folk rock*
  - *The scientific real blended with my father's falsification of events.*
  - *Classical music as the music of appearance and control, success/rock and blues as the music of the undercurrent struggle and the acknowledgment of breakdown*

Community (School)

Fayerweather St./Things Fall Apart. Fayerweather St. = Fair Weather spelled with a Y, street I grew up on, wealthy Cambridge intellectual establishment, awareness of a privileged demographic with its sheen of intelligentsia and power, named after General Fayerweather, implying the military power that is necessary to maintain hegemony. Things Fall Apart by Chinua Achebe, middle school reading, rise of multicultural education, the undercurrent or questioning of colonialism, token integration in my school but nevertheless very important, biracial makeout sessions in Longfellow Park.

Career Discourse

My first remembered painting, won first prize at a county fair, along with some vegetables we had grown: an orange dragon I called a "clobster" signed dislexically in blue: mailliW. My problem/asset of dyslexia: word and image doubling/mirroring. Boyhood fascination with butterfly collecting: butterfly wings unfolding mirror Y (WilliamImailliW), the Y of the antennae, the flapping of wings. My first artworld interest: Surrealism, Dalí/Magritte. The subconscious, image doubling. Rosalind Krauss: Moteur and Pulse from Formless—frame/beat as subconscious, reflexive, sequence as conscious, scopophilic gaze, illusion of continuity. Mike Kelley/Paul McCarthy Heidi, the contrast of Plato and the

*philosophic noncategory of abjection. Object-relations psychology, Winnicott's
part-object and his essay "The Good Enough Mother."*

Entertainment

First horror movie: Two Headed Killer *begins what I remember as a series
of nightmares.* 2001—*one of the most resonant movies for me, three stages of
development punctuated by an exposure and alignment of slabs which emit a
defining hum. First rock concert: the Doors. They were late arriving. Showed their
films instead. Morrison caught in a firing squad, shot, vomits; beginning interest
in abjection. A verse from a favorite Doors song, "When the Music's Over":
"I hear a very special sound with your ear down to the ground very near yet very
far very soft yet very clear. We want the world and we want it, now, NOW."*

The Y *eidos* from Upsilon Alarm had already produced the sting (punctum)
of involuntary memory that resonated with the childhood scene. Will enlarged
the family memory as the basis for a mystorical divination (deconsultation).

Family Becoming (Pappenheimer)

*Music. My mother and father were both classically trained musicians and
they wanted to pass these skills on to their children. To my father in particular,
playing classical music represented the fully rounded educated and successful person. Science and academics were the rational "real" and music was its
counterpart: emotional expression. Both categories seemed to be envisioned
by my father as part of the order of things, as part of the ideal life. My mother,
who was the more highly trained and gifted musician, was cast as the awesome
embodiment of female irrationality and deep emotion, as the quintessential
"otherness" of my father. The respect and sublimation of this otherness, as well
as many of the concepts my father tried to impart, seemed to derive from his
deep roots in the humanist tradition as it unfolded into the burgeoning field of
science in the mid-twentieth century.*

*Impossibility-incongruity. Every day my siblings and I were supposed to re-
treat to a sublime self-generated world of practicing our instruments, a peculiar
world of the crossing of self-discipline and emotional expression. My instrument was the cello. Invariably it began with the tuning process. The tuning fork
was the preferred method. To tune the A string the tuning fork was activated by
striking it against a hard object and then touching it to the instrument. Upon
contact the note would seem to emanate from deep within the instrument, or
from everywhere. The tuning then proceeded sympathetically: other strings
were tuned in harmonic fifths by ear.*

Skill and gift. Tuning was also connected to the notion of pitch, the learned

Figure 11. Will Pappenheimer, "Pom-Pom Trail."

process and gift (or lack thereof) to hear a perfect note, to play in tune. A good ear represented a high aptitude in this regard. Perfect pitch was applied to a rare few with amazing abilities to always hit the right note. These aspects mirrored family notions of acquiring skill, becoming educated, erudite, intelligent, and the ability to be persuasive conversationally.

Transfer. The tuning fork was mysterious in that it transferred its sound

*to another object. Even after it was struck, it put out very little sound until it
contacted another object. The sound that resulted seemed hard to locate, as if
it came from within the whole object. I remember discovering that touching
the tuning fork to the head caused the note to emanate from inside the head.
Touching the fork to the tongue produced an unbearably intense sensation of
tickling and burning.*

The initial commitment to the Y *eidos*, appropriated into Will's mystory
through this memory of tuning his cello, determined that Will's use of the
chance encounter to tune the choral zone of the disaster would differ from the
one Revelle used in Miami (that the fork tunes the A string confirms in its
rhyme with the "A" of EmerAgency, differAnce, and the rest of the theoretical A-effects that the scene is a good choice for the pattern). Revelle drifted
through the area surrounding the Miami River, interviewing whomever she
happened to meet, which could be anyone from a homeless derelict to an officer
of the Coast Guard. As the term "drift" suggests, the FRE use of "situation"
alludes to the French situationists and the connection between chorography
and psychogeography. The goal of the deconsultation is not (only) to solve the
querent's problem, but to use this hybrid divination as a way to test the categorical power of images to configure the site of the disaster in another way. The
mapping between the personal problem and the disaster measures the mood of
the place (the chora), and establishes an attunement whose singularity opens up
the problem to what Deleuze and Guattari call a "line of flight," an opportunity
for deterritorializing the zone as impasse or aporia and setting in motion a new
dynamic, new connections. If problems are dependent on category formation,
then the deconsultancy goes outside the problems to the frame of categorization
itself. The signifier that will be the answer to the burning question will at the
same time be generalized commemoratively as testimony of the group subject
and collective identity.

Rather than drifting or wandering through the streets of Lower Manhattan,
Will projected the Y *eidos* onto the streets of a neighborhood adjacent to
Ground Zero. The repetition of the tuning fork shape in the wishing Y meditation was revealed by the mystory as a confirmation of Will's decision to use
the divination ritual. His tour was not a drift but a ritual procession. Made of
a trail of pom-poms, this Y functioned as a dowsing rod to produce within the
area of the designated streets the chance meeting (the epiphany) that would be
the answer to his burning question. In MEmorial terms, the pom-pom Y is a
peripheral (even an *ephemorial*), anticipating, in this case, the official memorial whose design is still a matter of debate, to be constructed on the site of
Ground Zero.

Y Site in TriBeca (Pappenheimer)

Through processes of inquiry, attunement, and chance operations, the time, location, and size of the Y formation has been enumerated. The date of the action/installation will be April 20, 2002. The location is intentionally peripheral, at the intersection of West Broadway and Hudson Streets in TriBeca, with the total length extending eight to nine city blocks. The color of the pom-poms will be predominantly orange to suggest a state of E-mergency.

James Bogardus Triangle Park (at the confluence of the Y). The plaque reads: "James Bogardus (1800–1874) was an architect, engineer and inventor who devised the iron front building and the freestanding iron fire towers and shot towers that foretold the construction of the skyscraper as a building type. Bogardus built the world's first cast-iron building (184y) at the northwest corner of Washington and Murray Streets. Surviving cast-iron buildings can be seen nearby at 75 Murray Street (1857) and 85 Leonard Street (1860). David N. Dickens, Mayor. New York City Department of Transportation. Lucas J. Riccio, Ph.D., P.E. Commissioner." Note the use of the word "foretold." Note that the world's first cast-iron building was labeled "184y"—ending in Y. Need to investigate this building.

Finding Y and Sizing Y

Statistics:

20 street blocks = 1 mile = 5,280 feet

1 street block = 264 feet

5 blocks = 1,320 feet, each arm of Y

4×3 blocks = 3,168 feet, total Y

My shoe size = about 1 foot

my birthday = July 27, 1954

1,048,576 bytes (220) = 1 megabyte = 1,024 kilobytes

1,024 (210) bytes = 1 kilobyte

In terms of siting/situating the Y, I am headed, in my emotive memory, toward the intersection of West Broadway and Hudson Streets with the James Borgadus Triangle Park. The intersection is also near the center of TriBeca, so triangulation and 3s are very present. I am strangely attracted to this site rather than Battery Park also because it is peripheral, secondary, ficelle, minor compared to the major implications of the Battery Park site. But I will figure out how to include other Ys otherwise not chosen here.

Numerolog-Y

At this point I am thinking of starting with two five-block lengths for the bifurcation of the Y (along West Broadway and Hudson Streets) and a two *to three-block length for the joint section (along West Broadway), such that the figure still suggests the shape of the wishbone. It seems right that the distance between pom-poms should be the length of my shoe size, which is about a foot. Calculating the standard distance of street blocks in NYC to be twenty blocks to the mile, this would give me around 1,320 pom-poms for each arm of the Y (2,640). This would leave a little over one block (about 360 pom-poms) to bring the total number of pom-poms to about 3,000 (the approximate number of deaths from 9/11). Adding to this will be wishes/questions included by the Web site visitors. There are approximately three and something blocks left before excavation on the Trade Center site begins. This gives a leeway of about 696 pom-poms. I'm guessing that a wish/question sentence input into the Web site will be fairly long, about eighteen words, this gives about ninety-four characters with spaces. If I were to encode this directly into poms it would allow for only about six sentences. Therefore I think it might be a good idea to calculate the number of characters in a wish/question and then add numerals of the number together (94, 9 + 4 = 13) to give the number of pom-poms. Each wish/question would be separated by a blue pom. (This would allow for more like 60 wishes.)*

Associated with the MEmorial peripheral was a companion Web site on which visitors were asked to write a wish.

The Web of Wishes

Through the month of April, an accompanying Web site will collect wishes/ questions surrounding the 9/11 event as well as the audience's own personal wishes/questions. Consistent with the wishbone tradition, where the wish must be kept secret, visitors to the Web site will be invited to input wish/questions online that will be encrypted by replacing letters with password-type dots. The questions will then be stored and displayed on another Web page online. To determine the number of pom-poms, the approximate number of casualties from the 9/11 disaster will be added to compressed wishes/questions input into the Web site. The number of pom-poms will then determine the size of the Y and the ending place of the Wishing Walk. So we say that wishes/questions are encrypted and then compressed before they are added to the Y as poms. But let's keep the first encryption so that password dots appear as the original words and spaces so that users can "see" the outline proof of their wishes. A typical ninety-four-character sentence wish would become about twelve poms.

A former student of ours, Josh Weihnacht, programmed the Web site to encrypt the text wishes into emergency-colored asterisks.

Josh Weihnacht to Invent-L

I like the idea of adding up the number of characters. But I think that then adding the digits of this number together starts to become too cryptic. For example, someone who entered in an eighteen-character wish would have a longer string of pom-poms than someone who entered in an eighty-character wish. This is a little anti-intuitive for those looking at pom-poms. An alternate idea would be to add up the characters and have a pom-pom represent a fixed number of characters (eight characters would seem appropriate in making reference to the bytes used in the Web site, though four (half a byte) or sixteen (two bytes) would also work if you needed to fudge the number of pom-poms a bit). I like the idea of the blue pom-pom separators since it both makes the boundaries of the wishes more legible and reminds me of the EOL (end-of-line) and EOF (end-of-file) markers used in computer files. (e-mail from Weinacht)

For the Web site I composed a theoretical rationale explaining the function of the wishes.

The Y Fortune

The wish is

1. A pun (a catachresis): it is itself and stands in for the unnamable.
2. A ritual practice invoking the wisdom traditions concerned with fortuna.
3. A meditation on the relation between one's goals and one's actions.
4. A map showing the wisher's position on the grid of history.

1. Why Y?
The homophone connecting "Why?" and "Y" is a puncept—a category gathering and relating a semantic field based on similarity of signifier rather than of signified. Puncepts do not replace concepts but trace alternative paths through language and across languages (macaronic puns). Deleuze referred to this path as the "logic of sense." Rhizomes form around such switch points in discourse. In conditions of "problem" it is possible to move from aporia (dilemma) through the dialectical stages of diaporia and euporia (to untangle the knot), in which case the tension created by a question (why?) is released and resolved. Some conditions exceed the frame of "problem." These are conditions of absolute aporia: impossible dilemma. In these conditions the tension of a question (why?) is not released but builds until reaching a jump point

Figure 12. Will Pappenheimer, "Pom-Pom Map."

into a different logic. Puncepts support this discontinuous nonlinear mode of inference. The pun is a pivot, an Archimedian fulcrum, in discourse (puncepts may be nonverbal), of the kind exploited in haiku. As Basho advised, "learn about pine from the pine." That is, learn about pining from the pine tree; learn about the verb from the noun. The pine standing apart, evergreen in winter; I am alone. Learn about why from Y. The Y opens a line of flight. It shows the fly the way out of the fly bottle. It does not turn around (convert) but jumps, switches (the frog in the tracks).

2. What Wish?
Your wish is a vigil candle of desire. When everything has been explained regarding the history, theory, physics, and metaphysics of the institutions of business and religion that intersected on 9/11 (and we look forward to receiving these explanations), there will remain the incalculable dimension of human desire. Our wishes hold the place of and gesture toward this dimension. They are to desire what vigil candles are to fire as such. Desire built the twin towers, and desire destroyed them. When we make a wish, we are performing a ritual of fortune that has atrophied and all but disappeared from awareness and behavior in

modernity, reduced to a few superstitions, astrology columns in newspapers, and the New Age section of bookstores. The Wishing Y proposes a post-Enlightenment syncretism of science with fortune, to reinstill in the enterprise of the "Fortuna 500" the modality of wisdom, such as is embodied in divination traditions. The point is not to return to magic, but to move out of the time of opposition between the two meanings of enlightenment into a cooperation, a collaboration between worldviews. To make a wish counts first as a commemoration and acknowledgment of fortune (Bataille's General Economy whose operating principle is "death is necessary") as a force in human affairs, for better or worse.

3. Zone Y

In his science fiction masterpiece *Stalker,* the Russian filmmaker Andrei Tarkovsky told the story of a guide who took people into a special zone created in a particular region by the visit of a vehicle from another planet with a far superior civilization. At the heart of this devastated zone, which only a few such guides were able to navigate due to the supposed purity of their spirits, could be found a room that would grant to pilgrims any wish they might make. Even more dangerous than the risks of getting to the room was the fact that what was granted was not necessarily the wish one asked for, but the true wish in the petitioner's heart. Whatever wish one makes, the wishing Y is an opportunity to commemorate the wish manifested in the trace one makes through life (the zone).

4. Problems B Us

What makes Ground Zero sacred in part is its status as a new measure of the possible. The collapse of the towers included the fall of the letters I-M from impossible. I. Am. Possible. Perhaps one day someone will explain 9/11, but for now it explains us, within an epistemology of meaning determined through relationships within a field. September 11 makes perceptible the Lacanian Real, a macrocosmic limit of human ambition. At the same time, this Real in collective material history is marked with a spirit Y, the X of excess meaning, sometimes described as the "sublime." The a-causal synchronicity of the collapsing towers and the revelation of systemic corporate fraud manifests the intelligence of the Real.

The sublime is in me, in the microcosm within each person, bringing into experience the trauma of subjectivation, of identity formation. There is an uncanny moment of recognition, mediated through the wish, when I encounter the disaster—the limit border—in me: my death, my aporia. I find in some detail of the event-field a mirror that brings news (surprisingly) about my own self, as if I am posting my own photocopied visage on the kiosk or the protective fence, asking after my own whereabouts. The modality of the wish is that of a question in a contemporary divination practice, whose purpose is to rebuild the cognitive map connecting individuals with collective historical forces. If we gave it voice the wish would end in that rising note that spread through American English not long ago (?) signaling the beginning of a new era of doubt in our destination or destiny (?).

The wish is

1. A pun (a catachresis): it is itself and stands in for the unnamable.
2. A ritual practice invoking the wisdom traditions concerned with fortuna.
3. A meditation on the relation between one's goals and one's actions.
4. A map showing the wisher's position on the grid of history.

Will performed the marking of the Y site in the manner of a ritual rather than as a quest in an adventure story.

The Performance (Pappenheimer)

My performance plan is to stay quite focused on putting down poms and the practice of divining, which is what I am supposed to be doing. One might even say this is a trance state. I will have handout cards for people with questions that I and my documenters can pass out. We want to interact with any audience that gets interested but not get completely distracted. I'm going to start early in the morning around 7 a.m. and be there as long as it takes to create the Y from 3,000-plus poms. I'll start at the intersection of W. Broadway and Hudson, head up Hudson five blocks, cross over to W. Broadway and come back down past the intersection for a few more blocks to complete the Y. Look for a line of pom-poms mostly at street level, on windowsills, cracks, and at the intersection of buildings and sidewalk.

The FRE reviewed sixty minutes or so of edited video documenting Will's performance of the Y divination ritual, recorded April 20 in New York City.

Ulmer Sees the Video

The artist in deep concentration, wearing a transparent backpack (from Toys R Us?) filled with quarter-inch Day-Glo EmerAgency pom-poms. He lays down a trail of pom-poms articulating a predetermined Y figure on the city grid. The base of the stem touches the barricades cordoning off Ground

Zero; the site of division (of choice) is at a small green space dedicated to the man who invented the iron-frame engineering structure that is the basis for skyscraper architecture.

The artist begins with all-purpose glue squeeze bottle, ruler, bag of poms in hand, and meticulously places each pom in the mathematically determined site. Soon, however, the procedure evolved into a Hansel and Gretel venture into the woods, leaving a trail of breadcrumbs. The bright poms, small as they were, stood out sharply against the urban concrete stone storefront street asphalt iron. *Suddenly everything honked.* Documenting the operation were several camerapersons, one of whom seemed to be taking close-ups of each pom-pom, tracking its fall or confirming its fixed establishment.

The ritual motion, pursued with a determined purpose, carried the artist across the path of a family attempting to enter its residence (they respectfully stood back to let the crazy person pass); a car (miraculously) stopped midway through a turn so as not to run over the querent; pedestrians moving toward the farthest edge of the curb to be first across the intersection were intimidated and cut off by the passing dispenser egent for whom they stood aside (was it the phalanx of orbiting camera persons, like tourists taping a parade, that earned this respect?).

Encountered along the way: the crew of Emergency Medical Team unit 408, telling the tale of the partner (not on duty that day) who was the first to call in the incident of the plane striking the tower; a city work crew, garbed in Day-Glo safety jackets, using a small wheeled measuring device to determine exact figures for leveling the street; a business establishment called the Nautical Instrument Company, entered by the documenter, who was informed that the items for sale had everything to do with navigation (charts, sextants, compasses, and the like) but nothing to do with rescue or shipwreck gear. On the wall above the glass cases filled with sea-going tools hung a painting depicting a schooner under full sail; the exterior of a posh restaurant whose owner was persuaded to allow the pom-Y to trace his window ledge. As the trail approached the barricades pom distance shrunk to just a few inches, until the last of 3,064 individual EmerAgency pom-poms (number determined by the total figure of 9/11 casualties published that morning in the newspaper) bounced into place.

The artist's hand (close-up) bore a Band-Aid from a supply purchased along the route after a mishap. A soft but steady rain came down, marking the standing puddles with a rhythm of bouncing circles. The Glo-stripes on the sawhorse barriers outlining the threshold of disaster echoed the color of the tiny trail of stand-in asterisks, encoding the characters inscribed on the Web site as wishes, promising a future, each wish a vigil candle of desire.

The organizer of the Free Biennial visited the peripheral Y the day after the performance, and glimpsed an invasion of baby tribbles, suggesting that the walk had been a "trek."

Sal Randolph to Will Pappenheimer

I heard about you putting out the Y from your friend Alexa, who came on the tour. I'm afraid the tour never made it very far south. A rather bedraggled bunch trouped through the rain, but gave up about a third of the way through the tour route at Union Square. It was actually a very peculiar and increasingly funny tour because at each stop we found only traces or signs of art that had once been there, but had been removed.

I went down today, though, to look at the Y, and it was really spectacular. I was moved by the tender little pom-poms, fragile as wishes, blown around but still there. I watched a guy try to dig one out of a sidewalk crack with his toe and I asked him what he thought. "I don't know what they are!" he said, "but they're everywhere! They're multiplying!" I took lots of pictures—a few are attached. I imagine you documented things well, but I thought perhaps I could add the element of time and fate. I think it would be interesting to go back in a week, and two weeks, and see what was still there. I'd be happy to put the pics I took on a CD and hand them over or send them. I would be really interested to know what your experience has been with this piece—

Figure 13. Will Pappenheimer, "Nautical Instruments Company."

how it felt to do something so large and so ephemeral. I've been thinking a lot about this because it is also characteristic of the [free] biennial as a whole.

Discussion on the FRE Listserv (Invent-L) produced an important contribution to reading the pattern emerging from the consultation.

The Architectural Tuning Fork (Pappenheimer)

I must thank you, Becki, for your reference to MSN's Slate (http://slate.msn. com/?id=2060207). Last night it led me down the most important digital dowsing path to date. The article on Islamic correspondences/influences of Japanese architect Yamasaki in designing the WTCs as a plaza similar to Mecca, with two minarets, is nothing less than stunning and in all likelihood one of the reasons for bin Laden's focus on base buildings. Together with the suggestion you also made of associating the pointed arches with tuning forks and Ys, I set out by looking at my own video footage of the Trade Towers both before and after the attacks, and of course set off virtually through the Internet to look at Islamic architecture.

As you'll see once I set up some imagery and pages to deal with this issue, the resemblance of the WTC with many of the important religious and palace sites of the Middle East is undeniable. In particular I found a fascinating tomb in Iran called Monar-e-Jonban or the Shaking Minarets. In this landmark two minarets flank a central wishbone-shaped arch. The reason they are thought of as "shaking" is that the geometry of the architecture is such that if one walks up one tower the other one shakes identically. A veritable tuning fork. So powerful was its shaking that a couple of these mosques have lost two-thirds of their minarets. The British, as colonial powers, were often rumored to be responsible for this problem. This pair of tombs, the WTC, and Monar-e-Jonban so uncannily suggest the relationships between currently opposing cultures and show how reflecting the one is (always) in the other.

One more interesting event/phenomenon gets added to this mix. Last summer I had the wonderful privilege of seeing/hearing the concert debut of a piece by avant-garde guitar artist Glenn Branca performed in the plaza between the two Trade Center towers. It was called Symphony no. 13, Hallucination City, and consisted, as he is known for, of a piece for one hundred electric guitars. The sound created by these many different guitarists playing the same chords, itself like the mechanism of the tuning fork, rose and resonated to engulf the entire plaza beneath the towers, as if for a moment they were transformed from commerce to music, as Greg suggested, a giant tuning fork. I made a short video of this experience this past fall as part of a post-9/11 memorial project with my video class. Now of course, it has taken on another overtone.

The tuning fork, in its shape and in its generative power, I now realize takes hold within these images for me because it was the mysterious instrument with which I tuned my cello as a child.

There remained the question of divination: What was the answer to the burning question? What was the pattern emerging from the documentation? What image gathered the divergent elements of the zone into a mood revealing the situation of 9/11 as a potential hexagram of American wisdom?

The Oracle (Pappenheimer)

Following is a snapshot of relationships I have been thinking about as they pertain to the Soft Wishing Y Project, 9/11, and Mystory. Observations are formed in paired relations so they can be cross-referenced. I am still thinking about alignments that might lead to something practical.

    Will's burning question: "What is the situation of my artwork?"

- *Florida/NYC*
- *Decentered/centered artworlds*
- *Collaboration/solo—the judgment of institutions*
- *Artwork within the academy/artwork outside the academy, the gallery-museum?*
- *Image-artwork as record or representation/image-artwork as recognition (see Rosalind Krauss's* The Convulsive Image*)*
- *Photo doubling: (1) frame split/convergence; (2) signifying split: one image/thing looks like another; obviously Greg's work influences the latter trajectory*

    Patterns? The tuning fork is my personal experience of the Pythagorean Y (literally, the music of the spheres, tuning the world cello), with the shape as eidos *transversing the stories of family, New York City (the twin towers), and career (Pythagorean theory expressed in Plato's* Timaeus*).*

    Shipping: The starting point of this project in the aftermath of the WTC collapse as the condition of shipwreck (following from the Miami Miautre *focus on Haitian boats, both traders and refugees). Will's visits to the platforms overlooking the smoldering ruins of Ground Zero as if overlooking* aporia*. Will senses the analogy to conditions in his own biography and this image/site becomes a background to burning questions in both private and civic spheres.*

    Forbes: My father's family marrying into the Northeast WASPs, families like the Forbes. The Forbes had a penchant for the sea. Many of them sailed and sometimes in large vessels for recreation. Winslow Homer: The suitor of my great-grandmother Helena DeKay (my middle namesake, DeKay). Painted

*romantic paintings of eastern seaboard mariners. One of the first to extend this
image to landscapes and seascapes of Florida.*

Winston Murdock (Winston = Winslow): From working on the Miami
Miautre *project, burned boat, sabotaged by whom? Winston as mariner expert
from the third world caught in U.S. border politics. Free Biennial opening party
boat: held April 2, 2001, at the Frying Pan, a burned-out boat at the docks
in Manhattan transformed into a dance club, looks very similar to Winston
Murdock's boat.*

*New York Nautical Society encountered on the Y installation walk. Dave
Herman, while documenting the Wishing Y performance, asked the shop person if there were items to assist in a shipwreck. The answer is basically no, only
instruments to assist in navigation.*

Keys to the Response

*Is the Y found? I found it in the Ulmer/Walker correspondence, even if Ulmer
is collaborator. The suggestion/answer of the shop person in the New York
Nautical Society was: this is not about disaster, it's about navigation. Does the
Y separate as in "make a choice"? Does the Y converge as in "follow two tracks
simultaneously"?*

First Reading

Like the LMDC commemoration, the EmerAgency deconsultation on 9/11 is
a work in progress. Will at least has an answer to his burning question. The
answer is fundamentally ambiguous and depends on an emotional recognition
on the part of the querent. At the same time, the querent must submit to the
chance system for the selection of relevant stories or documents administered
by the diviner (the FRE). In this case, there were two strong patterns available:
the tuning fork and the ship. The experiment was to treat them as trigrams: two
trigrams make a hexagram in the I Ching oracle (tuning + navigation). The encounter with the nautical instruments shop was "instrumental" in the choice.
But how to read the scene? The reading must be metonymic, that is, taking the
initial sign as the index of a semantic field, and then examining the field to find
relevant material. "There just isn't any building, except maybe the Pyramids,
that could withstand the consequences of an enormous jetliner smashing into it
with a full load of fuel. 'You can't design for that, just like you can't design for the
epicenter of an earthquake,' David Childs said" (Goldberger 2001, 78). In our
brainstorming sessions we considered the possibility that the oracle assessed
Will's career situation as a need to prepare for a worst-case scenario (such as not
getting tenure). "You have enemies!" Ultimately, however, what felt right was
the wisdom that (as Bradley McGee might have said some day), "shit happens."

One expert observed, even if it were possible to anticipate total catastrophe in a design, the cost would be prohibitive "and the natural light would disappear" (ibid.). There needs to be a balance between safety and risk. The oracle is not saying "prepare for the worst," but "mind how you steer."

As a resident of New York, Will continued his engagement with the 9/11 project.

Pappenheimer Talks with the City

I signed up along with five thousand others in the New York City area to join today in what was described as a historic twenty-first-century town hall meeting at the Jacob Javits Center to help shape plans for the redevelopment of downtown New York and the creation of a memorial for 9/11. I found myself integrally involved and moved by the experience, and could not help noticing certain public choices echoing Soft Wishing Why discoveries.

The meeting was labeled "Listening to the City," with the logo showing the empty lower Manhattan area glowing with the sound of what must be emanating from a giant tuning fork (www.listeningtothecity.org). It involved advance registration on a Web site, and then upon arrival being seated at demographically diverse tables and discussing issues and decisions that were reported technologically to a central tabulation area. All this was guided by city officials and professionals with, hopefully, the eager ears of the Lower Manhattan Development Corporation (LMDC), the Port Authority, and other powers that be who now seem to be feeling some level of scrutiny due to various controversies emerging around the redevelopment plans. Once the six architectural plans for lower Manhattan were posted on the Web site of the LMDC, four thousand hits per second were received, demonstrating both the citywide and worldwide interest and intense desire for a participatory decision-making process.

My table included a facilitator from Minneapolis, a displaced lower Manhattan resident who watched the Trade Center towers get hit, burn, and collapse outside his window, a senior option analyst from Dean Witter, the largest employer in the South Tower, a Hispanic social worker working with families directly affected by the towers' collapse, an architect from Brooklyn working in Manhattan, a cultural promoter planner from New Jersey, a family member who lost two relatives as firemen, and myself, of course, self-described as an educator and artist having just moved to New York during this episode and interested in creating an Internet memorial. I was immediately and affectionately put to work translating the group discussions into summary notes on the computer to be sent to the central command center for the conference feedback.

There is not enough room to go into detail about the discussions we had, but some of the concerns were the primacy and development of the concept

of memorial space(s), equity and residency issues such as affordable housing,
allowing small service businesses to reenter and continue to flourish, not trying
to remake the highest skyscrapers, and in particular choosing architects that
would create a fascinating design, perhaps through competition, one that is not
evident in the plans so far. More than once the great architectural/city spaces
of Europe were evoked as a replacement for sterile towering skyscrapers.

Of the six architectural plans discussed, the most favored at the town meet-
ing was the last, called the Memorial Promenade. This plan includes a widening
of West Street to become a long grand walkway park stretching from Battery
Park up to the Trade Center site and then unfolding into a park. The ground
plan has a Y or tuning fork formation with a stress on the horizontal walk, echo-
ing the Y walk that figured so importantly in the Soft Wishing Y Memorial. A
secondary interest, particularly at our table, was in the Memorial Triangle plan,
confirming our interest in the related triangle form (the three points of the Y, dif-
ference plus syncretism, triangulation, Pythagoras, Tribeca, etc.). One member
of our table stated that Boston has its "squares" and New York has "triangles."

In one more instance of recognition, transportation planners discussed the
importance of creating an intermodal intersection of different transportation
systems stacked on top of one another, such that one could go from the subway
system to the train system to the walking system to the bus system. No doubt
they had been reading Greg's theory of Stimmung.

Will the Pomer

By July, 2003, 5,200 proposals for the memorial to be built at Ground Zero
had been received. After the announcement of the eight finalists, seventy of the

Figure 14. Will Pappenheimer, "Crossing Chambers."

nonwinners met in a forum to vent their frustrations. "The only thing more diverse than the nonwinners were their nonwinning entries. There were models on display with lots of trees, stairs, reflecting pools and light. There were flat stones laid in the ground to form the numbers 9/11. There was a 70-foot glass sculpture of a pair of hands cupped together reaching for the heavens, and a sort of paddle-wheel thing that people pushed, and when they pushed it, it generated energy, and the energy was used to power spotlights, and the spotlights shone up into the sky, and the intensity of the shine, well, it depended on how many people were pushing the wheel" (Alan Feuer, *New York Times*, December 7, 2003). As for the finalists, critics quickly judged the designs "disappointing." "No Vietnam Wall."

In the living monument of the Internet the winner/loser distinction is irrelevant, since the consultation gathers the individual testimonials into a networked civic sphere. Whatever permanent commemoration is put in place as part of Libeskind's overall design, the EmerAgency asterisk that marks the event of a MEmorial is prepared in advance. At the forum participants continued in person "what they had done for many months online, which is to say they thought, talked, argued, vented, ranted, complained and basically obsessed to the point of melt-down over how to build the best possible World Trade Center memorial" (ibid.) The lesson to be drawn from this effort to democratize monumentality is that this online conversation is itself an electrate commemoration.

THE WEB OF CHANGES

> The impossibility of seeing is followed by the impossibility of not seeing, of not foreseeing.
>
> —*Paul Virilio,* Open Sky

The Zone of Indistinction

How does the MEmorial peripheral contribute to a 9/11 consultation? The MEmorial does not commemorate the twin towers directly, since it recalls not the nationally validated loss of those killed on 9/11, but notices an abject sacrifice on behalf of an unrecognized or unappreciated value whose importance to American identity is made accessible through its association/juxtaposition with the public commemoration. Bradley McGee's death juxtaposed with the loss of the *Challenger* crew commemorated the family value that makes it impossible to eliminate child abuse in our society as presently constructed. The family value certainly is recognized, but the sacrifice required to maintain it is not. Although the connection between young McGee and Gus Grissom could be described as a conceit ("far-fet"), the same is not the case with the victims witnessed by the Soft Y. September 11 signals a contemporary condition of the group subject, in which ideals and abjects begin to merge. The twin towers disaster in Soft Y is adopted as an impresa, associated with undertaking a consultation on an abject value.

The obvious heroes of 9/11 are the firemen and police officers who responded

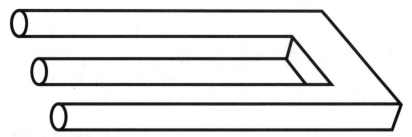

Figure 15. The devil's tuning fork.

to the emergency, especially those who lost their lives (such as the two fire chiefs who made it to the seventy-eighth floor in record time, only to die in the collapse of the tower). The passengers on the fourth airliner who prevented that plane from becoming another guided missile also are included in this conventional heroism. The more anonymous, ambiguous, but still collectively acknowledged loss is that of the tower occupants, especially the bond traders, stockbrokers, accountants, and similar professionals who worked in the financial sector (the symbolic target). While perhaps as many as a third of the victims' remains will never be identified, according to the city medical examiner (having been vaporized in the fire) several projects are under way to connect faces and biographies with the dead. An amateur artist declared his intention to produce individual portraits of every victim. A Florida company plans to market trading cards representing a cross-section of victims (the owner of the company lost his wife on one of the hi-jacked planes). Beginning the day after the attack the *Times* started a running story called "Portraits of Grief" that took on a life of its own.

> "Nobody involved in this had any idea early on that this would turn into some kind of national shrine," Jon Landman said recently. "It was a response to a journalistic problem: How can you write about victims when you don't know who they are or how many, and you can't assemble a comprehensive picture of them? And the answer was: One at a time." . . . In early October, as the number of people working on the project expanded, an editor named Wendell Jamieson circulated a memo admonishing contributors to avoid certain tropes. By then, evidently, the *Times* had filled its quota of bond traders who loved their wives and kids and were fanatical about golf. The Cantor Fitzgerald guys who always got the best tables at Smith & Wollensky had begun to blur. Whenever possible, Jamieson suggested, one should reach for illuminating details beyond how the deceased was such a devoted student of "The Simpsons" or Bruce Springsteen. And beware when interviewing women who identified themselves as fiancees. (Singer 2002, 31)

In the case of 9/11 the abject sacrifice was part of the same world and involved some of the same kinds of people as the heroic sacrifice. The abject loss was not loss of life, but of livelihood. "Enron," to give it a name, is a metonym for all the financial corporations involved in the worst fraud scandal in American history. Two disasters mutually illuminate one another: 9/11, Enron. The sacrifice was made by all those people who lost jobs, life savings, retirement years. The State of Florida retirement system, to note just one small example with personal relevance, lost $350 million on its Enron stocks (when the stock was plummeting the committee responsible for state investments, including one person also on the board of directors of Enron, refused to sell). Whether in terms of the oracle or of becoming, the clustering of the twin disasters in real time reveals the process within which the event becomes a narrative of global capital. The value? *Profit.* The sacrifice? Financial ruin. The MEmorial remembers that our values are conflicted, structured by inescapable contradictions. As one of the lyrics in the song "John Wesley Harding" says, some men rob you with a six-gun, some with a fountain pen.

What is the aporia, the impossibility of the event? Fraud is not an anomaly in business, but a constitutive possibility. If we are free to make money any way we can, as much as we can, then we are also free to cheat, to abuse the numbers game.

HOUSTON—The primary motive for creating Enron's complex web of partnerships was thought to have been to hide the company's debt, keep salaries high and make its stock ever more valuable. But new revelations by investigators and insider Michael Kopper indicate that whole deals may have been structured more to let executives skim money than to dress up Enron's books. (*Gainesville Sun*, August 23, 2002)

A more generous reading might take as its point of departure Mr. Skilling's praise of Mr. Fastow's bookkeeping innovations as examples of creative genius. "Former company insiders have said Fastow's aggressive and inventive approach to structuring deals appealed to Skilling. After CFO Magazine showered Fastow with the 'Excellence Award for Capital Structure' in 1999, Skilling told the publication: 'Andy has the intelligence and the youthful exuberance to think in new ways'" (*Gainesville Sun*, January 17, 2004). The excellence award for capital structure? At what point should one call for a Committee of Public Safety? Should we admire the greedy for throwing off the yoke of their internal Reign of Terror (morality)? The Enron executives voted democratically to suspend their own ethics rules during discussion of the illegal subsidiaries. A "capital" crime? Where is the internal ayatollah when you need him? In the context of electracy, the financial scandal is a symptom of the breakup of the collective identity formation established within literacy—the coordination of geography, economy, and symbology. The corporation is separating from the state now the way the state separated from the church at the beginning of modernity. Do we need an economic miranda warning? Carmen herself might say, "monee monee monee."

Terrorism (internal or external) by definition does not discriminate. There is no effort to distinguish the innocent from the guilty, the undeserving from the deserving, neither by al-Qaeda nor by the white-collar fifth column. That the only sound recording of the attack on the towers was made by an FBI agent wearing a wire, conducting a sting investigation of a corrupt accountant (a redundant phrase?) in a coffeeshop in one of the towers, is an abject conductive connection between the disasters in the Real. As one columnist said, the problem with American business is not what is illegal, but what is legal, and in any case the commemorative point has nothing to do with blame. We are not revulsed, making a shout, but mapping a value. President Bush and Vice President Cheney in their business dealings are reported to have profited by deals similar to those now being reclassified as illegal. There is no need to rehearse all the lines of this tangle (felt). The American wisdom highlighted in the event is *that's the way things are done; everyone does it; a fool and his money are soon parted; go along to get along (group think).* Collusion, conspiracy, are intimations of *ATH,* the blindness of a group subject. One measure of what we believe is found in the subject lines of our e-spam. These are our monuments: not pyramids, but pyramid schemes. Do you reply to the e-mail offer from the former official of an African nation to help him transfer millions of dollars via your personal bank account? Do you consider requesting the penis extension? The drunk-teen porn? Are these not tests? May the subject addressed by spam become wise?

The catastrophe covered everyone with the same ashen dust and produced a "frozen zone." The uncanny cartographer that is the Real continues a machinic index in the fact that "Houston street is the dividing line, the place where the world begins to end" (Gopnik 2001, 36). *Houston:* the headquarters of Enron.

> The smell, which fills the empty streets of SoHo from Houston to Canal, blew uptown on Wednesday night, and is not entirely horrible from a reasonable distance—almost like the smell of smoked mozzarella, a smell of the bubble time. Closer in it becomes acrid, and unbreathable. The white particulate smoke seems to wreathe the empty streets—to wrap right around them. The authorities call this the "frozen zone." In the "Narrative of A. Gordon Pym," spookiest and most cryptic of Poe's writings, a man approaches the extremity of existence, the pole beneath the Southern Pole, "The whole ashy material fell now continually around us," he records in his diary, "and in vast quantities." . . . Poe, whose house around here was torn down not long ago, is a realist now. (Ibid.)

Nothing is hidden. The physical smell evokes a spiritual smell. Disgust, repulsion. Cause and effect? Synchronicity? The terrorists, like the abusive fathers, were disgusted by the product that in the unconscious is indistinct (shit = lucre). The Real shows us a zone of indistinction, in which example and exception merge, localizing a "camp" in which bare life is exposed to death. Why did none of the 5,200 proposals include the smell of burned cheese as part of their commemorative atmosphere? Why not an *eternal stove* labeled *Invest in the Future* into which visitors are invited to toss their cash? No, such reminders are not the task of memorials, but of MEmorial peripherals.

The 9/11 Peripheral

The FRE proposes to commemorate the financial sacrifice made by the victims of corporate fraud on behalf of the profit motive by installing permanent twinkling emergency-colored Christmas lights along the route of Will Pappenheimer's Y tour of the streets of Lower Manhattan. Whenever the stock market has a winning day, the Y illuminates, as a reminder of Bataille's General Economy, the principle that accumulation is balanced necessarily by expenditure. When you see the gain, look also for the loss.

Neo-Baroque

Are we witnessing the death of the American Dream, as Slavoj Žižek suggested? "On September 11, the USA was given the opportunity to realize what kind of world it was part of" (2002, 47). A bifurcation point. What is to be done? Is there no perfect language, no universal communication capable of bringing together "the family of man"? "The actual universality is not the never-won neutral space of translation from one particular culture to another, but, rather, the violent experience of how, across the cultural divide, we share the same antagonism" (66). Each monad in isolation looks out obscurely "on the same river," Deleuze noted in his study of Leibniz. Here is the collusion between clarity and obscurity that we must learn to negotiate. The moment of clarity for each monad, however small an area it illuminates, comes in a flash. "Monads of the third species are flashing, twinkling in a way, through the difference of the illuminators and the illuminated" (Deleuze 1993, 117). The Christmas Y peripheral glimmers like the monads.

> No wonder that Leibniz is one of the predominant philosophical references of
> the cyberspace theorists: what reverberates today is not only his dream of a
> universal computing machine, but the uncanny resemblance between his on-
> tological vision of monadology and today's emerging cyberspace community

in which global harmony and solipsism strangely coexist. That is to say, does our immersion into cyberspace not go hand in hand with our reduction to a Leibnizean monad which, although "without windows" that would directly open up to external reality, mirrors in itself the entire universe? Are we not more and more monads with no direct windows onto reality, interacting alone with the PC screen, encountering only the virtual simulacra, and yet immersed more than ever in the global network, synchronously communicating with the entire globe? The impasse which Leibniz tried to solve by way of introducing the notion of the "reestablished harmony" between the monads, guaranteed by God Himself, the supreme, all-encompassing monad, repeats itself today, in the guise of the problem of communication: how does each of us know that he or she is in touch with the "real other" behind the screen, not only with spectral simulacra? (Žižek 2001, 26)

This problem of the screen replacing the window returns us to the educational challenge to replace the perspective window of the tourist-guide essay form of literacy with the MEmorial simulacrum of electracy.

A shorthand way to understand reasoneon (the relationship between the classic essay and the MEmorial) is as the relationship between the classical and baroque worldviews (aesthetics). A glance at any Western civilization textbook reveals in the features of the chronology of periods from ancient to modern an oscillation between the poles of classic and baroque forms of life. The formal features of the binary pair were codified by the art historian, Heinrich Wölfflin. One advantage of the postmodernist overview of the history of forms is the relativization of these alternatives as a relationship of interdependency. To get up to speed with the time accident requires a baroque morphology. The classical mood or state of mind is "ease," and the baroque mood is "disquiet" *(Unruhe)*. What forces and supports the alliance or cooperation of these two complementary (not opposed) states of mind is the syncretic possibilities of digital media, a text-graphics authoring environment. Adding imaging to writing creates the conditions of double or multiple perspectives that demand initially the formal resources of the baroque traditions to manage. Lyotard's theory of the figural, the visual supplement to discourse beyond the limits of natural language, is described as a version of anamorphic perspective. The immediate relevance to our context is the application of the evolution of linear perspective (from classic to baroque) to the evolution of the school assignment from essay to MEmorial. As this description of Lyotard's figural indicates, the MEmorial does not oppose or abandon the clarity of the idea, but it "blocks" (overprints) on it the obscurity of the scene (event).

The analogy in painting to the force of poetic rhetoricity as constituent and disruptive figure for language is anamorphosis. Anamorphosis rests upon the figural clash between the quasi-unmotivated geometric perspective and the

quasi-motivated force of curvature and diffusion in vision. The "textualiza-
tion" of the visual by Renaissance perspective or Cartesian optics is an attempt
to understand objects as in principle from a singular, immobile point. The
effect of this is to reduce vision to an affair of geometry, of straight lines, to exclude curvature and anamorphosis. The immobilization of the eye flattens the
visual field around a focal center, projecting the visible as a stable image clearly visible as on a transparent screen. Against this, Lyotard insists upon the
presence of the heterogeneity of curved space in vision: of the foveal periph-
ery alongside the focal center, of the evanescent, diffuse anelliptical margin
inseparable from distinct vision. . . . Lyotard thus juxtaposes clear and diffuse
vision as heterogeneous components of the visible. Anamorphosis plays upon
the co-presence of curved and geometric space in the visible. Anamorphosis is
the realization in painting of the co-existence of two radically heterogeneous
spaces of representation; as in Holbein's *Ambassadors* or the anamorphic portrait of Charles I discussed by Lyotard, the death's head often forms the mark
of the radical difference of the two spaces—the bar of death is the disjunction
of the two spaces in which vision is inscribed. (Readings 1991, 25–26)

ATH

To the extent that we are still writing as if we were looking through a window
(the model of the tourist guide), what we see is rendered in anamorphic perspective. Jacques Lacan uses the metaphor of anamorphosis to model the workings of tragedy *(Antigone)*, specifically with respect to *ATH*. Lacan is interested
in *ATH* as showing that exterior that is at the heart of me, the intersubjective
nature of the human identity. "One does or does not approach *Até*, and when
one approaches it, it is because of something that is linked to a beginning and a
chain of events, namely, that of the misfortune of the Labdacides family. As one
starts to come close to it, things come together in a great hurry" (Lacan 1992,
264). The name of the blindness at work in *Antigone* is badly translated, Lacan
says, as "resentment." We must understand it, in terms of how it is experienced,
as being overtaken by a bliss or *jouissance*, a "catastrophe" in the mathematical
sense of a sudden mutation of feeling as when in everyday life one lets anger or
lust override all good sense. In any case, her tragedy evokes the two "spaces"
that concern us, which Žižek relates with phenomenal reality and the noume-
nal Thing, each with its own logic.

> The horrifying, lethal, and at the same time fascinating borderline that we
> approach when the reversal into bliss is imminent is what Lacan, apropos of
> Sophocles's *Antigone*, endeavors to indicate by means of the Greek word *Até*.
> There is a fundamental ambiguity to this term: *Até* simultaneously denotes a

horrifying limit which cannot ever be reached, i.e., whose touch means death, and the space beyond it. The crucial point here is the primacy of the limit over the space: we do not have two spheres (that of reality and that of pure fantasy) which are divided by a certain limit; what we have is just reality and its limit, the abyss, the void around which it is structured. The fantasy space is therefore strictly secondary; it "gives body," it materializes a certain limit, or, more precisely, it changes the impossible into the prohibited. (Žižek 1993, 115–16)

As a figure for conceiving of this dimension of human disaster, Lacan proposed an anamorphic painting. Although he alludes to Holbein's *Ambassadors* several times, the example he discusses is, he says, a more modest work. "It is formed of a polished cylinder that has the function of a mirror, and around it you put a kind of bib or flat surface on which there are also indecipherable lines. When you stand at a certain angle, you see the image concerned emerge in the cylindrical mirror; in this case it is a beautiful anamorphosis of a painting of the crucifixion copied from Rubens" (1992, 135). Later in the seminar he explains the anamorphic character of tragedy. "What is the surface that allows the image of Antigone to rise up as an image of passion? The other day I evoked in connection with her the phrase, 'Father, why hast thou abandoned me?' which is literally expressed in one line. Tragedy is that which spreads itself out in front so that that image may be produced. When analyzing it, we follow an inverse procedure; we study how the image had to be constructed in order to produce the desired effect" (273).

The point of the new consultancy is that neither tragedy nor consulting are adequate to understand the work of *ATH* in the digital apparatus. This baroque relay helps update the question. The disaster spreads itself out in the media as a smear of statistical information. The MEmorial (as a collective practice distributed throughout the Internet) puts in place the *device* capable of imaging its passion, since ease, utility, and sufficient reason fail to notice *ATH* in modern experience: *Binge*. Binge eaters reported to researchers that although they did not feel hungry they were not able to stop eating and they did not know: Y. Is America as such obese? *Obese* is not an ideal but an abject. *Até*. We *ATH* ("ah-tay") too much. Personal blindness, collective catastrophe. Enron, 9/11. This connection may not be captured within the forms of tragedy or conventional consulting. It is not a question of catharsis or of statistics. It may not be eradicated by Jacobins or martyrs.

Syncretism

The MEmorial deconsultation uses commemoration to exceed the impasses revealed in disasters. Every disaster exposes a frozen zone. Abject or minor imaging of the disaster invents in these circumstances (thaws the zone) by finding a line of flight, making a map, forming new connections. The FRE learned in Miami *(Miami Virtue)* to syncretize its methodology with the epistemology of the Other (the quilting point) encountered in the choral zone. We opened a connection between poststructuralism and Vodou, the Other in that case being the Haitian targets of American policy. The Other of 9/11—the aggressors this time—is represented by Muslim extremists. In the context of theoria, syncretizing tourism and revolution, we easily recognize the Jacobinism of al-Qaeda: when the world resists a righteous call to virtue, the group becomes desperate. The terrorists are linked metonymically to Islam, but there is more to Islam than terrorism, just as there is more to Vodou than sorcery, and more to capitalism than fraud.

The choragraphic map shows that *the conducting link between capitalism and Islam is the ornamental design known as the arabesque.* The arabesque with its interlaced patterns of repeating shapes (whether floral or geometric) is said to be the most typical feature of Islamic aesthetics. "Spiritual states and musical tone which are mutable, impermanent qualities requiring an encounter or place in which to descend and then change the rhythm, both find a visual correspondence in the arabesque. The arabesque is a form which harmoniously renders a constantly changing rhythmical motion. Varying in density over the surface, it is a rhythmic outpouring of thought given precision by parallels, inversions and interlacings" (Bakhtiar 1976, 98). The abstractness of capital ("In capitalism power itself is carried to the highest abstraction of an idea" [Bataille 1985, 37]) found its perfect embodiment in the arabesque form. "In the middle of the 19th century, the modern arabesque is appropriated by capitalist aesthetics; it adorns stock certificates, bank notes, and the designs of industrial parks" (Menninghaus 1999, 74). The arabesque makes a map, opens a line of flight, between McWorld and Jihad, across and through the different, the incommensurable civilizations in this story. Here is a fold, a moment of overprinting to support the possibility of seeing multiple positions.

The Devil's Tuning Fork

Will Pappenheimer's musical family story attuned his theoria tour with the arabesque/Islam link in the community register of the popcycle. There is an uncanny necessity between Will's story and the conditions of the disaster. His becoming-music evokes the twin towers as tuning fork, but perhaps a devil's tuning fork (optical illusion, impossible figure): the symbol was not what it seemed. The heuristic metonym points to research on the history of tuning, since the emblematic story suggests that the world "lute" playing the music of the spheres is out of tune, producing a "howling wolf" so grating to the collective ear that the world tuning fork disintegrated. Henri Arnaut's "Pythagorean tuning" system (fifteenth century) attempted to keep as many fifths pure as possible. "Arnaut made every fifth within the scale a perfect consonance except for one, the interval between B and F-sharp. In the ripple effect that occurs with every system of tuning, this decision had consequences for all the other intervals. Only four thirds out of the twelve possible are pure under Arnaut's system, and the sound of the bad fifth is so grating that it was called the wolf, for its wild howl" (Levenson 1995, 57–58). The solution demonstrated in Johann Sebastian Bach's "well-tempered scale, distributed the imperfections of musical arithmetic across all the notes of the scale, preserving only the octave in its required absolute consonance of 2:1" (60). The "purity" here has a moral overtone that rebukes the righteous. Every demand for purity creates a howling wolf. Listen!

The writings and practices of Sufi mystics are filled with analogies between music and spirit. Deleuze and Guattari's "nomadism" (baroque monad becomes postmodern nomad) and interlaced logic of sense resonate with the arabesque pattern. Nomadism supports the navigational attunement as well, expressed aphoristically as "to think is to voyage" (Deleuze and Guattari 1987, 482). Music is a privileged dimension within the many plateaus of the theory. "The passage of the refrain. The refrain moves in the direction of the territorial assemblage and lodges itself there or leaves. In a general sense, we call a refrain any aggregate of matters of expression that draws a territory and develops into territorial motifs and landscapes (there are optical, gestural, motor, etc., refrains). In the narrow sense, we speak of a refrain when an assemblage is sonorous or 'dominated' by sound—but why do we assign this apparent privilege to sound?" (323).

What remains for the larger project—relating the Soft Y to the EmerAgency consultancy—is to develop a syncretic hybrid between this poststructural method and the mystical path of Sufism, representing a (if not the) Islamic epistemology. One point of connection is with the Sufi practice of *Sama,* whose most familiar manifestation is in the dance of the whirling dervishes. "Though usually translated as 'spiritual music,' *Sama* literally means 'hearing.' In the terminology of Sufism, it is listening with the ear of the heart to music in the most profound sense—poetry, melodies, tunes, and rhythmic harmonies—while being in a special state so deeply plunged in Love that there is no taint of self left within awareness. In this sense, *Sama* is named the 'call of God'" (Nurbakhsh 1978, 32). Here is a point of interface with miranda, the samba feeling of electrate justice. Sam(b)a: the new pedagogy. One function of the EmerAgency is to make syncretism an explicit part of online pedagogy.

Toward a Global American Wisdom

This goal of syncretizing with the epistemologies of the Other encountered in public policy conflicts is a point of departure for the design of an online global

American divination system. This proposed system is intended to be for postcolonial transculture what the I Ching was to premodern Chinese. Since research during the Miami consultation showed the similarity of the Chinese and Yoruban (IFA) oracles, and since we were not adopting pure divination but syncretizing divination operations with poststructural poetics, the FRE adopted the Chinese system as the relay for the interface. The FRE strategy offers a solution to the larger question of the EmerAgency, which is a need for an interface capable of transforming the MEmorials into a generative archive. As a registry of abject values, the MEmorials add up collectively to the first systematic cross-referencing of the beliefs that have replaced the virtues and vices as the guide to conduct in the emerging electrate society. The name of the Internet oracle—Cha-Ching—calls attention to the appropriation of the Book of Changes structure of a core of eight trigram/archetypes, generating a total of sixty-four situations, but that replaces the Taoist and Confucian philosophies informing Chinese wisdom with contemporary (capitalist) assumptions. The onomatopoeic word *cha-ching* (sometimes spelled "ka-ching"), evoking the sound of a cash register, is often used by sportscasters to describe a *score* in whichever game they are covering *(Barry Bonds goes deep—cha-ching—home run!)*. What is the music of these scores?

The sixty-four hexagrams of the I Ching acquire their divinatory power from their mapping of a complete process through multiple plateaus of becoming (the times of day, the seasons of a year, family relationships, the historical fall of one dynasty and the rise of another). Meaning is made possible by a correlational epistemology of correspondences common to nearly every premodern civilization, including European civilization, until displaced by science. To account for how each monad in Leibniz's philosophy is the entire world (which is what makes it possible for one querent/consultant to attune a zone for the collective community), Deleuze alludes to the Chinese worldview of correspondences: the microcosm reproduces the macrocosm. As above, so below. There is no transcendent realm in Chinese metaphysics, as there is in the West. Instead, the Chinese division of invisible/visible is between the potential and the actual. Deleuze sides with the Chinese reading. What happens in an event? In our given world Thomas Coe plunged his son Bradley McGee headfirst into a toilet; Mission Control decided to launch the *Challenger* despite the cold weather; suicide bombers targeted the World Trade Center; some passengers on a hi-jacked plane fought back.

> We find ourselves before events: Adam's soul is now sinning (following final
> causes), and thus his body is really absorbing the apple (according to efficient
> causes). My soul feels a current pain, my body receives a real blow. But what
> is it? What is this secret part of the event that is at once distinguished from its
> own realization, from its own actualization, even though realization does

not exist on the outside? This death, for example, is neither exterior reality nor
its intimacy in the soul. We have seen that it is pure inflection as ideality, a
neutral singularity, incorporeal as much as impassable, or if we use Blanchot's
words, "the part of the event as much as its accomplishment" can neither
actualize nor realize its carrying out. It is what can be conveyed by all expressions, or what can be realized by all realizations, the *Eventum tantum* to which
the body and soul attempt to be equal, but that never stops happening and
that never ceases to await us: a pure virtuality and possibility, the world in the
fashion of a Stoic Incorporeal, the pure predicate.

As the Chinese (or Japanese) philosopher would say, the world is the
Circle, the pure "reserve" of events that are actualized in every self and realized in things one by one. Leibniz's philosophy requires this ideal preexis-
tence of the world, this silent and shaded part of the event. We can speak of
the event only as already engaged in the soul that expresses it and in the body
that carries it out, but we would be completely at a loss about how to speak
of it without this withdrawn part. However difficult it may be, we must think
of the naval battle beginning with a potential that exceeds the souls that
direct it and the bodies that execute it. (Deleuze 1993, 105–6)

It is the beginning of "possible worlds" theory, and it is what makes divination useful, understood not as fortune-telling but in the practical way that it
actually works, as a means to ascertain my situation within what the Chinese
call "the propensity of things." "Propensity" is not "destiny." In Leibniz's version there is a multitude of possible worlds, but all the events of a given world
must be compossible. Thomas Coe may not both kill and not kill his son. "A
bifurcation is called a point in the neighborhood of series' divergence. Borges,
one of Leibniz's disciples, invoked the Chinese philosopher-architect Ts'ui Pen,
the inventor of the 'garden with bifurcating paths,' a baroque labyrinth whose
infinite series converge or diverge, forming a webbing of time embracing all
possibilities" (Deleuze 1993, 62). *ATH* is the propensity of the world, what
Deleuze with Leibniz calls the "inclination" of the soul (monad), which is not
the same as necessity. "Does Adam sin freely? In other words, at that instant his
soul has taken an amplitude that is found to be easily filled by the aroma and
taste of the apple, and by Eve's solicitations. Another amplitude—one having
retained God's defense—is possible. The whole question turns on 'laziness'"
(70). "Laziness" is Adam's *ATH*, his unwillingness to consider his options and
instead to follow his inclinations. The ubiquity of references to Borges's "fork-
ing paths" in hypermedia poetics is not (only) about linking, but about ethics.
In the face of a collective amnesia the Real presents us with a materialized re-
buke: *Don't you see that every action—every click—is a choice?* Causality in its

modern guise is too crude to grasp the shadows and dust of microrelations in which Adam's sin is contingent, not necessary.

"In Leibniz the formula is expressed time and again: the present portends the future and is burdened with the past. It is not a determinism—even an internal one—but an interiority that constitutes liberty itself. It is because the living present is essentially variable in both extension and intensity" (70). How to notice this *ATH*? "We have to begin from all of the smallest inclinations that ply our soul in every direction, in the flash of an instant, under the stress of a thousand 'little springs': disquiet" (69). This mood—whatever it might be in each case—is what the impresa helps the egent localize, recognize, and map. This mood is the *Stimmung* (attunement) that Heidegger says is the condition that makes knowledge *(bestimmen)* matter. Each monad is singular, a convergence of two series (soul and body), but all the monads collectively look out on the same river (the same world, the same antagonism). The purpose of the Cha-Ching is to make legible the traces of this compossibility. "It is because for Leibniz clarity comes of obscurity and endlessly is plunging back into it. Thus the Cartesian map of darkness-clarity-confusion-distinction is redrawn with an entirely new meaning and new set of relations. Inconspicuous perceptions constitute the obscure dust of the world, the dark depths of every monad contains. There are differential relations among these presently infinitely small ones that are drawn into clarity; that is to say, that establish a clear perception" (89). EmerAgency consultations map this circuit connecting obscurity and clarity of reason. Electrate humanities is about wisdom.

Winning the Trick

The Cha-Ching is a hybrid, a syncretic or postmodern formation drawing on the history of the world's wisdom traditions as an interface metaphor for designing an Internet civic sphere. The fact that playing cards entered Europe in the second half of the fourteenth century, brought back from Palestine by Crusaders (Pollack 1999, 25), suggests a second line of flight across the McWorld-Jihad differend. The Tarot deck, that is, developed from these cards into a Western style of divination, based on the adventure quest of the "fool." As for the specific design of the Tarot,

> The most influential theory comes from historian Gertrude Moakley, whose book *The Tarot Cards* links the trumps to the floats, or "triumphs," in grand parades held during the Renaissance. The modern tradition of Mardi Gras and Carnival, with its costumes, mystery, and broken rules comes from these trionfi held just before Lent. . . . Even more significant to Gertrude Moakley's theory, the word "trump" for the 22 Major Arcana cards probably comes

from the Italian word *trionf* or "triumph." In the popular card game *tarocchi*, the trumps, or *trionfi*, literally triumph over the lesser suit cards of the Minor Arcana. Two variations on Tarot images demonstrate the symbolic quality of the cards in their early days. The *Tarocchi dei Mantegna*, a set of 50 "cards" (prints) from around 1470, just 20 years after the Visconti-Sforza Tarot, is both a game and a set of lessons in moral, artistic, spiritual, mythological, and even cosmic ideas. (26)

Tarot is a popular survival of the hermetic memory palaces of universal knowledge that were the by-products of the search for a perfect language. The emblem-impresa relays for the MEmorial form are part of this context. The divination interface for the EmerAgency archive of MEmorials, then, may also take the form of a new Tarot, in which the trumps are updated to represent the formless values commemorated in the MEmorials. This postmodern oracle would do for the subject of the electrate apparatus what the festival parade of triumphs did for the identity institutions of literacy. The consequence of supplementing literacy with electracy is a shift away from alphabetic categories to image categories; from concept to concetto; from abstract to immanent or material forms; in ethics from ideals to abjects. The collapse of representation in imaging (the merging of superstructure and base in simulacra) corresponds in moral considerations to the dissolution of "ideals" as guides for conduct, replaced by investments in certain kinds of favored behaviors.

Diderot outlined this potentiality in *Rameau's Nephew*, in the contrast between the Philosopher (committed to the tradition of *virtu*) and the Nephew (a scoundrel). In one way the contrast may be read as the difference between the classical and baroque worldviews, in that the Nephew relied on the "agudeza" or acuity and wit ("flattery" is his chief skill) practiced by courtiers of the baroque period. The Nephew is not so much cynical as pragmatic. He proposed that schools teach not the utopias of the theorists but the practical behaviors that actually govern a society run by the aristocracy (the period is prerevolutionary France). The utilitarian Nephew recognized that the vices of his day were not anomalies but constitutive of the society. Indeed, it took a revolution to replace them with a different set of problems. Similarly, what some see as the vulgarization of American mores may be understood more affirmatively in terms of what Ralph Ellison described as a jazz approach to life:

> I believe that Hemingway, in depicting the attitudes of athletes, expatriates, bullfighters, traumatized soldiers, and impotent idealists, told us quite a lot about what was happening to that most representative group of Negro Americans, the jazz musicians—who also lived by an extreme code of withdrawal, technical and artistic excellence, rejection of the values of respectable society. They replaced the abstract and much-betrayed ideals of that

society with the more physical values of eating, drinking, copulating, loyalty to friends, and dedication to the discipline and values of their art. (Ellison, in O'Meally 1998, 120)

A more troubling view of what Bataille called the untransposed (formless) values (the big toe) is offered by Žižek's psychoanalytic position, who gives his own reading of Agamben's *Homo sacer:*

> The distinction between those who are included in the legal order and *Homo sacer* is not simply horizontal, a distinction between two groups of people, but more and more also the "vertical" distinction between the two (super-imposed) ways of how *the same* people can be treated—briefly: on the level of Law, we are treated as citizens, legal subjects, while on the level of its obscene superego supplement, of this empty unconditional law, we are treated as *Homo sacer.* Perhaps, then, the best motto for today's analysis of ideology is the line quoted by Freud at the beginning of his *Interpretation of Dreams:* "Acheronta movebo"—if you cannot change the explicit set of ideological rules, you can try to change the underlying set of obscene unwritten rules. (2002, 32)

He adds that the so-called clash of civilizations is really a clash between two kinds of nihilism: the West clinging to its life of "stupid pleasure" at all costs, and the Muslim radicals' readiness to give their lives for a transcendent cause (40). Žižek qualifies this point by noting that this clash is not between civilizations but within each civilization.

Whatever the causality of the transvaluation of values from ideals to formless, the purpose of the EmerAgency Tarot is to identify, record, and display the collection of contemporary investments. Taking the carnival parade of "triumphs" as a relay, the Web oracle represents each core behavior accompanied by its limit or violation. In the spirit of Virilio's museum of the accident (each invention includes its own disaster), the parade shows contemporary global America as emerging from a background of child rearing (abuse), bookkeeping (fraud), investment (scams), car driving (wrecks), beer drinking (alcoholism), drug taking (addictions), gun toting (murders), sweets eating (obesity), property owning (sprawl). We do not have to wait for Mardi Gras to see the world upside down, the celebration of greedy abusers. We have only to go to the movies (but leave the theater five minutes before the end of the film to avoid the ritual punishment meted out to the immoralists). What might be the effect on the group subject of confronting this collective character of American global behavior? Would we look in this mirror and have the eureka effect of the *infans* infant playing peek-a-boo? Would we experience the aha of recognition, or a revulsion of denial (to name a polarity of possible reactions)?

The oracle functions as a consultation in both the empirical and esoteric senses (learn consulting by consulting). The challenge of the interface design is to compose an oracle that relates individual quotidian problems with collective policy dilemmas. Through the oracle the obscurity of a multitude of little blindnesses achieves the clarity of collective catastrophe. Wisdom in practice means common sense—the plausible, what most people tend to do in that kind of situation. It circulates now in the form of proverbs and sayings ("no pain, no gain," "I'll be back"). To consult the oracle is to learn one's place in this scene. The ambition of the Cha-Ching is not to propagate conformity but to transvalue common sense itself. An awareness of the full set of hexagrams or triumphs allows one to understand the virtual, potential, propensity, the dimension of becoming (based on multiple close observations of the unfolding of the situations). The purpose of the EmerAgency consultancy is to compose rather than receive this wisdom—to enlist netizens in the creative process of designing contemporary wisdom, and to relate wisdom with knowledge. The intended users of the wisdom are group subjects, which, as part of the political process, may grasp the cost-benefit consequences of their cumulative behaviors. The political impact on public policy formation comes from the awareness of those in power that their actions are being monitored by egents worldwide, witnesses of disasters-in-progress.

The Tower

The FRE is at only the beginning of this project, still working to name and design a few hexagram/triumphs of the Cha-Ching as American wisdom for a global era. For this project to pass from a pedagogy and a conceptual critique into a practice of a virtual civic sphere will require its adoption and testing by many other groups and individuals. Meanwhile, perhaps Nietzsche's preface to "Twilight of the Idols" summarizes the critical implications for the EmerAgency of the tuning fork impresa that emerged in Pappenheimer's attunement of the Lower Manhattan zone. "This little essay is a great declaration of war; and regarding the sounding out of idols, this time they are not just idols of the age, but eternal idols, which are here touched with a hammer as with a tuning fork: there are altogether no older, no more convinced, no more puffed-up idols—and none more hollow. That does not prevent them from being those in which people have the most faith" (Nietzsche 1968, 466).

The next step of the EmerAgency is to move beyond the MEmorial, or to develop a poetics capable of generating the Cha-Ching from the accumulative MEmorials. A first step is to ask about the idols of choral Manhattan, in order to translate the Soft Y MEmorial into a triumph. The synchronistic clustering of two disasters in the fall of 2001 created a scene of sacrifice in the Real. Engineers explained that the ruins of the 110 floors of each tower could fit within a space of about eleven stories because the buildings were 90 percent air. The same could be said of the financial reports of many American corporations. Individuals are in a value environment the way they were in the skyscrapers (thinking with the group subject). It is this correspondence between the visible and spiritual (ethical) dimensions of experience that makes possible an intuitive operation of the oracular interface. MEmorials do not commemorate ideals, but "reals," "actuals," untransposed "abjects." They take into account not only declared values, but undeclared collective behaviors.

When the towers fell the nation asked why? The EmerAgency oracle interface proposes instead that we adopt the looped scene of the burning towers as an interface metaphor, introduced within the archetypal logic of the Tarot as a classification system for an image metaphysics.

> The Tarot is optimistic. Life, it teaches, does not allow us to remain immersed in illusions or oppression. However, if we do not free ourselves the pressure will build up until something explodes. The stone tower of our pain crashes around us and we discover ourselves flung free. We may not enjoy this experience. But it will liberate us.
>
> The Tower card evokes various tales. In the story of Rapunzel, the sorceress throws both Rapunzel and the prince from a tower without a door. In the modern fantasy *The Lord of the Rings*, the end of evil comes with the destruction of a "dark tower." And in the Biblical story of the Tower of Babel, God destroys human attempts to build a tower to heaven and confounds human language.
>
> All these images describe destruction, an idea that conveys the card's usual meanings. But we can also look at this card in a different way, as the lightning flash of revelation—the lightning releases us from the illusion we carry with us of normal consciousness. These are all very grand themes. In normal usage we can think of the lightning as a more conventional kind of revelation, as some kind of discovery that unlocks a secret or ends an illusion under which we are laboring.
>
> In readings, this card usually means chaos, upheaval, conflict. Something shatters a long-standing situation. Usually, however, the situation has "imprisoned" the person, so that the chaos releases him. Alternatively, the card may indicate some revelation, either joyous or disturbing. (Pollack 1999, 88)

Several methodological lessons follow from this connection between 9/11 and the Tower card of the major arcana. First, following the impresa rule, the MEmorial classifies its disaster within the archetypes of the oracle, and then updates the meaning of the category through the customizing and personalizing features of the peripheral and testimonial. The EmerAgency egents track the aftermath of 9/11 in order to formulate a contemporary Tower Trump for the postmodern arcana. Second, the familiarity of the Tarot in popular culture— New Age, self-help, Hollywood and TV narrative device—recommend it as an interface giving intuitive access to the databases of the Internet, thus providing a vehicle for the EmerAgency (amateur) consultancy. The interest of the Tarot not just as a device but as a worldview is measured by the frequency with which it is invoked in recent movies and TV series. HBO's original series *Carnivàle*, for example, is the most explicit exploration of the Tarot theme to date. The introductory title sequence includes an animated metamorphosis of the original tarrochi paintings into the world of 1930s America. The HBO Web site offers for sale a Tarot game. "A New Twist on Tarot! HBO invites you to play *Fate*, a tarot card game of strategy and intuition, based on the hit series *Carnivàle*. Match cards and wits against our resident Fortune Teller. If you beat her, you will learn more about your character's dark past. And as you master the game, more powerful wildcards will be added to your deck, adding consequences to every card you play. Step right up!"

Asian wisdom is invoked in another HBO series, *The Sopranos*, with the HBO Web site offering "a new book that illustrates the strange parallels between the universe of Tony Soprano and the world of *Tao Te Ching*. In *The Tao of Bada Bing! Words of Wisdom from The Sopranos*, principles are taken from the Eastern philosophy of the Tao Te Ching and juxtaposed against excerpts from all 52 episodes of 'The Sopranos,' showing similar ideas and themes that appear and reapppear throughout the show's four seasons." In the same vein, it was reported recently that representatives of several world religions endorsed the movie *Groundhog Day* as a faithful representation of their metaphysics.

What remains to be explored in the design of the Cha-Ching Web site is the usefulness of a hybrid oracle interface in reeducating world common sense. Commentators have noted for some time the need to update the classical Newtonian physics, which has become second nature, with a feeling for material reality that includes the principles of quantum mechanics. As numerous commentators have noted, the cosmology of the new physics of Einstein, Planck, Bohr, and Heisenberg fits well with that of esoteric or hermetic wisdom. Divination and its worldview of nonlocal a-causal synchronicity educates our intuitions to the notions of 4-D space-time described in contemporary physics. In our context it is important to keep in mind that the esoteric accounts are survivals of the correlational or correspondence cosmologies found in nearly all prescientific civilizations. The revelation announced by the falling towers may be just this appearance in everyday life of quantum common sense. Will the collective Euthyphro recognize itself in this card?

An oracle interface for contemporary wisdom further promises to provide a universal cultural translator, in that the New Age literature includes charts correlating the archetypes of most of the world's many divination systems. Tracy Porter's *Tarot Companion,* for example, coordinates the generative topoi of the Tarot with the I Ching, and such systems as numerology, astrology, kabbalah, runes, and chakras. The equivalent in the *I Ching* of the Tower card is hexagram 23, "Deterioration." The wisdom of all these systems expresses a similar theme: an upheaval results from a false sense of security, overconfidence. A radical change in lifestyle is needed to awaken from complacency. Is not this message the same one the United States has heard for some time from allies and enemies alike, with respect to the pose of the last remaining superpower? In any case we are not performing a reading but composing the deck. The EmerAgency is not New Age, but reads this phenomenon as a symptom of and opportunity for globalization, continuing the syncretism of cultures initiated by vanguard

Figure 16. *"The Tower"*:
Rider-Waite Tarot card.

primitivism. The online oracle is one answer to the crisis of the general accident posed by Paul Virilio. For the virtual civic sphere to function in the conditions of the dromosphere (speed pollution), netizens need a practice that supports thinking at the speed of light. The Cha-Ching proposes to learn *flash reason* from the mystics.

WORKS CITED

Achen, Sven Tito. 1978. *Symbols around Us.* New York: Van Nostrand.

Adler, Jerry. 1991. "Putting Names in the Sky." *Newsweek,* May 13.

Agamben, Giorgio. 1993. *The Coming Community.* Trans. Michael Hardt. Minneapolis: University of Minnesota Press.

———. 1998. *Homo Sacer: Sovereign Power and Bare Life.* Trans. Daniel Heller-Roazen. Stanford, CA: Stanford University Press.

Artaud, Antonin. 1958. *The Theater and Its Double.* Trans. Mary Caroline Richards. New York: Grove Press.

Babington, Bruce, and Peter William Evans. 1985. *Blue Skies and Silver Linings: Aspects of the Hollywood Musical.* Manchester, England: Manchester University Press.

Bakhtiar, Laleh. 1976. *Sufi: Expressions of the Mystic Quest.* London: Thames and Hudson.

Ballard, J. G. 1985. *Crash.* New York: Vintage.

Barber, Benjamin R. 1995. *Jihad vs. McWorld: How Globalism and Tribalism Are Reshaping the World.* New York: Ballantine.

Barnes, Hazel E. 1981. *Sartre and Flaubert.* Chicago: University of Chicago Press.

Barthes, Roland. 1972. *Critical Essays.* Trans. Richard Howard. Evanston, IL: Northwestern University Press.

———. 1974. *S/Z.* Trans. Richard Miller. New York: Hill and Wang.

———. 1986. *The Rustle of Language.* Trans. Richard Howard. New York: Hill and Wang.

Bataille, Georges. 1985. *Visions of Excess: Selected Writings, 1927–1939.* Ed. and trans. Allan Stoekl. Minneapolis: University of Minnesota Press.

———. 1986. "Writings on Laughter, Sacrifice, Nietzsche, Un-Knowing." Trans. Annette Michelson. *October* 36.

———. 1988. *The Accursed Share: An Essay on General Economy.* New York: Zone.

———. N.d. "Abjection and Miserable Forms." In *More & Less,* ed. Sylvère Lotringer. Pasadena, CA: Art Center College of Design.

Benedikt, Michael, ed. 1991. *Cyberspace: First Steps.* Cambridge, MA: MIT Press.

Benjamin, Walter. 1969. *Illuminations.* Trans. Harry Zohn. New York: Schocken.

———. 1978. *Reflections: Essays, Aphorisms, Autobiographical Writings.* Trans. Edmund Jephcott. New York: Harcourt Brace Jovanovich.

Bettelheim, Bruno. 1967. *The Empty Fortress: Infantile Autism and the Birth of the Self.* New York: Free Press.

263

Biel, Steven. 1996. *Down with the Old Canoe: A Cultural History of the "Titanic" Disaster.* New York: Norton.

Birnbaum, Daniel. 2000. "Stickup Artist." *Artforum* (November).

Birney, Hoffman. 1934. *Grim Journey.* New York: Minton, Balch.

Blanchot, Maurice. 1986. *The Writing of the Disaster.* Trans. Ann Smock. Lincoln: University of Nebraska Press.

Bois, Yve-Alain, and Rosalind E. Krauss. 1997. *Formless: A User's Guide.* New York: Zone.

Boltanski, Christian. 1988a. "Interview." *Bomb* 26.

———. 1988b. "Little Christians: Interview." *Artscribe International* (November/December).

Booth, Wayne C., Gregory G. Colomb, and Joseph M. Williams. 1995. *The Craft of Research.* Chicago: University of Chicago Press.

Bosso, Christopher J. 1994. "The Contextual Bases of Problem Definition." In *The Politics of Problem Definition: Shaping the Policy Agenda,* ed. David A. Rochefort and Roger W. Cobb, 182–203. Lawrence: University Press of Kansas.

Bower, B. 1992. "Desert Sands Yield Ancient Trading Center." *Science News* 141 (February 15).

Bowker, Geoffrey C., and Susan Leigh Star. 2000. *Sorting Things Out: Classification and Its Consequences.* Cambridge, MA: MIT Press.

Brint, Michael. 1991. *Tragedy and Denial: The Politics of Difference in Western Political Thought.* Boulder, CO: Westview Press.

Browning, Barbara. 1998. *Infectious Rhythm: Metaphors of Contagion and the Spread of African Culture.* New York: Routledge.

Bruce, Lenny. 1967. *The Essential Lenny Bruce.* Ed. John Cohen. New York: Ballantine Books.

Brunvand, Jan Harold. 1981. *The Vanishing Hitchhiker.* New York: Norton.

Bukatman, Scott. 1993. *Terminal Identity: The Virtual Subject in Postmodern Science Fiction.* Durham, NC: Duke University Press.

Bullock, Alan, and Oliver Stallybrass. 1977. *The Harper Dictionary of Modern Thought.* New York: Harper & Row.

Burson, Nancy, Richard Carling, and David Kramlich. 1986. *Composites: Computer-Generated Portraits.* New York: William Morrow.

Cadava, Eduardo, Peter Connor, and Jean-Luc Nancy, eds. 1991. *Who Comes after the Subject?* New York: Routledge.

Caputo, John D. 1978. *The Mystical Element in Heidegger's Thought.* Athens: Ohio University Press.

———. 1993. *Against Ethics: Contributions to a Poetics of Obligation with Constant Reference to Deconstruction.* Bloomington: Indiana University Press.

Carruthers, Mary. 1990. *The Book of Memory: A Study of Memory in Medieval Culture.* Cambridge: Cambridge University Press.

———. 1998. *The Craft of Thought: Meditation, Rhetoric, and the Making of Images, 400–1200.* New York: Cambridge University Press.

Caruth, Cathy, ed. 1995. *Trauma: Explorations in Memory.* Baltimore, MD: Johns Hopkins University Press.

Chaitin, Gilbert D. 1996. *Rhetoric and Culture in Lacan.* New York: Cambridge.

Chtcheglov, Ivan. 1981. *Situationist International Anthology*. Ed. Ken Knabb. Berkeley, CA: Public Secrets.

Cixous, Hélène. 1993. *Three Steps on the Ladder of Writing*. Trans. Sarah Cornell and Susan Sellers. New York: Columbia University Press.

Core, Philip. 1984. *Camp: The Lie That Tells the Truth*. New York: Delilah Books.

Cosgrove, Denis, ed. 1999. *Mappings*. London: Reaktion Books.

Courtine, Jean-Francois. 1991. "Voice of Conscience and Call of Being." In *Who Comes after the Subject*, ed. Eduardo Cadava, Peter Connor, and Jean-Luc Nancy. New York: Routledge.

Cushman, Robert F. 1976. *Cases in Civil Liberties*. 2nd ed. Englewood Cliffs, NJ: Prentice-Hall.

Daly, Carroll John. 1985. "Three Gun Terry." In *The "Black Mask" Boys: Masters in the Hard-Boiled School of Detective Fiction*, ed. William F. Nolan. New York: Morrow.

Daly, Peter M. 1988. "Modern Advertising and the Renaissance Emblem: Modes of Verbal and Visual Persuasion." In *Word and Visual Imagination: Studies in the Interaction of English Literature and the Visual Arts*, ed. Karl Josef Holtgen, Peter M. Daly, and Wolfgang Lottes. Erlangen: Universitätsbund Erlangen-Nurnberg.

———. 1998. *Literature in the Light of the Emblem: Structural Parallels between the Emblem and Literature in the Sixteenth and Seventeenth Centuries*. 2nd ed. Toronto: University of Toronto Press.

de Duve, Thierry. 1998. *Kant after Duchamp*. Cambridge, MA: MIT Press.

Deford, Frank. 1971. *There She Is: The Life and Times of Miss America*. New York: Viking Press.

Deleuze, Gilles. 1990. *The Logic of Sense*. Trans. Mark Lester. New York: Columbia University Press.

———. 1993. *The Fold: Leibniz and the Baroque*. Trans. Tom Conley. Minneapolis: University of Minnesota Press.

Deleuze, Gilles, and Félix Guattari. 1977. *Anti-Oedipus: Capitalism and Schizophrenia*. Trans. Robert Hurley, Mark Seem, and Helen R. Lane. New York: Viking Press.

———. 1986. *Kafka: Toward a Minor Literature*. Trans. Dana Polan. Minneapolis: University of Minnesota Press.

———. 1987. *A Thousand Plateaus: Capitalism and Schizophrenia*. Trans. Brian Massumi. Minneapolis: University of Minnesota Press.

Derrida, Jacques. 1986. *Memoires: For Paul de Man*. Trans. Cecile Lindsay, Jonathan Culler, and Eduardo Cadava. New York: Columbia University Press.

———. 1987. "Chora." In *Poikilia: Etudes Offertes à Jean-Pierre Vernant*. Paris: Editions de l'École des hautes études en sciences sociales.

———. 1991. "'Eating Well,' or The Calculation of the Subject," in Cadava, Connor, and Nancy, *Who Comes after the Subject*.

———. 1992. *Given Time: I, Counterfeit Money*. Trans. Peggy Kamuf. Chicago: University of Chicago Press.

———. 1993. *Aporias*. Trans. Thomas Dutoit. Stanford, CA: Stanford University Press.

———. 1994. *Specters of Marx: The State of the Debt, the Work of Mourning, and the New International*. Trans. Peggy Kamuf. New York: Routledge.

———. 1996. "Faith and Knowledge: The Two Sources of 'Religion' at the Limits of Reason Alone." In *Religion*, ed. Jacques Derrida and Gianni Vattimo. Stanford, CA: Stanford University Press.

———. 1998. *Demeure: Maurice Blanchot*. Paris: Galilee.

Dine, Jim. 1966. "The Car Crash." In *Happenings*, ed. Michael Kirby. New York: Dutton.

Doyle, Richard E. 1984. *ATH, Its Use and Meaning: A Study in the Greek Poetic Tradition from Homer to Euripides*. New York: Fordham University Press.

Dreyfus, Hubert L., and Stuart E. Dreyfus. 1986. *Mind over Machine: The Power of Human Intuition and Expertise in the Era of the Computer*. New York: Free Press.

duBois, Page. 1991. *Torture and Truth*. New York: Routledge.

Durham, Scott. 1998. *Phantom Communities: The Simulacrum and the Limits of Postmodernism*. Stanford, CA: Stanford University Press.

Düttmann, Alexander Garcia. 1996. *At Odds with AIDS: Thinking and Talking about a Virus*. Stanford, CA: Stanford University Press.

Dyer, Richard. 1991. "Charisma." In *Stardom*, ed. Christine Gledhill. New York: Routledge.

Eady, Cornelius. 2001. *Brutal Imagination*. New York: Putnam.

Eagleton, Terry. 1987. *Saints and Scholars*. London: Verso.

Eames, Charles, and Ray Eames. 1990. *A Computer Perspective: Background to the Computer Age*. Cambridge, MA: Harvard University Press.

Earnshaw, R. A., and N. Wiseman. 1992. *An Introductory Guide to Scientific Visualization*. New York: Springer-Verlag.

Eco, Umberto. 1995. *The Search for the Perfect Language*. Trans. James Fentress. Malden, MA: Blackwell.

Edelman, Murray. 1988. *Constructing the Political Spectacle*. Chicago: University of Chicago Press.

Enzensberger, Christian. 1972. *SMUT: An Anatomy of Dirt*. Trans. Sandra Morris. New York: Seabury Press.

Erdelyi, Matthew Hugh. 1985. *Psychoanalysis: Freud's Cognitive Psychology*. New York: W. H. Freeman.

Evans, Dylan. 1996. *An Introductory Dictionary of Lacanian Psychoanalysis*. New York: Routledge.

Felman, Shoshana. 1995. "Education and Crisis, or The Vicissitudes of Teaching." In *Trauma: Explorations in Memory*, ed. Cathy Caruth. Baltimore, MD: Johns Hopkins University Press.

Ffrench, Patrick. 1999. *The Cut: Reading Bataille's "Histoire d'Oeil."* Oxford: Oxford University Press.

Fletcher, John, and Andrew Benjamin, eds. 1990. *Abjection, Melancholia, and Love: The Work of Julia Kristeva*. London: Routledge.

Floch, Jean-Marie. 2000. *Visual Identities*. Trans. Pierre Van Osselaer and Alec McHoul. New York: Continuum.

Foreman, Richard. 1976. "How to Write a Play." *PAJ* 1: 84–92.

Foucault, Michel. 1972. *"The Archaeology of Knowledge" and "The Discourse on Language."* Trans. A. M. Sheridan Smith. New York: Pantheon.

Frampton, Kenneth. 1982. *Modern Architecture and the Critical Present*. London: Architectural Design.

Freud, Sigmund. 1965. *The Interpretation of Dreams*. Trans. James Strachey. New York: Avon.

Fulwiler, Toby, and Alan R. Hayakawa. 1994. *The Blair Handbook*. Englewood Cliffs, NJ: Prentice Hall.

Fynsk, Christopher. 2000. *Infant Figures: The Death of the 'Infans' and Other Scenes of Origin*. Stanford, CA: Stanford University Press.

Gasche, Rodolphe. 1999. *Of Minimal Things: Studies on the Notion of Relation*. Stanford, CA: Stanford University Press.

Gelernter, David. 1992. *Mirror Worlds*. New York: Oxford University Press.

Gibson, William. 1984. *Neuromancer*. New York: Ace Books.

Giddens, Anthony. 1991. *Modernity and Self-Identity: Self and Society in the Late Modern Age*. Stanford, CA: Stanford University Press.

Gilloch, Graeme. 1996. *Myth and Metropolis: Walter Benjamin and the City*. Cambridge, England: Polity Press.

Godard, Jean-Luc. 1972. *"Weekend" and "Wind from the East."* London: Lorrimer.

Godzich, Wlad. 1986. "Foreword: The Tiger on the Paper Mat." In *Paul de Man: The Resistance to Theory*. Minneapolis: University of Minnesota Press.

Goldberger, Paul. 2001. "Building Plans: What the World Trade Center Means." *New Yorker*, September 24.

Gopnik, Adam. 2001. "The City and the Pillars." *New Yorker*, September 24.

Goux, Jean-Joseph. 1993. *Oedipus, Philosopher*. Trans. Catherine Porter. Stanford, CA: Stanford University Press.

Greenaway, Peter. 1986. *A Zed and Two Noughts*. London: Faber.

Greimas, Algirdas Julien. 1987. *On Meaning: Selected Writings in Semiotic Theory*. Trans. Paul J. Perron and Frank H. Collins. Minneapolis: University of Minnesota Press.

———. 1990. *The Social Sciences: A Semiotic View*. Trans. Paul Perron and Frank H. Collins. Minneapolis: University of Minnesota Press.

Gross, Elizabeth. 1990. "The Body of Signification." In *Abjection, Melancholia, and Love: The Work of Julia Kristeva*, ed. John Fletcher and Andrew Benjamin. London: Routledge.

Guattari, Félix. 1984. *Molecular Revolution: Psychiatry and Politics*. Trans. Rosemary Sheed. New York: Penguin Books.

———. 1995. *Chaosmosis: An Ethico-Aesthetic Paradigm*. Trans. Paul Bains and Julian Pefanis. Sydney: Power Publications.

Guillermoprieto, Alma. 1990. *Samba*. New York: Vintage.

Gusfield, Joseph R. 1981. *The Culture of Public Problems: Drinking-Driving and the Symbolic Order*. Chicago: University of Chicago Press.

Hacking, Ian. 1999. *The Social Construction of What?* Cambridge, MA: Harvard University Press.

Havelock, Eric A. 1967. *Preface to Plato*. New York: Grosset and Dunlap.

———. 1978. *The Greek Concept of Justice: From Its Shadow in Homer to Its Substance in Plato*. Cambridge, MA: Harvard University Press.

Hermassi, Karen. 1977. *Polity and Theatre in Historical Perspective*. Berkeley: University of California Press.

Hillis, Ken. 1999. *Digital Sensations: Space, Identity, and Embodiment in Virtual Reality*. Minneapolis: University of Minnesota Press.

Himmelfarb, Gertrude. 1995. *The De-Moralization of Society: From Victorian Virtues to Modern Values*. New York: Alfred A. Knopf.

Hirsch, Edward. 2002. *The Demon and the Angel: Searching for the Source of Artistic Inspiration*. New York: Harcourt.

Hodges, Andrew. 1983. *Alan Turing: The Enigma*. New York: Simon and Schuster.

Hollier, Denis. 1995. "The Use-Value of the Impossible." In *Bataille: Writing the Sacred*, ed. Carolyn Bailey Gill. New York: Routledge.

James, David E. 1989. *Allegories of Cinema: American Film in the Sixties*. Princeton, NJ: Princeton University Press.

Jameson, Fredric. 1972. *The Prison-House of Language: A Critical Account of Structuralism and Russian Formalism*. Princeton, NJ: Princeton University Press.

———. 1981. *The Political Unconscious: Narrative as a Socially Symbolic Act*. Ithaca, NY: Cornell University Press.

———. 1985. "Class and Allegory in Contemporary Mass Culture: *Dog Day Afternoon* as a Political Film." In *Movies and Methods*, vol. 2, ed. Bill Nichols. Berkeley: University of California Press.

———. 2000. "Third-World Literature in the Era of Multinational Capitalism." In *The Jameson Reader*, ed. Michael Hardt and Kathi Weeks. Oxford, UK: Blackwell.

Jullien, François. 1995. *The Propensity of Things: Toward a History of Efficacy in China*. Trans. Janet Lloyd. New York: Zone Books.

Katz, Ephraim. 1979. *The Film Encyclopedia*. New York: Perigee.

Kopf, Biba. 1987. "Bacillus Culture." In *Tape Delay*, ed. Charles Neal. Harrow, England: SAF.

Krauss, Rosalind. 1994. *The Optical Unconscious*. Cambridge, MA: MIT Press.

Krell, David Farrell. 1992. *Daimon Life: Heidegger and Life Philosophy*. Bloomington: Indiana University Press.

Krips, Henry. 1999. *Fetish: An Erotics of Culture*. Ithaca, NY: Cornell University Press.

Kristeva, Julia. 1982. *Powers of Horror: An Essay on Abjection*. Trans. Leon S. Roudiez. New York: Columbia University Press.

Kubler, George. 1962. *The Shape of Time: Remarks on the History of Things*. New Haven, CT: Yale University Press.

Kurzweil, Raymond. 1992. *The Age of Intelligent Machines*. Cambridge, MA: MIT Press.

Lacan, Jacques. 1968. *Speech and Language in Psychoanalysis*. Trans. Leon S. Roudiez. New York: Columbia University Press.

———. 1970. "Of Structure as on Inmixing of an Otherness Prerequisite to Any Subject Whatever." In *The Structuralist Controversy*, ed. Richard Macksey and Eugenio Donato. Baltimore, MD: Johns Hopkins University Press.

———. 1977. "The Agency of the Letter in the Unconscious or Reason since Freud." In *Ecrits: A Selection*, trans. Alan Sheridan. New York: Norton.

———. 1992. *The Ethics of Psychoanalysis 1959–60.* The Seminar of Jacques Lacan, Book 7. Ed. Jacques-Alain Miller. Trans. Dennis Porter. New York: W. W. Norton.

LaCapra, Dominick. 1998. *History and Memory after Auschwitz.* Ithaca, NY: Cornell University Press.

Laplanche, J., and J.-B. Pontalis. 1973. *The Language of Psycho-Analysis.* New York: Norton.

Lefebvre, Henri. 1991. *The Production of Space.* Trans. Donald Nicholson-Smith. Cambridge, MA: Blackwell.

Leiris, Michel. 1988. "The Sacred in Everyday Life." In *The College of Sociology, 1937–39,* ed. Denis Hollier, trans. Betsy Wing. Minneapolis: University of Minnesota Press.

Leupin, Alexandre. 1991. "Introduction: Voids and Knots in Knowledge and Truth." In *Lacan and the Human Sciences,* ed. Alexandre Leupin. Lincoln: University of Nebraska Press.

Levenson, Thomas. 1995. *Measure for Measure: A Musical History of Science.* New York: Touchstone Books.

Lotman, Yuri M. 2000. *Universe of the Mind: A Semiotic Theory of Culture.* Trans. Ann Shukman. Bloomington: Indiana University Press.

Lukacher, Ned. 1986. *Primal Scenes: Literature, Philosophy, Psychoanalysis.* Ithaca, NY: Cornell University Press.

Lyotard, Jean-François. 1990. *Heidegger and "The Jews."* Trans. Andreas Michel and Mark S. Roberts. Minneapolis: University of Minnesota Press.

MacCannell, Dean. 1976. *The Tourist: A New Theory of the Leisure Class.* New York: Schocken.

MacIntyre, Alasdair. 1984. *After Virtue: A Study in Moral Theory.* 2nd ed. Notre Dame, IN: University of Notre Dame Press.

Mack, Richard N. 1990. "Catalog of Woes." *Natural History* (March).

Magill, Frank N., ed. 1961. *Masterpieces of World Philosophy in Summary Form.* New York: Harper.

Malcolm, Norman. 1958. *Ludwig Wittgenstein: A Memoir.* London: Oxford.

Marsh, Ken. 1982. *The Way the New Technology Works.* New York: Simon and Schuster.

Marth, Del, and Martha J. Marth, eds. 1992. *Florida Almanac, 1992–1993.* Gretna, LA: Pelican.

Martin, Elizabeth. 1994. "y-Condition." In *Architecture as a Translation of Music,* ed. Elizabeth Martin. Princeton, NJ: Princeton Architectural Press.

Martinich, A. P. 1996. *Philosophical Writing: An Introduction.* 2nd ed. Cambridge, MA: Blackwell.

McGowan, Chris, and Ricardo Pessanha. 1991. *The Brazilian Sound: Samba, Bossa Nova, and the Popular Music of Brazil.* New York: Watson-Guptill.

Menninghaus, Winfried. 1999. *In Praise of Nonsense: Kant and Bluebeard.* Trans. Henry Pickford. Stanford, CA: Stanford University Press.

Mercer, Charles. 1964. *Legion of Strangers: The Vivid History of a Unique Military Tradition— the French Foreign Legion.* New York: Holt, Rinehart, & Winston.

Mitchell, W. J. T. 1986. *Iconology: Image, Text, Ideology.* Chicago: University of Chicago Press.

————. 1994. *Picture Theory.* Chicago: University of Chicago Press.

Moeller, Susan D. 1999. *Compassion Fatigue: How the Media Sell Disease, Famine, War, and Death.* New York: Routledge.

Monk, Ray. 1990. *Ludwig Wittgenstein: The Duty of Genius.* New York: Free Press.

Monte, John, ed. 1978. *The Fred Astaire Dance Book.* New York: Simon and Schuster.

Moseley, Charles. 1989. *A Century of Emblems: An Introductory Anthology.* Brookfield, VT: Scholar Press.

Nietzsche, Friedrich. 1968. "The Twilight of the Idols." In *The Portable Nietzsche,* trans. Walter Kaufmann. New York: Viking Press.

Nurbakhsh, Javad. 1978. *In the Tavern of Ruin: Seven Essays on Sufism.* London: Khaniqahi-Nimatullahi.

Ogden, C. K. 1967. *Opposition: A Linguistic and Psychological Analysis.* Bloomington: Indiana University Press.

O'Meally, Robert G., ed. 1998. *The Jazz Cadence of American Culture.* New York: Columbia University Press.

Papert, Seymour. 1980. *Mindstorms: Children, Computers, and Powerful Ideas.* New York: Basic Books.

Pierson, Frank. 1988. "Writer's Revelations." In *Writing the Screenplay: TV and Film,* Alan A. Armer. Belmont, CA: Wadsworth.

Pippin, Steven. 1995. "The Continued Saga of an Amateur Photographer." *Grand Street: Space* 14, no. 54.

Pollack, Rachel. 1999. *The Complete Illustrated Guide to Tarot.* Boston: Element.

Pollock, Griselda, ed. 1996. Preface to *Generations and Geographies in the Visual Arts: Feminist Readings.* New York: Routledge.

Poundstone, William. 1992. *Prisoner's Dilemma: John von Neumann, Game Theory, and the Puzzle of the Bomb.* New York: Doubleday.

Pratkanis, Anthony R., and Elliot Aronson. 1991. *Age of Propaganda: The Everyday Use and Abuse of Persuasion.* New York: W. H. Freeman.

Propp, V. 1975. *Morphology of the Folktale.* Trans. Laurence Scott. 2nd ed. Austin: University of Texas Press.

Punin, Nikolai. 1992. "The Monument to the Third International." In *Art in Theory, 1900–1990: An Anthology of Changing Ideas,* ed. Charles Harrison and Paul Wood. Cambridge, MA: Blackwell.

Rasch, William. 2002. "The Self-Positing Society." In *Theories of Distinction: Redescribing the Descriptions of Modernity,* Niklas Luhmann, ed. William Rasch, trans. Joseph O'Neill et. al. Stanford, CA: Stanford University Press.

Readings, Bill. 1991. *Introducing Lyotard: Art and Politics.* New York: Routledge.

Remnick, David, et al. 2001. "September 11, 2001." *New Yorker,* September 24.

Rickels, Laurence A. 1988. *Aberrations of Mourning: Writings on German Crypts.* Detroit: Wayne State University Press.

Robins, Kevin. 1996. *Into the Image: Culture and Politics in the Field of Vision.* New York: Routledge.

Rochefort, David A., and Roger W. Cobb, eds. 1994. *The Politics of Problem Definition: Shaping the Policy Agenda.* Lawrence: University Press of Kansas.

Rose, Barbara. 1970. *Claes Oldenburg.* New York: Museum of Modern Art.

Royal, Robert F., and Steven R. Schutt. 1976. *The Gentle Art of Interviewing and Interrogation: A Professional Manual and Guide.* Englewood Cliffs, NJ: Prentice-Hall.

Ruthven, K. K. 1969. *The Conceit.* London: Methuen.

Sacks, Peter. 1985. *The English Elegy: Studies in the Genre from Spenser to Yeats.* Baltimore, MD: Johns Hopkins University Press.

Sadler, Simon. 1998. *The Situationist City.* Cambridge, MA: MIT Press.

Schank, Roger C. 1986. *Explanation Patterns: Understanding Mechanically and Creatively.* Hillsdale, NJ: Lawrence Erlbaum.

Serres, Michel. 1982. *The Parasite.* Trans. Lawrence R. Schehr. Baltimore, MD: Johns Hopkins University Press.

Shahn, Ben. 1957. *The Shape of Content.* New York: Vintage.

Sibley, David. 1995. *Geographies of Exclusion: Society and Difference in the West.* New York: Routledge.

Singer, Mark. 2002. "The Grief Desk." *New Yorker,* January 14.

Slotkin, Richard. 1993. *Gunfighter Nation: The Myth of the Frontier in Twentieth-Century America.* New York: Harper Perennial.

Smith, Rex Alan. 1985. *The Carving of Mount Rushmore.* New York: Abbeville.

Smithson, Robert. 1979. *The Writings of Robert Smithson.* Ed. Nancy Holt. New York: New York University Press.

Sperber, Dan, and Deirdre Wilson. 1986. *Relevance: Communication and Cognition.* Cambridge, MA: Harvard University Press.

Sternfeld, Joel. 1996. *On This Site: Landscape in Memoriam.* San Francisco: Chronicle Books.

Stewart, George R. 1960. *Ordeal by Hunger: The Story of the Donner Party.* New ed. Boston: Houghton Mifflin.

Stone, Allucquere Rosanne. 1991. "Will the Real Body Please Stand Up? Boundary Stories about Virtual Cultures." In *Cyberspace,* ed. Michael Benedikt, 81–118. Cambridge, MA: MIT Press.

Street, Brian V. 1984. *Literacy in Theory and Practice.* Cambridge: Cambridge University Press.

Stubbs, Tom. 1972. "Devil's Millhopper." *Florida Wildlife* (February).

Sturken, Marita. 1997. *Tangled Memories: The Vietnam War, the AIDS Epidemic, and the Politics of Remembering.* Berkeley: University of California Press.

Sutton, Horace. 1980. *Travelers: The American Tourist from Stagecoach to Space Shuttle.* New York: William Morrow.

Taylor, Simon. 1993. "The Phobic Object: Abjection in Contemporary Art." In *Abject Art: Repulsion and Desire in American Art.* New York: Whitney Museum.

Thomas, Francis-Noël, and Mark Turner. 1994. *Clear and Simple as the Truth: Writing Classic Prose.* Princeton, NJ: Princeton University Press.

Tisdall, Caroline. 1979. *Joseph Beuys.* New York: Guggenheim Museum.

Trend, J. B. 1968. *Bolivar and the Independence of Spanish America.* New York: Harper and Row.

Ulmer, Gregory L. 1989. *Teletheory: Grammatology in the Age of Video* New York: Routledge.

———. 1994a. *Heuretics: The Logic of Invention.* Baltimore, MD: Johns Hopkins University Press.

———. 1994b. "The Heuretics of Deconstruction." In *Deconstruction and the Visual Arts: Art, Media, Architecture,* ed. Peter Brunette and David Wills, 80–95. New York: Cambridge.

———. 2003. *Internet Invention: From Literacy to Electracy.* New York: Longman.

Vidler, Anthony. 2000. *Warped Space: Art, Architecture, and Anxiety in Modern Culture.* Cambridge, MA: MIT Press.

Virilio, Paul. 1997. *Open Sky.* Trans. Julie Rose. New York: Verso.

———. 1999. *Politics of the Very Worst: An Interview by Philippe Petit.* Trans. Michael Cavaliere. New York: Semiotexte.

———. 2003. *Unknown Quantity.* New York: Thames & Hudson.

Vogler, Christopher. 1992. *The Writer's Journey: Mythic Structure for Storytellers and Screenwriters.* Studio City, CA: Wiese.

Walter, Eugene Victor. 1988. *Placeways: A Theory of the Human Environment.* Chapel Hill: University of North Carolina Press.

Warner, Marina. 1994. *From the Beast to the Blonde: On Fairy Tales and Their Tellers.* London: Chatto & Windus.

Weber, John S. 1994. "Gerhard Richter." In *Public Information: Desire, Disaster, Document.* San Francisco: San Francisco Museum of Modern Art.

White, Hayden. 1999. *Figural Realism: Studies in the Mimesis Effect.* Baltimore, MD: Johns Hopkins University Press.

Wilber, Ken, ed. 1982. *The Holographic Paradigm and Other Paradoxes: Exploring the Leading Edge of Science.* Boulder, CO: Shambhala.

Wilden, Anthony. 1968. "Lacan and the Discourse of the Other." In *Speech and Language in Psychoanalysis,* Jacques Lacan, trans. Anthony Wilden. Baltimore, MD: Johns Hopkins University Press.

Williamson, Judith. 1978. *Decoding Advertisements: Ideology and Meaning in Advertising.* London: Marion Boyars.

Winston, Brian. 1986. *Misunderstanding Media.* Cambridge, MA: Harvard University Press.

Witt, Elder. 1988. *The Supreme Court and Individual Rights.* 2nd ed. Washington, DC: Congressional Quarterly.

Wittgenstein, Ludwig. 1961. *Tractatus Logico-Philosophicus* Trans. D. F. Pears and B. G. McGuinness. New York: Routledge.

———. 1968. *Philosophical Investigations.* Trans. G. E. M. Anscombe. Oxford: Basil Blackwell.

———. 1971. *Prototractatus.* Trans. D. F. Pears and B. F. McGuinness. Ithaca, NY: Cornell University Press.

Wodiczko, Krzysztof. 1996. "Memorial Projection." In *Theories and Documents of Contemporary Art,* ed. Kristine Stiles and Peter Selz. Berkeley: University of California Press.

Woll, Allen L. 1983. *The Hollywood Musical Goes to War.* Chicago: Nelson-Hall.

Yenser, Stephen. 1987. *The Consuming Myth: The Work of James Merrill.* Cambridge, MA: Harvard University Press.

Young, James E. 1993. *The Texture of Memory: Holocaust Memorials and Meaning.* New Haven, CT: Yale University Press.

Žižek, Slavoj. 1989. *The Sublime Object of Ideology.* London: Verso.

———. 1991. *For They Know Not What They Do: Enjoyment as a Political Factor.* London: Verso.

———. 1993. *Tarrying with the Negative: Kant, Hegel, and the Critique of Ideology.* Durham, NC: Duke University Press.

———. 1994a. "Introduction: The Spectre of Ideology." In *Mapping Ideology,* ed. Slavoj Žižek. New York: Verso.

———. 1994b. *The Metastases of Enjoyment: Six Essays on Woman and Causality.* London: Verso.

———. 2001. *On Belief.* New York: Routledge.

———. 2002. *Welcome to the Desert of the Real: Five Essays on September 11 and Related Dates.* New York: Verso.

Zulawski, David E., and Douglas E. Wicklander. 1992. *Practical Aspects of Interview and Interrogation.* New York: Elsevier.

INDEX

GREGORY L. ULMER is professor of English and media studies at the
University of Florida, Gainesville.